Anonymous

Selections illustrating economic history since the seven years war

Anonymous

Selections illustrating economic history since the seven years war

ISBN/EAN: 9783337204228

Printed in Europe, USA, Canada, Australia, Japan

Cover: Foto ©ninafisch / pixelio.de

More available books at **www.hansebooks.com**

SELECTIONS

ILLUSTRATING

ECONOMIC HISTORY

SINCE THE SEVEN YEARS' WAR.

COMPILED BY

BENJAMIN RAND, Ph.D.

———◆———

BOSTON:
A. A. WATERMAN & CO.,
36 BROMFIELD STREET.
1889.

Copyright, 1888,
BY BENJAMIN RAND.

PRESS OF
Rockwell & Churchill,
No. 39 Arch Street,
BOSTON.

PREFATORY NOTE.

THESE selections have been made for use as a text-book of required reading to accompany a course of lectures on economic history given at Harvard College. The work was undertaken at the request of Professor Charles F. Dunbar, to whose kind counsel the compiler has been throughout greatly indebted.

This book has already been adopted for a similar purpose as at Harvard by other leading American Universities. Although the compilation was prepared with special reference to the needs of students in courses of economic study, yet the nature and scope of the selections render them of value to any person who may desire to obtain a knowledge of some of the most important events and influences in modern economic history. B. R.

CAMBRIDGE, May, 1888.

CONTENTS.

I.

LEADING SECTIONS FROM THE ENGLISH NAVIGATION ACTS 1
From English Statutes at Large.

II.

THE COLONIAL POLICY OF EUROPE 5
From Adam Smith's Wealth of Nations.

III.

THE GREAT INVENTIONS 31
From Walpole's History of England.

IV.

ECONOMIC CAUSES OF THE FRENCH REVOLUTION . 52
From Von Sybel's French Revolution.

V.

THE EMANCIPATING EDICT OF STEIN . . . 78
From Seeley's Life and Times of Stein.

VI.

THE ORDERS IN COUNCIL 97
From Levi's History of British Commerce.

VII.

THE FINANCES OF ENGLAND, 1793–1815 . . . 111
From Porter's Progress of the Nation.

VIII.

THE ZOLLVEREIN 130
From Bowring's Report on the Prussian Commercial Union, Parl. Doc., 1840.

LE ZOLLVEREIN 153
From Legoyt's La France et l'Étranger.

IX.

THE CORN LAWS 163
From Levi's History of British Commerce.

X.

THE NEW GOLD 189
From Cairnes' Essays in Political Economy.

XI.

FRANCE SOUS LE SECOND EMPIRE 225
From Levasseur's Histoire des Classes Ouvrières.

XII.

THE FRENCH INDEMNITY: —
   THE PAYMENT OF THE FIVE MILLIARDS . . 237
   From Blackwood's Edinburgh Magazine.
   THE APPLICATION OF THE INDEMNITY . . . 259
   From Kolb's The Condition of Nations (Trans.).

XIII.

THE RECENT PROGRESS OF ITALY 263
From Wilson's The Resources of Modern Countries.

XIV.

THE UNITED STATES IN 1880: —

THE INCREASE OF POPULATION FROM 1790 TO
 1880 . . . . ·286
From Walker and Gannett's Report on the Progress of the Nation, Tenth Census.

THE FACTORY SYSTEM 308
From Wright's Report on the Factory System of the United States, Tenth Census.

THE COTTON MANUFACTURES 317
From Atkinson's Report on the Cotton Manufactures, Tenth Census.

THE IRON AND STEEL INDUSTRIES 339
From Swank's Statistics of the Iron and Steel Production, Tenth Census.

XV.

LES DETTES PUBLIQUES 352
From Neymarck's Les Dettes Publiques Européennes.

SELECTIONS.

I.

LEADING SECTIONS FROM THE ENGLISH NAVIGATION ACTS.

ACT OF 1660, 12 CAR. II., c. 18.

An Act for the Encouraging and Increasing of Shipping and Navigation.

For the Increase of Shipping and Encouragement of the Navigation of this Nation, wherein, under the good Providence and Protection of God, the Wealth, Safety and Strength of this Kingdom is so much concerned; (2) Be it enacted by the King's most Excellent Majesty, and by the Lords and Commons in this present Parliament assembled, and by the Authority thereof, That from and after the first day of *December*, one thousand six hundred and sixty, and from thenceforward, no Goods or Commodities whatsoever shall be imported into or exported out of any Lands, Islands, Plantations or Territories to his Majesty belonging or in his Possession, or which may hereafter belong unto or be in the Possession of his Majesty, his Heirs and Successors, in *Asia*, *Africa*, or *America*, in any other Ship or Ships, Vessel or Vessels whatsoever, but in such Ships or Vessels as do truly and without Fraud belong only to the People of *England* or *Ireland*, Dominion of *Wales*, or Town of *Berwick* upon *Tweed*, or are of the Built of and belonging to any the said Lands, Islands, Plantations, or Territories, as the Proprietors and right Owners thereof, and whereof the Master and three-fourths of the Mariners at least are *English*; . . . . .

III. And it is further enacted by the Authority aforesaid, That no Goods or Commodities whatsoever, of the Growth, Production or Manufacture of *Africa*, *Asia* or *America*, or of any Part thereof, or which are described or laid down in the usual Maps or Cards of those Places, be imported into *England*, *Ireland* or *Wales*, Islands of *Guernsey* and *Jersey*, or Town of *Berwick* upon *Tweed*, in other Ship or Ships, Vessel or Vessels whatsoever, but in such as do truly and without Fraud belong only to the People of *England* or *Ireland*, Dominion of *Wales*, or Town of *Berwick* upon *Tweed*, or of the Lands, Islands, Plantations or Territories in *Asia*, *Africa*, or *America*, to his Majesty belonging, as the Proprietors and right Owners thereof, and whereof the Master, and three-fourths at least of the Mariners are *English;* . . . . .

IV. And it is further enacted by the Authority aforesaid, That no Goods or Commodities that are of Foreign Growth, Production or Manufacture, and which are to be brought into *England*, *Ireland*, *Wales*, the Islands of *Guernsey* and *Jersey*, or Town of *Berwick* upon *Tweed*, in *English*-built Shipping, or other Shipping belonging to some of the aforesaid Places, and navigated by *English* Mariners, as aforesaid, shall be shipped or brought from any other Place or Places, Country or Countries, but only from those of the said Growth, Production or Manufacture, or from those Ports where the said Goods and Commodities can only, or are, or usually have been, first shipped for Transportation, and from none other Place or Countries; . . .

VIII. And it is further enacted by the Authority aforesaid, That no Goods or Commodities of the Growth, Production or Manufacture of *Muscovy*, or of any the Countries, Dominions or Territories to the Great Duke or Emperor of *Muscovy* or *Russia* belonging; as also that no Sort of Masts, Timber or Boards, no foreign Salt, Pitch, Tar, Rosin, Hemp or Flax, Raisins, Figs, Prunes, Olive-Oils, no Sorts of Corn or Grain, Pot-Ashes, Wines, Vinegar, or Spirits called *Aqua-Vitae*, or Brandy-Wine, shall from and after the first day of *April*, which shall be in the Year of our Lord one thousand six hundred sixty-one, be imported into *England*, *Ireland*, *Wales*, or Town of *Berwick* upon *Tweed*, in any Ship or Ships, Vessel or Vessels whatsoever, but in such as do truly and without fraud belong to the People thereof, or some of them, as the true Owners and Proprietors thereof, and whereof the Master and three-fourths of the Mariners at least are *English:* And that no Currans nor Com-

SECTIONS FROM ENGLISH NAVIGATION ACTS. 3

modities of the Growth, Production or Manufacture of any the Countries, Islands, Dominions or Territories to the *Ottoman* or *Turkish* Empire belonging, shall from and after the first day of *September*, which shall be in the year of our Lord one thousand six hundred sixty-one, be imported into any the afore-mentioned places in any Ship or Vessel, but which is of *English* built, and navigated, as aforesaid, and in no other, except only such foreign Ships and Vessels as are of the Built of that Country or Place of which the said Goods are the Growth, Production or Manufacture respectively, or of such Port where the said Goods can only be, or most usually are, first shipped for Transportation, and whereof the Master and three-fourths of the Mariners at least are of the said Country or Place ; . . . . .

XVIII. And it is further enacted by the Authority aforesaid, That from and after the first Day of *April*, which shall be in the Year of our Lord one thousand six hundred sixty-one, no Sugars, Tobacco, Cotton-Wool, Indigoes, Ginger, Fustick, or other dying Wood, of the Growth, Production or Manufacture of any *English* Plantations in *America*, *Asia* or *Africa*, shall be shipped carried, conveyed or transported from any of the said *English* Plantations to any Land, Island, Territory, Dominion, Port or Place whatsoever, other than to such other *English* Plantations as do belong to his Majesty, his Heirs and Successors, or to the kingdom of *England* or *Ireland*, or Principality of *Wales*, or Town of *Berwick* upon *Tweed*, there to be laid on shore ; . . .

ACT OF 1662, 14 CAR. II., C. 11.

XXIII. And whereas some Doubts and Disputes have arisen concerning the said late Act, *For increasing and encouraging of Shipping and Navigation*, about some of the Goods therein prohibited to be brought from *Holland* and the Parts and Ports thereabouts ; (2) Be it enacted and declared, that no Sort of Wines, (other than *Rhenish*) no Sort of Spicery, Grocery, Tobacco, Pot-Ashes, Pitch, Tar, Salt, Rozin, Deal-Boards, Fir, Timber, or Olive-Oil, shall be imported into *England*, *Wales*, or *Berwick*, from the *Netherlands* or *Germany*, upon any Pretence whatsoever, in any Sort of Ships or Vessels whatsoever ; . . . . .

ACT OF 1663, 15 CAR. II., C. 7.

V. And in regard his Majesty's Plantations beyond the Seas are inhabited and peopled by his subjects of this his Kingdom of *England*, for the maintaining a greater Correspondence and Kindness between them, and keeping them in a further Dependance upon it, and rendring them yet more beneficial and advantageous unto it in the further Imployment and Increase of *English* Shipping and Seamen, Vent of *English* Woollen and other Manufactures and Commodities, rendring the Navigation to and from the same more safe and cheap, and making this Kingdom a Staple, not only of the Commodities of those plantations, but also of the Commodities of other Countries and Places for the Supplying of them; and it being the Usage of other Nations to keep their Plantations Trade to themselves:

VI. Be it enacted, and it is hereby enacted, That from and after the five and twentieth Day of *March*, one thousand six hundred sixty-four, no Commodity of the Growth, Production or Manufacture of *Europe*, shall be imported into any Land, Island, Plantation, Colony, Territory, or Place to his Majesty belonging, or which shall hereafter belong unto or be in the Possession of his Majesty, his Heirs and Successors, in *Asia*, *Africa* or *America*, (*Tangier* only excepted) but what shall be *bona-fide*, and without Fraud, laden and shipped in *England*, *Wales*, or the Town of *Berwick* upon Tweed, and in English built Shipping, or which were *bona-fide* bought before the first day of *October* one thousand six hundred sixty and two, and had such Certificate thereof as is directed in one Act passed the last Sessions of this Present Parliament, intituled, *An Act for preventing Frauds, and Regulating Abuses in his Majesty's Customs;* and whereof the Master and three Fourths of the Mariners at least are *English*, and which shall be carried directly thence to the said Lands, Islands, Plantations, Colonies, Territories, or Places, and from no other Place or Places whatsoever; any Law, Statute, or Usage to the contrary notwithstanding; . . . . . .

See English Statutes at Large.

II.

THE COLONIAL POLICY OF EUROPE.

FROM ADAM SMITH'S WEALTH OF NATIONS, BOOK IV., CH. VII., PART II.

THE colony of a civilized nation which takes possession, either of a waste country or of one so thinly inhabited, that the natives easily give place to the new settlers, advances more rapidly to wealth and greatness than any other human society. The colonists carry out with them a knowledge of agriculture and of other useful arts, superior to what can grow up of its own accord in the course of many centuries among savage and barbarous nations. They carry out with them, too, the habit of subordination, some notion of the regular government which takes place in their own country, of the system of laws which supports it, and of a regular administration of justice; and they naturally establish something of the same kind in the new settlement. But among savage and barbarous nations, the natural progress of law and government is still slower than the natural progress of arts, after law and government have been so far established as is necessary for their protection. Every colonist gets more land than he can possibly cultivate. He has no rent, and scarce any taxes to pay. No landlord shares with him in its produce, and the share of the sovereign is commonly but a trifle. He has every motive to render as great as possible a produce, which is thus to be almost entirely his own. But his land is commonly so extensive, that with all his own industry, and with all the industry of other people whom he can get to employ, he can seldom make it produce the tenth part of what it is capable of producing. He is eager, therefore, to collect laborers from all quarters, and to reward them with the most liberal wages. But those liberal wages, joined to the plenty and cheapness of land, soon make those laborers leave him, in order to become landlords themselves. and to reward, with equal liberality, other laborers, who soon leave them for the same reason that they left their first master. The liberal reward of labor encourages marriage. The children, during the tender years of infancy, are well fed and properly taken care of, and when they are grown up, the value of their labor greatly overpays their maintenance. When arrived at maturity, the high price of labor, and the low price of land, enable them to establish themselves in the same manner as their fathers did before them.

In other countries rent and profit eat up wages, and the two superior orders of people oppress the inferior one. But in new colonies the interest of the two superior orders obliges them to treat the inferior one with more generosity and humanity; at least, where that inferior one is not in a state of slavery. Waste lands of the greatest natural fertility, are to be had for a trifle. The increase of revenue which the proprietor, who is always the undertaker, expects from their improvement, constitutes his profit; which in these circumstances is commonly very great. But this great profit cannot be made without employing the labor of other people in clearing and cultivating the land; and the disproportion between the great extent of the land and the small number of the people, which commonly takes place in new colonies, makes it difficult for him to get this labor. He does not, therefore, dispute about wages, but is willing to employ labor at any price. The high wages of labor encourage population. The cheapness and plenty of good land encourage improvement, and enable the proprietor to pay those high wages. In those wages consists almost the whole price of the land; and though they are high, considered as the wages of labor, they are low, considered as the price of what is so very valuable. What encourages the progress of population and improvement encourages that of real wealth and greatness.

The progress of many of the ancient Greek colonies towards wealth and greatness seems accordingly to have been very rapid. In the course of a century or two several of them appear to have rivalled, and even to have surpassed, their mother cities. Syracuse and Agrigentum in Sicily, Tarentum and Locri in Italy, Ephesus and Miletus in Lesser Asia, appear by all accounts to have been at least equal to any of the cities of ancient Greece. Though posterior in their establishment, yet all the arts of refinement, philosophy, poetry, and eloquence, seem to have been cultivated as early, and to have been improved as highly, in them, as in any part of the mother country. The schools of the two oldest Greek philosophers, those of Thales and Pythagoras, were established, it is remarkable, not in ancient Greece, but the one in an Asiatic, the other in an Italian colony. All those colonies had established themselves in countries inhabited by savage and barbarous nations, who easily gave place to the new settlers. They had plenty of good land, and as they were altogether independent of the mother city, they were at liberty to manage their own affairs in the way that they judged was most suitable to their own interest.

The history of the Roman colonies is by no means so brilliant. Some of them, indeed, such as Florence, have in the course of many ages, and after the fall of the mother city, grown up to be considerable States. But the progress of no one of them seems ever to have been very rapid. They were all established in conquered provinces, which in most cases had been fully inhabited before. The quantity of land assigned to each colonist was seldom very considerable, and, as the colony was not independent, they were not always at liberty to manage their own affairs in the way that they judged was most suitable to their own interest.

In the plenty of good land the European colonies established in America and the West Indies resemble, and even greatly surpass, those of ancient Greece. In their dependency upon the mother State they resemble those of ancient Rome; but their great distance from Europe has in all of them alleviated more or less the effects of this dependency. Their situation has placed them less in the view and less in the power of their mother country. In pursuing their interest their own way, their conduct has, upon many occasions, been overlooked, either because not known or not understood in Europe; and upon some occasions it has been fairly suffered and submitted to, because their distance rendered it difficult to restrain it. Even the violent and arbitrary government of Spain has, upon many occasions, been obliged to recall or soften the orders which had been given for the government of her colonies, for fear of a general insurrection. The progress of all the European colonies in wealth, population, and improvement, has accordingly been very great.

The crown of Spain, by its share of the gold and silver, derived some revenue from its colonies, from the moment of their first establishment. It was a revenue, too, of a nature to excite in human avidity the most extravagant expectations of still greater riches. The Spanish colonies, therefore, from the moment of their first establishment, attracted very much the attention of their mother country; while those of the other European nations were for a long time in a great measure neglected. The former did not, perhaps, thrive the better in consequence of this attention: nor the latter the worse in consequence of this neglect. In proportion to the extent of the country which they in some measure possess, the Spanish colonies are considered as less populous and thriving than those of almost any other European nation. The progress even of the Spanish colonies, however, in population and improvement, has certainly been very rapid and very great. The city of Lima, founded since the conquest, is represented in Ulloa, as containing fifty thousand inhabitants near thirty years ago. Quito, which had been but a miserable hamlet of Indians, is represented by the same author as in his time equally populous. Gemelli Carreri, a pretended traveller, it is said, indeed, but who seems everywhere to have written upon extreme good information, represents the city of Mexico as containing a hundred thousand inhabitants; a number which, in spite of all the exaggerations of the Spanish writers, is, probably, more than five times greater than what it contained in the time of Montezuma. These numbers exceed greatly those of Boston, New York, and Philadelphia, the three greatest cities of the English colonies. Before the conquest of the Spaniards there were no cattle fit for draught either in Mexico or Peru. The lama was their only beast of burden, and its strength seems to have been a good deal inferior to that of a common ass. The plough was unknown among them. They were ignorant of the use of iron. They had no coined money, nor any established instrument of commerce of any kind. Their commerce was carried on by barter. A sort of wooden spade was their principal instrument of agriculture. Sharp stones served them for knives and hatchets to cut with; fish-bones and the hard sinews of certain animals served them for needles to sew with; and these seem to have been their principal instruments of trade. In this state of things it seems impossible, that either of those empires could have been so much improved or so well cultivated as at present, when they are plentifully furnished with all sorts of European cattle, and when the use of iron, of the plough, and of many of the arts of Europe, has been introduced among them. But the populousness of every country must be in proportion to the degree of its improvement and cultivation. In spite of the cruel destruction of the natives which followed the conquest, these two great empires are, probably, more populous now than they ever were before; and the people are surely very different; for we must acknowledge, I apprehend, that the

Spanish creoles are in many respects superior to the ancient Indians.

After the settlements of the Spaniards, that of the Portuguese in Brazil is the oldest of any European nation in America. But as for a long time after the first discovery, neither gold nor silver mines were found in it, and as it afforded, upon that account, little or no revenue to the crown, it was for a long time in a great measure neglected; and during this state of neglect it grew up to be a great and powerful colony. While Portugal was under the dominion of Spain, Brazil was attacked by the Dutch, who got possession of seven of the fourteen provinces into which it is divided. They expected soon to conquer the other seven, when Portugal, recovered its independency by the elevation of the family of Braganza to the throne. The Dutch then, as enemies to the Spaniards, became friends to the Portuguese, who were likewise the enemies of the Spaniards. They agreed, therefore, to leave that part of Brazil, which they had not conquered, to the king of Portugal who agreed to leave that part which they had conquered to them, as a matter not worth disputing about with such good allies. But the Dutch government soon began to oppress the Portuguese colonists, who, instead of amusing themselves with complaints, took arms against their new masters, and by their own valor and resolution, with the connivance indeed, but without any avowed assistance from the mother country, drove them out of Brazil. The Dutch, therefore, finding it impossible to keep any part of the country to themselves, were contented that it should be entirely restored to the crown of Portugal. In this colony there are said to be more than six hundred thousand people, either Portuguese or descended from Portuguese, creoles, mulattoes, and a mixed race between Portuguese and Brazilians. No one colony in America is supposed to contain so great a number of people of European extraction.

Towards the end of the fifteenth and during the greater part of the sixteenth century Spain and Portugal were the two great naval powers upon the ocean; for though the commerce of Venice extended to every part of Europe, its fleets had scarce ever sailed beyond the Mediterranean. The Spaniards, in virtue of the first discovery, claimed all America as their own; and though they could not hinder so great a naval power as that of Portugal from settling in Brazil, such was, at that time, the terror of their name, that the greater part of the other nations of Europe were afraid to establish themselves in any other part of that great continent. The French, who attempted to settle in Florida, were all murdered by the Spaniards. But the declension of the naval power of this latter nation, in consequence of the defeat or miscarriage of, what they called, their Invincible Armada, which happened towards the end of the sixteenth century, put it out of their power to obstruct any longer the settlements of the other European nations. In the course of the seventeenth century, therefore, the English, French, Dutch, Danes, and Swedes, all the great nations who had any ports upon the ocean, attempted to make some settlements in the new world.

The Swedes established themselves in New Jersey; and the number of Swedish families still to be found there, sufficiently demonstrates, that this colony was very likely to prosper, had it been protected by the mother country. But being neglected by Sweden, it was soon swallowed up by the Dutch colony of New York, which again, in 1674, fell under the dominion of the English.

The small islands of St. Thomas and Santa Cruz are the only countries in the new world that have ever been possessed by the Danes. These little settlements too were under the government of an exclusive company, which had the sole right, both of purchasing the surplus produce of the colonists, and of supplying them with such goods of other countries as they wanted, and which, therefore, both in its purchases and sales, had not only the power of oppressing them, but the greatest temptation to do so. The government of an exclusive company of merchants is, perhaps, the worst of all governments for any country whatever. It was not, however, able to stop altogether the progress of these colonies, though it rendered it more slow and languid. The late king of Denmark dissolved this company, and since that time the prosperity of these colonies has been very great.

The Dutch settlements in the West, as well as those in the East Indies, were originally put under the government of an exclusive company. The progress of some of them, therefore, though it has been considerable, in comparison with that of almost any country that has been long peopled and established, has been languid and slow in comparison with that of the greater part of new colonies. The colony of Surinam, though very considerable, is still inferior to the greater part of the sugar colonies of the other European nations. The colony of Nova Belgia, now divided into the two provinces of New York and New Jersey, would probably have soon become considerable too, even though it had remained under the government of the Dutch. The plenty and cheapness of good land are such powerful causes of prosperity, that the very worst government is scarce capable of checking altogether the efficacy of their operation. The great distance too, from the mother country would enable the colonists to evade more or less, by smuggling, the monopoly which the company enjoyed against them. At present the company allows all Dutch ships to trade to Surinam upon paying two and a half per cent. upon the value of their cargo for a license; and only reserves to itself exclusively the direct trade from Africa to America, which consists almost entirely in the slave trade. This relaxation in the exclusive privileges of the company is probably the principal cause of that degree of prosperity which that colony at present enjoys. Curaçoa and Eustatia, the two principal islands belonging to the Dutch, are free ports open to the ships of all nations; and this freedom, in the midst of better colonies whose ports are open to those of one nation, only, has been the great cause of the prosperity of those two barren islands.

The French colony of Canada was, during the greater part of the last century, and some part of the present, under the government of an exclusive company. Under so unfavorable an administration its progress was necessarily very slow in comparison with that of other new colonies; but it became much more rapid when this company was dissolved after the fall of what is called the Mississippi scheme. When the English got possession of this country, they found in it near double the number of inhabitants which father Charlevoix had assigned to it between twenty and thirty years before. That Jesuit had travelled over the whole country, and had no inclination to represent it as less considerable than it really was.

The French colony of St. Domingo was established by pirates and freebooters, who, for a long time, neither required the protection, nor acknowledged the authority, of France; and, when that race of banditti became so far citizens as to acknowledge this authority, it was for a long time necessary to exercise it with very great gentleness. During this period the population and improvement of this colony increased very fast. Even the oppression of the exclusive company, to which it was for some time subjected, with all the other colonies of France, though it no doubt retarded, had not been able to stop its progress altogether. The course of its prosperity returned as soon as it was relieved from that oppression. It is now the most important of the sugar colonies of the West Indies, and its produce is said to be greater than that of all the English sugar colonies put together. The other sugar colonies of France are in general all very thriving.

But there are no colonies of which the progress has been more rapid than that of the English in North America.

Plenty of good land and liberty to manage their own affairs their own way, seem to be the two great causes of the prosperity of all new colonies.

In the plenty of good land, the English colonies of North America, though, no doubt, very abundantly provided, are, however, inferior to those of the Spaniards and Portuguese, and not superior to some of those possessed by the French before the late war. But the political institutions of the English colonies have been more favorable to the improvement and cultivation of this land than those of any of the other three nations.

First, the engrossing of uncultivated land, though it has by no means been prevented altogether, has been more restrained in the English colonies than in any other. The colony law which imposes upon every proprietor the obligation of improving and cultivating, within a limited time, a certain proportion of his lands, and which, in case of failure, declares those neglected lands grantable to any other person; though it has not, perhaps, been very strictly executed, has, however, had some effect.

Secondly, in Pennsylvania there is no right of primogeniture, and lands, like movables, are divided equally among all the children of the family. In three of the provinces of New England the oldest has only a double share, as in the Mosaical law. Though in those provinces, therefore, too great a quantity of land should sometimes be engrossed by a particular individual, it is likely, in the course of a generation or two, to be sufficiently divided again. In the other English colonies, indeed, the right of primogeniture takes place, as in the law of England. But in all the English colonies the tenure of the lands, which are all held by free socage, facilitates alienation, and the grantee of any extensive tract of land generally finds it for his interest to alienate, as fast as he can, the greater part of it, reserving only a small quit-rent. In the Spanish and Portuguese colonies, what is called the right of Majorazzo[1] takes place in the succession of all those great estates to which any title of honor is annexed. Such estates go all to one person, and are in effect entailed and unalienable. The French colonies, indeed, are subject to the custom of Paris, which, in the inheritance of land, is much more favorable to the younger children than the law of England. But, in the French colonies, if any part of an estate, held by the noble tenure of chivalry and homage, is alienated, it is, for a limited time, subject to the right of redemption, either by the heir of the superior or by the heir of the family ; and all the largest estates of the country are held by such noble tenures, which necessarily embarrass alienation. But, in a new colony, a great uncultivated estate is likely to be much more speedily divided by alienation than by succession. The plenty and cheapness of good land, it has already been observed, are the principal causes of the rapid prosperity of new colonies. The engrossing of land, in effect, destroys this plenty and cheapness. The engrossing of uncultivated land, besides, is the greatest obstruction to its improvement. But the labor that is employed in the improvement and cultivation of land affords the greatest and most valuable produce to the society. The produce of labor, in this case, pays not only its own wages, and the profit of the stock which employs it, but the rent of the land too upon which it is employed. The labor of the English colonists, therefore, being more employed in the improvement and cultivation of land, is likely to afford a greater and more valuable produce, than that of any of the other three nations, which, by the engrossing of land, is more or less diverted toward other employments.

Thirdly, the labor of the English colonists is not only likely to afford a greater and more valuable produce, but, in consequence of the moderation of their taxes, a greater proportion of this produce belongs to themselves, which they may store up and employ in putting into motion a still greater quantity of labor. The English colonists have never yet contributed anything towards the defence of the mother country, or towards the support of its civil government. They themselves, on the contrary, have hitherto been defended almost entirely at the expense of the mother country. But the expense of fleets and armies is out of all proportion greater than the necessary expense of civil government.

---

[1] Jus Majoratus.

The expense of their own civil government has always been very moderate. It has generally been confined to what was necessary for paying competent salaries to the governor, to the judges, and to some other officers of police, and for maintaining a few of the most useful public works. The expense of the civil establishment of Massachusetts Bay, before the commencement of the present disturbances, used to be but about £18,000 a year; that of New Hampshire and Rhode Island, £3,500 each; that of Connecticut, £4,000; that of New York and Pennsylvania, £4,500 each; that of New Jersey, £1,200; that of Virginia and South Carolina, £8,000 each. The civil establishments of Nova Scotia and Georgia are partly supported by an annual grant of Parliament. But Nova Scotia pays, besides, about £7,000 a year towards the public expenses of the colony; and Georgia about £2,500 a year. All the different civil establishments in North America, in short, exclusive of those of Maryland and North Carolina, of which no exact account has been got, did not, before the commencement of the present disturbances, cost the inhabitants above £64,700 a year; an ever-memorable example at how small an expense three millions of people may not only be governed, but well governed. The most important part of the expense of government, indeed, that of defence and protection, has constantly fallen upon the mother country. The ceremonial, too, of the civil government in the colonies, upon the reception of a new governor, upon the opening of a new assembly, etc., though sufficiently decent, is not accompanied with any expensive pomp or parade. Their ecclesiastical government is conducted upon a plan equally frugal. Tithes are unknown among them; and their clergy, who are far from being numerous, are maintained either by moderate stipends, or by the voluntary contributions of the people. The power of Spain and Portugal, on the contrary, derives some support from the taxes levied upon their colonies. France, indeed, has never drawn any considerable revenue from its colonies, the taxes which it levies upon them being generally spent among them. But the colony government of all these three nations is conducted upon a much more expensive plan and is accompanied with a much more expensive ceremonial. The sums spent upon the reception of a new viceroy of Peru, for example, have frequently been enormous. Such ceremonials are not only real taxes paid by the rich colonists upon those particular occasions, but they serve to introduce among them the habit of vanity and expense upon all other occasions. They are not only very grievous occasional taxes, but they contribute to establish perpetual taxes of the same kind still more grievous; the ruinous taxes of private luxury and extravagance. In the colonies of all those three nations too, the ecclesiastical government is extremely oppressive. Tithes take place in all of them, and are levied with the utmost rigor in those of Spain and Portugal. All of them besides are oppressed with a numerous race of mendicant friars, whose beggary being not only licensed but consecrated by religion, is a most grievous tax upon the poor people, who are most carefully taught that it is a duty to give, and a very great sin to refuse them their charity. Over and above all this, the clergy are, in all of them, the greatest engrossers of land.

Fourthly, in the disposal of their surplus produce, or of what is over and above their own consumption, the English colonies have been more favored, and have been allowed a more extensive market, than those of any other European nation. Every European nation has endeavored, more or less, to monopolize to itself the commerce of its colonies, and, upon that account, has prohibited the ships of foreign nations from trading to them, and has prohibited them from importing European goods from any foreign nation. But the manner in which this monopoly has been exercised in different nations has been very different.

Some nations have given up the whole commerce of their colonies to an exclusive company, of whom the colonies were obliged to buy all such European goods as they wanted, and to whom they were obliged to sell the whole of their own surplus produce. It was the interest of the company, therefore, not only to sell the former as dear, and to buy the latter as cheap as possible, but to buy no more of the latter, even at this low price, than what they could dispose of for a very high price in Europe. It was their interest not only to degrade in all cases the value of the surplus produce of the colony, but in many cases to discourage and keep down the natural increase of its quantity. Of all the expedients that can well be contrived to stunt the natural growth of a new colony, that of an exclusive company is undoubtedly the most effectual. This, however, has been the policy of Holland, though their company, in the course of the present century, has given up in many respects the exertion of their exclusive privilege. This, too, was the policy of Denmark till the reign of the late king. It has occasionally been the policy of France, and of late, since 1755, after it had been abandoned by all other nations, on account of its absurdity, it has become the policy of Portugal with regard at least to two of the principal provinces of Brazil, Pernambuco and Marannon.

Other nations, without establishing an exclusive company, have confined the whole commerce of their colonies to a particular port of the mother country, from whence no ship was allowed to sail, but either in a fleet and at a particular season, or, if single, in consequence of a particular license, which, in most cases, was very well paid for. This policy opened, indeed, the trade of the colonies to all the natives of the mother country, provided they traded from the proper port, at the proper season, and in the proper vessels. But as all the different merchants, who joined their stocks in order to fit out those licensed vessels, would find it for their interest to act in concert, the trade which was carried on in this manner would necessarily be conducted very nearly upon the same principles as that of an exclusive company. The profit of those merchants would be almost equally exorbitant and oppressive. The colonies would be ill supplied, and would be obliged both to buy very dear, and to sell very cheap. This, however, till within these few years, had always been the policy of Spain, and the price of all European goods, accordingly, is said to have been enormous in the Spanish West Indies. At Quito, we are told by Ulloa, a pound of iron sold for about four and sixpence, and a pound of steel for about six and ninepence sterling. But it is chiefly in order to purchase European goods, that the colonies part with their own produce. The more, therefore, they pay for the one, the less they really get for the other, and the dearness of the one is the same thing with the cheapness of the other. The policy of Portugal is in this respect the same as the ancient policy of Spain, with regard to all its colonies, except Pernambuco and Marannon, and with regard to these it has lately adopted a still worse.

Other nations leave the trade of their colonies free to all their subjects, who may carry it on from all the different ports of the mother country, and who have occasion for no other license than the common dispatches of the custom-house. In this case the number and dispersed situation of the different traders render it impossible for them to enter into any general combination, and their competition is sufficient to hinder them from making very exorbitant profits. Under so liberal a policy the colonies are enabled both to sell their own produce and to buy the goods of Europe at a reasonable price. But since the dissolution of the Plymouth company, when our colonies were but in their infancy, this has always been the policy of England. It has generally too been that of France, and has been uniformly so since the dissolution of what, in England, is commonly called their Mississippi company. The profits of the trade, therefore, which France and England carry on with their colonies, though no doubt somewhat higher than if the competition was free to all other nations, are, however, by no means exorbitant; and the price of European goods accordingly is not extravagantly high in the greater part of the colonies of either of those nations.

In the exportation of their own surplus produce too, it is only with regard to certain commodities that the colonies of Great Britain are confined to the market of the mother country. These commodities having been enumerated in the act of navigation and in some other subsequent acts, have upon that account been called *enumerated commodities*. The rest are called *non-enumerated*; and may be exported directly to other countries, provided it is in British or Plantation ships, of which the owners and three-fourths of the mariners are British subjects.

Among the non-enumerated commodities are some of the most important productions of America and the West Indies; grain of all sorts, lumber, salt, provisions, fish, sugar, and rum.

Grain is naturally the first and principal object of the culture of all new colonies. By allowing them a very extensive market for it, the law encourages them to extend this culture much beyond the consumption of a thinly inhabited country, and thus to provide beforehand an ample subsistence for a continually increasing population.

In a country quite covered with wood, where timber consequently is of little or no value, the expense of clearing the ground is the principal obstacle to improvement. By allowing the colonies a very extensive market for their lumber the law endeavors to facilitate improvement by raising the price of a commodity which would otherwise be of little value, and thereby enabling them to make some profit of what would otherwise be mere expense.

In a country neither half-peopled nor half-cultivated, cattle naturally multiply beyond the consumption of the inhabitants, and are often, upon that account, of little or no value. But it is necessary, it has already been shown, that the price of cattle should bear a certain proportion to that of corn before the greater part of the lands of any country can be improved. By allowing to American cattle, in all shapes, dead and alive a very extensive market, the law endeavors to raise the value of a commodity of which the high price is so very essential to improvement. The good effects of this liberty, however, must be somewhat diminished by the 4th of George III., c. 15, which puts hides and skins among the enumerated commodities, and thereby tends to reduce the valuation of American cattle.

To increase the shipping and naval power of Great Britain, by the extension of the fisheries of our colonies, is an object which the legislature seems to have had almost constantly in view. Those fisheries, upon this account, have had all the encouragement which freedom can give them, and they have flourished accordingly. The New England fishery in particular was, before the late disturbances, one of the most important, perhaps, in the world. The whale-fishery, which, notwithstanding an extravagant bounty, is in Great Britain carried on to so little purpose, that, in the opinion of many people (which I do not, however, pretend to warrant) the whole produce does not much exceed the value of the bounties which are annually paid for it, is in New England carried on without any bounty to a very great extent. Fish is one of the principal articles with which the North Americans trade to Spain, Portugal, and the Mediterranean.

Sugar was originally an enumerated commodity which could be exported only to Great Britain. But in 1731, upon a representation of the sugar-planters, its exportation was permitted to all parts of the world. The restrictions, however, with which this liberty was granted, joined to the high price of sugar in Great Britain, have rendered it, in a great measure, ineffectual. Great Britain and her colonies still continue to be almost the sole market for all the sugar produced in the British plantations. Their consumption increases so fast, that, though in consequence of the increasing improvement of Jamaica, as well as of the Ceded Islands, the importation of sugar has increased very greatly within these twenty years, the exportation to foreign countries is said to be not much greater than before.

Rum is a very important article in the trade which the Americans carry on to the coast of Africa, from which they bring back negro slaves in return.

If the whole surplus produce of America in grain of all sorts, in salt provisions, and in fish, had been put into the enumeration, and thereby forced into the market of Great Britain, it would have interfered too much with the produce of the industry of our own people. It was probably not so much from any regard to the interest of America, as from a jealousy of this interference, that those important commodities have not only been kept out of the enumeration, but that the importation into Great Britain of all grain, except rice, and of all salt provisions, has, in the ordinary state of the law, been prohibited.

The non-enumerated commodities could originally be exported to all parts of the world. Lumber and rice, having been once put into the enumeration, when they were afterwards taken out of it, were confined, as to the European market, to the countries that lie south of Cape Finisterre. By the 6th of George III., c. 52, all non-enumerated commodities were subjected to the like restriction. The parts of Europe which lie south of Cape Finisterre, are not manufacturing countries, and we were less jealous of the colony ships carrying home from them any manufactures which could interfere with our own.

The enumerated commodities are of two sorts: first, such as are either the peculiar produce of America, or as cannot be produced, or at least are not produced, in the mother country. Of this kind are, molasses, coffee, cocoanuts, tobacco, pimento, ginger, whale-fins, raw silk, cotton-wool, beaver, and other peltry of America, indigo, fustic, and other dyeing woods: secondly, such as are not the peculiar produce of America, but which are and may be produced in the mother country, though not in such quantities as to supply the greater part of her demand, which is principally supplied from foreign countries. Of this kind are all naval stores, masts, yards, and bowsprits, tar, pitch, and turpentine, pig and bar iron, copper ore, hides and skins, pot and pearl ashes. The largest importation of commodities of the first kind could not discourage the growth or interfere with the sale of any part of the produce of the mother country. By confining them to the home market, our merchants, it was expected, would not only be enabled to buy them cheaper in the Plantations, and consequently to sell them with a better profit at home, but to establish between the Plantations and foreign countries an advantageous carrying trade, of which Great Britain was necessarily to be the centre or emporium, as the European country into which those commodities were first to be imported. The importation of commodities of the second kind might be so managed too, it was supposed, as to interfere, not with the sale of those of the same kind which were produced at home, but with that of those which were imported from foreign countries; because, by means of proper duties, they might be rendered always somewhat dearer than the former, and yet a good deal cheaper than the latter. By confining such commodities to the home market, therefore, it was proposed to discourage the produce, not of Great Britain, but of some foreign countries with which the balance of trade was believed to be unfavorable to Great Britain.

The prohibition of exporting from the colonies, to any other country but Great Britain, masts, yards, and bowsprits, tar, pitch, and turpentine, naturally tended to lower the price of timber in the colonies, and consequently to increase the expense of clearing their lands, the principal obstacle to their improvement. But about the beginning of the present century, in 1703, the pitch and tar company of Sweden endeavored to raise the price of their commodities to Great Britain, by prohibiting their exportation, except in their own ships, at their own price, and in such quantities as they thought proper. In order to counteract this notable piece of mercantile policy, and to render herself as much as possible independent, not only of Sweden, but of all the other northern powers, Great Britain gave a bounty upon the importation of naval stores from America, and the effect of this bounty was to raise the price of timber in America, much more than the confinement to the home market could lower it; and, as both regulations were enacted at the same time, their joint effect was rather to encourage than to discourage the clearing of land in America.

Though pig and bar iron too have been put among the enumerated commodities, yet as, when imported from America, they are exempted from considerable duties to which they are subject when imported from any other country, the one part of the regulation contributes more to encourage the erection of furnaces in America, than the other to discourage it. There is no manufacture which occasions so great a consumption of wood as a furnace, or which can contribute so much to the clearing of a country overgrown with it.

The tendency of some of these regulations to raise the value of timber in America, and thereby to facilitate the clearing of the land, was neither, perhaps, intended nor understood by the legislature. Though their beneficial effects, however, have been in this respect accidental, they have not upon that account been less real.

The most perfect freedom of trade is permitted between the British colonies of America and the West Indies, both in the enumerated and in the non-enumerated commodities. Those colonies are now become so populous and thriving, that each of them finds in some of the others a great and extensive market for every part of its produce. All of them taken together, they make a great internal market for the produce of one another.

The liberality of England, however, towards the trade of her colonies has been confined chiefly to what concerns the market for their produce, either in its rude state, or in what may be called the very first stage of manufacture. The more advanced or more refined manufactures even of the colony produce, the merchants and manufacturers of Great Britain choose to reserve to themselves, and have prevailed upon the legislature to prevent their establishment in the colonies, sometimes by high duties, and sometimes by absolute prohibitions.

While, for example, Muscovado sugars from the British plantations, pay upon importation only 6s. 4d. the hundred weight; white sugars pay £1, 1s. 1d.; and refined, either double or single, in loaves £4, 2s. 5d. $\frac{8}{20}$. When those high duties were imposed, Great Britain was the sole, and she still continues to be the principal market to which the sugars of the British colonies could be exported. They amounted, therefore, to a prohibition, at first of claying or refining sugar for any foreign market, and at present of claying or refining it for the market, which takes off, perhaps, more than nine-tenths of the whole produce. The manufacture of claying or refining sugar accordingly, though it has flourished in all the sugar colonies of France, has been little cultivated in any of those of England, except for the market of the colonies themselves. While Grenada was in the hands of the French there was a refinery of sugar, by claying at least, upon almost every plantation. Since it fell into those of the English, almost all works of*this kind have been given up, and there are at present, October, 1773, I am assured, not above two or three remaining in the island. At present, however, by an indulgence of the custom-house, clayed or refined sugar, if reduced from loaves into powder, is commonly imported as Muscovado.

While Great Britain encourages in America the manufactures of pig and bar iron, by exempting them from duties to which the like commodities are subjected when imported from any other country, she imposes an absolute prohibition upon the erection of steel furnaces and slit-mills in any of her American plantations. She will not suffer her colonists to work in those more refined manufactures even for their own consumption; but insists upon their purchasing of her merchants and manufacturers all goods of this kind which they have occasion for.

She prohibits the exportation from one province to another by water, and even the carriage by land upon horseback or in a cart, of hats, of wools and woollen goods, of the produce of America; a regulation which effectually prevents the establishment of any manufacture of such commodities for distant sale, and confines the industry of her colonists in this way to such coarse and household manufactures, as a private family commonly makes for its own use, or for that of some of its neighbors in the same province.

To prohibit a great people, however, from making all that they can of every part of their own produce, or from employing their stock and industry in the way that they judge most advantageous to themselves, is a manifest violation of the most sacred rights of mankind. Unjust, however, as such prohibitions may be, they have not hitherto been very hurtful to the colonies. Land is still so cheap, and, consequently, labor so dear among them, that they can import from the mother country almost all the more refined or more advanced manufactures cheaper than they could make them for themselves. Though they had not, therefore, been prohibited from establishing such manufactures, yet in their present state of improvement, a regard to their own interest would, probably, have prevented them from doing so. In their present state of improvement those prohibitions, perhaps, without cramping their industry, or restraining it from any employment to which it would have gone of its own accord, are only impertinent badges of slavery imposed upon them, without any sufficient reason, by the groundless jealousy of the merchants and manufacturers of the mother country. In a more advanced state they might be really oppressive and insupportable.

Great Britain too, as she confines to her own market some of the most important productions of the colonies, so in compensation she gives to some of them an advantage in that market; sometimes by imposing higher duties upon the like productions when imported from other countries, and sometimes by giving bounties upon their importation from the colonies. In the first way she gives an advantage in the home market to the sugar, tobacco, and iron of her own colonies, and in the second to their raw silk, to their hemp and flax, to their indigo, to their naval stores, and to their building-timber. This second way of encouraging the colony produce by bounties upon importation, is, so far as I have been able to learn, peculiar to Great Britain. The first is not. Portugal does not content herself with imposing higher duties upon the importation of tobacco from any other country, but prohibits it under the severest penalties.

With regard to the importation of goods from Europe, England has likewise dealt more liberally with her colonies than any other nation.

Great Britain allows a part, almost always the half, generally a larger portion, and sometimes the whole of the duty which is paid upon the importation of foreign goods, to be drawn back upon their exportation to any foreign country. No independent foreign country, it was easy to foresee, would receive them if they came to it loaded with the heavy duties to which almost all foreign goods are subjected on their importation into Great Britain. Unless, therefore, some part of those duties was drawn back upon exportation, there was an end of the carrying trade; a trade so much favored by the mercantile system.

Our colonies, however, are by no means independent foreign countries; and Great Britain, having assumed to herself the exclusive right of supplying them with all goods from Europe, might have forced them (in the same manner as other countries have done their colonies) to receive such goods loaded with all the same duties which they paid in the mother country. But, on the contrary, till 1763, the same drawbacks were paid upon the exportation of the greater part of foreign goods to our colonies as to any independent foreign country. In 1763, indeed, by the 4th of George III., c. 15, this indulgence, was a good deal abated, and it was enacted, " That no part of the duty called the old subsidy should be drawn back for any goods of the growth, production, or manufacture of Europe or the East Indies, which should be exported from this kingdom to any British colony or plantation in America; wines, white calicoes and muslins excepted." Before this law, many different sorts of foreign goods might have been bought cheaper in the plantations than in the mother country; and some may still.

Of the greater part of the regulations concerning the colony trade, the merchants who carry it on, it must be observed, have been the principal advisers. We must not wonder, therefore, if, in the greater part of them, their interest has been more considered than either that of the colonies or that of the mother country. In their exclusive privilege of supplying the colonies with all the goods which they wanted from Europe, and of purchasing all such parts of their surplus produce as could not interfere with any of the trades which they themselves carried on at home, the interest of the colonies was sacrificed to the interest of those merchants. In allowing the same drawbacks upon the re-exportation of the greater part of European and East India goods to the colonies, as upon their re-exportation to any independent country, the interest of the mother country was sacrificed to it, even according to the mercantile ideas of that interest. It was for the interest of the merchants to pay as little as possible for the foreign goods which they sent to the colonies, and consequently, to get back as much as possible of the duties which they advanced upon their importation into Great Britain. They might thereby be enabled to sell in the colonies, either the same quantity of goods with a greater profit, or a greater quantity with the same profit, and, consequently, to gain something either in the one way or the other. It was, likewise, for the interest of the colonies to get all such goods as cheap and in as great abundance as possible. But this might not always be for the interest of the mother country. She might frequently suffer both in her revenue, by giving back a great part of the duties which had been paid upon the importation of such goods; and in her manufactures, by being undersold in the colony market, in consequence of the easy terms upon which foreign manufactures could be carried thither by means of those drawbacks. The progress of the linen manufacture of Great Britain, it is commonly said, has been a good deal retarded by the drawbacks upon the re-exportation of German linen to the American colonies.

But though the policy of Great Britain with regard to the trade of her colonies has been dictated by the same mercantile spirit as that of other nations, it has, however, upon the whole, been less illiberal and oppressive than that of any of them.

In everything, except their foreign trade, the liberty of the English colonists to manage their own affairs their own way is complete. It is in every respect equal to that of their fellow-citizens at home, and is secured in the same manner, by an assembly of the representatives of the people, who claim the sole right of imposing taxes for the support of the colony government. The authority of this assembly overawes the executive power, and neither the meanest nor the most obnoxious colonist, as long as he obeys the law, has anything to fear from the resentment, either of the governor, or of any other civil or military officer in the province. The colony assemblies, though, like the house of commons in England, they are not always a very equal representation of the people, yet they approach more nearly to that character; and as the executive power either has not the means to corrupt them, or, on account of the support which it receives from the mother country, is not under the necessity of doing so, they are perhaps in general more influenced by the inclinations of their constituents. The councils, which, in the colony legislatures, correspond to the house of lords in Great Britain, are not composed of an hereditary nobility. In some of the colonies, as in three of the governments of New England, those councils are not appointed by the king, but chosen by the representatives of the people. In none of the English colonies is there any hereditary nobility. In all of them, indeed, as in all other free countries, the descendant of an old colony family is more respected than an upstart of equal merit and fortune: but he is only more respected, and he has no privileges by which he can be troublesome to his neighbors. Before the commencement of the present disturbances, the colony assemblies had not only the legislative, but a part of the executive power. In Connecticut and Rhode Island they elected the governor. In the other colonies they appointed the revenue officers who collected the taxes imposed by those respective assemblies, to whom those officers were immediately responsible. There is more equality, therefore, among the English colonists than among the inhabitants of the mother country. Their manners are more republican, and their governments, those of three of the provinces of New England in particular, have hitherto been more republican too.

The absolute governments of Spain, Portugal, and France, on the contrary, take place in their colonies; and the discretionary powers which such governments commonly delegate to all their inferior officers are, on account of the great distance, naturally exercised there with more than ordinary violence. Under all absolute governments there is more liberty in the capital than in any other part of the country. The sovereign himself can never have either interest or inclination to pervert the order of justice, or to oppress the great body of the people. In the capital his presence overawes more or less all his inferior officers, who in the remoter provinces, from whence the complaints of the people are less likely to reach him, can exercise their tyranny with much more safety. But the European colonies in America are more remote than the most distant provinces of the greatest empires which had ever been known before. The government of the English colonies is perhaps the only one which, since the world began, could give perfect security to the inhabitants of so very distant a province. The administration of the French colonies, however, has always been conducted with more gentleness and moderation than that of the Spanish and Portuguese. This superiority of conduct is suitable both to the character of the French nation, and to what forms the character of every nation, the nature of their government, which, though arbitrary and violent in comparison with that of Great Britain, is legal and free in comparison with those of Spain and Portugal.

It is in the progress of the North American colonies, however, that the superiority of the English policy chiefly appears. The progress of the sugar colonies of France has been at least equal, perhaps superior, to that of the greater part of those of England; and yet the sugar colonies of England enjoy a free government nearly of the same kind with that which takes place in her colonies of North America. But the sugar colonies of France are not discouraged, like those of England, from refining their own sugar; and, what is of still greater importance, the genius of their government naturally introduces a better management of their negro slaves.

In all European colonies the culture of the sugar-cane is carried on by negro slaves. The constitution of those who have been born in the temperate climate of Europe could not, it is supposed, support the labor of digging the ground under the burning sun of the West Indies; and the culture of the sugar-cane, as it is managed at present, is all hand labor, though, in the opinion of many, the drill plough might be introduced into it with great advantage. But, as the profit and success of the cultivation which is carried on by means of cattle, depend very much upon the good management of those cattle ; so the profit and success of that which is carried on by slaves, must depend equally upon the good management of those slaves ; and in the good management of their slaves the French planters, I think it is generally allowed, are superior to the English. The law, so far as it gives some weak protection to the slave against the violence of his master, is likely to be better executed in a colony where the government is in a great measure arbitrary, than in one where it is altogether free. In every country where the unfortunate law of slavery is established, the magistrate, when he protects the slave, intermeddles in some measure in the management of the private property of the master ; and, in a free country, where the master is perhaps either a member of the colony assembly, or an elector of such a member, he dare not do this but with the greatest caution and circumspection. The respect which he is obliged to pay to the master renders it more difficult for him to protect the slave. But in a country where the government is in a great measure arbitrary, where it is usual for the magistrate to intermeddle even in the management of the private property of individuals, and to send them, perhaps, a *lettre de cachet* if they do not manage it according to his liking, it is much easier for him to give some protection to the slave ; and common humanity naturally disposes him to do so. The protection of the magistrate renders the slave less contemptible in the eyes of his master, who is thereby induced to consider him with more regard, and to treat him with more gentleness. Gentle usage renders the slave not only more faithful, but more intelligent, and therefore, upon a double account, more useful. He approaches more to the condition of a free servant, and may possess some degree of integrity and attachment to his master's interest, — virtues which frequently belong to free servants, but which never can belong to a slave, who is treated as slaves commonly are in countries where the master is perfectly free and secure.

That the condition of a slave is better under an arbitrary than under a free government, is, I believe, supported by the history of all ages and nations. In the Roman history the first time we read of the magistrate interposing to protect the slave from the violence of his master is under the emperors. When Vedius Pollio, in the Augustus, ordered one of his slaves, who had committed a slight fault, to be cut into pieces, and thrown into his fish-pond in order to feed his fishes, the emperor commanded him, with indignation, to emancipate immediately, not only that slave but all the others that belonged to him. Under the republic no magistrate could have had authority enough to protect the slave, much less to punish the master.

The stock, it is to be observed, which has improved the sugar colonies of France, particularly the great colony of St. Domingo, has been raised almost entirely from the gradual improvement and cultivation of those colonies. It has been almost altogether the produce of the soil and of the industry of the colonists, or, what comes to the same thing, the price of that produce gradually accumulated by good management, and employed in raising a still greater produce. But the stock which has improved and cultivated the sugar colonies of England has, a great part of it, been sent out from England, and has by no means been altogether the produce of the soil and industry of the colonists. The prosperity of the English sugar colonies has been, in a great measure, owing to the great riches of England, of which a part has overflowed, if one may say so, upon those colonies. But the prosperity of the sugar colonies of France has been entirely owing to the good conduct of the colonists, which must therefore have had some superiority over that of the English; and this superiority has been remarked in nothing so much as in the good management of their slaves.

Such have been the general outlines of the policy of the different European nations with regard to their colonies.

The policy of Europe, therefore, has very little to boast of, either in the original establishment, or, so far as concerns their internal government, in the subsequent prosperity of the colonies of America.

Folly and injustice seem to have been the principles which presided over and directed the first project of establishing those colonies; the folly of hunting after gold and silver mines, and the injustice of coveting the possession of a country whose harmless natives, far from having ever injured the people of Europe, had received the first adventurers with every mark of kindness and hospitality.

The adventurers, indeed, who formed some of the later establishments, joined, to the chimerical project of finding gold and silver mines, other motives more reasonable and more laudable; but even these motives do very little honor to the policy of Europe.

The English Puritans, restrained at home, fled for freedom to America, and established there the four governments of New England. The English Catholics, treated with much greater injustice, established that of Maryland; the Quakers, that of Pennsylvania. The Portuguese Jews, persecuted by the Inquisition, stripped of their fortunes, and banished to Brazil, introduced, by their example, some sort of order and industry among the transported felons and strumpets, by whom that colony was originally peopled, and taught them the culture of the sugar-cane. Upon all these different occasions, it was, not the wisdom and policy, but the disorder and injustice, of the European governments, which peopled and cultivated America.

In effectuating some of the most important of these establishments, the different governments of Europe had as little merit as in projecting them. The conquest of Mexico was the project, not of the council of Spain, but of a governor of Cuba; and it was effectuated by the spirit of the bold adventurer to whom it was entrusted, in spite of everything which that governor, who soon repented of having trusted such a person, could do to thwart it. The conquerors of Chili and Peru, and of almost all the other Spanish settlements upon the continent of America, carried out with them no other public encouragement, but a general permission to make settlements and conquests in the name of the king of Spain. Those adventures were all at the private risk and expense of the adventurers. The government of Spain contributed scarce anything to any of them. That of England contributed as little towards effectuating the establishment of some of its most important colonies in North America.

When those establishments were effectuated, and had become so considerable as to attract the attention of the mother country, the first regulations which she made with regard to them had always in view to secure to herself the monopoly of their commerce; to confine their market, and to enlarge her own at their expense, and, consequently, rather to damp and discourage, than to quicken and forward, the course of their prosperity. In the different ways in which this monopoly has been exercised, consists one of the most essential differences in the policy of the different European nations with regard to their colonies. The best of them all, that of England, is only somewhat less illiberal and oppressive than that of any of the rest.

In what way, therefore, has the policy of Europe contributed either to the first establishment, or to the present grandeur of the colonies of America? In one way, and in one way only, it has contributed a good deal. *Magna virum Mater!* It bred and formed the men who were capable of achieving such great actions, and of laying the foundation of so great an empire; and there is no other quarter of the world of which the policy is capable of forming, or has ever actually and in fact formed, such men. The colonies owe to the policy of Europe the education and great views of their active and enterprising founders; and some of the greatest and most important of them, so far as concerns their internal government, owe to it scarce anything else.

III.

THE GREAT INVENTIONS.

FROM WALPOLE'S HISTORY OF ENGLAND, VOL. I., PP. 50–76.

The manufacturing industries of the country had never previously experienced so marvellous a development. The hum of the workshop was heard in places which had previously only been disturbed by the whirr of the grouse; and new forces, undreamed of a century before, were employed to assist the progress of production. The trade of the United Kingdom acquired an importance which it had never previously enjoyed, and the manufacturing classes obtained an influence which they had never before known. The land-owners were slowly losing the monopoly of power which they had enjoyed for centuries. Traders and manufacturers were daily obtaining fresh wealth and influence. A new England was supplanting the old country; and agriculture, the sole business of our forefathers, was gradually becoming of less importance than trade. In 1793, the first year of the war, the official value of all the imports into Britain was less than £20,000,000. In 1815, the year of Waterloo, it exceeded £31,000,000. In 1792, the official value of British and Irish exports was only £18,000,000: it rose in 1815 to £41,000,000. The official values, however, give only a very imperfect idea of the extent of our export trade. They are based on prices fixed so far back as 1696, and afford, therefore, an inaccurate test of the extent of our trade. No attempt was made to ascertain the declared or real value of the exports till the year 1798, when it slightly exceeded £33,000,000. The declared value of the exports of British and Irish produce in 1815 exceeded £49,000,000. The rise in the value of the exports and imports was attributable to many causes. The predominance of the British at sea had driven every enemy from the ocean, and had enabled British merchants to ply their trade in comparative safety. The numerous possessions, which the British had acquired in every quarter of the globe, had provided them with customers in all parts of the world; and the most civilized, as well as the most savage, of nations were purchasing the produce of the looms of Manchester and of the factories of Birmingham. Even the taxation which the war had necessitated had stimulated the manufacturers to fresh exertions. The merchants were continually discovering fresh outlets for British trade; the manufacturers were constantly encouraged to increase their produce.[1]

Wool was the most ancient and most important of English manufactures. Custom seemed to point to the permanent superiority of the woollen trade. The Chancellor of England sat on a sack of wool; and when men spoke of the staple trade, they always referred to the trade in wool. For centuries British sovereigns and British statesmen had, after their own fashion, and according to their own ideas, actively promoted this particular industry. Edward III. had induced Flemish weavers to settle in this country. The Restoration Parliament prohibited the exportation of British wool, and had ordered that the very dead should be interred in woollen shrouds. The manufacturers spread over the entire kingdom. Wherever there was a running stream to turn their mill, there was at any rate the possibility of a woollen factory. Norwich, with its contiguous village of Worsted, was the chief seat of the trade. But York and Bradford, Worcestershire and Gloucestershire, Manchester and Kendal, were largely dependent on it.

The steps, which Parliament took to promote this particular industry, were not always very wise; in one point they were not very just. Ireland, in many respects, could have competed on advantageous terms with the woollen manufacturers of England. English jealousy prohibited in consequence the importation of Irish manufactured woollen goods. The result hardly answered the sanguine anticipations of the selfish senators who had secured it. The Irish, instead of sending their fleeces to be worked up in Great Britain, smuggled them, in return for contraband spirits, to France. England failed to obtain any large addition to her raw material; and Ireland was driven into closer communication with the hereditary foe of England. The loss of the Irish fleeces was the more serious from another cause. The home supply of wool had originally been abundant and good; but its production, at the commencement of the century, was not increasing as

---

[1] McCulloch's " Commercial Dictionary," imports and exports; cf., however, Porter's " Progress of the Nation," p. 357, where the figures are slightly different. Nothing is more difficult than to ascertain the correct figures.

rapidly as the demand for it; the quality of home-grown wool was rapidly deteriorating. The same sheep do not produce both wool and mutton in the greatest perfection. Every improvement in their meat is effected at the cost of their fleece. English mutton was better than it had ever been; but English manufacturers were compelled to mix foreign with native wool. Had trade been free this result would have been of little moment. The English could have easily obtained an ample supply of raw material from the hills of Spain and other countries. But, at the very time at which foreign wool became indispensable, the necessities of the country, or the ignorance of her financiers, led to the imposition of a heavy import duty on wool. Addington, in 1802, levied a duty upon it of 5*s*. 3*d*. the cwt.; Vansittart, in 1813, raised the tax to 6*s*. 8*d*. The folly of the protectionists had done much to ruin the wool trade. But the evil already done was small in comparison with that in store.

Nowithstanding, however, the restrictions on the wool trade, the woollen industry was of great importance. In 1800, Law, as counsel to the manufacturers, declared, in an address to the House of Lords, that 600,000 packs of wool, worth £6,600,000, were produced annually in England and Wales, and that 1,500,000 persons were employed in the manufacture. But these figures, as McCulloch has shown, are undoubtedly great exaggerations.[1] Rather more than 400,000 packs of wool were available for manufacturing purposes at the commencement of the century; more than nine-tenths of these were produced at home; and some 350,000 or 400,000 persons were probably employed in the trade. The great woollen industry still deserved the name of our staple trade; but it did not merit the exaggerated descriptions which persons, who should have known better, applied to it.

If the staple trade of the country had originally been in woollen goods at the commencement of the present century, cotton was rapidly gaining upon wool. Cotton had been used in the extreme East and in the extreme West from the earliest periods of which we have any records. The Spaniards, on their discovery of America, found the Mexicans clothed in cotton. " There are trees," Herodotus had written, nearly 2,000 years before, " which grow wild there (in India), the fruit whereof is a wool exceeding in beauty and goodness that of sheep. The

---

[1] " McCulloch," ad verb. Wool; Porter's " Progress of the Nation," pp. 170-175.

natives make their clothes of this tree wool."[1] But though the use of cotton had been known from the earliest ages, both in India and America, no cotton goods were imported into Europe; and in the ancient world both rich and poor were clothed in silk, linen, and wool. The industrious Moors introduced cotton into Spain. Many centuries afterwards cotton was imported into Italy, Saxony, and the Low Countries. Isolated from the rest of Europe, with little wealth, little industry, and no roads; rent by civil commotions; the English were the last people in Europe to introduce the manufacture of cotton goods into their own homes.

Towards the close of the sixteenth century, indeed, cotton goods were occasionally mentioned in the Statute Book, and the manufacture of the cottons of Manchester was regulated by Acts passed in the reigns of Henry VIII., Edward VI. and Elizabeth. But there seem to be good reasons for concluding that Manchester cottons, in the time of the Tudors, were woollen goods, and did not consist of cotton at all. More than a century elapsed before any considerable trade in cotton attracted the attention of the legislature. The woollen manufacturers complained that people were dressing their children in printed cottons; and Parliament was actually persuaded to prohibit the introduction of Indian printed calicoes. Even an Act of Parliament, however, was unable to extinguish the growing taste for Indian cottons. The ladies, according to the complaint of an old writer, expected "to do what they please, to say what they please, and wear what they please." The taste for cotton led to the introduction of calico-printing in London; Parliament, in order to encourage the new trade, was induced to sanction the importation of plain cotton cloths from India under a duty. The demand, which was thus created for calicoes, probably promoted their manufacture at home; and Manchester, Bolton, Frome, and other places, gradually acquired fresh vitality from the creation of a new history.

Many years, however, passed before the trade attained anything but the slenderest proportions. In the year 1697 only 1,976,-359 lbs. of cotton wool were imported into the United Kingdom. In the year 1751 only 2,976,610 lbs. were imported. The official value of cotton goods exported amounted in the former year to

---

[1] Rawlinson's "Herodotus," vol. ii. p. 411. The German name for cotton is Baumwolle — tree wool.

only £5,915; in the latter year to only £45,986. At the present time Britain annually purchases about 1,500,000,000 lbs. of cotton wool. She annually disposes of cotton goods worth £60,000,000. The import trade is 500 times as large as it was in 1751; the value of the exports has been increased 1,300 fold. The world has never seen, in any similar period, so prodigious a growth of manufacturing industry. But the trade has not merely grown from an infant into a giant; its conditions have been concurrently revolutionized. Up to the middle of the last century cotton goods were really never made at all. The so-called cotton manufactures were a combination of wool or linen and cotton. No Englishman had been able to produce a cotton thread strong enough for the warp; and even the cotton manufacturers themselves appear to have despaired of doing so. They induced Parliament in 1736 to repeal the prohibition, which still encumbered the Statute Book, against wearing printed calicoes; but the repeal was granted on the curious condition "that the warp thereof be entirely linen yarn." Parliament no doubt intended by this condition to check the importation of Indian goods without interfering with the home manufacturers. The superior skill of the Indian manufacturers enabled them to use cotton for a warp; while clumsy workmanship made the use of cotton as a warp unattainable at home.

In the middle of the eighteenth century, then, a piece of cotton cloth, in the true sense of the term, had never been made in England. The so-called cotton goods were all made in the cottages of the weavers. The yarn was carded by hand; it was spun by hand; it was worked into cloth by a hand-loom. The weaver was usually the head of the family; his wife and unmarried daughters spun the yarn for him. Spinning was the ordinary occupation of every girl, and the distaff was, for countless centuries, the ordinary occupation of every woman. The occupation was so universal that the distaff was occasionally used as a synonym for woman. "Le royaume de France ne tombe point en *quenouille.*"

"See my royal master murdered,
His crown usurped, a *distaff* in the throne."

To this day every unmarried girl is commonly described as a "spinster."

The operation of weaving was, however, much more rapid than

that of spinning. The weaver consumed more weft than his own family could supply him with; and the weavers generally experienced the greatest difficulty in obtaining sufficient yarn. About the middle of the eighteenth century the ingenuity of two persons, a father and a son, made this difference more apparent. The shuttle had originally been thrown by the hand from one end of the loom to the other. John Kay, a native of Bury, by his invention of the fly-shuttle, saved the weaver from this labor. The lathe, in which the shuttle runs, was lengthened at both ends; two strings were attached to its opposite ends; the strings were held by a peg in the weaver's hands, and, by plucking the peg, the weaver was enabled to give the necessary impulse to the shuttle. Robert Kay, John Kay's son, added the drop-box, by means of which the weaver was able " to use any one of the three shuttles, each containing a different colored weft, without the trouble of taking them from and replacing them in the lathe." By means of these inventions the productive power of each weaver was doubled. Each weaver was easily able to perform the amount of work which had previously required two men to do; and the spinsters found themselves more hopelessly distanced than ever in their efforts to supply the weavers with weft.

The preparation of weft was entirely accomplished by manual labor, and the process was very complicated. Carding and roving were both slowly performed with the aid of the clumsy implements which had originally been invented for the purpose. " Carding is the process to which the cotton is subjected after it has been opened and cleaned, in order that the fibres of the wool may be disentangled, straightened, and laid parallel with each other, so as to admit of being spun. This was formerly effected by instruments called hand-cards, which were brushes made of short pieces of wire instead of bristles, the wires being stuck into a sheet of leather, at a certain angle, and the leather fastened on a flat piece of wood about twelve inches long and five wide, with a handle. The cotton being spread upon one of the cards, it was repeatedly combed with another till all the fibres were laid straight, when it was stripped off the card in a fleecy roll ready for the rover. In ' roving ' the spinner took the short fleecy rolls in which the cotton was stripped off the hand-cards, applied them successively to the spindle, and whilst with one hand she turned the wheel and thus made the spindle revolve, with the other she drew out the cardings, which, receiving a slight twist from the spindle, were made into thick threads called rovings, and wound upon the spindle so as to form cops." In spinning, " the roving was spun into yarn; the operation was similar, but the thread was drawn out much finer and received much more twist. It will be seen that this instrument only admitted of one thread being spun at a time by one pair of hands, and the slowness of the operation and consequent expensiveness of the yarn formed a great obstacle to the establishment of a new manufacture."

The trade was in this humble and primitive state when a series of extraordinary and unparalleled inventions revolutionized the conditions on which cotton had been hitherto prepared. A little more than a century ago John Hargreaves, a poor weaver in the neighborhood of Blackburn, was returning home from a long walk, in which he had been purchasing a further supply of yarn for his loom. As he entered his cottage, his wife Jenny accidentally upset the spindle which she was using. Hargreaves noticed that the spindles, which were now thrown into an upright position, continued to revolve, and that the thread was still spinning in his wife's hand. The idea immediately occurred to him that it would be possible to connect a considerable number of upright spindles with one wheel, and thus multiply the productive power of each spinster. " He contrived a frame in one part of which he placed eight rovings in a row, and in another part a row of eight spindles. The rovings, when extended to the spindles passed between two horizontal bars of wood, forming a clasp which opened and shut somewhat like a parallel ruler. When pressed together this clasp held the threads fast; a certain portion of roving being extended from the spindles to the wooden clasp, the clasp was closed, and was then drawn along the horizontal frame to a considerable distance from the spindles, by which the threads were lengthened out and reduced to the proper tenuity; this was done with the spinner's left hand, and his right hand at the same time turned a wheel which caused the spindles to revolve rapidly, and thus the roving was spun into yarn. By returning the clasp to its first situation and letting down a piercer wire, the yarn was wound upon the spindle."

Hargreaves succeeded in keeping his admirable invention secret for a time; but the powers of his machine soon became known. His ignorant neighbors hastily concluded that a machine, which enabled one spinster to do the work of eight, would throw multitudes of persons out of employment. A mob broke into his house and destroyed his machine. Hargreaves himself had to retire to Nottingham, where, with the friendly assistance of another person, he was able to take out a patent for the spinning-jenny, as the machine, in compliment to his industrious wife, was called.

The invention of the spinning-jenny gave a new impulse to the cotton manufacture. But the invention of the spinning-jenny, if it had been accompanied by no other improvements, would not have allowed any purely cotton goods to be manufactured in England. The yarn spun by the jenny, like that which had previously been spun by hand, was neither fine enough nor hard enough to be employed as warp, and linen or woollen threads had consequently to be used for this purpose. In the very year, however, in which Hargreaves moved from Blackburn to Nottingham, Richard Arkwright took out a patent for his still more celebrated machine. It is alleged that John Wyatt, of Birmingham, thirty years before the date of Arkwright's patent, had elaborated a machine for spinning by rollers. But in a work of this description it is impossible to analyze the conflicting claims of rival inventors to the credit of discovering particular machinery; and the historian can do no more than record the struggles of those whose names are associated with the improvements which he is noticing. Richard Arkwright, like John Hargreaves, had a humble origin. Hargreaves began life as a poor weaver; Arkwright, as a barber's assistant. Hargreaves had a fitting partner in his industrious wife Jenny. Mrs. Arkwright is said to have destroyed the models which her husband had made. But Arkwright was not deterred from his pursuit by the poverty of his circumstances or the conduct of his wife. "After many years' intense and painful application," he invented his memorable machine for spinning by rollers; and laid the foundations of the gigantic industry which has done more than any other trade to concentrate in this country the wealth of the world. The principle of Arkwright's great invention is very simple. He passed the thread over two pairs of rollers, one of which was made to revolve much more rapidly than the other. The thread, after passing over the pair revolving slowly, was drawn into the requisite tenuity by the rollers revolving at a higher rapidity. By this simple but memorable invention Arkwright succeeded in producing thread capable of employment as warp. From the circumstance that the mill at which his machinery was first erected was driven by water power, the machine received the somewhat inappropriate name of the water-frame; the thread spun by it was usually called the water-twist. The invention of the fly-shuttle by John Kay had enabled the weavers to consume more cotton than the spinsters had been able to provide; the invention of the spinning-jenny and the water-frame would have been useless if the old system of hand-carding had not been superseded by a more efficient and more rapid process. Just as Arkwright applied rotatory motion to spinning, so Lewis Paul introduced revolving cylinders for carding cotton. Paul's machine consisted of "a horizontal cylinder, covered in its whole circumference with parallel rows of cards with intervening spaces, and turned by a handle. Under the cylinder was a concave frame, lined internally with cards exactly fitting the lower half of the cylinder, so that when the handle was turned, the cards of the cylinder and of the concave frame worked against each other and carded the wool." "The cardings were of course only of the length of the cylinder, but an ingenious apparatus was attached for making them into a perpetual carding. Each length was placed on a flat broad riband which was extended between two short cylinders and which wound upon one cylinder as it unwound from the other."[1]

This extraordinary series of inventions placed an almost unlimited supply of yarn at the disposal of the weaver. But the machinery, which had thus been introduced, was still incapable of providing yarn fit for the finer qualities of cotton cloth. "The water-frame spun twist for warps, but it could not be advantageously used for the finer qualities, as thread of great tenuity has not strength to bear the pull of the rollers when winding itself on the bobbin." This defect, however, was removed by the ingenuity of Samuel Crompton, a young weaver residing near Bolton. Crompton succeeded in combining in one machine the various excellences of "Arkwright's water-frame and Hargreaves' jenny." Like the former, his machine, which from its nature is happily called the mule, "has a system of rollers to reduce the roving; and, like the latter, it has spindles without bobbins to give the twist, and the thread is stretched and spun at the same time by the spindles after the rollers have ceased to

---

[1] Baines'" Hist. of the Cotton Manufacture," p. 173, from which work the preceding quotations are also taken.

give out the rove. The distinguishing feature of the mule is that the spindles, instead of being stationary, as in both the other machines, are placed on a movable carriage, which is wheeled out to the distance of fifty-four or fifty-six inches from the roller beam, in order to stretch and twist the thread, and wheeled in again to wind it on the spindles. In the jenny, the clasp, which held the rovings, was drawn back by the hand from the spindles; in the mule, on the contrary, the spindles recede from the clasp, or from the roller beam, which acts as a clasp. The rollers of the mule draw out the roving much less than those of the water-frame, and they act like the clasp of the jenny by stopping and holding fast the rove, after a certain quantity has been given out, whilst the spindles continue to recede for a short distance farther, so that the draught of the thread is in part made by the receding of the spindles. By this arrangement, comprising the advantages both of the roller and the spindles, the thread is stretched more gently and equably, and a much finer quality of yarn can therefore be produced."[1]

The effects of Crompton's great invention may be stated epigrammatically. Before Crompton's time it was thought impossible to spin eighty hanks to the pound. The mule has spun three hundred and fifty hanks to the pound! The natives of India could spin a pound of cotton into a thread 119 miles long. The English succeeded in spinning the same thread to a length of 160 miles.[2] Yarn of the finest quality was at once at the disposal of the weaver, and an opportunity was afforded for the production of an indefinite quantity of cotton yarn. But the great inventions, which have been thus enumerated, would not of themselves have been sufficient to establish the cotton manufacture on its present basis. The ingenuity of Hargreaves, Arkwright, and Crompton had been exercised to provide the weaver with yarn. Their inventions had provided him with more yarn than he could by any possibility use. The spinster had beaten the weaver, just as the weaver had previously beaten the spinster, and the manufacture of cotton seemed likely to stand still because the yarn could not be woven more rapidly than an expert workman with Kay's improved fly-shuttle could weave it.

Such a result was actually contemplated by some of the leading manufacturers, and such a result might possibly have temporarily

---

[1] Baines' "Hist. of the Cotton Manufacture," pp. 197, 198.
[2] Ibid., p. 200, and "Colchester," vol. ii. p. 75.

occurred if it had not been averted by the ingenuity of a Kentish clergyman. Edmund Cartwright, a clergyman residing in Kent, happened to be staying at Matlock in the summer of 1784, and to be thrown into the company of some Manchester gentlemen. The conversation turned on Arkwright's machinery, and "one of the company observed that, as soon as Arkwright's patent expired, so many mills would be erected and so much cotton spun that hands would never be found to weave it." Cartwright replied "that Arkwright must then set his wits to work to invent a weaving mill." The Manchester gentlemen, however, unanimously agreed that the thing was impracticable. Cartwright "controverted the impracticability by remarking that there had been exhibited an automaton figure which played at chess;" it could not be "more difficult to construct a machine that shall weave than one which shall make all the variety of moves which are required in that complicated game." Within three years he had himself proved that the invention was practicable by producing the power-loom. Subsequent inventors improved the idea which Cartwright had originated, and within fifty years from the date of his memorable visit to Matlock there were not less than 100,000 power-looms at work in Great Britain alone.[1]

The inventions, which have been thus enumerated, are the most remarkable of the improvements which stimulated the development of the cotton industry. But other inventions, less generally remembered, were hardly less wonderful or less beneficial than these. Up to the middle of last century cotton could only be bleached by the cloth being steeped in alkaline lyes for several days, washed clean, and spread on the grass for some weeks to dry. The process had to be repeated several times, and many months were consumed before the tedious operation was concluded. Scheele, the Swedish philosopher, discovered in 1774 the bleaching properties of chlorine, or oxymuriatic acid. Berthollet, the French chemist, conceived in 1785 the idea of applying the acid to bleaching cloth. Watt, the inventor of the steam-engine, and Henry of Manchester, respectively introduced the new acid into the bleach-fields of Macgregor of Glasgow and Ridgway of Bolton. The process of bleaching was at once reduced from months to days, or even hours.[2]

In the same year in which Watt and Henry were introducing

---
[1] Baines' "Cotton," pp. 229, 235.
[2] Ibid., pp. 247-249.

the new acid to the bleacher, Bell, a Scotchman, was laying the foundations of a trade in printed calicoes. "The old method of printing was by blocks of sycamore, about 10 inches long by 5 broad, on the surface of which the pattern was cut in relief in the common method of wood engraving." As the block had to be applied to the cloth by hand, "no more of it could be printed at once than the block could cover, and a single piece of calico, 28 yards in length, required the application of the block 448 times."[1] This clumsy process was superseded by cylinder printing. "A polished copper cylinder, several feet in length, and 3 or 4 inches in diameter, is engraved with a pattern round its whole circumference and from end to end. It is then placed horizontally in a press, and, as it revolves, the lower part of the circumference passes through the coloring matter, which is again removed from the whole surface of the cylinder, except the engraved pattern, by an elastic steel blade placed in contact with the cylinder, and reduced to so fine and straight an edge as to take off the color without scratching the copper. The color being thus left only in the engraved pattern, the piece of calico or muslin is drawn tightly over the cylinder, which revolves in the same direction, and prints the cloth." The saving of labor "effected by the machine" is "immense; one of the cylinder machines, attended by a man and a boy, is actually capable of producing as much work as could be turned out by one hundred block printers, and as many tear boys."[2]

Such are the leading inventions, which made Great Britain in less than a century the wealthiest country in the world. "When we undertook the cotton manufacture we had comparatively few facilities for its prosecution, and had to struggle with the greatest difficulties. The raw material was produced at an immense distance from our shores, and in Hindustan and in China the inhabitants had arrived at such perfection in the arts of spinning and weaving, that the lightness and delicacy of their finest cloths emulated the web of the gossamer, and seemed to set competition at defiance. Such, however, has been the influence of the stupendous discoveries and inventions of Hargreaves, Arkwright, Crompton, Cartwright, and others, that we have overcome all these difficulties, — that neither the extreme cheapness of labor in Hindustan, nor the excellence to which the natives had attained,

---

[1] Baines' "Cotton," pp. 264, 265.
[2] Ibid., pp. 265, 266.

has enabled them to withstand the competition of those, who buy their cotton, and who, after carrying it 5,000 miles to be manufactured, carry back the goods to them."[1]

If Great Britain entirely monopolized the woollen and the cotton trades, she had done her best, in her own way, to promote the manufacture of linen in Ireland. In 1698 Parliament, while rigorously prohibiting the exportation of Irish woollen goods, sedulously attempted to encourage the linen manufacture in Ireland. Bounties were paid on all linen goods imported into this country from the sister island ; and the great linen trade acquired, especially in Ulster, the importance which it still retains. In 1800, 31,978,039 yards of linen were exported from Ireland to Great Britain, and 2,585,829 yards to other countries. In 1815, the export trade had risen to 37,986,359 and 5,496,206 yards respectively. A formidable rival to Ulster was, however, slowly rising in another part of the kingdom. At the close of the great French war Dundee was still an insignificant manufacturing town, but the foundations were already laid of the surprising supremacy which she has since acquired in the linen trade. Some 3,000 tons of flax were imported into the Scotch port in 1814. But the time was rapidly coming when the shipments of linen from this single place were to exceed those from all Ireland, and Dundee was to be spoken of by professed economists as the Manchester of the linen trade.[2]

The silk manufacturers of Britain have never yet succeeded in acquiring the predominance which the woollen, cotton, and linen factors have virtually obtained. The worm, by which the raw material is produced, has never been acclimatized on a large scale in England ; and the trade has naturally flourished chiefly in those countries where the worm could live and spin, or where the raw material could be the most easily procured. Insular prejudice, moreover, should not induce the historian to forget another reason which has materially interfered with the development of this particular trade. The ingenuity of the British was superior to that of every other nation; but the taste of the British was inferior to that of most people. An article which was only worn by the rich, and which was only used for its beauty and delicacy, was naturally produced most successfully by the most artistic people. English woollen goods found their way to every

---

[1] McCulloch's " Commercial Dict.," ad verb. Cotton.
[2] McCulloch, ad verb. Linen; Porter's " Progress of the Nation," p. 230.

continental nation; but the wealthy English imported their finest lustrings and à les modes from Italy and France. The silk trade would, in fact, have hardly found a home in England at all had it not been for the folly of a neighboring potentate. Louis XIV., in a disastrous hour for France, revoked the Edict of Nantes; and the French Huguenots, to their eternal honor, preferring their consciences to their country, sought a home amongst a more liberal people. The silk weavers of France settled in Spitalfields, and the British silk trade gained rapidly on its foreign rivals. Parliament adopted the usual clumsy contrivances to promote an industry whose importance it was no longer possible to ignore. Prohibitory duties, designed to discourage the importation of foreign silk, were imposed by the legislature; monopolies were granted to successful throwsters, and every precaution was taken which the follies of protection could suggest, to perpetuate the supremacy which Great Britain was gradually acquiring in the silk trade. The usual results followed this short-sighted policy. Prohibitory duties encouraged smuggling. Foreign silk found its way into England, and the revenue was defrauded accordingly. The English trade began to decline, and Parliament again interferred to promote its prosperity. In that unhappy period of English history which succeeds the fall of Chatham and the rise of Pitt, Parliament adopted fresh expedients to promote the prosperity of the silk trade. Prohibitory duties were replaced with actual prohibition, and elaborate attempts were made to regulate the wages of the Spitalfields weavers. The natural consequences ensued. Smuggling, which had been created by prohibitive duties, flourished with fresh vitality under the influence of actual prohibition. The capitalists transferred their mills from Spitalfields, where the labors of their workmen were fixed by law, to Macclesfield and other places, where master and workmen were free to make their own terms.

The silk trade was hardly being developed with the same rapidity as the three other textile industries. But silk, like wool, cotton, and linen, was affording a considerable amount of employment to a constantly growing population. The textile industries of this country could not indeed have acquired the importance which they have since obtained, if the inventions of Hargreaves, Arkwright, Crompton, and Cartwright had not been supplemented by the labors of explorers in another field. Machinery makes possible what man by manual labor alone would find it impossible to perform. But machinery would be a useless incumbrance were it not for the presence of some motive power. From the earliest ages men have endeavored to supplement the brute force of animals with the more powerful forces which nature has placed at their disposal. The ox was not to be perpetually used to tread out the corn; women were not always to pass their days laboriously grinding at a mill. The movement of the atmosphere, the flow of running water, were to be taken into alliance with man; and the invention of wind-mills and water-mills was to mark an advance in the onward march of civilization. But air and water, mighty forces as they are, proved but fickle and uncertain auxiliaries. When the wind was too low its strength was insufficient to turn the cumbrous sails of the mill; when it was too high it deranged the complicated machinery of the miller. The miller who trusted to water was hardly more fortunate than the man who relied upon air. A summer drought reduced the power of his wheel at the very time when long days and fine weather made him anxious to accomplish the utmost possible amount of work. A flood swept away the dam on which his mill depended for its supply of water. An admirable auxiliary during certain portions of each year, water was occasionally too strong, occasionally too weak, for the purposes of the miller.

The manufacturing industry of the country stood, therefore, in need of a new motive power; and invention, which is supposed by some thinkers to depend like other commodities on the laws of demand and supply, was busily elaborating a new problem, — the use of a novel power, which was to revolutionize the world. The elasticity of hot water had long been noticed, and, for a century and a half before the period of this history, a few advanced thinkers had been speculating on the possibility of utilizing the expansive powers of steam. The Marquis of Worcester had described, in his "Century of Inventions," "an admirable and most forcible way to drive up water by means of fire." Steam was actually used early in the eighteenth century as a motive power for pumping water from mines; and Newcomen, a blacksmith in Dartmouth, invented a tolerably efficient steam-engine. It was not, however, till 1769, that James Watt, a native of Greenock, and a mathematical instrument-maker in Glasgow, obtained his first patent for "methods of lessening the consumption of steam, and consequently of fuel, in fire-engines." James Watt was born in 1736. His father was a magistrate, and had the good sense to encourage the good turn for mechanics which his son displayed at a very early age. At the age of nineteen Watt was placed with a mathematical instrument-maker in London. But feeble health, which had interfered with his studies as a boy, prevented him from pursuing his avocations in England. Watt returned to his native country. The Glasgow body of Arts and Trades, however, refused to allow him to exercise his calling within the limits of their jurisdiction; and had it not been for the University of Glasgow, which befriended him in his difficulty, and appointed him their mathematical instrument-maker, the career of one of the greatest geniuses whom Great Britain has produced would have been stinted at its outset.

There happened to be in the University a model of Newcomen's engine. It happened, too, that the model was defectively constructed. Watt, in the ordinary course of his business, was asked to remedy its defects, and he soon succeeded in doing so. But his examination of the model convinced him of serious faults in the original. Newcomen had injected cold water into the cylinder in order to condense the steam and thus obtain a necessary vacuum for the piston to work in. Watt discovered that three-fourths of the fuel which the engine consumed was required to reheat the cylinder. "It occurred to him that, if the condensation could be performed in a separate vessel, communicating with the cylinder, the latter could be kept hot, while the former was cooled, and the vapor arising from the injected water could also be prevented from impairing the vacuum. The communication could easily be effected by a tube, and the water could be pumped out. This is the first and the grand invention by which he at once saved three-fourths of the fuel, and increased the power one-fourth, thus making every pound of coal produce five times the force formerly obtained from it."[1] But Watt was not satisfied with this single improvement. He introduced steam above as well as below the piston, and thus again increased the power of the machine. He discovered the principle of parallel motion, and thus made the piston move in a true straight line. He regulated the supply of water to the boiler by the means of

---

[1] Lord Brougham's "Men of Letters and Science," p. 367.

"floats," the supply of steam to the cylinder by the application of "the governor," and, by the addition of all these discoveries, "satisfied himself that he had almost created a new engine, of incalculable power, universal application, and inestimable value."[1] It is unnecessary to relate in these pages the gradual introduction of the new machine to the manufacturing public. Watt was first connected with Dr. Roebuck, an iron-master of Glasgow. But his name is permanently associated with that of Mr. Boulton, the proprietor of the Soho Works near Birmingham, whose partner he became in 1774. Watt and Boulton rapidly supplemented the original invention with further improvements. Other inventors succeeded in the same field, and, by the beginning of the present century, steam was established as a new force; advanced thinkers were considering the possibility of applying it to purposes of locomotion.

The steam-engine indeed would not have been invented in the eighteenth century, or would not at any rate have been discovered in this country, if it had not been for the vast mineral wealth with which Great Britain has fortunately been provided. Iron, the most useful of all metals, presents greater difficulties than any other of them to the manufacturer, and iron was probably one of the very last minerals which was applied to the service of man. Centuries elapsed before the rich mines of our own country were even slightly worked. The Romans indeed established iron works in Gloucestershire, just as they obtained tin from Cornwall or lead from Wales. But the British did not imitate the example of their earliest conquerors, and the little iron which was used in this country was imported from abroad. Some progress was, no doubt, made in the southern counties; the smelters naturally seeking their ores in those places where wood, then the only available fuel, was to be found in abundance. The railings which but lately encircled our metropolitan cathedral were cast in Sussex. But the prosperity of the trade involved its own ruin. Iron could not be made without large quantities of fuel. The wood gradually disappeared before the operations of the smelter, and the country gentlemen hesitated to sell their trees for fuel when the increase of shipping was creating a growing demand for timber. Nor were the country gentlemen animated in this respect by purely selfish motives. Parliament

---

[1] Lord Brougham's "Men of Letters and Science," p. 371.

itself shared their apprehensions and endorsed their views. It regarded the constant destruction of timber with such disfavor that it seriously contemplated the suppression of the iron trade as the only practical remedy. "Many think," said a contemporary writer, "that there should be no works anywhere, they so devour the woods."[1] Fortunately, so crucial a remedy was not necessary. At the commencement of the seventeenth century, Dud Dudley, a natural son of Lord Dudley, had proved the feasibility of smelting iron with coal; but the prejudice and ignorance of the work-people had prevented the adoption of his invention. In the middle of the eighteenth century, attention was again drawn to his process, and the possibility of substituting coal for wood was conclusively established at the Darby's works at Coalbrook Dale. The impetus which was thus given to the iron trade was extraordinary. The total produce of the country amounted at the time to only 18,000 tons of iron a year, four-fifths of the iron used being imported from Sweden. In 1802 Great Britain possessed 168 blast-furnaces, and produced 170,000 tons of iron annually. In 1806 the produce had risen to 250,000 tons; it had increased in 1820 to 400,000 tons. Fifty years afterwards, or in 1870, 6,000,000 tons of iron were produced from British ores.[2]

The progress of the iron trade indicated, of course, a corresponding development of the supply of coal. Coal had been used in England for domestic purposes from very early periods. Sea coal had been brought to London; but the citizens had complained that the smoke was injurious to their health, and had persuaded the legislature to forbid the use of coal on sanitary grounds. The convenience of the new fuel triumphed, however, over the arguments of the sanitarians and the prohibitions of the legislature, and coal continued to be brought in constantly though slowly increasing quantities to London. Its use for smelting iron led to new contrivances for ensuring its economical production. Before the commencement of the present century there were two great difficulties which interfered with the operations of the miner. The roof of the mine had necessarily to be propped, and, as no one had thought of using wood, and coal itself was employed for the purpose, only 60 per cent. of the produce of each mine was

---

[1] Smiles' "Industrial Biography," p. 43.
[2] "Dict. Hist." vol. iv. p. 689; McCulloch, "Dict. of Commerce," ad verb. Iron; Porter's "Progress of the Nation," p. 520; statistical abstract of the United Kingdom.

raised above ground. About the beginning of the nineteenth century, timber struts were gradually substituted for the pillars of coal, and it became consequently possible to raise from the mine all the coal won by the miner. A still more important discovery was made at the exact period at which this history commences. The coal-miner in his underground calling was constantly exposed to the dangers of fire-damp, and was liable to be destroyed without a moment's notice by the most fearful catastrophe. In the year in which the great French war was concluded, Sir Humphrey Davy succeeded in perfecting his safety-lamp, an invention which enabled the most dangerous mines to be worked with comparative safety, and thus augmented to an extraordinary extent the available supplies of coal.[1]

Humphrey Davy was the son of a wood-carver of Penzance, and early in life was apprenticed to a local apothecary. Chance — of which other men would perhaps have failed to avail themselves — gave the lad an opportunity of cultivating his taste for chemistry. A French surgeon, wrecked on the coast, to whom Davy had shown some kindness, gave him a case of surgical instruments, and " the means of making some approximation to an exhausting engine." Watt's son, Gregory Watt, was ordered to winter in Cornwall for his health, and happened to take apartments in the house of Davy's mother. " Another accident threw him in the way of Mr. Davies Giddy, a cultivator of natural as well as mathematical science." Giddy " gave to Davy the use of an excellent library;" he " introduced him to Dr. Beddoes," who made his young friend the head of " a pneumatic institution for the medical use of gases," which he was then forming. The publication, soon afterwards, of a fanciful paper on light and heat gave Davy a considerable reputation. He was successively chosen assistant lecturer in chemistry, and sole chemical professor of the Royal Institution. While he held this office his inquiries induced him to investigate the causes of the fearful explosions which continually took place in coal mines. He soon satisfied himself that carburetted hydrogen is the cause of fire-damp; and that it will not explode unless mixed with atmospheric air " in proportions between six and fourteen times its bulk;" and " he was surprised to observe in the course of his experiments, made for ascertaining how the inflammation takes place, that the flames

---

[1] Porter's " Progress of the Nation," p. 277; McCulloch, ad verb. Coal.

will not pass through tubes of a certain length and smallness of bore. He then found that, if the length be diminished and the bore also reduced, the flames will not pass; and he further found that, by multiplying the number of the tubes, this length may be safely diminished provided the bore be proportionally lessened. Hence it appeared that gauze of wire, whose meshes were only one twenty-second of an inch in diameter, stopped the flame and prevented the explosion."[1] These successive discoveries, the results of repeated experiments and careful thought, led to the invention of the safety-lamp. The first safety-lamp was made in the year 1815. There is some satisfaction in reflecting that the very year which was memorable for the conclusion of the longest and most destructive of modern wars, was also remarkable for one of the most beneficial discoveries which have ever been given to mankind. Even the peace of Paris did not probably save more life or avert more suffering than Sir Humphrey Davy's invention. The gratitude of a nation properly bestowed titles and pensions, lands and houses, stars and honors, on the conqueror of Napoleon. Custom and precedent only allowed inferior rewards to the inventor of the safety-lamp. Yet Hargreaves and Arkwright, Crompton and Cartwright, Watt and Davy, did more for the cause of mankind than even Wellington. Their lives had more influence on their country's future than the career of the great general. His victories secured his country peace for rather more than a generation. Their inventions gave Great Britain a commercial supremacy, which neither war nor foreign competition has yet destroyed.

A series of extraordinary inventions, at the commencement of the present century, had supplied Great Britain with a new manufacturing vigor. Hargreaves, Arkwright, Crompton, and Cartwright had developed, to a remarkable degree, the producing power of man; Watt had given a new significance to their inventions by superseding the feeble and unequal forces, which had hitherto been used, with the most tractable and powerful of agents. And Davy, by his beneficent contrivance, had enabled coal to be won with less danger, and had relieved the miner's life from one of its most hideous perils. The ingenuity of these great men had been exercised with different objects; but the inventions of each of them had given fresh importance to the

---

[1] See Brougham's "Men of Letters and Science," p. 462. The life of Davy is admirably told by Lord Brougham.

THE GREAT INVENTIONS.

discoveries of the others. The spinning-jenny, the water-frame, and the mule would have been deprived of half their value, if they had not been supplemented with the power-loom; the power-loom would, in many places, have been useless without the steam-engine; the steam-engine would have been idle, had it not been for coal; the coal would not have been won without danger, had it not been for Sir H. Davy. Coal, then, was the commodity whose extended use was gradually revolutionizing the world; and the population of the world, as the first consequence of the change, gradually moved towards the coal fields. The change was just commencing at the beginning of the present century; it was proceeding with rapid strides at the period at which this history opens; its ultimate effects will be seen later on in this work. The time was to come when the coal measures of England were to draw away the population of Ireland; to weaken the power of the southern agricultural counties; to give predominance to the north of England; and by these results to involve a political revolution.

IV.

ECONOMIC CAUSES OF THE FRENCH REVOLUTION.

FROM VON SYBEL'S FRENCH REVOLUTION, VOL. I., pp. 21-53.

IN order to bring this matter, in its details, more clearly before us, we may pass in review the three great classes into which the French people were divided according to their occupation.[1] By far the most important of these occupations, at that period, was agriculture. Nearly 21,000,000 out of 25,000,000 of inhabitants were employed in tilling the soil. Of the 51,000,000 *hectares* of which the whole kingdom is composed, 35,000,000 were destined for cultivation, that is, rather less than at the present day, but more than twice as much as is now under cultivation in England. It has often been imagined that the property of these great masses of land was almost entirely in the hands of the church, the monasteries, the nobility, and the financiers; and that before 1789 only large estates existed, while the class of small proprietors was created by the Revolution. Some consider this supposed change as the highest glory, and others as the greatest calamity of modern times; but all are agreed as to the fact, and the more so, because it was continually proclaimed in the debates of the revolutionary assemblies. But, on closer examination, we shall find that the effects of the feudal system upon agriculture are not to be looked for in this direction. We cannot rank the authority of the revolutionary orators very high, both because they had a political interest in breaking up the large estates for the advantage of the city proletaries, and because they always showed themselves fabulously ignorant of statistics. If we examine the state of things before 1789, we shall find that — apart from the feudal tenures and the church property — even the old French law of inheritance by no means favored the accumulation of estates. The nobility, indeed, were often heard to complain that the *roturiers* were constantly get-

---

[1] In drawing up the following statement we have chiefly consulted the "Statistique ministerielle de la France," and the admirable works of Moreau de Yonne; and also Lavergne, "Économie rurale." The latter gives much information respecting the earlier state of things, which now and then, however, requires examination and correction.

ting possession of land; which is intelligible enough, since the moneyed classes were continually gaining ground on the ancient aristocracy. It follows that there was nothing in the circumstances of the age to render the division of land impossible; and one of the most credible witnesses, after three years' investigation in all the French provinces, tells us, as the result of his observations, that about a third of the land was held by small proprietors, who were sufficiently prosperous in Flanders, Alsace, Bearn, and the north of Bretagne; but in other parts, especially in Lorraine and Champagne, poor and miserable. The division of property, he observes, is carried to too great an extent; "I have frequently seen properties of ten roods with a single fruit-tree; excessive division ought to be forbidden by law."

The witness is Arthur Young, one of the first agriculturists of the period in Europe, who gave this testimony after indefatigable inquiry; and his report is confirmed by native authorities.

"The subdivision of land," says Turgot, "is carried to such an extent, that a property, only just sufficient for one family, is divided among five or six children." "The landed estates," writes an *intendant*, "are broken up systematically to a very alarming degree; the fields are divided and subdivided *ad infinitum*." Such was the case among the small proprietors;[1] the other two-thirds of the soil was entirely in the possession of the great land-owners — consisting partly of the nobility and clergy, and partly of magistrates and financiers. We shall presently inquire, in what manner they turned their lands to profit; but we may first of all observe that a middle class of proprietors, substantial enough to derive from their land a sufficient livelihood, and yet humble enough to be bound to constant and diligent labor, was entirely wanting. In the present day the landed proprietors of France may be divided into three sections, each of which possesses about one-third of the productive soil of the country. Eighteen million *hectares* belong to 183,000 great landed owners; fourteen millions to 700,000 proprietors of the middle class, and fourteen millions to not quite four millions of peasant owners.[2] When we compare these figures with those of the pre-revolutionary period, we find the number of poor possessors exactly corresponding to one another; and, what is very re-

---

[1] Quoted by Tocqueville, "L'Ancien Régime," 60.
[2] Cochut, "Revue de Deux Mondes," Sept., 1848; Rossi, "Economie politique," p. 325, et seq.

markable, they are almost exactly the same in 1831 as in 1815. The most fearful storms pass over the surface of the land without producing any change in these relations. But what the movement of 1789 — the emancipation of the soil, and civil equality — did produce, is this middle class of proprietors, which now possesses one-third of the land. It must be confessed that this is a most remarkable result. How often has it been announced by feudalists and socialists, that entire freedom of trade would inevitably lead to the annihilation of the middle classes, and leave nothing but millionnaires and proletaries! We here see the very contrary proved by one of the grandest historical facts. The feudal system, by its restrictions, crushed the agricultural middle class; the rule of freedom created it afresh. Let us, however, consider the position of these lords of the soil and their dependents more closely.

The first fact which meets us in this investigation is an unhappy one. It was only an excessively small minority of the great land-owners who concerned themselves about their estates and tenants. All who were at all able to do so hurried away to the enjoyments of the court or the capital, and only returned to their properties to fill the purse which had been emptied by their excesses. There they lived in miserly and shabby retirement; sometimes in wretchedly furnished castles, shunned by the peasants as pitiless creditors; sometimes in the midst of forests and wastes, that they might have the pleasures of the chase close at hand. They took as little interest in intellectual subjects as in agricultural affairs, and cherished little or no intercourse with their neighbors; partly from parsimony, and partly from the entire want of local roads. When the period of fasting was over, they rushed eagerly back to the alluring banquets of Paris and Versailles. The number of exceptions to this melancholy rule was so small as to exercise no influence on the general condition of the country.

While these gentlemen were squandering the produce of their estates in aristocratic splendor, their fields were let out in parcels of ten or, at most, fifteen *hectares*, to the so-called *métayers*, who did not pay a fixed rent, but generally half the gross produce, and received from the owner, in return, their first seed-corn, their cattle, and agricultural implements.[1] This system yielded a

---

[1] Quesnay in Daire, "Physiocrates," p. 219, et seq.; Young's "Travels," II. 190; Lullin de Chateauvieux, I. 270.

wretched existence for the tenants themselves, and reduced the estates to a miserable condition, but it brought the owners a large though uncertain income. The latter, who only saw their estates as travellers, were accustomed to farm out the collection of their dues, generally to a notary or an advocate, who treated the tenants with merciless severity.

The peasants, in their turn, neglected the cultivation of corn — of which they had to give up a moiety — for any chance occupation, the whole profit of which fell to themselves; they used their oxen rather for purposes of transport than for ploughing, fattened their geese in their own wheat fields, and, above all, introduced the system of alternating crop and fallow, in order to get a greater extent of pasture, and consequently a larger number of cattle. This was a personal gain to themselves, but evidently brought no advantage to the estate. A system of tillage, in short, prevailed without industry, without science, and, above all, without capital. It has been calculated that the average amount of capital employed at that period in the French *métairies*, was from 40 to 60 francs to the *hectare;* while in England, at the same time, the average amounted to 240 francs.[1] The result was, of course, a wretched one; they only reckoned upon a crop from seven to eight *hectolitres* of wheat to the *hectare*,— the increase being from five to six fold; while the English farmer of that time obtained a twelve-fold increase. It was impossible for the peasant under such circumstances to gain a livelihood; the produce of ten *hectares* was scarcely sufficient to support his family, and sale and profit were out of the question. The man who is thus condemned to pass his life in starvation, soon learns to fold his hands in idleness. A constantly increasing extent of country lay uncultivated, which Quesnay, in 1750, estimated at a quarter of the arable land of France, and Arthur Young, in 1790, at more than 9,000,000 *hectares*. Millions of rural dwellings had no aperture in them but the door, or at most one window;[2] the people had no clothing but a home-made, coarse, and yet not thick, woollen cloth; in many provinces every one went barefoot, and in others only wooden shoes were known. The food of the people was gruel with a little lard; in the evening a piece of bread, and on great occasions a little bacon; but, besides this, no meat

---

[1] Arthur Young, II. 249. The elder Mirabeau reckons for the whole of France, 66 francs to the *arpent*.
[2] This is still the case.

for months together, and in many districts no wine at all.[1] The mental condition of the people was in accordance with their external circumstances. Books and newspapers were as little known in the villages as reading and writing. The peasants depended for instructions on their pastors and parish clerks, proletaries like themselves, who very seldom got beyond the horizon of the church steeple. The Church was, after all, the only institution that threw an intellectual spark into their wretched life; but unfortunately their religious impulses were strongly mixed with barbarism and superstition. In many large districts of the south the peasants had no other idea of a Protestant than as of a dangerous magician who ought to be knocked on the head. Their own faith, moreover, was interwoven with a multitude of the strangest images of old Celtic heathenism. Of the world outside they heard nothing, for there was next to no traffic or travelling in the country. There were some royal roads, magnificently made, and sixty feet in breadth — splendid monuments of monarchical ostentation. On these, however, up to 1776, only two small coaches ran,[2] throughout the whole of France; and the traveller might pass whole days without getting sight of any other vehicle.[3] Only few villages, in the most favored provinces, possessed cross-roads to these great highways, or to the nearest market town. And thus the whole existence of these people was passed in toil and privation; without any pleasures except the sight of the gaudy decorations of a few church festivals; without any change, save when hunger drove an individual, here and there, to seek day-labor in the towns, or into military service. It was seldom that such a one ever returned to his father's house, so that his fellow-villagers gained no advantage from his wider experience.

Under these circumstances the relation between peasant and lord was naturally a deplorable one. What we have already said, sufficiently characterizes a community, in which all the enjoyments fell to the rich, and all the burdens were heaped upon the poor. In aristocratic England at this period, a quarter of the gross proceeds was considered a high rent for a farm, and the owner, moreover, paid large tithes and poor-rates.[4] In France,

---

[1] Reports of the Prefects to the Ministry, 1803.
[2] E. Daire, " Introduction aux Œuvres de Turgot."
[3] Young's " Travels."
[4] Yvernois, " Tableau des Pertes," etc.

half the proceeds was the usual rent; and the owners were exempted by their privileges from many public burdens, which fell with double weight upon the wretched *métayers*. Thus, the produce of the French land, as compared with the English, was nine to fourteen, while the rents of an English land-owner were at the rate of two and three-fourths per cent., and those of the French land-owner three and three-fourths per cent.[1]

The deficiency in the product of the land, therefore, affected the gains of the little farmer doubly. In addition to this he was burdened by a number of feudal services, by forced labor on the lands of his lord, by tithes to the church, and by the obligation to make roads for the State. The landlord who tried to sell his rent in kind as dearly as possible, wished for high prices of corn; the peasant, who, after paying his dues, did not raise enough for his own family, longed, like the city proletary, for low prices. In short, these two classes, so intimately connected with one another, had nothing at all in common; in education, in interests and enjoyments, they were as widely separated as the inhabitants of different quarters of the globe, and regarded each other respectively with contempt and hatred. When the peasant looked upon the towers of his lord's castle, the dearest wish of his heart was to burn it down, with all its registers of debt. Here and there a better state of things existed; but we can only bring forward two exceptions to the melancholy rule, extending over large tracts of country. In Anjou the system of *métairie* prevailed as in Lower Bretagne and Guienne; and yet in the former province, the peasants were prosperous, and the noblemen beloved. Lower Poitou was the only province from which the nobles had not allowed themselves to be enticed into the whirlpool of court life. The nobleman dwelt in his own castle, the real lord of his domains, the cultivator of his fields, the guardian of his peasants. He advanced them money to purchase the necessary stock, and instructed them in the management of their cattle;[2] the expulsion of a tenant was a thing unheard of; the laborer was born on the estate, and the landlord was the godfather of all his farmers' children. He was often seen going to market with his peasants, to sell their oxen for them as advantageously as possible. His mental horizon, however, did not extend beyond these honorable cares; he honored God and the King, labored in his own fields,

---

[1] Young.
[2] Sauvegrain, "Considérations sur la Population," etc. Paris, 1806.

was a good sportsman and toper, and knew as little of the world and its civilization as his tenants.

In the north of the kingdom a more modern state of things had grown up. There, wealthy farmers were to be seen, who held their land on lease at a fixed money rental, — which was settled according to the amount of the taxes to which they were liable, — and who brought both skill and capital to the management of their land. This was the regular practice in Flanders, Artois, Picardy, Normandy, the Islè of France, and other smaller districts. In these parts the landlords had a certain revenue, and their land yielded twice as much as that which was in the hands of the *métayers*. The whole country wore the appearance of a garden, and the poorer neighbors found lucrative employment at the stately farm-houses. These were the same provinces in which Arthur Young met with small proprietors in a tolerable condition. If a peasant in this part of the country possessed a small strip of land near his cottage, large enough to grow some vegetables, food for a goat, or a few vines, he earned sufficient to supply the rest of his wants, in day wages from the farmers, or, as a weaver, from the neighboring manufacturers.

His was a condition similar to the normal one of the peasant proprietors in France at the present day; who are not reduced farmers, but laborers who have invested their savings in land.[1] It was more difficult for these people to make a livelihood at that time than now, because there were fewer manufacturers and wealthy agriculturists. Except in the above-mentioned provinces, these petty proprietors were equally wretched and hopeless with the *métayers*, by whom they were surrounded; their only object was to rent a *métairie* in addition to their own pittance of land. They were in fact entirely lost sight of among the *métayers*, and this is the reason that French writers, in their descriptions of the so-called *petite culture* (plot farming), never make any special mention of them, but always confound them with the more numerous class by which they were surrounded. All authorities are agreed in estimating the amount of land cultivated in small parcels, at 27,000,000 *hectares*, while only 9,000,000 were held at a money rent. The former, therefore, was nearly equally divided between the small owners and the *métayers*, who paid their rent in kind.

---

[1] Rossi, l. c.

In France, at the present day, nearly 23,000,000 *hectares* are cultivated by small proprietors and *métayers;* about 8,000,-000[1] (the same as in 1780) by tenants paying a money rent, and rather more than nine and a half millions, by wealthy landlords.[2] Hence we can clearly see what the French Revolution has done for French agriculture. Not only did it create the middle class of land-owners, but greatly promoted a more rational system of tillage. About four million *hectares* have been rescued from the *petite culture*, and an equal number redeemed from utter barrenness. The breadth of land standing at a money rent is exactly the same as before the Revolution. The increase is entirely in the properties of rich or substantial land-owners, who manage their own estates, — which indicates a change to more zealous industry, coupled with the employment of greater capital. The extent occupied by the *métayers* is still very great, and the condition of those who are subject to it but little improved, notwithstanding the abolition of socage and seigniorial rights. It will be one of our most important tasks to examine the several events and tendencies of the Revolution, in relation to their effects on the rural population.

If we turn our attention to the towns of ancient France we find that similar causes produced effects corresponding to those we have just described. The civic offices, to which persons had formerly been elected by the districts or the guilds. had been frequently filled up by the crown in the 17th century; and in the 18th, the great majority of them were sold in hereditary possession to fill the exchequer.[3] The government of the towns, therefore, was in the hands of a close corporation consisting of a few families, who, generally speaking, allowed themselves to be infected with the indolent and self-seeking spirit of the central government. Associated with these were the families of the moneyed aristocracy, the members of the great financial companies, the farmers of the indirect, and the collectors of the direct, taxes, the shareholders of the trading monopolies, and the great bankers. These circles, too, were either legally or virtually closed to the general world. The *bourse* was ruled by an aristocracy, to which only birth, or the permission of government, could give

---

[1] Quesnai, Turgot, Young.
[2] On this point Lullinde, Chateauvieux, and Cochut are in the main agreed. Lavergens' figures are somewhat different, but the general result is the same.
[3] Depping, " Correspondence administrative de Louis XIV.," Vol. II., Introduction.

access. Their activity was of course necessarily centred in Paris. Indeed, they stamped their own character on this city to a degree which would be impossible in our age, notorious though it be as the epoch of the rule of paper. Every one knows to what a dizzy and ruinous height stock-jobbing was carried by law, in the beginning of the century; and from that time forward its operations were never suspended, and all who had wealth or credit engaged in it with reckless greediness. Kings, nobles, ministers, clergy, and parliaments, one and all, took part in these transactions; and the chronic deficit, and increasing debts, of the treasury afforded constant opportunities of involving the State, and making a profit out of its embarrassments. We may confidently assert that, as compared with the present day, the speculative swindling of that age was as prevalent and as shameless as its immorality. Paris was not at that time a manufacturing town, and its wholesale trade was insignificant; with few exceptions, therefore, the industry of the city consisted in retail trade and the negotiation of bills of exchange. It is not the least characteristic feature of the indolent and selfish licentiousness, into which the higher classes of a great nation had fallen, that of all securities, life annuities were most in favor; by means of which the purchaser procured high interest for himself, while he robbed his children of the capital.

The trade and commerce of the whole empire was fettered by the restrictions of guilds and corporations. The principles on which they were conducted dated from Henry III., who was the first to promulgate the proposition that the king alone can grant the right to labor, — a maxim which contains the whole doctrine of the socialists from a monarchical point of view. The masters of every handicraft managed its internal affairs, allowed no one to practise it who did not belong to their guild, and admitted no one to their privileges, until he had passed an examination of his qualification before themselves. Originally many trades were free from this organization, until these too were injuriously affected by the financial necessities of the State; when the exclusive rights of a guild were sold to the artisans, as their offices were to the judges. The government soon further proceeded to divide each trade into several guilds, and made an exclusive corporation of the most insignificant occupation. Thus the workers in ebony were distinguished from the carpenters, the sellers of old clothes from the tailors, and the pastry-cooks from the bakers.

The fruit-women and flower-girls formed separate exclusive associations, regulated by formal and binding statutes. In the guilds of the seamstresses, embroiderers, and dress-makers, only men were admitted to the privileges of masters. A number of these statutes, by imposing excessive fees and duties, rendered it doubly difficult for an apprentice, however capable, to obtain the rank of master. Other enactments only admitted the sons of masters, or the second husbands of the widows of masters, to the privileges of the guild. In short, the power of the State was abused in the most glaring manner for the furtherance of exclusive class interests. Those who did not belong to this aristocracy of trade, could only support themselves by the labor of their hands, in a state of eternal servitude. Despair and famine drove the peasants from the country into the towns, where they found no employment open to them but that of day-laborers. The important influence which this system exercised over the State was clearly understood, both by the privileged and the excluded classes. When Turgot abolished the guilds in 1776, the Parliament of Paris, the princes, peers, and doctors, unanimously declared that all Frenchmen were divided into close corporations, the links of a mighty chain extending from the throne to the meanest handicraft; and that this concatenation was indispensable to the existence of the State and of social order. It was not long before the guilds were reëstablished in accordance with this declaration; we shall see how the journeymen and apprentices replied to this unctuous manifesto some fifteen years later.

The great manufacturing interests of the country were confined by the same narrow restrictions. Since the time of Colbert, who was the real creator of them, manufactures had been the darling child of the government; and, as is usually the case with darling children, had been petted and tyrannized over at the same time. When Colbert began his operations, France produced neither the finer kinds of cloth, nor stockings — neither silks nor glass — neither tar nor soap. The previously existing handicraft — which had been for a century in the fetters of the guild — had done so little to develop the native manufacturing talent of the country that the minister was obliged to introduce German, Swedish, and Italian workmen. To secure a sale in foreign countries he prescribed with great exactness the sort of fabric which he wished to be produced; and, to prevent competition from without he enacted a number of prohibitory and protective duties. Here, again, the power of the State intruded itself into the sphere of private business, to the advantage of the manufacturer and the injury of the consumer. The same system was continued by his successors with still worse effects, because it was carried out with all the fickleness and irregularity of Louis XV.'s government. It is true that manufacturers made great progress, and increased their annual products six-fold, from the time of Colbert to that of Necker.[1] But the statutes became more oppressive every year; every new invention and improvement was excluded by them; and after 1760, no legislation could keep pace with the progress of machinery. Manufacturers, therefore, as is everywhere the case under such circumstances, no longer adapted themselves to the natural wants and capacities of men, but immediately took an artificial and aristocratic direction. During Colbert's ministry, while only 60,400 hands were employed in the manufacture of wool, no less than 17,300 were engaged in lace-making; and a hundred years later, while the manufacture of soap only produced 18,000,000 of francs a year, that of hair-powder was estimated at not less than 24,000,000. The contrast between the aristocratic luxury of the rich and the uncleanly indigence of the populace can hardly be more glaringly displayed.

Agriculture experienced in every way the disadvantages of a system which crippled communication with foreign countries, raised the price of farming implements, and injuriously affected the home trade. In their eagerness to protect manufactures the government had learned to look on the interests of agriculture as of secondary importance. They accustomed themselves, like the modern socialists, to apply the word *people* exclusively to the manufacturing classes in the towns; and though they sacrificed the interests of the latter in a thousand ways to the privileged monopolist, yet philanthropy and love of quiet coöperated in inducing them to supply the necessities of the poorer artisans, at the cost of the agricultural population. As supplements to the protective and prohibitory duties in favor of manufactures decrees were issued forbidding the exportation of corn and other raw agricultural products. By these artifices the price of the *hectolitre* of wheat, 'which on the average is at present 19 to 20 francs, was in 1764 forced down to less than 8 francs.[2] Choiseul then opened the trade, and the price rose to more than 15

---

[1] This was the proportion in the woollen manufacture.
[2] Melier, in 10th vol. of the " Mémoires de l'Académie royale de Médicine."

CAUSES OF THE FRENCH REVOLUTION. 63

francs. A similar result followed the same measure in 1775, during the ministry of Turgot; but a return to protection reduced the price once more to 12¾ francs, until the Revolution. The city artisans had tolerably cheap bread, but nowhere in the kingdom were the farmers prosperous. In spite of the most violent complaints from all the provinces the cause of the evil, and consequently the evil itself, remained unchanged. The government adhered to the conviction that it was their immediate duty to provide for the maintenance of the population of the towns. It seemed to them a matter of course that the State should use its political power for the advantage of its rulers and their favorites. No one considered the remoter consequences of such a principle; no one asked the question: "What if this power should fall into democratic hands?"

Let us endeavor to obtain a general view of the wealth of France at this period. From the imperfection of official information, the task is a difficult one, and its results uncertain. Even an approximation to the truth, however, will not be without interest, since, in order not to bring forward unmeaning figures, we shall constantly institute a comparison with the new existing state of things.

The well-informed Tolosan — the only authority on this subject — estimates the total produce of manufactures at 931 million francs; that of handicraft at 60 millions. At the present day[1] the manufactures of Eastern France alone — not reckoning handicraft — produce 2,282 millions; the sum total therefore has been at least quadrupled. At the former period it amounted to 39 francs per head of the whole population; at present we might unhesitatingly place it at more than 100 per head. The emancipation of the internal trade since 1789 has not raised the amount of property produced, but — what has so often been called in question — has favorably influenced the manner in which it is distributed. The daily wages of the manufacturing laborers in 1788, according to a rather high estimate, were for men 26 sous, and for women 15.[2] They are now, according to the most numerous and trustworthy observation, 42 sous for men, and 26 for women. The daily wages of the agricultural laborers, too, can certainly not be reckoned at more than 15 sous[3] for the year 1789, or less

---
[1] In 1853. In 1860 a total of five milliards was reached. Boiteau, "État de la France en 1789," pr. 506.
[2] Boiteau thinks 19 to 20 sous.
[3] Lavergne says 30 sous, p. 57.

than 25[1] in the present day. If we further take into account the very considerable increase in the number of working days, — arising from the abolition of thirty holidays, — we shall find the annual wages of the earlier period to be little more than half what they now are, viz., 351 francs for the manufacturing, and 157 for the agricultural, laborer, against 630 and 300 at the present day. To appreciate the significance of these results we must compare the prices of provisions at these two periods. It appears, then, that before 1789 bread was considered very cheap at three sous per pound, and it was only in Paris that this rate was a common one; in the provinces, the price was generally higher. In our own times the average price for the whole of France from 1820 to 1840 was 17 centimes, while at Paris, in 1851, it was 14 cents, — less, therefore, than the old rate of 3 sous. This seems out of proportion to the price of corn; since the *hectolitre* of wheat in 1780 cost from 12-13 francs, and in 1840 from 19-20. This apparent incongruity, however, is accounted for by the improvement in the method of grinding and baking, by which a third, or even a half, more weight of bread is now obtained from the same quantity of corn than in the former period.[2] We find, therefore, that the laborer received for his wages little more than half the quantity of bread which the modern workman can obtain for what he earns. The same proportion holds good in other kinds of food, and in regard to clothing the comparison is still more unfavorable to the ante-revolutionary period.

We shall discover the determinate cause of these differences when we come to consider the main wealth of the French empire, — the produce of the soil in the widest sense of the word. It would carry us too far if we were to examine every branch of the subject, and discuss all the difficulties connected with it; it will be sufficient to dwell on a few of the principal points of interest. Of wheat, the great staff of life, the soil of France produced before the Revolution about 40,000,000 *hectolitres*, or 167 *litres* per head of the population; and in 1840, 70,000,000, or 208 litres per head. At the former period the number of cattle was calculated at 33,000,000 head, and at the present day at 49,000,000; and there is an equal increase in the number of the other domestic animals. The vineyards formerly yielded 27,000,000 *hecto-*

---

[1] Before 1789 the *septier* (240 pounds) of wheat yielded only 180 pounds of bread. —*Moniteur*, 12 July, 1792, supplement.

[2] Young, "Assemblée nationale," 15th Jan., 1790, 11th Aug., 1791.

litres, and at present 37,000,000, so that the proportion, per head, is at any rate not lower than it was.¹ And if we take into consideration that a number of useful agricultural products were at that time unknown, that a violent controversy was carried on about the wholesomeness of potatoes, that the forests were allowed to run to waste far more than at the present day,² we shall not be astonished that the best statist of modern France estimates the vegetable product of the French soil (which now exceeds in value the sum of 6,000 millions), not more than 2,000 millions at the period before the Revolution.³ The importance of this fact is sufficiently evident; and we may gain an idea of the state of the population before 1789, by remembering that even now the total consumption of food in France is not greater in proportion to the population than in Prussia, and much less than in England.⁴

Respecting commerce, the third great branch of national wealth, I have but little to say. I am not aware that any statistical data exist of the internal traffic of France before the Revolution; it was, no doubt, smaller than at the present day, in consequence of the multitude of inland duties. And with regard to the foreign commerce of the earlier period we have no means of dividing the sum totals which lie before us into the value of the raw materials, and the cost of manufacture, on the one hand, and the clear profits of trade on the other. It must suffice us to gain a general idea of the relation between the two periods, from the summary statement, that in the custom-house registers, immediately before the Revolution, the annual imports are stated at 576,000,000, and the exports at 540,000,000; while, as early as 1836, the former amounted to 905,000,000, and the latter to 961,000,000; and in 1857, both imports and exports had risen to a value of more than 1,800,000,000. Taking all in all, therefore, France under the old monarchy was four times as poor in manufactures, three times as poor in agriculture, and more than three times as poor in commerce, as it is in the present day. We must bear this result well in mind when we try to form a judgment

---

¹ Moreau de Yonne, from contemporary sources. I have followed him because space does not allow me to give my reasons for thinking a much more unfavorable state of things in 1770 highly probable.

² "Mémoire remis aux Notables, 1781;" Young's "Travels," III.—111; Moreau, "Agriculture," 366.

³ The calculation of Young agrees with this. Tolosan, Dedeley d'Agier, Lavoisier, make amounts higher. (Boiteau, "État de la France en 1789," p. 481, compares their statements). But the uncertainty of their calculations is very perceptible.

⁴ Communications from the Prussian Statistical Bureaus, 1851.

respecting the finances of the *ancien régime*. A budget of 600 millions weighed as heavily upon the resources of the country at that period, as a budget of 1,800,000,000 would now; and, consequently, a deficit of 100,000,000 was equivalent to one of 300,000,000 in our own times. Such a deficit actually existed when Louis XVI. mounted the throne; it is therefore easy to conceive that his attention should be strongly turned to the restoration of the balance between income and expenditure, and that his vain endeavors in this direction should shake the fabric of the State to its very foundation.

A whole volume would be necessary to detail the different schemes of reform, which were brought forward between the accession of Louis XVI. and the outbreak of the Revolution. It will be sufficient for our purpose to notice the chief points, which have an important bearing on the antecedents and the actual events of that mighty movement.

Louis the XVI. himself — as no one can doubt who has approached the sources of the history of this period — entered on the task of government with a heart full of piety, philanthropy, and public spirit. He was earnest and pure-minded, penetrated by a sense of his own dignity and the responsibilities attached to it; and firmly resolved to close forever the infamous paths in which his predecessor had walked.

But, unhappily, his capacity bore no proportion to his good will. He was incapable of forming a decision; his education was deficient; he was awkward both in person and speech, and slow of comprehension. As he had a very limited knowledge both of the people and the condition of his empire, the selection of his ministers was, from the very outset, determined by accident, — the influence of his aunts, his queen, or the contending court factions; and as he was immovable wherever morality was concerned, but utterly helpless in the practical execution of his ideas, his was just a case in which almost everything depended on the aid of his nearest advisers. He possessed just sufficient sense of justice and benevolence to encourage every effort for useful reforms; but lacked entirely that firmness of an enlightened judgment which knows how to bring about a positive result, in spite of the opposition of existing interests. The inevitable consequences soon showed themselves. Anarchy, which under Louis XV. had reigned in the minds of men, now broke forth into overt acts. The sufferings of the people, which individuals had hitherto borne in silent apathy, now occupied the attention of the masses.

The same chance which in his reign directed the management of public business, had given him, as his first minister, Turgot, the greatest reformer of the day.

This great minister's strokes fell heavily on the existing system in every direction. Among his measures we find free trade in corn; abolition of the *corvée* in the country districts; liberation of trade from the trammels of the guilds; the erection of the *caisse d'escompte*;[1] a number of improvements and alleviations in the mode of raising the public taxes; and a prospect held out to all possessors of property, of a gradual increasing share in political rights: and it is under these heads that the restless activity of this liberal statesman may be best arranged. We may easily conceive that there was scarcely one of the privileged classes which did not consider its previous existence imperilled.

Opposition rose in every quarter: the courtiers, the parliaments, the landed aristocracy, and the members of the guilds — all threw themselves into an attitude of defence, with noisy zeal. The contest penetrated into the royal family itself, — Louis's younger brother, Count Charles of Artois, abused the minister, who, he said, was undermining the aristocracy, the prop and rampart of the throne; and a cousin of the king, the rich and abandoned Philip, Duke of Orleans, began, amid the general excitement, to play the demagogue on his own account. Then, for the first time, a spectacle was seen in Paris, which was subsequently repeated in ever darker colors, — the spectacle of the police authorities of the capital stirring up the mob against the crown, and, on this occasion, in the interest of the privileged classes.

At first Louis XVI. declared that he and Turgot were the only friends of the people, and stood firm against the parliament of Paris and the street rioters; but he was not proof against the feebleness of his own character and the wearing influence of those by whom he was daily surrounded. After an administration of nearly a year and a half Turgot was obliged to yield to the reaction of the *ancien régime*, and almost all his creations collapsed at once. Then followed a long period of experiments and palliatives; the successors of Turgot would gladly have gone on

---

[1] An institution for lending money for the furtherance of manufactures and commerce.

in the broad track of traditional privileges if their increasing financial difficulties had left them any peace. It was just at this time that Louis resolved to support the North Americans against England, which he really did against his own will and the views of his ministers, who dreaded the expense of a great war, and clearly saw that the emancipation of the colonies would not weaken England. But the undefined longing for freedom, and the liberal political doctrines which had taken root far and wide in the land, prevailed over the scruples of the king and his counsellors. The Marquis of Lafayette, then a tall light-haired youth, full of vanity and ambition, who, on account of his ungraceful manners, had no success at court, fitted out a ship at his own expense, and sailed across the Atlantic. A number of influential persons cried out for vengeance upon England for the humiliation sustained in the Seven Years' War; in a word, the warlike party carried their point, and war was declared against England. The consequence to France was a rapid spread of democratic sentiments on the American pattern. The followers of Rousseau were triumphant; here, they said, might be seen the possibility of a democracy on a broad basis, — the construction of a State on the foundation of the natural rights of man. Another consequence of the war was to throw fresh burdens on the public exchequer. The minister of finance at this time was Necker, a native of Geneva. Having come to Paris as a poor clerk, he had risen by his talents and skill in business to the position of a rich banker, and with great self-complacency had made his house the *rendezvous* of the more distinguished members of the liberal party. By his influence with the *bourse* he procured a certain degree of credit for the State, and raised loan after loan to the amount of 500 millions, without any increase of the taxes, or any provision for a liquidation of the debt incurred. This was evidently sacrificing the future to the present, since the deficit became larger every year, as the interest of the public debt increased. Necker had the real merit of bringing some of the departments of finance into better order; he enjoyed, for the time being, unbounded popularity, and basked with delight in the universal acknowledgment that he was the greatest statesman in Europe. Public confidence was freely given to a minister who endeavored to found his administration on credit alone,— *i.e.* on the confidence of mankind. He was looked on as a perfect hero when he introduced, with good results, provincial assemblies into Berry and Guyenne,

CAUSES OF THE FRENCH REVOLUTION. 69

and soon afterwards — breaking through all the traditions of the ancient monarchy — published a detailed, but unfortunately very inexact and highly colored, report on the state of the finances. But, as he nowhere laid the axe to the root of the evil, he only roused a number of powerful interests by his attempts at innovation, but was utterly unable to close the source of financial confusion. He, too, soon saw no other means of recovery but limitation of the budget and economy in the expenses of the court, by avowing which he made himself hateful to all the grandees of the antechamber, and was deprived of his office in May, 1781. After two insignificant and inexperienced ministers had exhausted their strength, in the years immediately following, the *intendant* of Lille, the gifted but frivolous Calonne, was called to the helm. He began with the proposition, that whoever wished for credit must cultivate luxury; and he renewed the prodigality of the court, in the style of Louis XV. After matters had gone on in this jubilant course for some years and the public debt had been increased by 400 millions, and the taxation by twenty-one millions, the ruin of the country became palpable at the beginning of the year 1787 and the catastrophe inevitable.

Let us here cast a glance at the budget of the *ancien régime*, the disorder of which was to give the signal of convulsion to every quarter of the civilized world. After Necker and Calonne, the Notables and the Revolution, have quarrelled about its contents with equal mendacity, this budget now lies, in its most secret details, before the eyes of the historical inquirer.[1]

And first, with regard to the national income, which, as is well known, amounted to about 500 millions before 1789, nearly 800 under Napoleon, and then increased, during the period between 1815 and 1848, to 1,500 million francs. However definite these figures may appear, we can by no means draw a conclusion from them as to the cheapness of the respective modes of government above-mentioned. We have already observed, that in proportion to the national wealth, a taxation of 500 millions before 1789 would be about equivalent to one of 1,500 millions at the present day. In the next place, we must make several additions to the round sum of 500 millions.

The income of the State in the year 1785 was calculated at 558 millions, to which were added 41 millions more, for the local

---

[1] Bailly, "Hist. financ. de la France," II. 278.

administration of the provinces; a sum which was never paid into the treasury, but immediately expended in the different places where it was raised. Thus we find that the nation was bearing an annual burden of from 599 to 600 millions. At the same time the Church, whose expenses now figure in the budget of the State, raised 133 millions in tithes, and 16 millions in other dues and offerings.[1] The fees, which served as a compliment to the judicial salaries, amounted to 29 millions;[2] the seigniors raised about 2,500,000 in tolls of various kinds, and at least 37,000,000 in stamp duties.[3] I pass over the feudal rents and services, the valuation of which is quite impossible. These, from their very nature, cannot be taken into account in speaking of the public burdens, and may very well be set off against the mortgage debts of the modern peasant proprietors.

The items already mentioned, however, in addition to some of a similar character, amounted to 280 millions; so that the French people had, at that period, to bear a total annual taxation of 880 millions. If we compare this sum with the national wealth, we may unhesitatingly set it down as equivalent to an amount of 2,400 millions at the present day; it follows, therefore, that from the time of Louis XV. to that of Napoleon III. there existed but one government in France, which appropriated to itself a still larger proportion to the public income than the *ancien régime* — and that one was the government of the Jacobins during the Reign of Terror. The Empire, the Restoration, and Louis Philippe contented themselves with far smaller sums; here, too, feudalism finds its counterpart among the socialists.

When we inquire into the distribution of these taxes among the different classes of the people, we discover a glaring inequality. The higher ranks were not, indeed, exempt from taxation, but they were in many respects favored. Of the taxes on consumption — which were valued at 308 millions — they bore, of course, a full share; but of the land and capitation taxes (171 millions) they ought, as was discovered during the Revolution, to have paid, on a fair distribution, 33 millions more than they actually did. In the next place, the maintenance of the public

---

[1] Louis Blanc, B. III. c. 3, estimates them, according to other authorities, not at 16, but at 30 millions.
[2] According to other estimates, 42 millions. Boiteau, "État de la France en 1781." Paris, 1861.
[3] For the sake of brevity I use this term to denote all the fees paid on change of property, *e.g.*, *lods*, *relods*, *quints*, etc.

roads, which were entirely kept up by means of the *corvée*, at a cost of 20 millions; and, further, the expenses of the provincial militia — about six and one-fourth millions — rested entirely on the shoulders of the lower classes. If we take into consideration the 40 millions quoted above, which the seigniors received from the peasants,— the fact that the poorer classes of every town were responsible for the taxes of their *commune*, — even when their rich fellow-citizens escaped payment by the purchase of privileged offices; and, lastly, the scandalous unfairness in the imposition of the taxes on consumption, to which the helpless multitude was subjected by their superiors, we shall easily understand the triumphant fury with which, in 1789, the peasants, more especially, received the joyful intelligence of the utter destruction of the system above described.

Great as was the proportion which it exacted of the national income the government found itself, nevertheless, in a state of ever-increasing need and embarrassment. Disorder on the one side and selfishness on the other scattered its treasures to the wind. The case was the same in the financial administration as in that of justice; no one had ever tried to organize it on any grand principle of wise adaptation to the end in view; on the contrary, a number of isolated jurisdictions — distinguished from one another according to provinces, or sources of income, or the destination of the funds in question — existed side by side, interfering with each other's operations and destroying all responsibility. The amount of arrears due the treasury — equal perhaps to half the annual budget — not even the Revolution has been able to ascertain, and it could only get hold of the profits of the farmers of the revenue by means of the guillotine. When once familiarized with deficits the government soon fell into the stream of floating debts. The anticipation of the revenue of future years, at a usurious discount paid to the collectors themselves, the putting off the payment of debts which had fallen due, and the omission of expenditure prescribed by law, were the cause of equally enormous losses, when the day for liquidation at last arrived. How widely this confusion spread, may be gathered from the actual cash accounts of the year 1785. By the side of the regular income of the treasury, of not quite 357 millions, there is another account of 493 millions income, and 407 millions expenditure, consisting of items which belong either to the earlier or later years of the period between 1781 and 1787; so that the sum total amounts to nearly 850 millions. We see what a field was opened to speculators and the lovers of plunder, and to what a state such proceedings had reduced the prosperity of an empire, which a hundred years earlier, and twenty years later, dictated its will to Europe as a law.

The last feature in this State economy which reveals to us its character is the kind of expenditure in which these treasures, collected with so much difficulty, were employed. The expenses of the court were stated in the official budget at thirty-three or thirty-five millions, but they were in reality forty millions, which did not include the royal hunting expeditions and journeys, the salaries of the great officers of the court, or the maintenance of the royal palaces. The war office — the cost of which Necker states at ninety-nine millions and Calonne at 114 millions — received 131 millions, of which rather more than thirty-nine millions went to the administration, forty-four millions for the pay and commissariat of the troops, and forty-six millions for the salaries of the officers.

Entirely removed from all ministerial calculation were the money orders of the king himself, "for presents, etc., to courtiers, to the minister of finance and magistrates; repayment of foreign loans; interest and discount to the treasury officials; remission of certain personal taxes, and unforeseen expenses of every kind." This class of expenditure, which is well characterized by the above heading, amounted in 1785 to 136 millions; in other years the sum was rather smaller; but we may fairly assume that the annual average was more than 100 millions.[1] And whilst we thus see nothing but abundance and superfluity among the highest classes of society, the bridges and roads are only set down at four millions; the public buildings at scarcely two millions, and the scientific institutions at rather more than one million; for which objects the budget of 1832 and the following years granted 59 millions! The hospitals and foundling institutions received six millions from the State, six from the church, and had a revenue of twenty-four millions of their own; while the benevolent institutions of modern France (1832) had an annual sum of 119 millions at their disposal. In short, whatever portion of the financial affairs of this feudal state we investi-

---

[1] We arrive at this result from the debates of the "Assemblée Constituante" (in April, 1790) on the pensions, the *ordonnances à comptant*, and the *livre rouge*. Louis Blanc gives a number of details from these in B. IV., ch. 5.

CAUSES OF THE FRENCH REVOLUTION. 73

gate, we arrive at the same result, and find the people separated into two great classes, one of which was enriched at the cost of the other.

But as every such draining of the wealth of a nation bears within itself the germs of ruin, by drying up, on the one hand, the sources of income, and increasing, on the other, the passion for extravagance, the government found itself at the end of 1786 in the following condition : The regular annual income was 327 millions. The annual expenditure, according to the treasury accounts, amounted to 340 millions. In addition to this there were 27 millions for pensions, and 72 millions of urgent arrears from former years; and, lastly, in the year 1787, there was a loss of 21 millions from the cessation of a tax, which had only been imposed for a period ending with that year. The deficit, therefore, amounted to 198 millions. Up to this time the government had helped itself by all the artifices, both bad and good, of a credit strained to the very utmost and now utterly exhausted. An increase of the taxes was not to be thought of, on account of the enormous burdens by which the nation was already crushed. Under these circumstances Calonne, with genial frivolity, recurred to the serious and noble plans of Turgot.

He had hitherto lived on the favor of the privileged classes; he now endeavored, by sacrificing them, to relieve the commonwealth. He congratulated the State on having within it so many great abuses by the removal of which new sources of prosperity might be opened !

The opposition which Turgot had met with was of course directed, with redoubled fury, against Calonne.

A closely crowded throng of privileges rose tumultuously against his plans. The court nobility, the provincial estates, the tax-collectors, the courts of law, the police officers, the councillors of the *commune*, and the heads of the guilds, took up the contest against the will of the king and his ministers. But the development of modern ideas had made such progress that the parties competed with one another for the power of public opinion. The ministry itself emancipated the press, in order to expose the advocates of the old system to the national contempt. The young nobles of the court and in the provinces armed the mob of Paris and the peasants of Auvergne against the ministers, and instigated them to violent excesses. An assembly of aristocratic notables, to whom Calonne submitted his schemes of reform, refused their assent, claimed the right of inspecting and superintending every department of the public service, and ended by declaring, that as they were nominees of the king, and not representatives of the nation, they were not competent to make new grants. Immediately after their dismissal the parliament of Paris, which, next to the ministry, was the highest authority in the State, brought forward, as a positive demand, what the notables had only negatively suggested. In a formal decree they demanded that an Assembly of the States-general should be called, — an Assembly which the monarchy had dispensed with for 200 years. The ministry at first received this proposal with great disfavor; but as the want of money grew more and more urgent, the alluring hope arose in their minds of finding in the States-general, which was chiefly composed of burghers, a powerful support against the privileged classes. We shall never understand the extraordinary success of the first revolutionary movements, unless we bear in mind what a large share in the government of the country was possessed by the higher orders and the corporations, and how they now mutually sought each other's destruction.

Calonne was not long able to make head against this noisy opposition. The last of the many blows which caused his fall was dealt by the queen, whom he afterwards persecuted with inextinguishable hatred. His successor, Brienne, after a violent contest with the parliaments, resigned his office, when the convocation of the States-general had already been determined on, and the national bankruptcy virtually proclaimed. Louis had recourse to Necker again, who really relieved the financial embarrassment for the moment, and, recognizing the necessity of a liberal policy, fixed the meeting of the States-general for the 27th of April, 1789. The ferment which, owing to the preceding disputes, had for the first time since the religious wars penetrated the mass of the people, increased from hour to hour. The agitation was principally caused by the question, whether the States-general should meet as before in three separate chambers, or form a single assembly, in which the *tiers état* should have a double number of votes. On this point the hitherto allied opposition parties differed, — the aristocrats advocating the separation, the liberals the union of the three estates. Necker, with great want of tact, betrayed his own views by assigning the double number of votes to the *tiers état* while he induced the government to observe an obstinate silence on the main point in question. The public debates on this subject were all the more violent in consequence of this reticence; and in Bretagne it came to an open civil war between the nobility and the burghers.

The radical elements in France saw that their time for action was come; and the great dearness of provisions which prevailed during the winter months placed a large number of desperate men at the disposal of every conspirator. In Paris the revolutionary demagogues gathered round the agents of the Duke of Orleans, and at the end of April tried their strength in a sanguinary street riot, which was professedly directed against the usurious avarice of a rich manufacturer, but really had no other object than to intimidate the moderate party, before the impending election of the States-general.[1] In other respects external quiet still prevailed in the provinces; but the feverish agitation of men's minds increased with every day; and in this state of things the elections by almost universal suffrage began to be held. Every electoral college was to intrust its instructions and complaints to its deputies according to mediæval custom. In every district, therefore, a long list of abuses was drawn up and examined and brought home to the minds of the people at large by means of discussion. A modern historian has justly observed that these complaints do not leave a single particle of the *ancien régime* untouched; that everything was rejected by the restless desire of innovation, and that, unfortunately, neither the possibility nor the method of introducing reforms is anywhere pointed out. Revolution — universal and radical revolution — speaks in every line of these documents. There was but one thought through the whole of France, that thenceforward a new era was to commence for the people and the empire, and that the work begun must be completed in spite of every opposition.

Whilst the millions in every part of the country were thus emancipating themselves from the bonds of traditional law — uncertain about their future, but firm in their resolution to proceed — the government was daily sinking more and more into utter helplessness. It had indeed a presentiment of the dangers which would accompany the breaking out of the new epoch, but its destitution was so complete that it eagerly longed for the commencement of the crisis. Money, one of the great factors of material power, was not to be found in its coffers; and even the

---

[1] This has been clearly and concisely shown by Croker in his "Essays on the French Revolution," p. 50.

other, the army, was already affected by the general process of dissolution. This is perhaps the most important circumstance, with respect to the subsequent course of the French Revolution, and its difference from all those which have since taken place in Europe. The reason is simple enough: the French army was, in the main, organized according to the same principles as the other departments of the State, and, like them, had been thoroughly unhinged by the contests between the crown and the feudal orders, long before the breaking out of the Revolution. The nobility alone were eligible for commissions in the army; and though single exceptions to this rule really occurred, yet the monopoly was actually limited by a law of 1781 to noblemen of four descents. Twenty-seven regiments belonged to foreign or native grandees, and in these the owner of each regiment appointed the colonel, from a list drawn up by the minister at war; and the colonel appointed the other officers. The influence of the king's government, therefore, in the selection of officers, was limited to the composition of the list of candidates for the single office of colonel. In the other divisions of the army, indeed, the highest rank was in the gift of the king alone; but of the other commissions only one-half were bestowed by the king, and the other half by the colonel. The officer, moreover, received his commission, after giving proofs of his fitness, on payment of a sum of money; it was a purchase for life, as, in the case of the courts of law, it was a purchase of an hereditary right. The duty of unconditional obedience was not indeed abrogated by this system; but it was inevitable, especially under a weak government, that the corps of officers should feel itself, what it really was, a part of that great aristocracy which shared with the King the ruling power of France in every department of public life. The contest between this nobility and the ministry, by which the last years of the *ancien régime* were filled, must, therefore, have had a deep effect upon the army. It frequently occurred that the officers, like the judges, with their colonels at their head, refused obedience. And as in the rural districts the opposition of the aristocracy was followed by excitement among the peasants, and the opposition of the towns by excitement among the artisans, so, in the case of the army, the popular movement found its way into the minds of the soldiers, and operated side by side with the class resistance of the officers. The common soldiers had felt the oppression of the *ancien*

CAUSES OF THE FRENCH REVOLUTION. 77

régime, perhaps, more deeply than the peasants themselves; for they were starving on a pay of ten sous, whilst countless sums were employed in rich endowments for 1,171 generals. They suffered all the insolence of the nobility towards the *canaille*, embittered by the weight of a severe and often brutal discipline; and, like their fellow-citizens, they looked forward to the meeting of the States-general as the signal of liberation from intolerable slavery. The number of regiments on which the government could reckon was extremely small. The bands of discipline were loosened in every rank; the officers inveighed against the despotism of the ministers, and the soldiers promised one another to do nothing against the people.

The ancient polity, therefore, was destroyed by its own internal discord and dissolution, before a single revolutionary word had been uttered. The government was destitute of money and troops to defend its position; and the feudal seigniors, though they had important individual rights, had no general organization which could enable them to replace the government. As soon as public opinion — which, guided by radical theories, emphatically rejected both the government and the aristocracy — obtained an organ of power in the States-general, it only needed to declare its will, nay, only to give expression to the facts before them, and the old system hopelessly collapsed in its own rottenness. What was to follow no man at that time was able to foresee. As most men were extremely ill-informed respecting the condition of the country, they indulged in hopes which were all the more ardent in proportion as they were undefined. But there were many who knew the poverty and brutality of the masses, the bitter hatred between rich and poor, and the selfish immorality of the upper classes, and looked, some with ambitious pleasure, others with patriotic anxiety, towards a stormy future.

V.

THE EMANCIPATING EDICT OF STEIN.

FROM SEELEY'S LIFE AND TIMES OF STEIN, VOL. I., PP. 287-305.

I CALL by this name the great Edict which was signed on the 9th of October, i.e. only five days after Stein had received his powers, not solely because it contains the provision that from a certain date there shall be only free persons in the States of the King of Prussia. It is indeed to be remarked that the principal authors of the measure are so intoxicated with the pride of being the bestowers of freedom upon bondsmen, that they forget to remark how much more and how many other emancipations they accomplished by the same act. Stein's own account of the Edict of October runs as follows: —

" The measures adopted to reach the above-mentioned general object were: —

" (1) Abolition of personal serfdom in the Prussian Monarchy: by an Edict of October, 1807, it was decreed that from October 8th, 1809 (*sic;* it should be 1810), personal serfdom with its consequences, especially the very oppressive obligation of menial service, should be abolished; but the obligations of the peasant, as far as they flowed from his possession of property, remained unaltered. It was reserved for the Chancellor Hardenberg's love of innovation (on the advice of a H. Scharrenweber, a dreamer who died in a madhouse at Eberbach in 1820) to transform in 1811 the relations of the landlord to the peasant class, and its inner family relations in a manner pernicious to it; in this I had no share.

" (2) The transformation of the peasants on the Domain in East and West Prussia into free proprietors."

Here not a word is said of any changes made by the Edict of October, except those which affected the peasant. It is the same aspect of the Edict which interests Schön. This Edict, he says. " has made the figure of the king stand higher, since he is henceforth no longer a king of slaves, but of free men." And again: " Thus came into existence the law of Oct. 9th, 1807, that

Habeas Corpus Act of our State. The idea of freedom had begun to live. With ninety-nine hundredths of the people it made a deep and elevating impression; the few friends of slavery intrigued and murmured no doubt a good deal, so that, according to Rhediger's story, a prejudiced man said at the Berlin Casino after reading the law, ' Rather three battles of Auerstädt than such a law!' But the king stood firm, and God maintained the right."

In stating pretty strongly his claims to be considered the real author of the law, Schön uses language which shows that he is thinking almost exclusively of this part of it. " All else that I did in life," he says, " was as nothing compared to calling into life the idea of freedom." Only from one casual expression do we learn that he even knew that the measure had another side, where he says, "I represented that hereditary serfdom, that scourge of our country, must be brought to an end, and that a proclamation of free trade in landed property would be sufficient to promote material interests."

Here we are suddenly introduced to something quite new and very different from the abolition of serfdom, namely, free trade in landed property.

Up to a certain point it is true that these two things coincide. One part of the burden of serfdom lay in the incapacity of the serf to alienate his land; but this is a small matter. The proclamation of free trade in land affected all classes of society at once, and the upper and middle classes much more than the peasantry. When, therefore, we observe that the Edict of the 9th of October, at the same time that it abolished personal serfdom, removed all the principal restrictions that interfered with traffic in land, we see that it is in fact not a single law, but two laws in one, and two laws of such magnitude that each by itself might be considered equivalent to a social revolution.

But, when we look closer still, we discover that the Edict goes even further, and should be rather described as threefold than as twofold. Englishmen are only too familiar with the notion of a depressed class of agricultural laborers; but such depression may be of two kinds, and may spring from two very different causes. We are not to suppose that the peasantry of Prussia were in a condition resembling that of our own laborers any further than as it was bad. The evils afflicting the Prussian peasantry were those arising out of *status;* those which afflict

English laborers arise mainly out of contract. The English laborer is nominally free, and at liberty to carry his industry to the best market; he is reduced to real dependence by his inability to make a favorable bargain for himself. The Prussian peasant was nominally a serf, but in reality some very important rights were secured to him. We are not to suppose, for instance, that cruel punishments were allowed, or that he was subject to the caprice of the landlord. He was far more of a proprietor than the English laborer, for, though on a degrading tenure, he did for practical purposes own land. Nor were his interests neglected as those of a freeman, who is supposed able to take care of himself, may be neglected. Not only was he a member of an ancient and organized village community, but the Government also took, and was obliged to take, the greatest possible interest in his class, for these serfs were neither more nor less than the Prussian army.

Now it might very plausibly be maintained that the proclamation of free trade in land would not create a happy peasant class, but would simply substitute for a peasantry laboring under certain evils that class of famished drudges whom we know in England, and who if they cannot be called serfs can still less be called peasants, for a peasant properly so called must have a personal interest in the land. Hence the conservative opponents of Stein, such as Marwitz, actually declare that there existed no slavery or serfdom in the land when he professed to abolish it, but "that it then for the first time began to appear, namely, the serfdom of the small holder towards the creditor, of the poor and sick towards the police and the work-houses;" and again, "that with the proclamation of free trade disappeared the previous security of the peasantry in their holdings; every rich landowner could now buy them out and send them off— fortunately scarcely anybody was rich any longer!"

These were the criticisms of the conservative party, which might have been very truly applicable to a simple measure of free trade in land. But the Edict of October had in fact taken account of the danger, and contained an express provision to meet it. Hence, as I have said, it was actually a threefold enactment, for not only did it first abolish serfdom and, secondly, establish free trade in land; but, thirdly, it endeavored to guard the peasantry against the danger, which in so many countries has proved serious, of being gradually driven out or turned from proprietors into wage-receivers by the effects of the unequal competition to which they are exposed.

At the same time that we carefully distinguish these different enactments all included in one Legislative Edict, let us be as careful to remark what was not included in it. Englishmen are apt to attribute to the legislation of Stein all the innovations introduced in this period. In particular it has been supposed that he created the peasant-proprietorship of modern Prussia. But this he did not do, except, as he says in the passage quoted above, on the Domain Lands of West and East Prussia. Proprietors in a certain sense the peasantry were before this Edict, that is, they cultivated land for themselves, and with a considerable sense of security; proprietors in the full sense they were not, because they held of a landlord to whom they owed various dues and services. Now Stein's Edict altered the nature of these services, and abolished the most oppressive; but it did not destroy the rights of the landlord, or leave the peasant sole master of the land he cultivated. It was reserved for Hardenberg to do this by an Edict issued on Sept. 14th, 1811, and it should be noticed that Stein expressly declines to accept any responsibility for this innovation. Again, it is not to be supposed that the provision just mentioned, by which Stein tried to prevent the absorption of the small holdings by the great proprietors, has actually proved the means of preserving the peasant class in Prussia; for all this passed away with the legislation of Hardenberg, and it has been by its own vitality, and not by State interference that peasant-proprietorship has maintained itself.

Further, it is to be remarked that Stein is quite accurate when he describes his Land Reform as not consisting solely in the Edict of October, but as including also another quite distinct act of legislation, which applied only to the provinces of East and West Prussia. This act belongs to July, 1808, and is confined not simply to the peasants of these two provinces, but to a particular class of peasants, viz., those sometimes called *immediate* peasants, or, in other words, those who, living on the Royal Domains, had no other landlord but the King. It is evident that the Government could deal with these more easily than with those peasants whose condition it could not improve without meddling with the rights of another class. The extreme distress in which these two provinces lay, and which the Government was in no condition to relieve directly, was the justification for granting privileges to these particular immediate peasants, which, for the moment, were not extended to those of the other provinces.

Such, then, defined in general terms, was the extent of this reform. It needs, however, a much closer description. In the first place the reader must guard against a misapprehension of the phrase, "free trade in land," into which he is likely to be led by his English experience. Free trade in land is also a cry of our own reformers; but we must beware of supposing that what they call for is the same thing that was granted in Prussia by Stein's Edict. The complaint in England is that a number of practical obstructions prevent land from being the object of such free purchase and sale as other commodities. Much of the land of the country, it is said, is in the hands of persons who in family settlements have given up the right to alienate it; the system under which landed property is conveyed is so cumbrous and expensive as to deter people from transactions of the kind; and, lastly, by recognizing the principle of primogeniture with respect to land and not with respect to personal property in cases of intestacy, the law itself countenances the notion that landed property stands in a class by itself, and is not to be dealt with or transferred as if it were purely a commodity. Now, it is an instance of the confusing and misleading inaccuracy of our party cries, when the removal of these restrictions is called free trade in land. Free trade in other cases means the removal of restrictions imposed by the law or by the government; but these restrictions are of quite another kind. Only the last mentioned is the work of the law, and it cannot in any proper sense be called a restriction, for the only way in which it operates restrictingly is by lending the moral influence of the law to the support of a restrictive system. The cumbrousness of our conveyancing is merely the result of the gradual way in which our land system has been formed, and as to the system of settlements, so far from being a restriction of freedom, it is the direct result of freedom of contract, so much so that the reformers themselves demand an interference of the law to prevent it; in other words, wish to promote what they call free trade by a new legal prohibition.

Now, when Stein is said to have established free trade in land, the expression is to be understood literally. The hindrances to the sale and purchase of land which he removed were not accidental practical obstacles, but formal legal prohibitions. In the old law of Prussia and in the Code of Frederick or Allgemeines Landrecht, which came into force in 1794, it is laid down that noble estates (adelige Güter) can only be held by nobles, and that persons of civic origin (bürgerlicher Herkunft) can only acquire them by express permission of the sovereign. In the same way peasant-land could, as a rule, only be held by peasants, and land belonging to towns only by citizens. We are familiar with the idea of caste as applied to human beings, that is, of an unalterable *status* stamped upon a man from his birth; in Prussia it may be said that caste extended actually to the land, so that every rood of soil in the country was of a definite and unalterable rank, and, however it might change its owners, always remained either noble or citizen or peasant land. Now, the first innovation contained in Stein's Edict consisted in cancelling in the fewest and simplest words all the regulations which established caste in land.

When the Edict is examined more closely it will be seen to be much more comprehensive even than it was represented above, when I pointed out how much more comprehensive it was than was commonly supposed, or than Stein himself described it. For at the same time that it abolishes caste in land, it accomplishes another act of emancipation, which is in no way expressed in the phrase free trade in land; it removes another quite distinct set of restrictions, and abolishes caste in persons. The Code of Frederick prohibited the nobleman from engaging in any occupation properly belonging to the citizen, and only allowed under certain conditions the citizen to pass into the class of peasants or the peasant into the class of citizens. The Nobles, the Citizens, the Peasants; these were the three castes into which the Prussian population, outside the professions, was divided; into one or other of them each person was born, and in the same, as a rule, he died. To each caste was assigned its special pursuit. The Noble cultivated his estate and exercised jurisdiction over the peasantry who held under him, though he could not himself hold or cultivate peasant-land; he also served the king in civil or military office. The Peasant cultivated his plot of ground, rendering fixed services to the lord, and subject to his jurisdiction, and belonged at the same time to the rank and file of the army. Between them stood the Citizen, holding a monopoly of trades and industries, which by law were confined, with few exceptions, to the towns. It is remarkable that the military profession was, for the most part, closed to him. This must be borne in mind when we compare the Seven Years' War with the War of Liberation. We have read of the fearful consumption of men caused by the Seven Years' War, and of the desperate shifts of Frederick to procure recruits; but we must understand that no *levée en masse* took place then, and that the citizen class had scarcely any share in what was going forward. This is the more to be noted because the connection between the citizen class and the learned class was closer than in other countries. The learning, literature, and philosophy, which flourished so remarkably in that age, took the tone of the middle class, and a curious result followed. In the most military of all modern States, literature, because it sprang from a class which enjoyed an exemption from military service, and as a consequence, the tone of public feeling which is determined by literature, was in an especial degree wanting in the military spirit — Scharnhorst describes the army as being generally hated and despised, and Kant speaks with contempt of a man of education who had embraced a military life — and this fact goes some way to explain that phenomenon of a military state fighting exceptionally ill which we have so long had before us.

This state of society is very foreign to our ideas, and may, perhaps, because we have no experience of it, fascinate some imaginations. No Laissez faire here; every man's place is assigned to him from his birth; his occupations are prescribed, and a great taskmaster, or earthly Providence, stands at the head of the whole society, which may be called army or nation at pleasure, since even the unmilitary citizens were regarded by the State principally as a sort of commissariat department. And, for the immediate purpose of Frederick William I. and Frederick the Great, the system was well adapted, for that purpose was simply military. A place for every man, and every man in his place; the "productive forces of the country perfectly inventoried, and a debtor and creditor account of its resources kept";[1] by such a system the rulers could wield the whole force of the country most easily and certainly. Nevertheless, the destruction of this whole system by a stroke of Stein's pen, was now regarded as the greatest of reforms, and the commencement of the restoration of Prussia. For it will be evident that the same

---

[1] Morier.

system which concentrated so powerfully and measured so exactly the forces of the country at the same time entirely prevented them from growing, not to mention the intellectual stagnation, outside the University world, which was produced by such rigid uniformity of life. A country in which no man can follow his natural bent, take to agriculture if he does not like trade, or to trade if he does not succeed in agriculture, is evidently not an industrial country; its material resources under such a system will remain undeveloped, and if it be a poor country, as Prussia was, the system will actually in the end defeat its own object, for such a country from mere poverty will be weak in war.

As the first section of the Edict abolished what I have called "caste in land," so the second, consisting of about three lines, abolished caste in persons. And here it may perhaps be observed that I omitted above one principal circumstance which made such sweeping changes so easy to Stein. Before the Peace of Tilsit it would have been scarcely possible to carry out such reforms, however much the rulers might have been convinced of their necessity. Frederick had shrunk from the emancipation of the serfs because he felt that it would introduce disorder into his army, and for the same reason these reforms also would have been scarcely practicable so long as the army existed. The disasters brought with them the compensation that they destroyed for a moment this incubus; the necessity of maintaining a great position in Europe, the necessity even of defending the country, ceased when the country actually fell into French occupation, and thus, as we may say, the building being down, it was for the first time possible to mend a defect in the foundations.

These reforms, favored as they were by circumstances and requiring but few lines in the Edict, were yet much more fundamental and pregnant with consequences than any such practical reforms as may be called for in England to make the purchase of land more easy. They were a sort of Magna Charta to the Prussians, and Schön might well have applied to them the enthusiastic expressions which he keeps for the sections which emancipated the serf. In v. Rönne's standard text-book of Prussian Constitutional Law, I find in the chapter on Rights, under the first title, Freedom or Security of the Person, that this freedom is composed of three rights: (1) the right of movement and free choice of abode (Freizügigkeit); (2) the right of emigration (Auswanderungsrecht) ; (3) *the right of choosing a calling or trade* (Freie Wahl von Beruf und Gewerbe) ; and this third right we are informed was given to the Prussians by the Edict of October, 1807. The same is said of the first of the rights which go to make up the second Title ; viz., free right to the acquisition and possession of property (Freies Recht zum Erwerbe und Besitze des Eighenthums).

I proceed to give the text of this Edict, the vast importance of which will have by this time become clear. The less important sections are printed in a smaller type, and of §§ III. and V., as purely technical, only the heading is given.

"*Edict concerning the facilitation of possession and the free use of landed property, as well as the personal relations of the inhabitants of the country.*

"WE, Frederick William, by the grace of God King of Prussia, &c., &c.,

"Make known hereby and give to understand. Since the beginning of the peace We have been before all things occupied with the care for the depressed condition of Our faithful subjects, and the speediest restoration and greatest improvement of it. We have herein considered that in the universal need it passes the means at Our command to furnish help to each individual, and yet We could not attain the object; and it accords equally with the imperative demands of justice and with the principles of a proper national economy, to remove all the hindrances which hitherto prevented the individual from attaining the prosperity which, according to the measure of his powers, he was capable of reaching; further, We have considered that the existing restrictions, partly on the possession and enjoyment of landed property, partly on the personal condition of the agricultural laborer, specially thwart Our benevolent purpose and disable a great force which might be applied to the restoration of cultivation, the former by their prejudicial influence on the value of landed property and the credit of the proprietor, the latter by diminishing the value of labor. We purpose, therefore, to reduce both within the limits required by the common well-being, and accordingly ordain as follows : —

" § I. Freedom of Exchange in Land.

"Every inhabitant of our States is competent, without any limitation on the part of the State, to possess either as property or pledge landed estates of every kind ; the nobleman therefore to possess not only noble but also non-noble, citizen, and peasant lands of every kind, and the citizen and peasant to possess not only citizen, peasant, and other non-noble, but also noble, pieces of land, without either the one or the other needing any special permission for any acquisition of land whatever, although, henceforward as before, each change of possession must be announced to the authorities.

"§ II. Free Choice of Occupation.

" Every noble is henceforth permitted without any derogation from his position, to exercise citizen occupation; and every citizen or peasant is allowed to pass from the peasant into the citizen class, or from the citizen into the peasant class.

"§ III. How far a legal right of Pre-emption and a First Claim still exist.

"§ IV. Division of Lands.

" Owners of Estates and Lands of all kinds, in themselves alienable either in Town or Country, are allowed, after due notice given to the provincial authority, with reservation of the rights of Direct Creditors and of those who have the right of pre-emption (§ III.), to separate the principal estate and its parts, and in general to alienate piecemeal. In the same way Co-proprietors may divide among them property owned in common.

"§ V. Granting of Estates under Leases for a Long Term.

"§ VI. Extinction and Consolidation of Peasant Holdings.

" When a landed proprietor believes himself unable to restore or keep up the several peasant holdings existing on an estate which are not held by a hereditary tenure, whether of a long lease or of copyhold, he is required to give information to the government of the province, with the sanction of which the consolidation, either of several holdings into a single peasant estate, or with demesne land, may be allowed as soon as hereditary serfdom shall have ceased to exist on the estate. The provincial Authorities will be provided with a special instruction to meet these cases.

"§ VII. If, on the other hand, the peasant tenures are hereditary, whether of long lease or of copyhold, the consolidation or other alteration of the condition of the lands in question, is not admissible until the right of the actual possessor is extinguished, whether by the purchase of it by the lord or in some other legal way. In this case the regulations of § VI. also apply.

"§ VIII. Indebtedness of Feudal and Entailed Estates in consequence of the Ravages of War.

" Every possessor of feudal or entailed property is empowered to raise the sums required to replace the losses caused by war, by mortgaging the substance of the Estates themselves, as well as the revenues of them, provided the application of the money is attested by the Administrator (Landrath) of the Circle or the Direction of the Department. At the end of three years from the contracting of the debt the possessor and his successor are bound to pay off at least the fifteenth part of the capital itself.

"IX. Extinction of Feudal Relations, Family Settlements, and Entails, by Family Resolution.

"Every feudal connection not subject to a Chief Proprietor, every family settlement and entail may be altered at pleasure or entirely abolished by a Family Resolution, as is already enacted with reference to the East Prussian Fiefs (except those of Ermeland) in the East Prussian Provincial Law, Appendix 36.

"§ X. Abolition of Villainage.

"From the date of this Ordinance no new relation of villainage, whether by birth, or marriage, or acquisition of a holding, or by contract, can come into existence.

"§ XI. With the publication of the present Ordinance the existing condition of villainage of those villains with their wives and children who possess their peasant-holdings by hereditary tenures, of whatever kind, ceases entirely both with its rights and duties.

"§ XII. From Martinmas, 1810, ceases all villainage in Our entire States. From Martinmas, 1810, there shall be only free persons, as this is already the case upon the Domains in all Our provinces; free persons, however, still subject, as a matter of course, to all the obligations which bind them as free persons by virtue of the possession of an estate or by virtue of a special contract.

"To this declaration of Our royal Will every man whom it may concern, and in particular Our provincial and other governments, are exactly and loyally to conform themselves, and the present Ordinance is to be made universally known.

"Authentically, under Our royal Signature. Given at Memel, Oct. 9th, 1807.

"FRIEDRICH WILHELM,
"Schrötter, Stein, Schrötter II."

The elder Schrötter was at this time Minister for the province of Prussia, and he with his brother was entrusted with the task of publishing the Ordinance in the province where it had received the king's signature. It is for this reason that their names are affixed to it along with Stein's.

That threefold character of the Edict which was pointed out above, will appear very visibly by observing the three groups of sections, which on account of their especial importance have been printed in large type. The abolition of caste, both in land and in persons, is accomplished in the first two sections; the abolition of villainage in the last three, which, it is evident, might as well have composed a separate edict. Sections 6 and 7 are introduced to prevent the system of free trade in land from bearing too hard on the peasant and making the proprietorship of land a monopoly of the richer classes.

Having traced the history of the preparation of this Edict, and examined its nature and the changes it introduced, we are in a condition to inquire who are the persons to whom the Prussians may consider themselves chiefly indebted for it.

In such cases the popular mind invariably makes a misapprehension which it is almost in vain to attempt to correct. It attributes to the unassisted intelligence and will of a single author what was necessarily the joint-work of many. In this instance Stein has obtained a popular fame to which he has little right, and which partly compensates for much unjust neglect. While his real life and actions have been little known, he has gained a sort of legendary reputation, such as has gathered round many other legislators, and has been credited with all the judgment, technical skill and wisdom implied in the framing of a law which has revolutionized a country. His admirers need not hesitate for a moment to disown for him all such ungrounded pretensions. In the construction of the Emancipating Edict Stein had no great share. Before it reached his hands it was almost complete, and we may distinguish two agents by whom it had been made such as it then was. The first agent was what we call the Spirit of the Age, that is, the sum of influence proceeding partly from the humanitarian writers, partly from the economists of the eighteenth century, by which the majority of those who guided public affairs had been convinced of the necessity of certain great changes. When a man like Hardenberg, who had no special or professional learning, confidently sanctioned such sweeping proposals as those which Altenstein laid before him, he proclaimed in effect that the work of the Zeitgeist was done. From that moment the matter of the law existed, and the question of the form came under consideration. Then began the work of the second agent, that is, the Immediate Commission. We have seen who the men were from whose deliberations the law came forth clothed in form. But perhaps the question may be asked which member, or members, of the Commission deserved best of the law; and this question can only be answered partially and doubtfully, many of the documents being missing in the archives. We have the fact that Niebuhr separated himself deliberately from his colleagues because he would not take the responsibility of their plans. For the rest we have Schön's Report, of which an abstract has been given above, and we have some reminiscences of Schön, which were written down at a much later period and not published till 1875. The latter indeed give us many statements, but we are embarrassed when we find that their drift is to claim the whole credit of the Edict for Schön. It seems hardly fair to the other members of the Commission to accept a representation which is made at their expense and published after their death. When we test it in the only way open to us, that is, by comparing it with Schön's Report, which for what it asserts is far better testimony, we find the suspicions decidedly strengthened, which the claim itself by its exorbitant and egotistic character suggests. That Schön deserved a great share of the credit we are quite prepared, from what we hear of the influence he exerted, to believe; nay, after a reasonable deduction for evident self-conceit, we might be willing to think that perhaps his claim to have been the guiding spirit of the Commission was substantially well-founded. But when we compare his late reminiscences with his own report written at the time, as well as with other evidence, we discover that his self-conceit was of an unusual intensity, and that it certainly clouded and corrupted his remembrances. His statement is not merely exaggerated; it is certainly untrue, and gives an incorrect impression of the nature as well as of the degree of the influence he exerted.

We have gathered from Niebuhr's hints that he had friends on the Commission who applied certain doctrinaire theories with a consistency which appalled him, and in fact frightened him away. It is scarcely possible to doubt who is pointed at. Schön was just such a doctrinaire, and such inexorable consistency was just in his character, while nothing similar seems to be true of Altenstein or Stägemann. It seems also unquestionable what rigorous applications of theory are pointed at. The introduction of free trade in land created so manifest a danger of the absorption of the peasant-holdings by the rich, that it was found in the end necessary to protect those holdings by a special limitation. Now the theory of free trade was precisely that which at the moment possessed the heads of the Prussian doctrinaires under the influence of Kraus, and it was precisely that of which Schön was the mouth-piece on the Immediate Commission. " Kraus," says Schön himself, " was my great teacher; he mastered me entirely, and I followed him without reserve." The theory was still so new, that it is not likely that the Prussian legislators could have adopted it with such courageous completeness as they did in the Emancipating Edict unless there had been among them some strongly convinced free-trader, whose arguments were heard at the Immediate Commission. Schön's influence is necessary to account for the result, and we can fancy how hard and ruthless his language must sometimes have sounded, particularly to one so timid by temperament as Niebuhr. Thus Niebuhr's evidence and the nature and known facts of the case concur to show us Schön advocating with all his influence, and with more energy than any one else, that part of the Edict which introduces free trade in land.

On the other hand we do not expect to be told that Schön had much influence in deciding the Commission to propose the abolition of serfdom, not because he did not feel strongly on the question, but because there was no difference of opinion about it. How did we find Hardenberg treating this subject? " The abolition of serfdom," he wrote, " must be decreed by a law briefly, and at once." In other words, it is a matter on which argument has long been exhausted. That this was really the case, that, to use the vigorous words of—what writer?—of Schön himself: —

" The great majority of the nation, a few weak and wicked persons only excepted, have long been agreed upon the principle that there is no greater injustice than that a reasonable being should be prevented from using his energies for his own welfare in a way not prejudicial to the State, by a fellow-subject, simply because he was born on this or that clod," all evidence concurs to show. To abolish serfdom had been a favorite object of Frederick William III. since his accession, " towards which," as he himself said in his Cabinet Order of August 23d, " he had undeviatingly striven." The question had been agitated in every way, in the Estates of West Prussia as early as 1799, in writings by Kraus, Leopold Krug, and others; Stein himself, as has been remarked above, had been busy with it in Westphalia. A good notion of the general state of public opinion on the subject may be formed from the following statement given in Bassewitz's " State of the Electoral Mark of Brandenburg in 1806 " : —

" Though the peasant, used to routine, had, in his fettered condition, little industry, and did not yet appreciate the advantages which were offered him for the future in a perfectly free proprietorship, yet he felt keenly enough the pressure of the service-payments, and of the compulsory service. This, and the views of the rights of man that were diffused among the people, created among the peasantry the wish to be relieved from their services, from their dependence on the landlords, and from the compulsory menial service, as it subsisted under the Servants Ordinance (Gesinneordnung) for the country districts of the Electoral Mark of Feb. 11, 1769, and the later interpretations of it."

Now what startles us in Schön's reminiscences and excites the suspicion that he does not merely exaggerate, but deliberately distorts and misrepresents the truth, is this, that he describes himself as having carried the abolition of serfdom in spite of general opposition, while he is not only silent about his exertions in the cause of free trade, but endeavors by studied turns of language to convey the impression that he took no interest in that question. What curious freak of vanity can have actuated him we can only guess; I suppose he thought the glory of a liberator of bondsmen more desirable than a mere reputation for enlightened views of political economy. It is, however, the fact that he, the enthusiastic disciple of Kraus, describes one of the most memorable triumphs of the free trade theory in such a way that it can only be discovered from a single casual expression that free trade triumphed at all. Meanwhile he describes his zeal for the abolition of serfdom as resembling that of a martyr or apostle, and has a pathetic picture of his own devotedness, when, as he was engaged in composing his report, he received intelligence that his wife was at the point of death, if he would see her again alive he must leave his work and hurry to her side; but, " though deeply afflicted, he felt he must not betray the great idea, and with violent self-mastery, wrote on till his task was ended, and then setting out, found his wife, the angel that hovered over him, no longer living." And he repeats several times that this had been " his sole and single object in public life," that " he had desired only this," which assertions of course imply, and seem intended to imply, that he had never taken the smallest interest in free trade. Equally strong are his assertions that the abolition of serfdom was owing to his own efforts. The reform is described, not as one about the desirableness of which all were agreed, not as one which had long been agitated and over every part of the monarchy, which the king had always had at heart, and the peasantry themselves were eagerly looking forward to, but in a strain which might have suited the Abolition of the Slave Trade by Clarkson and Wilberforce. It is a grand philanthropic idea conceived by a few Königsberg philosophers and diffused from them to a band of faithful disciples, but remaining for a long time a doctrine peculiar to the Prussian province, so that it " seemed a mere brain-cobweb to Westphalians and Markers." This idea he personally has the glory of representing in the Immediate Commission. Stägemann is the first convert, then Beyme raises himself to the level of the Idea, his conversion being helped by the authority of another Königsberger, Morgenbesser; Klewitz is the last to come in. While the abolition of serfdom required so much preaching, the doctrines of free trade, we are asked to believe, were received as a matter of course. But in the moment of his triumph this Prussian Wilberforce sank down exhausted; no sooner was the struggle over than the sense of his bereavement overcame him. Accordingly he could not draught the law, — here at least is an important statement, — and Stägemann, " faithful companion on the great journey," undertook this task. " All else that I have done in the world is nothing compared to calling into life the idea of freedom." And this hymn to himself Schön introduces with the mock-modest heading, *What did I do? Answer: Nothing worth speaking of.*

The report which cost Schön such "violent self-mastery" is now before us, and we cannot read it without feeling that the Frau v. Schön was somewhat hardly used. It is from this very report that I have just extracted the statement, that "the great majority of the nation had long been agreed on the principle of the abolition of serfdom." So far from arguing strongly and eloquently against serfdom, so far from directing his argument principally to this point, he puts serfdom last among six causes to which he refers the impoverishment of the country. He does indeed describe it as the most important of the six, but he refrains from treating it with the same fulness as the others, because, as he says, "on the necessity and safety of abolishing it Your Majesty has heard so much that it would tire you to hear more." And in the short preface which he has prefixed to the Report he says expressly:—

"This matter (*i. e.*, the abolition of serfdom) had occupied all good heads and hearts in Prussia many years before the war. The number of those who were slavishly disposed was small, but they were powerful."

At the same time it refutes the reminiscences not less completely on the subject of free trade in land. It shows, as we should expect, that Schön's mind is fully occupied with this question, and that he gives it precedence over the question of the abolition of serfdom. We find in this report just those hard and cruel-sounding statements of economic principle which Niebuhr had led us to expect. We find him attacking as a mischievous prejudice the accepted rule that the number of peasant-holdings on an estate should never be diminished, and declaring that "there is no reason why the land-owner should not have an unlimited right to dispose at pleasure of his land and soil," and that, "as a matter of fact it would be found impossible to keep up as many peasant-holdings as before the war," and throwing out hard assertions that "the government can never have an interest in securing A or B in the possession of his property."[1]

It is, however, a mistake to suppose that Stein's reputation is in any way concerned in the question of the trustworthiness of Schön's account. Schön's sphere was the Immediate Commission, while Stein's sphere was altogether outside it. What Schön has snatched at is not any reputation belonging to Stein, but that which ought to fall to his colleagues, Stägemann, Klewitz, and in some degree also Altenstein and Niebuhr. An achievement which officially belonged to the whole Commission jointly he has tried to appropriate in the main to himself. Fortunately evidence enough remains to defeat this attempt, and to show that the only statement in his whole narrative which we can safely accept is the statement that the draughting of the Edict was the work of Stägemann. As to Stein, his share in the

---

[1] I have carefully avoided depending upon the narrative given in Pertz of the party-contest at the Immediate Commission, which I agree with the anonymous author of "Zu Schutz und Trutz am Grabe Schöns" in regarding as somewhat legendary. I trust I have made it appear that the statements of Schön's Autobiography can be disproved without assuming the truth of a narrative equally unsatisfactory that has unfortunately crept into Pertz, and in any case that Stein is not at all concerned in the controversy.

EMANCIPATING EDICT OF STEIN. 95

achievement is altogether distinct from that of the Commission, and, therefore, from that of any member of the Commission. It is to be divided into two parts, of which the one can be precisely stated, and the other is essentially indefinable, though not necessarily the smaller on that account.

The first consists in any alterations he may have made in the Edict after it was laid before him. Of these the principal was the extension of the Edict to all the provinces of the monarchy. That the credit of this belongs to Stein we find Schön himself, who, when he wrote his Autobiography, had formed the habit of denying him all share in the Edict beyond that of putting his name to it, fully acknowledging while the facts were still fresh in memory. In a diary written about the time of Stein's fall Schön writes of him: " He made his *début* with the Edict of October, which he found ready, and which it is his merit only to have made universal. Besides this, as we have seen, the incorporation of Stägemann's suggestion into Art. 6 is due to Stein.

But it is strangely perverse to limit Stein's share in the Edict to those alterations in the text of it which are known to be due to him. It is not thus that the merit of an act of legislation ought to be, or commonly is, awarded. When Lord Grey is called the author of the Reform Bill, is it intended that he first thought of reforming Parliament, or that he devised and draughted all or most of the provisions of the bill? Plainly his title to the achievement would be entirely unaffected if it could be shown that no single word of the bill was suggested or determined by him. It is not draughting a bill, but passing it, that is the difficulty. What we say of Lord Grey is that he gained that ascendency both in his own party and in the nation by the height and firmness of his character, that he was able to guide them safely through a legislative enterprise which, with an inferior leader, they would either have feared to attempt, or, in attempting, would have stumbled into revolution and civil bloodshed. When we call the Edict of October Stein's Edict we mean something similar. But it may be thought that the cases were not parallel, because in Prussia there was no parliament to guide, no turbulent public opinion to control. And, indeed, I imagine that no one would pretend to equal this single act of Stein's to the passing of the Reform Bill. Still, between the draughting of the Emancipating Edict and the making it law in Prussia there was a space to be traversed, though not so wide a space as that over which Lord Grey carried the Reform Bill. Not a parliament or a people, but officials and the king, had to be inspired with courage. No noisy parliamentary opposition indeed, but tenacious interests exceedingly strong in the court and in the army had to be defied. When Hardenberg and Altenstein and the Commission recommended these reforms, they did so with the knowledge that Stein was at hand to carry them out. Would they have made the same suggestions if Voss or Schulenburg or Struensee had been at the head of affairs? Hardenberg's recommendations proceed avowedly upon the assumption that Stein is to be minister, and we cannot even be sure that he would himself have had courage to attempt what he felt sure Stein would not shrink from. Much more may we doubt whether the king would have borne the weight of such responsibility unsupported, or supported only by a common minister.

In one word, we must not confound the reforming legislator with the jurist and parliamentary draughtsman. It is not inventiveness, or originality, or technical skill, that we honor in those who have presided over the transitions of States. It is chiefly the massive courage that moves freely under responsibility and lightens the burden of responsibility to all around; it is the "Atlantean shoulders."

On these principles we ought perhaps to regard the rapidity with which Stein hurried the reform through as an essential and principal part of the reform itself. It was most material that the nation should feel the stay and sway of a powerful hand. Stein always acted with an almost Napoleonic swiftness, but in this instance we are particularly struck with his promptitude. It was perhaps rather instinctive than calculated, and yet he may have been aware of the importance of justifying without a moment's delay the great expectations that had been formed of him. He receives his powers on October 4th, and on the 9th the most comprehensive measure ever passed in Prussia, affecting every class and the whole framework of society, appears, not as a proposal, but as an accomplished act with the king's signature, as a part of the law of the country.

VI.

THE ORDERS IN COUNCIL.

FROM LEVI'S HISTORY OF BRITISH COMMERCE (2D ED.), PP. 101-120.

THE political horizon was ominously darkening at the commencement of the nineteenth century. Whilst grievously suffering from the high prices of corn and provisions, and oppressed by the burden of a contest already sufficiently prolonged, England was threatened by the renewal of another armed neutrality on the part of the Northern powers, — a neutrality based on a new code of maritime law, then deemed utterly inconsistent with the rights of this country. The Northern powers wished to proclaim that free ships should make free goods; but England was determined that the trade of the enemy should not be carried on by neutrals. The Northern powers asserted that only contraband goods should be excluded from the trade of neutrals, and these of certain definite and known articles. England did not wish the enemy to obtain timber, hemp, and other articles, which, though not contraband of war, are still essential for warfare. The Northern powers declared that no blockade should be held valid unless real. England had already assumed the right to treat whole coasts as blockaded, in order to prevent the enemy receiving supplies from any quarter. And when the Northern powers added that a merchant vessel accompanied and protected by a belligerent ship ought to be safe from the right of search, England was not prepared to recognize the authority of such ships, and would place no limit to the action of her cruisers. When, therefore, Russia, Denmark, and Sweden entered into a convention to enforce the principles of the armed neutrality, and, in pursuance of the same, Russia caused an embargo to be laid on all British vessels in her ports, the British Government, ill-disposed to bear with such provocation, issued a proclamation on Jan. 14, 1801, authorizing reprisals, and laying an embargo on all Russian, Swedish, and Danish vessels in British ports. What followed is well known, and with the battle of Copenhagen the Northern confederacy was completely dissolved. By this time Mr. Pitt had given in his resignation, and a change of government took place, which led to a change of policy towards France, and to negotiations which ended with the conclusion of the treaty of Amiens.[1]

But, alas! from whatever cause it was, that peace was of short duration, and, more than ever, the patriotic spirit of the people was evoked to defend British soil against Britain's inveterate enemies.[2] From class to class the national enthusiasm spread and increased, and even the merchants, setting aside their books and business, issued a declaration, promising, in a solemn manner, to use every exertion to rouse the spirit and to assist the resources of the kingdom; to be ready with their services of every sort and on every occasion in its defence; and rather to perish altogether than live to see the honor of the British name tarnished, or that sublime inheritance of greatness, glory, and liberty destroyed, which descended to them from their forefathers, and which they were determined to transmit to their posterity. Again was Mr. Pitt called to be prime minister, as the only man who could really be trusted in times of so much anxiety and peril. And then it was that that continental system was inaugurated, which made of oceans and seas one vast battlefield of strife and bloodshed.

Fully to understand the policy of this country as regards these orders in council, we must briefly retrace our steps, by examining the measures taken in previous wars. During the Seven Years' War, which ended in 1763, France hemmed in on all sides by England, and hindered by the British naval force from carrying on any trade with her West India colonies, adopted the plan of relaxing her colonial monopoly, and allowing neutral ships to carry the produce of those islands to French or foreign ports in Europe. The produce being thus carried really or ostensibly on neutral account, it was assumed that no danger of capture could be incurred. But the prize courts of England condemned such vessels as were captured while engaged in the trade, and the rule was then adopted, called the rule of 1756,[3] that a neutral has no

---

[1] Peace was ratified on October 10, 1801; and the treaty of Amiens was concluded March 25, 1802.

[2] On May 16, 1803, an order in council was made, issuing letters of marque and reprisals against France, and another laying an embargo on all ships belonging to the French and Batavian republics. Reprisals against Spain were ordered December 19, 1805; against Prussia on May 14, 1806; and against Russia on December 18, 1807.

[3] The rule of 1756 had been acted upon even by France on previous occasions. See Note 1, On the practice of the British Prize Courts with regard to the Colonial trade of the Enemy during the American War, in 6 Rob. Rep. App.; and *Considérations sur l'Admission des Navires neutres aux Colonies françoises de l'Amérique ens Tems de Guerre*, p. 13, 1779; and see the Wilhelmina, 4 Rob. Rep., p. 4; and the Immanuel Tudor. — Leading cases of mercantile war, p. 814.

right to deliver a belligerent from the pressure of his enemy's hostilities by trading with his colonies in time of war in a way that was prohibited in time of peace. As Sir William Scott said, " The general rule is, that the neutral has a right to carry on in time of war his accustomed trade to the utmost extent of which that accustomed trade is capable. Very different is the case of a trade which the neutral has never possessed; which he holds by no title of use and habit in time of peace ;'and which, in fact, he can obtain in war by no other title than by the success of the one belligerent against the other, and at the expense of that very belligerent under whose success he sets up his title." During the American war this principle did not come practically into action, because, although then also the French government opened the ports of her West India islands to the ships of neutral powers, it had the wisdom to do so before hostilities were commenced, and not after.

In accordance with these principles, when the war of the French Revolution commenced, instructions were given, on Nov. 6, 1793, to the commanders of British ships of war and privateers, ordering them " to stop and detain for lawful adjudication all vessels laden with goods, the produce of any French colony, or carrying provisions or other supplies for the use of any such colony." And this order was the more necessary from the fact that American ships were crowding the ports of the French West Indies, where the flag of the United States was made to protect the property of the French planters. Great numbers of ships under American colors were thus taken in the West Indies and condemned, the fraudulent pretences of neutral property in the cargoes being too gross to be misunderstood. Complaints were, however, made of the hardship of this practice on the *bond-fide* American trader, and in January, 1794, the instructions were so far amended that the direction was to seize " such vessels as were laden with goods the produce of the French West India Islands, *and coming directly from any ports of the said islands to Europe.*" This rule continued in force till 1798, when again it was relaxed, by ordering that vessels should be seized "laden with the produce of any island or settlement of France, Spain, or Holland, and coming directly from any port of the said island or settlement to any port in Europe, not being a port of this kingdom, or of the country to which the vessel, being neutral, should belong." European neutrals were thus permitted to bring the produce of the hostile colonies from thence to ports of their own countries; and European or American neutral ships might carry such produce direct to England. But when the war was resumed in 1803, the rule of 1798 was again put in force, and instructions were given "not to seize any neutral vessels which should be found carrying on trade directly between the colonies of the enemy and the neutral country to which the vessel belonged, and laden with property of the inhabitants of such neutral country, provided that such neutral vessel should not be supplying, nor should have on the outward voyage supplied, the enemy with any articles of contraband of war, and should not be trading with any blockaded ports."

By thus allowing, however, neutrals to trade safely to and from neutral ports, means were opened to them to clear out for a neutral port, and under cover of that pretended destination to make a direct voyage from the colony to the parent state, or really to proceed to some neutral country, and thence reëxport the cargo in the same or a different bottom to whichever European market, neutral or hostile, they might prefer. The former, on an assumed voyage to the parent State, being the shortest and most convenient method, was chiefly adopted by the Dutch on their homeward voyages, because a pretended destination for Prussian, Swedish, or Danish ports in the North Sea, or the Baltic, was a plausible mask, even in the very closest approach the ship might make to the Dutch coast down to the moment of her slipping into port. The latter method, or the stopping at an intermediate neutral country, was commonly preferred by the Spaniards and French in bringing home their colonial produce, because no pretended neutral destination could be given that would consist with the geographical position and course of a ship coming directly from the West Indies, if met with near the end of her voyage in the latitude of their principal ports. The American flag in particular was a cover that could scarcely ever be adapted to the former method of eluding our hostilities, but it was found peculiarly convenient in the latter. Such is the position of the United States, and such was the effect of the trade-winds, that European vessels, homeward bound from the West Indies, could touch at their ports with very little inconvenience or delay; and such was also the case, though in a less degree, with regard to vessels coming from the remotest parts of South America or the East Indies. The passage from the Gulf of Mexico, especially, runs so close along the North American shore that ships bound from the Havannah, from Vera Cruz, and other great Spanish ports bordering on that gulf, to Europe, could touch at certain ports in the United States with scarcely any deviation. On an outward voyage to the East and West Indies the proper course would be more to the southward than would well consist with touching on North America; yet the deviation for that purpose was not a very formidable inconvenience. From these causes the protection given by the American flag to the intercourse between our European enemies and their colonies was chiefly in the way of a double voyage, in which America was the half-way house or central point of communication. The fabrics and commodities of France, Spain, and Holland were brought under American colors to ports in the United States, and from thence reëxported, under the same flag, for the supply of the hostile colonies. Again, the produce of these colonies was brought in a like manner to the American ports, and thence reshipped to Europe. But the Americans went still farther. The ports of this kingdom having been constituted, by the royal instructions of 1798, legitimate places of destination for neutrals coming with cargoes of produce directly from the hostile colonies, the American merchants made a pretended destination to British ports a convenient cover for a voyage from the hostile colonies to Europe, which their flag could not otherwise give, and thus rivalled the neutrals of the old world in this method of protecting the West India trade of the enemy, while they nearly engrossed the other. As the war advanced, after the Peace of Amiens, the neutrals became bolder and more aggressive. American ships were constantly arriving at Dutch and French ports with sugar, coffee, and other productions of the French and Spanish West Indies. And East India goods were imported by them into Spain, Holland, and France.

By these and other means, Hamburgh, Altona, Emden, Gottenburgh, Copenhagen, Lisbon, and other neutral markets were glutted with the produce of the West Indies and the fabrics of the East, brought from the prosperous colonies of powers hostile to this country. By the rivers and canals of Germany and Flanders these were floated into the warehouses of the enemy, or circulated for the supply of his customers in neutral countries. He rivalled the British planter and merchant throughout the continent of Europe, and in all ports of the Mediterranean, and even supplanted the manufacturers of Manchester, Birmingham, and Yorkshire; and by these means the hostile colonies derived benefit, and not inconvenience, from the enmity of Great Britain. What, moreover, especially injured the commerce of this country, was the increase in the cost of importation into this country from the British colonies, from freight, insurance, and other charges, which, taken together, were as much as, if not superior to, those to which the enemy was subjected in his covert and circuitous trade. It was a general complaint, therefore, that the enemy carried on colonial commerce under the neutral flag cheaply, as well as safely; that he was enabled not only to elude our hostilities, but to rival our merchants and planters in the European markets; that by the same means the hostile treasuries were filled with a copious stream of revenue; and that by this licentious use of the neutral flag, the enemy was enabled to employ his whole military marine in purposes of offensive war, without being obliged to maintain a squadron or a ship for the defence of their colonial ports. It was, moreover, contended that, since neutral states have no right, but through our own gratuitous concession, to carry on the colonial trade of the enemy, we might, after a reasonable notice, withdraw that ruinous indulgence; that the comparative cheapness of his navigation gives him, in every open market, a decisive advantage; that in the commerce of other neutral countries he could not fail to supplant the belligerent; and that he obtained an increase of trade by purchasing from one belligerent, and selling to his enemies the merchandise for which, in time of peace, they depended on each other.

Such complaints made against neutral states found a powerful echo by the publication of a work entitled "War in Disguise and the Frauds of the Neutral Flag," supposed to have been written by Mr. James Stephen, the real author of the orders in council. The British government did not see its way at once to proceed in the direction of prohibiting to neutral ships the colonial trade, which they had enjoyed for a considerable time; but the first step was taken to paralyze the resources of the enemy, and to restrict the trade of neutrals, by the issue of an order in council in May, 1806, declaring that all the coasts, ports, and rivers from the Elbe to Brest should be considered blockaded, though the only portion of those coasts rigorously blockaded was that included between Ostend and the mouth of the Seine, in the ports of which preparations were made for the invasion of England. The northern ports of Germany and Holland were left partly open, and the navigation of the Baltic altogether free.

Napoleon, then in the zenith of his power, saw, in this order in council, a fresh act of wantonness, and he met it by the issue of the Berlin decree of Nov. 21, 1806. In that document, remarkable for its boldness and vigor, Napoleon charged England with having set at naught the dictates of international law, with having made prisoners of war of private individuals, and with having taken the crews out of merchant ships. He charged this country with having captured private property at sea, extended to commercial ports the restrictions of blockade applicable only to fortified places, declared as blockaded places which were not invested by naval forces, and abused the right of blockade in order to benefit her own trade at the expense of the commerce of continental states. He asserted the right of combating the enemy with the same arms used against himself, especially when such enemy ignored all ideas of justice, and every liberal sentiment which civilization imposes. He announced his resolution to apply to England the same usages which she had established in her maritime legislation. He laid down the principles which France was resolved to act upon until England should recognize that the rights of war are the same on land as on sea, that such rights should not be extended either against private property or against persons not belonging to the military or naval forces, and that the right of blockade should be restricted to fortified places, truly invested by sufficient forces. And upon these premises the decree ordered, 1st, That the British islands should be declared in a state of blockade. 2d, That all commerce and correspondence with the British islands should be prohibited; and that letters addressed to England or Englishmen, written in the English language, should be detained and taken. 3d, That every British subject found in a country occupied by French troops, or by those of their allies, should be made a prisoner of war. 4th, That all merchandise and property belonging to British subjects should be deemed a good prize. 5th, That all commerce in English merchandise should be prohibited, and that all merchandise belonging to England or her colonies, and of British manufacture, should be deemed a good prize. And, 6th, That no vessel coming direct from England or her colonies be allowed to enter any French port, or any port subject to French authority; and that every vessel which, by means of a false declaration, should evade such regulations should at once be captured.

The British government lost no time in retaliating against France for so bold a course; and on Jan. 7, 1807, an order in council was issued, which, after reference to the orders issued by France, enjoined that no vessel should be allowed to trade from one enemy's port to another; or from one port to another of a French ally's coast shut against English vessels; and ordered the commanders of the ships of war and privateers to warn every neutral vessel coming from any such port, and destined to another such port, to discontinue her voyage, and that any vessel, after being so warned, which should be found proceeding to another such port should be captured and considered as lawful prize. This order in council having reached Napoleon at Warsaw, he immediately ordered the confiscation of all English merchandise and colonial produce found in the Hanseatic Towns. Bourrienne, Napoleon's commissioner at Hamburg, declared that all who carried on trade with England supported England; that it was to prevent such trading that France took possession of Hamburg; that all English goods should be produced by the Hamburghers for the purpose of being confiscated; and that in forty-eight hours domiciliary visits would be paid and military punishments inflicted on the disobedient. But Britain in return went a step further, and by order in council, Nov. 11, 1807, declared all the ports and places of France, and those of her allies, and of all countries where the English flag was excluded, even though they were not at war with Britain, placed under the same restrictions for commerce and navigation as if they were blockaded, and consequently that ships destined to those ports should be liable to the visit of British cruisers at a British station, and there subjected to a tax to be imposed by the British Parliament.

Napoleon was at Milan when this order in council was issued, and forthwith, on December 17, the famous decree appeared, by which he imposed on neutrals just the contrary of what was prescribed to them by England, and further declared that every vessel, of whatever nation, that submitted to the order in council of November 11 should by that very act become denationalized, considered as British property, and condemned as a good prize. The decree placed the British islands in a state of blockade, and ordered that every ship, of whatever nation, and with whatever cargo, proceeding from English ports or English colonies to countries occupied by English troops, or going to England, should be a good prize. This England answered by the order in council of April 26, 1809, which revoked the order of 1807 as regards America, but confirmed the blockade of all the ports of France and Holland, their colonies and dependencies. And then France, still further incensed against England, issued the tariff of Trianon, dated Aug. 5, 1810, completed by the decree of St. Cloud of September 12, and of Fontainebleau of October 19, which went the length of ordering the seizure and burning of all British goods found in France, Germany, Holland, Italy, Spain, and in every place occupied by French troops. Strange infatuation! and how many States took part in this mad act of vindictiveness! The princes of the Rhenish Confederation hastened to execute it, some for the purpose of enriching themselves by the wicked deed, some out of hatred towards the English, and some to show their devotion towards their master. From Carlsruhe to Munich, from Cassel to Dresden and Hamburg, everywhere, bonfires were made of English goods. And so exacting were the French, that when Frankfort exhibited the least hesitation in carrying out the decree French troops were sent to execute the order.

By means such as these the commerce of the world was greatly deranged, if not destroyed altogether, and none suffered more from it than England herself. Was it not enough to be effectually shut out from all commerce with French ports, that we should have provoked the closing of neutral ports also? Was it politic, at a time when our relations with the principal powers were in a condition so critical, to alienate from us all the neutral states of Europe? Was it wise to inflict so grievous an injury upon neutral states, as to force them to make common cause with the enemy? It is scarcely possible to describe at what peril the commerce of the world was carried on. The proceedings of the Court of Admiralty are full of the most romantic incidents. An American ship,[1] with a cargo of tobacco, was sent from America to Vigo, or to a market, for sale. At Vigo the tobacco was sold under contract to deliver it at Seville, at the master's risk, and the vessel was going to Seville to deliver the cargo when she was captured. A British vessel[2] was separated from her convoy during a storm, and brought out by a French lugger which came up, and told the master to stay by her till the storm moderated,

---

[1] The "Atlas," 3 Rob. Rep., p. 299.
[2] The "Edward and Mary," 3 Rob. Rep., p. 305.

when they would send a boat on board. The lugger continued alongside, sometimes ahead, and sometimes astern, and sometimes to windward, for three or four hours. But a British frigate coming in sight gave chase to the lugger and captured her, during which time the ship made her escape, rejoined the convoy, and came into Poole. Ships were taken because they were sailing to false destinations, under false papers, false flags, false certificates of ownership, and false bills of sale. They were seized for running the blockade, and for escaping from blockaded ports. They were arrested for carrying despatches, military men, and contraband of war. In every way, at every point of the ocean, the pursuit was carried on, till the seas were cleared of merchant ships, and the highway of nations, the widest and freest arena for trade, was converted into an amphitheatre for the display of the wildest and worst excesses of human cupidity and passions.

But a greater evil than even this extreme derangement of maritime commerce was that which flowed from the system of licenses,[1] an evil which undermined the first principles of commercial morality. It was forcibly stated by the Marquis of Lansdowne that the commerce of the country was one mass of simulation and dissimulation; that our traders crept along the shores of the enemy in darkness and silence, waiting for an opportunity of carrying into effect the simulative means by which they sought to carry on their business; that such a system led to private violation of morality and honor of the most alarming description; and that, instead of benefiting our commerce, manufactures, and resources, the orders in council diminished our commerce, distressed our manufactures, and lessened our resources. Yet all these warnings and expostulations were unheeded. The national mind was preoccupied by the *one* thought of compelling France and her military leader to a complete submission; and no consideration of a commercial or pecuniary character, no regard to the bearing of her measures upon other countries, were sufficient to induce a reversal of this military and naval policy.

Upwards of fifteen years had elapsed since the first shot was fired between England and France after the great revolution, and yet the two nations were as intent as ever on securing their mutual destruction. England had indeed learnt, by this time, to

---

[1] The number of commercial licenses granted for Imports and exports was 68 in 1802, 836 in 1803, 1,141 in 1804, 791 in 1805, 1,620 in 1806, 2,606 in 1807, 4,910 in 1808, 15,226 in 1809, 18,356 in 1810, and 7,602 in 1811.

make light of all such decrees, and she had found by experience that British goods found their way to the Continent in spite of all vindictive measures. But the attitude of the United States became more and more threatening, and the nations saw an absolute necessity for revising the policy of the orders in council. For years past Lord Temple, Lord Castlereagh, Mr. Perceval, Sir John Nichols, had brought the subject before the House, and many a long discussion had taken place on the subject. In their opinion this country had, without any alleged provocation from the United States of America, interrupted nearly the whole of their commerce with Europe, and they held that such orders in council were unjust and impolitic, and that the issuing of them, at the time and under the circumstances, was an act of the utmost improvidence and rashness. Yet the nation was disposed to be guided by the government; and when Lord Grenville moved resolutions of similar import, in 1809, he met with no better response. When, however, the United States, after having passed the Non-intercourse Act, proceeded still further in the way of preparation for open hostilities, the merchants began to speak their mind on the subject; and from London, Hull, Bristol, and all the chief ports, petitions came to the legislature praying for the revocation of the obnoxious orders. The merchants of London represented that trade was in a miserable condition, chiefly from the want of the customary intercourse with the continent of Europe; that employment was very scarce, and the wages of labor very low; that the aspect of affairs threatened additional suffering to those then experienced; that since all the evils then suffered were owing to the continuance of the war, it was all-important to obtain if possible an early restoration of the blessings of peace; that it was not from any dread of the enemy that they made such a request, but from a desire that no opportunity might be lost of entering into negotiations for the purpose; that in their opinion it was a great error to suppose that the policy of the orders of the council could in any way be beneficial to trade; but that, on the contrary, they regarded with extreme apprehension its effect on our relations with the United States of America. The merchants of Hull complained that the system of license sapped public morals. Those of Bristol represented that they suffered intensely in their general trade; and riots occurred in Lancashire, Yorkshire, and Cheshire.

On April 28, 1812, the House of Commons agreed, without a

division, to hear evidence in support of these petitions; and, on June 16, Mr., afterwards Lord, Brougham moved, "That an humble address be presented to his Royal Highness the Prince Regent, representing to his Royal Highness that this House has, for some time past, been engaged in an inquiry into the present depressed state of the manufactures and commerce of the country, and the effects of the orders in council issued by his majesty in the years 1807 and 1809; assuring his royal highness that this House will at all times support his royal highness to the utmost of its powers, in maintaining those just maritime rights which have essentially contributed to the prosperity and honor of the realm; but beseeching his royal highness that he would be graciously pleased to recall or suspend the said orders, and to adopt such measures as may tend to conciliate neutral powers, without sacrificing the right and dignity of his majesty's crown." In the most graphic manner Lord Brougham depicted the distress of the country, showed how erroneous was the idea that what we lost in the European trade we gained in any other quarter, and warned the country of the certainty of a war with America if the orders were not at once rescinded. "I know," he said, "I shall be asked, whether I would recommend any sacrifice for the mere purpose of conciliating America. I recommend no sacrifice of honor for that or for any purpose; but I will tell you that I think we can well and safely, for our honor, afford to conciliate America. Never did we stand so high since we were a nation in point of military character. We have it in abundance, and even to spare. This unhappy and seemingly interminable war, lavish as it has been in treasure, still more profuse of blood and barren of real advantage, has at least been equally lavish of glory. Its feats have not merely sustained the warlike fame of the nation, which would have been much; they have done what seemed scarcely possible, — they have greatly exalted it. They have covered our arms with immortal renown. Then, I say, use this glory, — use this proud height on which we now stand for the purpose of peace and conciliation with America. Let this and its incalculable benefits be the advantage which we reap from the war in Europe, for the fame of that war enables us safely to take it. And who, I demand, give the most disgraceful counsels, — they who tell you we are in military character but of yesterday, we yet have a name to win, we stand on doubtful ground, we dare not do as we list for fear of being thought afraid;

we cannot, without loss of name, stoop to pacify our American kinsmen? or I, who say we are a great, a proud, a warlike people ; we have fought everywhere, and conquered wherever we have fought ; our character is eternally fixed — it stands too firm to be shaken ; and, on the faith of it, we may do towards America safely for our honor that which we know our interests require? This perpetual jealousy of America! Good God! I cannot, with temper, ask on what it rests! It drives me to a passion to think of it! Jealousy of America! I should as soon think of being jealous of the tradesman who supplies me with necessaries, or the client who entrusts his suits to my patronage. Jealousy of America! whose armies are as yet at the plough, or making, since your policy has willed it, so awkward (though improving) attempts at the loom — whose assembled navies could not lay siege to an English harbor! Jealousy of a power which is necessarily peaceful as well as weak, but which, if it had all the ambition of France, and her armies to back it, and all the navy of England to boot — nay, had it the lust of conquest which marks your enemies, and your own army as well as navy, to gratify, it is placed at so vast a distance as to be perfectly harmless! And this is the nation of which, for our honor's sake, we are desired to cherish a perpetual jealousy for the ruin of our best interests. I trust, sir, that no such phantom of the brain will scare us from the path of our duty. The advice which I tender is not the same which has at all times been offered to this country. There is one memorable era in our history when other uses were made of our triumphs from those which I recommend. By the treaty of Utrecht, which the reprobation of ages has left inadequately censured, we were content to obtain, as the whole price of Ramillies and Blenheim, an additional share of the accursed slave trade. I give you other counsels. I should have you employ the glory which you have won at Talavera and Corunna in restoring your commerce to its lawful, open, honest course, and rescue it from the mean and hateful channels in which it has lately been confined. And, if any thoughtless boaster, in America or elsewhere, should vaunt that you have yielded through fear, I would not bid him wait until some new achievement of our arms put him to silence, but I would counsel you in silence to disregard him."

The effect of such an appeal was fatal to the whole system. The government saw that resistance was no longer possible, and on April 21 the Prince Regent made a declaration that the orders in council would be revoked as soon as the Berlin and Milan decrees should be repealed. But it was too late. America had by this time ceased to maintain a neutral attitude. And, having made a secret treaty with Napoleon, she issued an embargo on all British vessels in American ports, declared war against England, and proceeded to make an ineffectual attack upon Canada. The political condition of Europe, however, at this stage happily assumed a bright aspect. The long-desired peace began to dawn on the horizon, and in rapid succession the news came of the battle of Leipzig, the entry of the Allies into Paris, and the abdication of Bonaparte. Negotiations then commenced in earnest, and they issued in a treaty of peace and Congress of Vienna, which once more restored order and symmetry in the political organization of Europe.[1] On Dec. 24, 1814, a treaty of peace was signed between the United Kingdom and the United States. On June 9, 1815, the principal act of the Congress of Vienna was signed, which established the future political relations of the European States, and laid down the regulations for the free navigation of rivers ; and on July 27, of the same year, a Treaty of Commerce was concluded between Great Britain and the United States of America.

---

[1] The total cost of the war with France, from 1793 to 1815 (the war expenditure continued till 1817), was £831,446,449. The national debt, which, in 1793, amounted to £247,874,434, rose in 1815 to £861,039,049.

VII.

THE FINANCES OF ENGLAND 1793-1815.

FROM PORTER'S PROGRESS OF THE NATION, SECTION IV.

CHAPTER I.

IN order to give an intelligible account of the financial state of the kingdom at the beginning of the present century, it is necessary to explain briefly the system which had been brought into operation by Mr. Pitt during the preceding three years.

In November, 1797, that minister had recourse to what he was pleased to call "a perfectly new and solid system of finance." The public expenditure of that year amounted to twenty-five and a half millions, of which sum only six and a half millions were provided for by existing unmortgaged taxes, leaving nineteen millions to be raised by extraordinary means. In the then condition of the money market, it was felt to be impossible to borrow such an amount in the ordinary manner, that is, providing by new taxes for the payment of only the permanent annual burthen occasioned by the increased debt; and a new impost, calculated to produce seven millions, was sanctioned by parliament, which impost was to be continued until it should, in conjunction with the produce of the sinking-fund, repay the twelve millions that would be still deficient. This new system of finance might have been entitled to the character given of it by Mr. Pitt, if it had not been probable — nay, certain — that in the following years an equal expenditure must be met by similar means, until the seven millions would prove inadequate even for the payment of the annual interest of the sums for which the tax was imposed, when it would become part of the permanent burthens of the country. This new impost, to which the name of "triple assessment" was given, was in fact an addition made to the assessed taxes, "in a triplicate proportion to their previous amount — limited, however, to the tenth of each person's income."

The adoption of this, or some similar plan of financial arrangement, was hardly a matter of choice with the minister, by whom the funding system, as ordinarily practised, could not have been any further pursued at that time. Unfortunately for the success of the principle which it was thus sought to establish, the mode in which it was proposed to raise the seven millions of additional revenue was highly unpopular, and indeed it has always excited dissatisfaction on the part of the public to be called on for the payment of any tax from which they have not the power to protect themselves, by abstaining from the use of the taxed commodity. It is this consideration which has always made our finance ministers prefer indirect to direct taxation, and which led, during the progress of a long and expensive war, to the imposition of duties that weighed with destructive force upon the springs of industry. The financial difficulties by which the government was then embarrassed may be known from the fact that a loan of three millions was raised in April, 1798, at the rate of £200 three per cent. stock, and 5s. long annuity for each £100 borrowed, being at the rate of six and a quarter per cent., and that the "triple assessment," which was calculated to produce seven millions, yielded no more than four and a half millions. In the following December the triple assessment was repealed, and in lieu of it an income-tax was imposed at the rate of 10 per cent. upon all incomes amounting to £200 and upwards, with diminishing rates upon smaller incomes, down to £60 per annum, below which rate the tax was not to apply. This tax was estimated to produce ten millions; it was called a war tax; but, when the minister proceeded to mortgage its produce to defray the interest of loans to a large amount, such a name appeared to be little better than a delusion. Like the triple assessment, the produce of the income-tax fell greatly short of its estimated amount, and yielded no more than seven millions, a large part of which was quickly absorbed to defray the interest of loans for which it was successively pledged. In 1801, after deducting the sums thus chargeable on it, this tax produced only four millions towards the national expenditure. In proposing a loan of twenty-five and a half millions for the service of that year, it was considered inexpedient to mortgage the income tax any further, and new taxes were imposed, estimated to yield £1,800,000 per annum. In March, 1802, peace was made with France, and in the same month notice was given by the Chancellor of the Exchequer, Mr. Addington, of his intention to repeal the income-tax, which was felt to be highly oppressive, and had become more and more odious to the people. In effecting this repeal, and at the same time to keep faith with the public creditors, to whom its produce had been mortgaged to the extent of fifty-six and a half millions of 3 per cent. stock, additional taxes were imposed upon beer, malt, and hops, and a considerable increase was made to the assessed taxes, besides which an addition, under the name of a modification, was made to the tax on imports and exports, previously known under the name of the convoy duty.

At this time the aggregate amount of permanent taxes was thirty-eight and a half millions, exactly double what it had been at the breaking out of the war in 1793. During those nine years, taxes to the amount of £280,000,000, exclusive of the cost of collection, had been levied from the people; and a few words are necessary in order to account for the seeming contradiction implied in the fact, that, notwithstanding this ruinous rate of expenditure, many of the great interests throughout the country wore the outward appearance of prosperity. A nation engaged in an expensive war, which calls for the systematic expenditure of large sums beyond its income, may be likened to an individual spendthrift during his career of riot and extravagance; all about him wears the aspect of plenty and prosperity, and this appearance will continue until his means begin to fail, and those who have fattened upon his profusion are at length sent away empty. The enormous expenditure of the government, joined to the state of the currency (as already explained), necessarily caused a general and great rise of prices; as regarded agricultural produce, this effect was exaggerated by the ungenial nature of the seasons. Rents had risen throughout the country in a far greater degree than the necessary expenditure of the land-owners, who thence found their situations improved, notwithstanding the additional load of taxation. The great number of contractors and other persons dealing with the government had derived a positive benefit from the public expenditure, and, being chiefly resident at the seat of government, they were enabled greatly to influence the tone of public opinion. The greater command of money thus given to considerable classes occasioned an increased demand for luxuries of foreign and domestic production, from which the merchants and dealers derived advantage. There were, besides, other classes of persons who profited from the war expenditure. These were the producers of manufactured goods, and those who dealt in them, and who found their dealings greatly increased by means of the foreign expenditure of the government in subsidies and expeditions, the means for which were furnished through those dealings; the manufacturers were at the same time beginning to reap the advantages that have since been experienced in a more considerable degree from the series of inventions begun by Hargreaves and Arkwright, and which acted in some degree as palliatives to the evil effects of the government profusion.

As in the case of the spendthrift, while all these causes were in operation, there was an appearance of prosperity, and those who were profiting from this state of things were anxious to keep up the delusion. That it was no more than delusion will be at once apparent to all who examine below the surface, and who inquire as to the condition of poverty and wretchedness into which the great mass of the people were then plunged. In some few cases there had been an advance of wages; but this occurred only to skilled artisans, and even with them the rise was wholly incommensurate with the increased cost of all the necessaries of life. The mere laborer — he who had nothing to bring to market but his limbs and sinews — did not participate in this partial compensation for high prices, but was, in most cases, an eager competitor for employment, at the same or nearly the same wages as had been given before the war. Nor could it well be otherwise, since the demand for labor can only increase with the increase of the capital destined for the payment of wages; and we have seen that capital, so far from being suffered to accumulate, was dissipated by the government expenditure more rapidly than it could be accumulated by individuals. In London and its vicinity the rates of wages are necessarily higher, because of the greater expense of living, than in country districts; and it is asserted, from personal knowledge of the fact, that at the time in question there was a superabundant supply of laborers constantly competing for employment at the large government establishments, where the weekly wages did not exceed 15s., while the price of the quartern loaf was 1s. 10d., and the other necessary outgoings of a laborer's family were nearly as high in proportion. If we contrast the weekly wages at the two periods of 1790 and 1800, of husbandry laborers, and of skilled artisans, measuring them both by the quantity of wheat which they could command, it will be seen that the former could, in 1790, purchase eighty-two pints of wheat, and in 1800 could procure no more than fifty-three pints, while the skilled artisan, who in 1790 could buy one hundred and sixty-nine pints, could procure in 1800 only eighty-three pints. To talk of the prosperous state of the country under such a condition of things involves a palpable contradiction. It would be more correct to liken the situation of the community to that of the inhabitants of a town subjected to a general conflagration, in which some became suddenly enriched by carrying off the valuables, while the mass were involved in ruin and destitution.

It may be objected to the view here taken, but which is founded upon facts that hardly admit of controversy, that, had the condition of the country been such as is represented, we must have sunk under the greater efforts we were so soon after called on to sustain; and there is every reason to believe that, but for the invention of the spinning-jenny, and the improvements in the steam-engine, which have produced such almost magical effects upon the productive energies of this kingdom, it would have been impossible to have withstood the combination with which, single-handed, we were called upon to contend. The manner and degree in which these powerful agents have enabled us to withstand and to triumph over difficulties unparalleled in the history of the world, have been shown in a preceding section of this inquiry.

CHAPTER II.

THE public expenditure of England during the war which was begun in 1793, and continued (with short intermissions in 1801 and 1814) until the final overthrow of Napoleon in 1815, was conducted throughout upon a truly gigantic scale. In 1792, the last year of peace, the entire public expenditure of the kingdom was £19,859,123, which sum included £9,767,333 interest upon the public debt. In 1814 the current expenditure amounted to £76,780,895, and the interest upon the debt to £30,051,365, making an aggregate sum of £106,832,260 paid out of the public exchequer for the disbursements of that one year. This is the largest annual outlay ever made; that of the previous year was within one million of the same amount.

It is hardly possible to conceive that the public expenditure could have been long continued upon this scale of magnitude; the state of exhaustion under which the country was made to suffer, during the first few years of the peace that followed, sufficiently attests the truth of this opinion. The financial efforts of the government had been made for several preceding years with a degree of lavish profusion that was continually augumented until it reached the height above mentioned; the expenditure, including interest upon the debt, during the ten years, from 1806 to 1815, inclusive, averaged £84,067.761 per annum,' sums which, until the years in which they were actually expended, it would have been considered wholly chimerical to expect to raise. The experience of that period has shown how impossible a thing it is to judge correctly from the past as to the growing resources of our country, or it might be confidently affirmed that, during the concluding years of this series, we had assuredly reached the limit of possibility. Without that experience for their guidance, our ancestors, in former but not very remote times, gave way to gloomy forebodings as to their future prospects, at which we cannot but smile, when thinking of the comparatively pigmy efforts which called them forth. Some of those forebodings have been recorded by Sir John Sinclair, in his work on the public revenue of this kingdom. A few passages upon the subject, taken from that work, and with the dates at which they were written, may not be without interest to the reader at the present moment.

1736. " The vast load of debt under which the nation still groans is the true source of all those calamities and gloomy prospects of which we have so much reason to complain. To this has been owing that multiplicity of burthensome taxes which have more than doubled the price of the common necessaries of life within a few years past, and thereby distressed the poor laborer and manufacturer, disabled the farmer to pay his rent, and put even gentlemen of plentiful estates under the greatest difficulties to make a tolerable provision for their families." — *The Craftsman*, No. 502, 14th Feburary, 1736.

At the time this gloomy picture was drawn the public debt did not exceed £50,000,000, and the annual charge on that account was somewhat under £2,000,000, being considerably below the sums added to the public burthens in the single year 1814.

1749. " Our parliamentary aids, from the year 1740 exclusively, to the year 1748 inclusively, amount to £55,522,159 16s. 3d., a sum that will appear incredible to future generations, and is so almost to the present. Till we have paid a good part of our debt, and restored our country in some measure to her former wealth and power, it will be difficult to maintain the dignity of Great Britain, to make her respected abroad, and secure from injuries or even affronts on the part of her neighbors." — *Some Reflections on the present state of the Nation*, by Henry St. John, Lord Bolingbroke.

The debt, to the effects of which so much evil is here attributed, was still under £80,000,000, and the annual interest scarcely more than £3,000,000.

1756. "It has been a generally received notion among political arithmeticians, that we may increase our debt to £100,000,000, but they acknowledge that it must then cease, by the debtor becoming bankrupt." — *Letters* by Samuel Hannay, Esq.

In the few years that preceded the publication of Mr. Hannay's letters the debt had been somewhat diminished, so that it amounted to about £75,000,000, and the annual charge on the country to £2,400,000.

1761. "The first instance of a debt contracted upon parliamentary security occurs in the reign of Henry VI. The commencement of this pernicious practice deserves to be noted, — a practice the more likely to become pernicious the more a nation advances in opulence and credit. The ruinous effects of it are now become apparent, and threaten the very existence of the nation." — Hume's *History of England*, 8vo edition, 1778, vol. iii, p. 215.

The public burthens had by this time so far exceeded the possible limit assigned by Mr. Hannay, that the debt amounted to nearly £150,000,000, and the annual interest to £4,800,000. The amount was somewhat reduced between, that period and the breaking out of the American war, when a succession of loans again became necessary. On winding up the accounts of that contest, the debt amounted to £268,000,000, and the annual charge to £9,500,000. On the 5th of January, 1793, just before the beginning of the war of the French Revolution, the debt continued nearly the same as at the beginning of the peace (the exact amount of funded and unfunded debt, including the value of terminable annuities, was £261,735,059, and the annual charge was £9,471,675). From that time to the peace of Amiens hardly a year passed without witnessing some increase to the national burthens, so that at midsummer 1802, the capital of the funded and unfunded debt amounted to £637,000,000. On the 5th of January, 1816, the capital was £885,186,323, and the annual charge was £32,457.141. The following statements exhibit the progressive state of the public income and expenditure from 1792 to

Abstract of Public Income and Expenditure in the United Kingdom in each year, from 1792 to 1849.

Years.	INCOME.			EXPENDITURE.			
	Amount of Revenue paid into the Exchequer, the produce of taxation.	Amount received on account of Loans and Exchequer bills, beyond the amount redeemed in the year.	Total amount raised for public uses.	Interest paid on public debt, funded and unfunded.	Sums applied to redemption of public debt beyond the amount of loans, etc., in the year.	Current annual public expenditure.	Total amount paid and expended in the year.
1792	£19,258,814	£	£19,258,814	£9,767,333	£2,421,681	£ 7,670,109	£19,859,123
1793	19,845,705	4,877,956	24,723,661	9,437,862	....	14,759,208	24,197,070
1794	20,193,074	6,998,389	27,191,463	9,890,904	....	17,851,213	27,742,117
1795	19,883,520	30,464,831	50,348,351	10,810,728	....	37,603,449	48,414,177
1796	21,454,728	22,244,982	43,699,710	11,841,204	....	30,334,087	42,175,291
1797	23,126,940	30,356,873	53,483,813	14,270,616	....	36,469,993	50,740,609
1798	31,035,363	16,858,503	47,893,866	17,585,518	....	33,541,727	51,127,245
1799	35,602,444	21,714,863	57,317,307	17,220,983	....	38,403,421	55,624,404
1800	34,145,534	23,030,529	57,176,113	17,381,561	....	39,439,706	56,821,267
1801	34,113,146	27,305,271	61,418,417	19,945,624	....	41,383,555	61,329,179
1802	36,368,149	14,638,254	51,006,403	19,855,588	....	29,693,619	49,549,207
1803	38,609,392	8,752,761	47,362,153	20,699,864	....	28,298,366	48,998,230
1804	46,176,492	14,570,763	60,747,255	20,726,772	....	38,649,436	59,376,208
1805	50,897,706	16,849,801	67,747,507	22,141,426	....	45,027,892	67,169,318
1806	55,796,086	13,035,344	71,831,430	23,000,000	....	45,941,205	68,941,211
1807	59,339,321	10,432,934	69,772,255	23,362,685	....	44,250,357	67,613,042
1808	62,998,191	12,095,044	75,093,235	23,158,982	....	49,984,105	73,143,087
1809	63,719,400	12,298,379	76,017,779	24,213,867	....	52,352,146	76,566,013
1810	67,144,542	7,792,444	74,936,986	24,246,946	....	52,618,602	76,865,548
1811	65,173,545	19,143,953	84,317,498	24,977,915	....	58,757,308	83,735,223
1812	65,037,850	24,790,697	84,828,547	25,546,508	....	63,210,816	88,757,324
1813	68,748,363	39,649,282	108,397,645	28,030,239	....	77,913,488	105,943,727
1814	71,134,503	34,563,603	105,698,106	30,051,365	....	76,780,895	106,832,260
1815	72,210,512	20,241,807	92,452,319	31,576,074	....	60,704,106	92,280,180
1816	62,264,546	514,059	62,778,605	32,938,751	....	32,231,020	65,169,771
1817	52,055,913	....	52,055,913	31,436,245	1,826,814	22,018,170	55,281,238
1818	53,747,795	....	53,747,795	30,880,244	1,624,606	20,843,728	53,348,578
1819	52,648,847	....	52,648,847	30,807,249	3,163,130	21,436,130	55,406,509
1820	54,282,958	....	54,282,958	31,157,846	1,918,019	21,381,382	54,457,247
1821	55,834,192	....	55,834,192	31,955,304	4,104,457	21,070,825	57,130,586
1822	55,663,650	....	55,663,650	29,021,493	2,962,564	20,826,567	53,710,624
1823	57,672,999	....	57,672,999	29,215,905	5,261,725	21,746,110	56,223,740
1824	59,362,403	....	59,362,403	29,066,350	6,456,559	23,708,252	59,231,161
1825	57,273,869	....	57,273,869	28,060,287	9,900,725	23,559,741	61,520,753
1826	54,894,989	....	54,894,989	28,076,957	1,195,531	25,808,585	55,081,073
1827	54,932,518	....	54,932,518	28,239,847	2,023,028	25,560,446	55,823,321
1828	55,187,142	....	55,187,142	28,095,506	4,667,965	21,407,670	54,171,141
1829	50,786,682	....	50,786,682	29,155,612	2,760,003	19,919,522	51,835,137
1830	50,056,616	....	50,056,616	29,118,858	1,935,465	18,024,085	49,078,108
1831	46,424,440	....	46,424,440	28,341,416	2,673,858	18,781,882	49,797,156
1832	46,988,755	....	47,322,744	28,323,751	5,696	18,050,245	46,379,692
1833	46,271,326	333,989	46,271,326	28,522,507	1,023,784	16,235,735	45,782,026
1834	46,425,263	....	46,425,263	28,504,096	1,776,378	16,397,605	46,678,079
1835	45,893,369	....	45,893,369	28,514,610	1,270,050	15,884,649	45,669,309
1836	48,591,180	....	48,591,180	29,243,598	1,590,727	17,258,871	48,093,196
1837	46,475,194	....	46,475,194	29,489,571	1,985,885	17,641,383	49,116,839
1838	47,333,460	....	47,333,460	29,260,230	7,496	18,418,449	47,686,183
1839	47,844,899	....	47,844,899	29,454,062	....	19,903,629	49,357,691
1840	47,567,565	....	47,567,565	29,381,718	8,016	19,779,818	49,169,552
1841	48,084,360	853,037	48,937,397	29,450,145	....	20,735,584	50,185,729
1842	46,965,631	1,614,395	48,580,026	29,428,120	....	21,517,049	50,945,169
1843	52,582,817	....	52,582,817	29,269,160	8,741	21,870,353	51,148,254
1844	54,003,754	....	54,003,754	30,495,459	1,563,361	20,152,189	52,211,009
1845	53,060,354	....	53,060,354	28,251,872	4,143,831	20,988,840	59,386,603
1846	53,790,138	....	53,790,138	28,077,987	....	22,865,843	50,943,830
1847	51,546,265	7,476,353	59,022,617	28,141,531	....	26,361,416	54,502,947
1848	53,388,717	1,593,945	54,982,662	28,563,517	....	26,621,610	54,185,136
1849	52,951,749	374,568	53,326,317	28,323,961	21,074	22,529,661	50,874,696

FINANCES OF ENGLAND.

Statements showing the Amount of Money raised by Loans and the Finding of Exchequer Bills, with the Amount and description of Stock created, and the Annual Charge thereon in the Years undermentioned.

Years.	Amount of Money raised on Loan.	Amount of Exchequer Bills Funded.	Amount and Description of Stock Created.					Rate of Interest per cent. for Money.	Amount of Annual Charge incurred.
			3 per cent.	4 per cent.	5 per cent.	Total of Perpetual Annuities.	Annuities to terminate in 1860.		
	£.	£.	£.	£.	£.	£.	£.	£. s. d.	£.
1801	20,500,000	....	32,185,000	....	....	32,185,000	....	4 14 2	965,550
1802	29,000,000	8,910,450	49,210,000	....	....	49,210,000	....	5 5 5½	1,476,300
1803	25,000,000	....	4,455,225	4,455,225	2,227,612	11,138,062	7,796	5 16 7¾	431,043
1804	12,000,000	....	34,097,615	....	....	34,097,615	....	5 19 2 0	969,713
1805	14,500,000	....	19,200,000	....	....	19,200,000	38,500	5 2 0	614,500
1806	22,500,000	....	26,390,000	....	....	26,390,000	....	5 9 2	791,700
...	1,500,000	....	38,700,000	....	....	38,700,000	....	5 3 2	1,161,000
1807	20,000,000	....	....	....	360,000	360,000	75,000	5 17 0½	93,000
1808	14,200,000	....	33,200,000	....	....	33,200,000	....	4 19 7	996,000
"	1,500,000	....	24,580,000	....	1,505,000	21,385,200	....	4 14 7	743,948
1809	....	....	2,409,615	....	....	2,409,615	....	4 16 6½	72,288
"	10,500,000	4,000,000	....	237,900	4,001,353	4,239,253	....	5 4 4½	209,583
1810	....	7,932,100	....	12,406,375	7,873,308	12,408,375	64,483	4 14 9¾	402,135
"	14,600,000	....	....	336,336	....	8,353,644	....	5 14 6½	408,878
1811	13,400,000	8,311,000	5,760,000	8,760,000	....	17,520,000	....	5 3 1	677,683
1812	12,000,000	12,007,000	18,310,250	....	8,581,107	27,391,357	....	4 11 6	993,392
"	12,000,000	....	....	2,400,000	12,444,712	12,444,712	....	5 3 8	622,236
1813	22,500,000	12,075,043	....	....	16,800,000	16,800,000	41,500	4 14 1¾	569,500
1814	49,000,000	15,755,700	14,400,000	....	13,199,031	52,799,031	....	4 6 10½	1,317,951
1815	24,000,000	....	39,600,000	5,220,423	13,860,000	103,920,423	89,250	5 10 0	3,561,707
1816	36,000,000	18,189,682	84,340,000	....	7,200,000	32,040,000	....	4 12 10	1,105,200
1819	....	....	24,340,000	3,600,000	21,208,402	87,148,492	....	3 13 10	3,003,620
1820	12,000,000	27,262,000	62,640,000	....	....	34,695,356	....	5 16 10	1,046,860
"	....	....	34,895,160	....	....	17,152,000	....	3 10 9	514,560
1821	5,000,000	7,000,000	17,152,000	....	6,930,000	14,040,000	....	4 11 7½	559,800
			7,110,000						

1849, including the annual charge on account of the public debt, and the amount of money raised by loans and the funding of Exchequer Bills, with the amount and description of stock created, and the annual charge in respect of the same, in each year from the beginning of the present century.

An extraordinary degree of delusion is observable in the proceedings of the different finance ministers by whom the support of the sinking-fund was advocated during the war. It has been pretended that the purchases made by means of that fund had the effect of keeping up the market value of the public debt, and thereby enabled the minister to contract loans upon more advantageous terms than, without this machinery, would have been possible. It may well be doubted, however, whether the repurchase in this manner, from time to time, of parts only of that surplus portion of the public debt which was created for the express purpose of such operations, had any real effect in raising the price of the remaining portion of the public securities; in other words, whether the price, thus factitiously acted upon, of the larger amount of debt, was at any time greater than the price would have been of the smaller amount of debt that would have existed if the sinking-fund had not been created, the purchases of the commissioners never having in fact accomplished more than the repurchase of the so-needlessly-created part of the debt. It has been further urged in defence of the sinking-fund, that the prospect which it enabled the minister to hold out of the speedy redemption of the whole debt had the effect of reconciling the people to the payment of a larger amount of taxes than they would otherwise have been willing to pay. Allowing that the effect here stated was produced, we may still doubt the wisdom of that government which is obliged to resort to a juggle in order to reconcile the people to its measures, and especially when, as in the case under examination, the delusion was so expensive and likely to prove so permanently injurious in its nature.

The average rate at which 3 per cent. stock was created between 1793 and 1801 was £57 7s. 6d. of money for £100 stock, and the average market price during that period was £61 17s. 6d. for £100 stock. The loss to the public upon the additional sum borrowed in order that it might be redeemed during that period, which was £49,655,531, amounted to four and a half per cent., or £2,234,500. Between 1803 and the termination of the war, the average price at which loans were contracted was £60 7s. 6d.

per £100 stock, and the average market price during that time was £62 17s. 6d. per £100. The loss was, therefore, two and a half per cent. upon the sum redeemed during that time, £176,173,240, or £4,404,331, making together an amount of £6,638,831 absolutely lost to the public by these operations. This amount, reckoned at the average price of the various loans, is equivalent to a capital of more than eleven millions of 3 per cent. stock, with which the country is now additionally burthened through the measure of borrowing in a depressed market more money than was wanted in order to its being repaid when the market for public securities was certain to be higher. The fallacy attending this system is now so fully recognized that it is not likely any minister will in future make a show of redeeming debt at the moment when circumstances compel him actually to increase its amount for that purpose.

Another error of a still more important nature, involved in this system, remains to be noticed. The absurdity of borrowing money in order to extinguish debt could never have been seriously adopted but with the anticipation of the good effects that might be drawn from such a course after the necessity for further borrowing should cease, when it might be beneficial to apply towards the redemption of the debt the high scale of taxation which that system rendered practicable. There never could have existed any doubt of the fact, that whenever the necessity for borrowing should cease, the market value of the public funds would advance greatly, and would therefore in an equal degree limit the redeeming power of the surplus income, however arising. The knowledge of this fact should have led the ministers, by whom successive additions were made to the public debt, to the adoption of a course which would have enabled them to turn this rise of prices to the advantage of the public, instead of its being, as it has proved, productive of loss; and this end would certainly have been accomplished, if at the expense of a small present sacrifice, the loans had been contracted at a high rate of interest, instead of their having been contracted, as for the most part they were, in 3 per cent. annuities. It is presumable that, if the borrowing had been restricted to the sums actually wanted from time to time, without thought of a sinking-fund, the public might possibly have had to pay at the outside a quarter per cent. more of annual interest than they actually paid. At this rate the deficiency of income compared with expenditure, between 1793 and 1815, which amounted, as will be shown in the next Table, to £425.482,761, would have occasioned an addition to the capital of the debt to the amount of £455,266,554 of 5 per cent. stock, the annual interest of which would have been £22,763,-327, instead of a nominal capital of £547,292,764, with the annual additional charge of £20,690,871. At the close of the war the nominal capital of the debt would have then amounted to £724.285,729, and the annual charge to £32,530,660, instead of £816.311,939 of capital, and £30,458,204 of annual charge, which was the state of the unredeemed public debt on the 5th of January, 1816. The government would then have been in the most favorable position for taking advantage of the lowering of the rate of interest which was certain to follow, and many years before the present time the whole of the 5 per cent. annuities might have been converted, without any addition to the capital, into annuities of the same amount, bearing interest at the rate of three and a half per cent., or perhaps lower. Assuming, however, that the reduction would not have gone lower than three and a half per cent., and taking into consideration the surplus revenue which has been actually applied to the redemption of debt between 5th January, 1816, and 5th January, 1849, which, as will be seen, amounted to £45,779,046, the funded debt existing on 5th of January, 1837, would have amounted to £678,506,683, and the annual charge to £23,747,734, instead of its actual amount, £773,-168,316, and its actual annual charge, £27,686,458; showing that the loss entailed on the country by the plan pursued, of funding the debt in stock bearing a nominal low rate of interest, is £94,661,-633 of capital, and £3,938,724 of annual charge. It is not possible to calculate with certainty the further benefits that must have resulted from the repeal of five millions and a half of annual taxes, which would have been practicable beyond the amount actually repealed; but it is probably much under-estimating those benefits to state, that among their results the amount of public income over expenditure would have been so far augmented that the unredeemed debt would not at this time have exceeded six hundred millions, while the annual charge upon the same would have been twenty-one millions, a state of things at which, if the peace of Europe should continue undisturbed, and if our progress should only equal our past experience, we may possibly hope to arrive in about half a century.

The charge of inconsistency on the part of our finance ministers is fully deserved by their adoption of two measures having for their objects results exactly opposed to each other. These measures are, first, the creation of what is called the dead-weight annuity; and secondly, the conversion of perpetual annuities into annuities for lives or for terms of years; the effect of the first being to bring present relief at the expense of future years, while the second increases the present burthen with the view of relieving posterity. When the measure for commuting the half-pay and pensions was brought forward in May, 1822, the charge upon the country on that account was estimated at about five millions. This was necessarily a decreasing charge, and from year to year the public would have been relieved by the falling in of lives, until at the end of forty-five years the whole, according to probability, would have been extinguished. In order to turn to present advantage this prospective diminution of burthen, it was attempted to commute the whole of those annually diminishing payments into an unvarying annuity to last during the whole probable term of forty-five years, and it was computed that, by the sale of a fixed annuity of £2,800,000, funds might be obtained in order to meet the diminishing demands of the quarterly claimants. This scheme was only partially carried into execution by means of an arrangement made with the Bank of England, under which that corporation advanced to the government, in nearly equal payments, during the six years from 1823 to 1828, the sum of £13,089,419 as the purchase money of an annual annuity of £585,740 to be paid until 1867. The result of this operation has been to save the immediate payment during the years in which it was in progress of £9,574,979, and in return to fix upon the country the annual payment for thirty-nine years thereafter of £585,740.

In the prosecution of the opposite plan of converting perpetual annuities into annuities terminable at stated periods, or upon the occurrence of certain natural contingencies, the amount of terminable annuities has advanced from £1,888,835, at which it stood at the end of the war, to £3,755,099 at the beginning of the year 1850. It would occupy considerable space to exhibit the progress of this conversion from year to year, and it will probably suffice to exemplify the result of the operation during one year (1834). In that year the perpetual annuities received in exchange amounted to £6,500,169 of capital, bearing an annual charge of £202,831, and there were granted, in lieu of the same —

Annuities for lives £195,337
" for terms of years . . . 313,138
Deferred annuities 2,871

Together . . £511,346

making a present annual increase of £308,514 to the public burthens in order to ensure the earlier extinction of the charge of £202,831.

It is not necessary here to inquire which of these two modes of proceeding is preferable. Under different circumstances either of them might be wise or prudent, but it is quite impossible that at the same time, and consequently under the same circumstances, both could be either wise or prudent, and the minister and legislators by whom the plans were proposed and sanctioned must be allowed to have stultified themselves by the operations. Of the two courses that is assuredly the most generous, which subjects the parties by whom it is adopted to additional burthen in order to lighten the load for their successors, and indeed it would seem no more than an act of justice on the part of those by whom the debt was contracted to adopt every means within their power for its extinction.

It is singular that, with so much experience and so much of scientific acquirement that could have been brought to the correct elucidation of this subject, the tables adopted for the creation of terminable annuities were incorrect, to a degree which entailed a heavy loss upon the public. The system was established in 1808, and during the first year of its operation annuities were granted to the amount of £58,506 10s. per annum. Of that amount there continued payable £23,251 per annum at the beginning of 1827, when, to adopt the calculation of the actuary of the national debt, as given in a report to the Chancellor of the Exchequer, the public had already sustained a loss of more than £10,000 by the transactions, besides having the above annual sum of £23,251 still to pay for an indefinite term. In this report of Mr. Finlaison he states that the loss to the public through miscalculation in these tables was then (April, 1827) proceeding at the rate of £8,000 per week, and during the three preceding months had exceeded £95,000. The discovery of this blunder had been made and pressed upon the attention of the finance minister as early as 1819, but no active steps were taken to remedy it until 1828, and even then the rates at which annuities were granted upon the lives of aged persons were, after a time, found to be so unduly profitable to the purchasers, that the government was again obliged to interfere and to limit the ages upon which life annuities could be obtained.

It is quite impossible that any similar series of blunders could have been committed by any private persons or association of individuals, whose vigilance would have been sufficiently preserved by their private interest; and it is disgraceful that the government, which could at all times command the assistance of the most accomplished actuaries, should have fallen into them. It is yet more disgraceful that, after the evil had been discovered and pressed upon its notice, so many years were suffered to elapse before any step was taken to put a stop to the waste of public money.

It would require a voluminous account to explain all the financial operations of the government during the period embraced in the foregoing statements. In the earlier years of that time, while on the one hand the minister was annually borrowing immense sums for the public service, an expensive machinery was, as we have seen, employed to keep up a show of diminishing the debt, and by this means the people were brought to view with some degree of complacency the most ruinous addition to their burthens, under the expectation of the relief which, through the magical effect of the sinking-fund, was to be experienced by them in future years. The establishment and support of this sinking-fund was long considered as a master-stroke of human wisdom. Having since had sufficient opportunity for considering its effects, we have arrived at a different conclusion, and can no longer see any wisdom in the plan of borrowing larger sums than were wanted, and paying in consequence more dearly for the loan of what was actually required, in order to lay out the surplus to accumulate into a fund for buying up the debt at a higher price than that at which it was contracted.

In the fourth report of the Select Committee on Public Income and Expenditure, which was printed by order of the House of Commons, in 1828, there are three statements showing the difference between the public receipts and disbursements in the ten years ended 5th January, 1802; the fourteen years ended 5th January, 1816; and the twelve years ended 5th January, 1828; an abstract of which is here given, and the statement is further continued for the twenty-two years ended 5th January, 1850:—

BALANCE OF INCOME AND EXPENDITURE.

Ten Years ended 5th January, 1802.

Expenditure .	£447,812,773	Raised by creation of debt			£380,997,380
Income . .	258,659,322	Applied to redemption of debt	£180,346,440		
		Money raised for Austria	4,600,000		
		Discount and charges of receipt . . .	2,416,497		
					187,362,937
					£193,634,443
		Balance 5th January, 1802	£9,027,021		
		Balance 5th January, 1792	4,546,029		
Expenditure more than income . .	£189,153,451				4,480,992
					£189,153,451

Fourteen Years ended 5th January, 1816.

Expenditure	£1,059,683,370	Raised by creation of debt			900,107,717
Income . .	823,354,060	Applied to redemption of debt	£651,952,651		
		Raised for East India Company	2,500,000		
		Discount, etc. . . .	2,887,199		
					657,339,850
					£242,767,867
		Balance 5th January, 1816	£15,465,578		
		Balance 5th January, 1802	9,027,021		
Expenditure more than income . .	236,329,310				6,438,557
					£236,329,310

Twelve Years ended 5th January, 1828.

Income . .	670,198,286	Applied to redemption of debt			580,454,422
Expenditure .	640,966,521	Discount and charges of receipt . . .			544,588
					£580,999,040
		Raised by creation of debt			540,530,450
					£40,468,590
		Balance 5th January, 1816	£15,465,578		
		Balance 5th January, 1828	4,228,753		
Income more than expenditure . .	£29,231,765				11,236,825
					£29,231,765

FINANCES OF ENGLAND. 127

Twenty-two Years ended 5th January, 1850.

Income . .	£1,092,219,672	Applied to redemption of debt, beyond the amount of debt created		£11,054,495
Expenditure	1,075,645,391			
		Balance 5th January 1850	£9,748,539	
		Balance 5th January, 1828	4,228,753	
Income more than expenditure . .	£16,574,281			5,519,786
				£16,574,281

It appears from this statement that during the ten years from 5th Jan., 1792 to 5th Jan., 1802 —

The public expenditure exceeded the income £189,153,451
Between 1802 and 1816 the excess of expenditure was 236,329,310

Excess of expenditure during twenty-four years of war £425,482,761
During thirty-four years of peace, between 1816 and 1850, the excess of income over expenditure has been 45,779,046

At this rate it would require three hundred and sixteen years of peace to cancel the debt incurred during twenty-four years of war, or thirteen years for one; but the comparison is even more unfavorable than this, because at the time of borrowing the rate of interest is high and the value of public securities low, whereas at the time of liquidation the reverse of these circumstances is experienced, so that on the most favorable supposition it requires fifteen years of saving in peace to repair the evil consequences of one year of war expenditure; at which rate, our successors who may be living about the close of the twenty-second century will find themselves relieved from that portion of the public debt which has been contracted since 1792. On the other hand, this period would be somewhat hastened through the extinction of that part of public debt which consists of terminable and life annuities.

It is necessary here to explain briefly the financial plans which have at different times within the present century been proposed by the Government and sanctioned by Parliament.

At the breaking out of the war in 1803, it became necessary to meet as far as possible the increased expenditure of the country by the imposition of new taxes, among which was included the income-tax, under the name of a property-tax. The greater part of these taxes were declared to be of a temporary character, and were to cease in six months after the reëstablishment of peace. It soon became apparent, however, that to adhere to this stipulation would be impossible, since the exigencies of the country required the contraction of loans, the interest of which could not be provided, except by the gradual appropriation of one portion after another of the proceeds of the war taxes. Under these circumstances, it was proposed, in 1807, by Lord Henry Petty, then Chancellor of the Exchequer, to depart from the usual practice of confining the financial arrangements to the current year, and to determine at once, as far as was possible, the amount which it would be necessary to raise during each one of a series of years, providing beforehand the means for meeting the increasing burthen. It was assumed that the loans to be raised in 1807 and the two following years should be each £12,000,000; that for 1810 was stated at £14,000,000, and during each of the ten ensuing years the amount was assumed at £16,000,000. It was calculated that the interest upon those loans would be met, up to that for the year 1811, by the falling in of annuities, after which, the war taxes were to be pledged, at the rate of ten per cent., upon each loan: five per cent. to pay the interest, and five per cent. to accumulate as a sinking-fund for discharging the principal. The deficiency that would be occasioned by this appropriation year by year of the war taxes was to be met by supplementary loans for the interest on which, and to provide a sinking-fund for their redemption, it would be necessary to impose new taxes. By these means it was expected that the country would have been able to meet the charges of an expensive war during a series of years with only a moderate addition to the public burthens. The ministry, of which Lord Henry Petty formed a part, having gone out of office before the next annual finance arrangement was brought forward, his plan was abandoned, and no attempt has since been made by any minister to form financial arrangements embracing the circumstances of future years.

The explanations offered each year in the House of Commons by the Chancellor of the Exchequer, concerning the financial condition of the country, are not given in such a form as to be readily understood. In the accounts by which the statements are accompanied, the interest of the debt and other permanent charges are not included, and on the other hand nothing is stated regarding the produce of the permanent taxes, forming what is called the consolidated fund, except the amount of its surplus or deficiency, as the case may be, after providing for the permanent charge upon it. The *Budget*, as it is the practice to call this annual exposition, explains on the one hand the sums required for the public service during the year, under the different heads of Navy, Army, Ordnance, and Miscellaneous Services, together with any incidental charges which may apply to the year; and on the other hand, are given the *ways and means* for meeting the same. These ways and means consist of the surplus (if any) of the consolidated fund, the annual duties, and such incidental receipts as come in aid of the national resources.

The detail of these *budgets* would consequently throw but little light upon the financial condition of the country, if even they had been preserved in an authentic form, which has not been done. Any statements of the kind that could be offered must be drawn from unauthorized publications, in which they have been given without regard to methodical arrangement, while, as respects some years of the series, we should seek in vain for any statement whatever.

VIII.

THE ZOLLVEREIN.

FROM BOWRING'S REPORT ON THE PRUSSIAN COMMERCIAL UNION, PARL. DOC. 1840, VOL. XXI., PP. 1-17.

IN compliance with the instructions which I had the honor to receive from your lordship, dated Foreign Office, July 14, 1839, I proceed to report on the progress, present state, and future prospects of the Prussian Commercial League.

No doubt this great Union, which is known in Germany by the name of the *Zoll Verein* or *Zoll Verbande* (Toll Association or Alliance), derived its first and strongest influence from a desire to get rid of those barriers to intercommunication which the separate fiscal legislation of the various States of Germany raised among a people whom natural and national feelings, as well as common interests, would otherwise have connected more intimately and permanently together.

The Zoll Verein represents, in Germany, the operation of the same opinions and tendencies which have already effected so many changes in the commercial legislation of other countries. In the United Kingdom the custom-house laws which separated Scotland and Ireland from England, have been superseded by a general system applicable to the whole. In France the local barriers and the local tariffs have given way to a general and uniform system of taxation. Even before the Commercial League associated so many States in a common union, several less extensive combinations had prepared the way for a more diffusive intercourse. Between the States which do not form part of the Prussian League — as, for example, between Hanover and Brunswick and Oldenburgh the same tariffs have been adopted, and the payment of duties in one of the States is sufficient to secure free sale or transit in the other.

The Commercial League is, in fact, the substantial representative of a sentiment widely, if not universally, spread in Germany — that of national unity. It has done wonders in breaking down petty and local prejudices, and has become a foundation on which future legislation, representing the common interests of the German people, may undoubtedly be hereafter raised. If well directed in its future operation, the Zoll Verein will represent the fusion of German interests in one great alliance. The peril to its beneficial results will grow out of the efforts which will be made, and which are already made, to give by protections and prohibitions an undue weight to the smaller and sinister interests of the Verein. But if its tariffs be so moderate and so judicious as to allow full play to the interests of the consumers in the field of competition — if there should be no forcing of capital into regions of unproductiveness or of less productiveness — if the claims of manufacturers to sacrifices in their favor from the community at large be rejected — if the great agricultural interests of Germany recover that portion of attention from the *commercial* union to which they are justly entitled — if the importance of foreign trade and navigation be duly estimated — the Zoll Verein will have the happiest influence on the general prosperity. And that the League has been much strengthened by the experience of its benefits — that its popularity is extending — that its further spreading may be confidently anticipated — appears to be indubitable. In fact, the Zoll Verein has brought the sentiment of German nationality out of the regions of hope and fancy into those of positive and material interests; and representing, as it does, the popular feeling of Germany, it may become, under enlightened guidance, an instrument not only for promoting the peace and prosperity of the States that compose it, but of extending their friendly relations through the world.

Considerations both of morality and economy were not wanting to recommend the Commercial Union to the German people. Not only were the numerous barriers and various legislation of the German States great impediments to trade, but they created a considerable amount of contraband traffic, and caused the country to swarm with petty smugglers, who lived upon the profits which the varieties of the tariffs placed within their reach. The custom-house administration was costly, and generally inefficient, from the extent of frontier to be guarded; so that the establishment of one large instead of a variety of small circles has led at the same time to a great diminution of cost and a great increase of efficiency, while it has removed from all the interior of Germany that demoralizing influence which the presence of multitudes of illicit traders and smugglers always brings with it.

The Zoll Verein was not, as it has been often asserted to be, a union formed in hostility to the commercial interests of other States — it was not intended prematurely to create a manufacturing population in rivalry with or opposition to the manufacturing aptitudes of Great Britain — it was by no means the purpose of its founders to misdirect capital to unprofitable employment, to sacrifice agriculture to trade, or to encourage less the field than the factory. The Zoll Verein was the substantial expression and effect of a general desire among a great nation, split into many small States, but still of common origin, similar manners, speaking the same language, educated in the same spirit, to communicate, to trade, to travel, without the annoyance and impediments which the separate fiscal regulations of every one of their governments threw in the way. If, in the natural process of things, the tariffs of the Zoll Verein have become hostile to the importation of foreign, and especially of British, produce, it is because *our* laws have prevented the greater extension of commercial relations with Germany. We have rejected the payments they have offered — we have forced them to manufacture what they were unable to buy — and we have put in their hands the means of manufacturing cheaply, by refusing to take the surplus of their agricultural produce, the non-exportation of which has kept their markets so low that small wages have been sufficient to give great comforts to their laborers.

There can be no doubt that the hostile tariffs of other nations, and especially the corn and timber laws of Great Britain, served greatly to strengthen the arguments in favor of Commercial Union. It was felt necessary to extend the home market while foreign markets were closed, or only partially and irregularly opened, to the leading articles of German production.

"We should not have complained," says a distinguished German writer, in 1835, "that all our markets were overflowing with English manufactures — that Germany received in British cotton goods alone more than the hundred millions of British subjects in the East Indies — had not England, while she was inundating us with *her* productions, insisted on closing her markets to *ours*. Mr. Robinson's Resolutions in 1815 had, in fact, excluded our corn from the ports of Great Britain; she told us we were to buy, but not to sell. We were not willing to adopt reprisals; we vainly hoped that a sense of her own interest would lead to reciprocity. But we were disappointed, and we were compelled to take care of ourselves "[1]

Thus, while on the one hand, the Zoll Verein was advocated as a measure of self-defence against the hostile legislation of foreign nations, it should not be forgotten that, as respects the confederated States, it represented the principles of unrestricted intercommunication.

As between more that twenty-six millions of Germans, it was the establishment of *free trade;* restrictions, duties, prohibitions, custom-houses, there are none, as far as regards the various States that comprise the Commercial Union. Whatever impediments the tariffs create to commercial communication with foreign lands, the League has thrown down every barrier which stood in the way of trading intercourse between the different branches of the great German family, which the League represents. And, as the conception of the League was popular and national, so it cannot be denied that its workings have been, *on the whole*, favorable to the prosperity and to the happiness of the German community. Tariffs less hostile to the manufactures and foreign commerce of nations would, as I conceive, have greatly added to the beneficial effects of the Union. Its more extended communications with other countries would have given greater energy, and opened a wider field to the increased activity of the home trade. There is no reason why foreign commerce should not have been benefitted to the same or even a wider extent than internal industry, by the overthrow of that local legislation which impeded intercourse, and by the introduction of a uniform and liberal system of custom-house legislation.

The Zoll Verein now represents the interests (well or ill understood) of more than twenty-six millions of inhabitants of the most civilized and opulent parts of Europe, and has accomplished one important result, namely, of exciting the attention and of awakening the apprehensions of more than one neighboring nation. What the Zoll Verein is to become may depend as much upon others as upon themselves; and, should its course be guided by enlightened economy and sound commercial policy, it may become an instrument of incalculable and boundless good.

Long before the Zoll Verein came into operation, the same spirit which led to its formation had been exhibited in various

---

[1] Kauke's " Historisch-politische Zeitschrift."

parts of Germany, leading to sundry local and even national reforms in the commercial policy of the German States.

Some steps had been taken in Prussia, during the years 1816 and 1817, by sundry ordinances to introduce " a general and simple system of custom-house legislation,[1] and on the 26th May, 1818, a new tariff was published, which is, in fact, the groundwork of the existing arrangements. Before this period a different fiscal system prevailed in different parts of the Prussian kingdom. The imposts in Brandenburg amounted to 69 groschen — 7s. 4d. per individual; in Silesia they were only 22 groschen — 2s. 3d. The new law allowed the unrestricted circulation of all foreign products which had once passed the frontier, and the free transit of all home productions. The intention of this tariff of 1818 was to establish 10 per cent. as the maximum of protection; and, had the intention of the Prussians been carried into effect, there would have been no grounds for complaint.

In speaking of the Prussian tariff to the House of Commons, on the 7th May, 1827, Mr. Huskisson stated "that the duties on the internal consumption of British goods are what we should consider very low upon most articles, fluctuating from 5 to 10 per cent. — upon no one article, I believe, exceeding 15 per cent.;" but this was undoubtedly an incorrect view of things, for it will appear, on the investigation of the matter, that the duties on many articles of British manufacture vary from 20 to 100 per cent. upon the value; and though no doubt the duty (being levied on the weight) has much increased in *ad valorem* amount since 1827, it was, even then, from 20 to 60 per cent. on various low-priced manufactures; nor was Mr. Huskisson warranted in saying that the low-priced manufactures; nor was Mr. Huskisson warranted in saying that, " in the whole Prussian tariff, there is not a single prohibition," inasmuch as imports of salt and playing-cards are wholly prohibited, except for government account.

The most important step by which evidence was given of the tendency of the different States of Germany to amalgamate their interests and to establish, instead of many tariffs, one single system, was the union of Bavaria, Würtemberg, Hollenzollern-Sigmaringen, and Hollenzollern-Hechingen, in the commercial league of 28th July, 1824. Baden, the two Hesses, and Saxony were afterwards invited to join the League. The government of

---

[1] See especially the ordinance of 11th June, 1816—" Zur Aufhebung der Wasser-Binnen und Provinzialzölle zunächst in den alten Provinzen der Monarchie."

THE ZOLLVEREIN. 135

Prussia, alive to the state of public opinion, had entered by various treaties, from 1819 to 1830, into a commercial league with Grand Ducal Hesse, Lippe Detmold, and some smaller states, and in December, 1826, the *enclaves* (such portions of the territory as are surrounded by another State) of Mecklenburg-Schwerin, Ripen-Hesseland, Schœnberg, Anhalt-Kothen, Anhalt-Dessau, Hesse-Homburg, and other States, joined the Prusso-Hessian Union; while, in 1831, Saxony, Electoral Hesse, Saxe Weimar, Saxe Meiningen, Saxe Coburg, Saxe Altenburg, and other united themselves to the Bavaro-Wurtemberg league. Each of these two great branches naturally sought to extend its influence, and each prepared the way for a fusion of the whole in one great association.

On the 22d March, 1833, a treaty was concluded between Prussia, Bavaria, Wurtemberg, Electoral and Ducal Hesse; on the 30th March of the same year, Saxony joined the association; on the 11th of May, Anhalt and Ducal Saxony united themselves. The ratifications were exchanged on the 11th of May. This treaty is the basis of the Zoll Verein, or Commercial League. It will be found at length in the Appendix I. (Parl. Doc. p. 73-78) ; In 1835 Baden united itself to the League, and Nassau and Frankfort-on-the-Maine have also become parties.

The first Prusso-Hessian Union, taking the name of the *Preussisch-Hessischen Zoll Verbande*, comprising many smaller States, such as Anhalt Dessau, Anhalt Neuberg, Saxe Coburg Gotha, Anhalt Kothen, Schwartzburg Sondenhausen, Hesse Homburg, Schwartzburg Rudolstadt, etc., represented, according to the census of 1831, a population of 13,936,087 souls, and contained a territory of 5,278 square German miles. In 1833 it had, by the union of Electoral Hesse and the increase of population, augmented the number of souls to 14,827,418, and the territory to 5,460 square German miles. The States of Thuringia, containing about 900,000 inhabitants, had also their commercial and toll union before they joined the Prussian League in 1833, while Bavaria, Wurtemberg, Saxony, and Baden, brought between 8 and 9 millions of population, and nearly 2,500 square German miles of territory into the confederation.

The following table exhibits the population of the States now comprising the German Custom-house Union, to serve as a basis for the Division of the Receipts at Triennial Periods.

No. in Order.	Designation of the States which have given their assent in their own name.	Extent of territorial superficies in square miles.	Extent of the Custom-house frontier in miles.	Population according to the Census agreed upon on the 31st of December, in		Observations.
				1834.	1837.	
1	Prussia, and the States which have come to an agreement with her	5,157 $\frac{21}{100}$	774 $\frac{88}{100}$	13,692,889	14,318,250	
2	Bavaria	1,477 $\frac{36}{100}$	151 $\frac{60}{100}$	4,251,118	4,319,887	
3	Saxony	271 $\frac{88}{100}$	58	1,595,668	1,652,114	
4	Wurtemberg	385 $\frac{15}{100}$	3 $\frac{10}{100}$	1,627,122	1,667,901	
5	Grand Duchy of Baden	279 $\frac{6}{100}$	60 $\frac{80}{100}$	1,237,657	1,264,614	
6	Electorate of Hesse	182 $\frac{10}{100}$	16 $\frac{40}{100}$	640,674	652,761	
7	Grand Duchy of Hesse	179 $\frac{22}{100}$		769,691	791,736	
8	Thuringian States	283 $\frac{49}{100}$		908,478	931,340	
9	Duchy of Nassau	84 $\frac{70}{100}$		373,601	383,730	
				25,090,898	25,982,333	Total for Divi'n.
10	Frankfort[1]	4 $\frac{33}{100}$		60,000	60,000	
		8,252 $\frac{71}{100}$	1,064 $\frac{48}{100}$	25,150,898	26,042,333	Total for Population.

[1] Note.—The population of Frankfort is not taken into the Division of the Revenues, as this town receives an inalienable and invariable sum calculated on the basis of a population of 60,000 souls (63,936).

The *Zoll Verein* had to contend with a strong opposition in its origin, not only from some of the States whose local position forced them into the union, but from other German States that continued independent, for the tariff pressed equally on all, not parties to the League, whether neighbors or foreigners. The Prussian tariffs of 1818 had been strongly resisted by Electoral Hesse, Cassel and other States. Saxony denounced them as hostile, nay, fatal to her manufacturing and commercial interests. Yet it cannot be denied that the tariffs of 1818 were a great improvement upon the previously existing legislation, for they replaced multitudes of prohibitions and prohibitory duties by moderate imports. In 1826 the question of a union between Prussia, and Hesse Darmstadt was discussed, and an inquiry was made, in case Hesse Darmstadt should unite with Bavaria and Wurtemberg, whether Prussia would be willing to entertain the subject of a commercial treaty. The first answer of Prussia was unfavorable, but the difficulties were at last surmounted, and the League before referred to was formed between Prussia and Hesse Darmstadt, of which the Prussian tariff of 1818 was the basis, the custom-houses between the two countries being wholly removed — each State, however, reserved the right to establish duties of consumption on sundry articles of food and drink; and Prussia was allowed to maintain the monopoly of salt and playing-cards.

The objects proposed by the Zoll Verein were the removal of all restrictions to communication and transit, the abolition of all internal custom-houses, the establishment of a common tariff and system of collection, and the repartition of the receipts on all imports and exports according to the population among all the members of the League. The States reserved to themselves the right of introducing any local arrangements which did not interfere with the general principles — of nominating the functionaries of their own districts, and of examining the accountancy of any part of the League. The League is bound not to interfere with matters of local revenue, such as port-dues, turnpikes, tolls, etc. The Prussian tariff of 1818 was recognized as establishing the maximum of duties. It was determined that a common system of moneys, weights, and measures, should replace, as soon as possible, the various, complicated, and discordant usages of the different States of the union, and that the whole influence of the union should be directed towards the extension of its commercial relations with other States. The intention of the tariff is to admit raw materials without any, or on merely a nominal, duty. The lightest duty levied is on silk goods, amounting to 110 dollars per cwt., or about 3 shillings sterling per lb.[1] The common rate of duty is half a dollar, or 1s. 6d. per cwt. on all articles not specially excepted. The tariff, as fixed by the Congress which has just closed its labors, will be found in the Appendix II. (Parl. Doc., p. 76).

It would ill become me, in this report, to discuss — though I cannot pass over in absolute silence — the probable political consequences of the establishment of the Zoll Verein. They certainly were not lost sight of by its founders. The intimate connection between commercial and political interests is obvious; and the advocates of the League did not fail to perceive that no political alliance would be so strong as that based upon a community of pecuniary and social interests. The jarring of differently constituted institutions, the local jealousies which still exert

---

[1] The duty levied by the English tariff on silk goods is from 11s. to 27s. 6d. per lb.

their influences, the clashing of personal and privileged interests with the public weal, have prevented, to a certain extent, the fusion which would otherwise have taken place, so that the political and the commercial policy are not always identified; but it cannot be denied that under a wise direction the machinery of the Zoll Verein would become a very mighty political engine, which would be brought to bear with great power upon the future concerns of Europe and the world at large.

The general feeling in Germany towards the Zoll Verein is, that it is the first step towards what is called the *Germanization* of the people. It has broken down some of the strongest holds of alienation and hostility. By a community of interests on commercial and trading questions it has prepared the way for a political nationality, — it has subdued much local feeling, prejudice, and habit, and replaced them by a wider and stronger element of German nationality.

The Zoll Verein, by directing capital to internal, in preference to external, trade, has already had a great influence in improving the roads, the canals, the means of travelling, the transport of letters; in a word, in giving additional impulse to inland communications of every sort. The isolation of the several German States, with separate fiscal interests, and often hostile legislation, prevented those facilities from being given to intercourse which are alike the evidence and the means of civilization. On every side beneficial changes are taking place. Railways are being constructed in many parts of the German territory, steamboats are crowding the German ports and coasting along the German shores; everything is transported with greater cheapness and rapidity.

But whatever opinions may be formed as to the effect of the Commercial League upon British interests, it is now too late to discuss them beneficially. The League exists, and is not likely to be broken up; the separate interests of the different States are blended in the common interests of the Zoll Verein; all the topics of comparison between the general tariff and the tariffs which previously existed in the various independent States of the union are now removed; whatever existed of local fiscal influence is merged in the common alliance, and the League must now be accepted and treated with as a body more influential than were any of its members, — capable of controlling the smaller influences of its component parts by the concentrated influence of the whole.

It is natural that a body so powerful as the Commercial League should seek to extend its influence. More coasts, more ports, and more shipping are the three *desiderata* which are put forward by its advocates and members. For the coasts and the ports of the Baltic belonging to the union are so much cramped and prejudiced by the Sound dues that they cannot meet, in any of the great emporiums of trade out of the Baltic, the competition of the ports and coast south of the Baltic; while the ports, such as Hamburg, Rotterdam, etc., which are the natural outlets of the great rivers which run through the provinces of the League, all belong to States not associated with it. The subject has been discussed of giving a flag to the Zoll Verein, as it has already a coinage; but to possess a marine, both warlike and commercial, in order to compete with the growing squadrons of Russia, and to be on a level with the Hanse Towns and with Holland, is an object much insisted on, but which does not seem to present any immediate prospects of realization.

On the 30th of July, 1838, an arrangement was made (Appendix, III., P. D. p. 95,) for introducing a unity of currency, to take effect from the 1st of January, 1841, the unity to consist of the mark, weighing $233\frac{855}{1000}$ grammes.

The mark to be represented by 14 dollars; the dollar by $1\frac{3}{4}$ florins; and the florin to be $\frac{4}{7}$ of a dollar.

The accounts to be kept either in dollars (Prussian crowns) or florins (guilders).

Two millions of pieces of two dollars each are to be coined before the 1st of January, 1842. The coinage has already been introduced: it bears the effigies of the King of Prussia, and has on the reverse the inscription of *Vereins Münze*, or "Association's Money."

The future influences and direction of the Zoll Verein will be determined not alone by the growing strength of the interests it represents, but by the direction which foreign nations trading with Germany may be able or willing to give to their own commercial legislation; for, however enlightened may be the policy, and however sincere the purpose, of the statesmen of Germany to prevent the League becoming an instrument for advancing the minor interests of certain classes of producers, as opposed to the major interests of greater producers, and to the general interests of the whole body of consumers, all experience shows that the minor interest, being more youthful, vigorous, and concentrated, weighs in the balance for much more than its real value. The agricultural interest, for example, which in the States of the union is the most diffused, the most important, and the most productive, will not, in the contest with the rising manufacturing interest, obtain its full share of power, dependent as it must naturally be to a great extent on the demands of foreign markets. For it is to foreign markets alone it can look for the sale of that surplus produce which home demand does not consume, and which, as ong as it remains without vent, must create a depression in the price of the whole quantity produced. Hitherto the operation of the Zoll Verein has been to strengthen the manufacturing interest at the expense of the agricultural. As the foreign demand for agricultural produce has been uncertain and capricious, the low average prices have operated, on the one hand, in forcing capital out of agricultural into manufacturing channels; while the cheap price of food has given to the German artisan great advantages in his competition with the labor of countries in which the price of food is relatively higher.

Were foreign markets accessible to the German agriculturist, there is no doubt the flow of capital towards manufactures would be checked, first by the increased demand for agricultural labor, and, secondly, by the loss of the advantage which the German artisan now possesses in the comparative cheapness of food. For the prices of the countries which would be importers of German corn, for example, would determine the prices of corn in the German markets for the German consumer. In his own market he must give the same price as the foreign buyer who comes into that market.

One of the great difficulties with which sound commercial principles have had to contend, in Germany as elsewhere, is the too general adoption of a phraseology which has grown out of a vicious legislation, and has to a great extent popularized error. High duties on imported articles are justified by the plea that it is necessary to afford *protection to the producer*, while the substantial fact of the consequent *sacrifice of the consumer* is wholly kept out of view. For one case in which the *loss to the many* is put forward, there are a thousand in which the *profits to the few* are urged as sufficient sanction to perverse legislation.

Dieterici[1] gives a very curious table (p. 127), showing the operation of the Zoll Verein, during the years 1833 to 1835, on imported articles.

On foreign articles of consumption not coming into competition with German articles the increase in the three years is as 54 to 46; in foreign articles of consumption competing with German articles the decrease is as 24 to 29; in half-manufactured articles serving for further labor the increase is only from 9,161 to 9,520; while in wholly manufactured articles the decrease is from 13 to 10. . . .

The facilities created for communication by the improvement of roads, canals, etc., have greatly aided the inland trade of Germany. At the close of the last war there were no roads of the first class either in Pomerania, Posen, or Prussia proper. In 1816 the number of German miles laid down in Chausées was $523\frac{3}{8} = 2,408$ English; in 1828 it was $1,062\frac{7}{8} = 4,889$; and in 1831, $1,228\frac{1}{2} = 5,610$; and this amount has been greatly increased at the present time.

Of the activity of communication, the following official returns of the quantities of goods which passed through Priegnitz will furnish remarkable evidence: —

Years.	Saxony and Bohemia.	Magdeburg.	Berlin.	Cottbus.	Breslau.	Halle.	Warsaw.	Other places.	Total in Cwt.
	Cwt.	Cwt.	Cwt.	Cwt.	Cwt.	Cwt.	Cwt.	Cwt.	
1830 . . .	246,934	683,020	446,557	48,322	138,813	. . .	. . .	153,314	1,716,963
1831 . . .	229,412	595,610	519,086	45,574	158,195	46,988	. . .	34,088	1,628,954
1832 . . .	246,145	720,289	540,246	53,297	147,617	57,213	18,489	94,899	1,878,199
1833 . . .	260,564	700,858	477,979	32,962	132,612	50,948	9,694	80,595	1,746,196
1834 . . .	307,087	927,764	755,038	26,575	221,623	70,728	11,067	906,112	3,225,998

It must not be forgotten that Great Britain had long enjoyed peculiar advantages in the facilities of communication; and to these facilities much of the activity and success of her manufacturing and commercial industry is attributable. For many years her progress in this respect created almost a monopoly of benefit; but

---

[1] I have had occasion constantly to consult Dieterici's "Statistische Uebersicht der wichtigsten Gegenstände des Verkehrs und Verbrauchs im Preussischen Staate und im Deutschen Zollverbande, von 1831 bis 1836, aus amtlichen Quellen dargestellt," Berlin, 1838. The valuable facts he has collected will be found scattered over the whole of this report.

the advantages she enjoyed are now participated in by other nations; and in Germany especially great advances have been made, and continue to be made, in all those improvements which facilitate intercourse.

It is obvious that England cannot long maintain exclusive possession of advantages which civilized man is everywhere successfully struggling to obtain. Railroads are now being introduced between the principal towns in the Zoll Verein, — those between Dresden and Leipzig and between Berlin and Potsdam are completed, many others are begun, and a still greater number are projected; and in these enterprises the undertakers have all the advantages of our experience. The number of canals has considerably increased; steamers are giving great development to river navigation; and even in those branches of industry in which our superiority is the most marked, such as the manufacture of machinery, competition is marching after us with rapid strides.

But, independently of the progress of Germany towards a participation in the advantages which for a series of years have been almost exclusively possessed by Great Britain, she has aptitudes and facilities of her own which must greatly aid her in the development of her industry. The frugal and economical habits of the German people enable them to procure a far greater proportion of comforts for the same proportional rate of wages than are generally obtained by the English laborer; added to which a simpler mode of life, a smaller consumption of animal food, and a less costly class of garments, leave out of their smaller earnings a larger amount of savings. Their savings are, for the most part, invested in the purchase of the house in which they dwell, and the garden which they cultivate, — whose cultivation is alike a source of health, enjoyment, and profit, being in most cases a valuable auxiliary to manufacturing industry. Nor ought the general, the almost universal education of the population, be forgotten as immensely contributory to the public prosperity. Elementary instruction is provided for all, and special instruction for those who, in any department of art or industry, exhibit any particular aptitude. I have given in the Appendix (IV., P.D. pp. 96–7), a short account of the Gewerbe-Schule at Berlin, which under the admirable superintendence of M. Banth (whose services to his country are beyond all estimate, and above all praise), has first gathered from every part of the kingdom the youths best fitted for scientific training; and, after a thorough course of education,

THE ZOLLVEREIN. 143

has again dispersed them over the country. The gradual diffusion of a knowledge and a taste for art over the whole field of German industry, its happy influence upon all manufactures, exhibited in a thousand evidences of improvement, are obvious to every observer. Manual skill and experience, more and more intimately associated with scientific instruction, have been long preparing the most important results; and when the ' rising generation of intelligent artisans bring their information and taste into the wide region of manufacturing and commercial competition, there can be no doubt of their contributing largely to the general wealth and weal.

The tariff of the Zoll Verein has no other prohibitions than those of salt and playing-cards, which are monopolies in Prussia; and the principle of the tariff is to admit raw material, and materials serving the ends of agriculture and manufactures, either on very low, or without any, duties. Thus, raw cotton, wool, coals, pig-iron, ores, raw hides, and skins, hare and rabbit skins, potashes, common pottery, turpentine, common furniture, chalk, rags, raw refuse of sundry manufactures, trees for planting, manure, earths, fish, grass and hay, garden produce, birds, blacklead, worn clothes, precious metals, wood, turf, fresh fruit, milk, seeds, etc., pay no duties at all.

The objections to the tariff of the Zoll Verein are twofold; they refer to the amount of duties levied, and to the manner in which they are levied.

The duties are far higher than the Prussian government professed its intention to levy. They were intended to represent the tariffs of Prussia. Now, in the communication of Baron Maltzahn to Mr. Canning, dated Dec. 25, 1825, and laid before Parliament, by order of Her Majesty, in answer to the address of the House of Commons of 1st July, 1839, the words of the Prussian minister are as follows:—

" No one of the duties on imports is sufficiently high to prevent the importation of foreign products, as is proved by their extensive sale in all parts of the monarchy. The duties levied on the products of foreign fabrics or manufactures are generally only 10 per cent. on their value; on some they amount to 15 per cent., but there are many which are more moderate."

But these representations are certainly not borne out by facts; for, not only do the duties levied on manufactures vary from 20 to 80 per cent. (instead of from 10 to 15 per cent.), but there are great varities of goods which are wholly excluded from the Prussian markets in consequence of the elevation of the tariff.

The manner in which the duties are levied is such as to press most severely, with reference to their cost, on coarse, inferior and heavy articles; those least able to bear a high rate of duty are most imposed, the same amount of duty being taken on all species of goods made of the same raw material — the finest qualities pay the least, and the lowest qualities the highest amount. The *ad valorem* principle, which is in its nature the fairest, because it distributes taxation by the measure of wealth and expenditure, is wholly lost sight of, and the goods employed by the poor are visited by a much heavier rate of taxation than those by the opulent. The richest muslin and the coarsest calico, the cloth of Sedan and the serge of Devon pay the same amount per cwt. Hence articles of low quality — such as are used by the many, such as would have the largest sale — are wholly excluded from the markets of the League.

It cannot be disputed that the *ad valorem* system, as applied to manufactures, has many inconveniences and difficulties. It is not easy always to ascertain even the approximative value; and with the number of custom-houses by which goods are allowed to be imported through a frontier, both of sea and land so various and extensive as that of the Commercial League, it would be out of the question to seek for a sufficiency of custom-house functionaries, with knowledge and experience competent to the protection of the revenue against fraud. There is no system so simple as that of weight; it is intelligible to everybody; it is, too, a generally popular system, as it affords no latitude for the caprice of the officer, and opens no door to the frauds of the importer. It might probably be associated with some classification of articles, if not too detailed or complicated, into a few great divisions; but the desirableness of a thorough change in the system itself may well be doubted, and such a proposal is not likely to be entertained.

The Americans have strongly objected to the system of levying duties by weight, instead of on value. They have represented that the duty of $5\frac{1}{2}$ dollars on their tobacco, being the same as that levied on the tobaccos of the Havana and the Spanish colonies, is, in fact, a discriminating duty on their produce, even to the extent of 200 to 300 dollars per cent. They complain that while the duties in the United States on the articles imported from Germany do not upon the whole amount pay more than an average of 5⅝ per cent., the imports from the United States into the Zoll Verein pay 46 per cent. duty. They represent that Prussia levies on American produce a gross revenue of 776,606 dollars; and while the United States receive only 159,663 dollars from imports of the Zoll Verein. Of about 4 millions of dollars exported from the Commercial League to the United States 3 millions (1½ millions of linens, 1 million of silk, and half a million merino and other similar articles) pay no duty at all. The remaining million is principally composed of glass, hardware, hosiery, etc., paying from 20 to 25 per cent.

The original intention of the Prussian tariff has certainly been much departed from, and the general principle which was put forward has not been carried out in its details. For not only did the Prussian government, in its official correspondence, declare that it was its purpose not to lay duties exceeding from 10 to 15 per cent., but the Commercial League itself professed to make the Prussian tariff the basis of the legislation of the union; and the maximum intended to be established by the Prussian tariff was an *ad valorem* 10 per cent. on manufactures; for that tariff provides that " The duty on consumption in foreign fabrics and manufactured goods shall not exceed 10 per cent. ; and it shall be less, whenever a smaller duty can be imposed without injury to the national industry."[1] But the duties levied being, on cotton manufactures £7 10s. per cwt., on woollens £4 10s., on hardwares £8 5s., on common linens 33s., on fine linens £3 6s., and on silks £16 10s., per cwt., do, on the whole, greatly exceed the proposed 10 per cent. The system of imposing the duty by weight has the advantage of great simplicity, but it acts in complete hostility to the *ad valorem* principle, as the duty increases, instead of diminishing, with the lowness and coarseness of the article; so that the operation of the tariff is as complete an exclusion of every low-priced manufacture as if it were absolutely prohibited. Under the influence of this state of things the duty on cotton goods varies from 3½ to 120 per cent.

It has been remarked that this system fails in the very ends proposed, namely, to distribute the amount of protection in proportion to the backwardness of the manufacture. On certain articles the amount of duty is so heavy as completely to exclude

---

[1] "Allgemeine Zeitung," 2d December, 1834.

foreign competition, where the home production requires no such encouragement as that afforded by the tariff; and on others, where a protecting duty is required by the condition of the home production, the duty on the foreign article is small, and insufficient to check its introduction. But the general result of the tariff is to exclude the foreign articles of low quality and general consumption, and thus to keep the large demand exclusively for the home manufacturers. One baneful effect is, however, that the increased price is levied on those who are least able to pay, and levied on articles of the lowest value, for the piece goods which are consumed by the opulent are precisely those upon which the smallest amount of duty is collected.

It has, indeed, been argued that the levying heavy duties upon manufactures of ordinary quality, so as to exclude them from the markets of the League, is, in fact, to create a demand for superior articles, and so confer a benefit upon the German consumer; but to the immense multitude of consumers, *cost* is the all-important consideration; and, to deny access to low-priced articles, — or by prohibitory duties on foreign fabrics, considerably to elevate the price of the home-made article, — is, in all cases, to levy an unfair and unequal contribution on the poor, and in many cases wholly to exclude them from the enjoyment of what would otherwise be accessible to them. In fact, to exclude the ordinary manufactures of foreign countries is to give a special premium to the production of ordinary manufactures at home, is to create for the least advanced, the least intelligent industry, a field of peculiar favor; and it may be well doubted if the monopoly thus established for the manufacture of low articles is beneficial to them. That it is prejudicial to the consumers is obvious, but some of the ablest writers on the Zoll Verein have expressed their conviction that the uncontrolled power given to the German manufacturer of low articles in the German market is baneful as well to his own as to the public interest.[1]

The tendency of opinion in Germany is towards free trade. Almost every author of reputation represents the existing system as an instrument for obtaining changes in favor of commercial liberty. One of the most distinguished writers on the commercial league, in cautioning the capitalist from embarking his wealth in the protected branches of industry, says, "You are

---

[1] See Osiander, " Betrachtungen über den Zoll Preussischen Tarif." Stutgart, 1837, pp. 89, 90.

building ships which are not prepared for the storm. You are creating interests which cannot make their way through a crisis; you are erecting edifices upon sand."[1]

It should be borne in mind, however, that the tariffs of the Zoll Verein are far more liberal than the old tariffs of Prussia, which were intended wholly to exclude foreign manufactures. But diminished duties have not injured her own manufactures. No man is found to deny that they have made a much greater progress under a less protection than they made when the home market was, by a greater protection, closed against foreign competition.

The Prussian tariff of 1818 was a great improvement on preceding legislation, but it contained many incongruities, which were changed by the tariff of 1822. On many articles the duties varied between the eastern and western provinces. Common cloths, which paid 26 rix-d. 22½ gr., and fine cloths paying 47 rix-d. 10 5/6 gr. in the eastern provinces, paid only 22 rix-d. 18¾ gr. and 43 rix-d. 7½ gr. in the western; cotton twist paid 2 rix-d. 10 gr. in the eastern, and only half that amount in the western provinces; while dyed twist paid 6 rix-d. 17½ gr. in the former, and 5 rix-d. 17½ gr. in the latter. White and colored woven cottons and cottons mixed with thread paid the same duties as fine woollens, viz., 47 rix-d. 10 5/8 gr. and 43 rix-d. 7½ gr.; and printed and fine cottons, 61 rix-d. 3⅓ gr. in eastern, and 57 rix-d. in western districts; gray linens 2 rix d. and 1 rix-d. 22½ gr., and bleached, 12 rix-d. 6⅔ and 8 rix-d. 8⅓ gr.; silks, 171 rix-d. 3⅓ gr. in the eastern, and 167 rix-d. in the western department; half-silks, 79 rix-d. 13½ gr., and 75 rix-d. 10 gr. Common iron goods paid 6 rix-d. 17½ gr. in the east, and 5 rix-d. 2½ gr. in the west; fine iron goods, 24 rix-d. 12½ gr., and 20 rix-d. 10 gr.; and cutlery and fine hardware, 79 rix-d. 13½ gr. and 75 rix-d. 10 gr. The tariff of 1822 left the distinction only existing on cotton twist; introduced a uniform duty of 30 rix-d. on woollens, and 6 rix-d. on dyed twist; 50 rix-d. on cottons generally, but reduced the duty on cottons mixed with thread to 10 rix-d., which it also levied on bleached linens; lowered the duties on silks to 100 rix-d., and on half-silks to 50 rix-d.; on common iron goods levied 6 rix-d., on fine 10 rix-d., and on cutlery, and hardware 50 rix-d.

Thus the tariff of 1822 was in every respect an improvement

---

[1] See Osiander, " Betrachtungen," p. 97.

on that of 1818. In 1825 the duties on woollen warps were reduced from 30 rix-d. to 10 rix-d.; and those on carpets of wool and thread from 30 rix-d. to 20 rix-d.; those on fine linens and cottons mixed with flax were raised from 10 rix-d. to 20 rix-d. In 1828 the duties on flannels, meltons, etc., were reduced from 30 rix-d. to 10 rix-d., and on woollen carpets from 30 to 20 rix-d.

Up to this period half the duty was payable in *friederichs d'or*, which was an augmentation of about 6 per cent. upon the tariff. In 1832 the duty on woollen yarn was lowered from 6 rix-d. to 15 silver gr.; on carpets in general it was lowered from 30 rix-d. to 22 rix-d.; on woollens it was raised from 30 rix-d. to 33 rix-d.; on cotton yarns 2 rix-d. were established as a general duty; 55 rix-d. on cottons and cutlery, instead of 50, which 50 continued to be levied on cotton and flax manufacturers; and the duties on silk were raised from 100 rix-d. to 110 rix-d. The tariff of the Zoll Verein, in 1834, reduced the duty on carpets from 32 rix-d. to 20 rix-d.; and on woollens generally from 33 rix-d. to 30 rix-d.; on cottons from 55 rix-d. to 50 rix-d. The duty on linen thread was raised, in 1837, from 6 rix-d. to 8 rix-d.; and on twisted cotton to the same amount. The tariff of 1840 has lowered the duties on cutlery and hardware from 55 rix-d. to 50 rix-d.

The changes introduced by the Congress of 1839 into the tariffs of 1837-9, are not very considerable. The adoption of the unity of 50 kil. as the cwt. of the tariff, operates as an elevation of $2\frac{2}{7}$ per cent., in all cases, when it applies to articles, the duty on which is charged by weight, as is the case with the major part of the goods mentioned in the tariff. The system of tarification has been simplified throughout by the cutting off all fractions of lbs. The most important change is the reduction of the sugar, rice, and hardware duties. . . . The standard of the florin is altered from 24 gold standard to $24\frac{1}{2}$ gold standard; so that, under the new tariff, the rix dollar is now represented by $1\frac{3}{4}$ fl., instead of $1\frac{2}{3}$, as in the former tariff. Thus, the general rate of import duty (when there is no special exception) was, in 1837-9, one-half Prussian dollar, or 15 silver gr., represented by 50 kreutzers; but at present the general import duty of one-half Prussian dollar is represented by $52\frac{1}{2}$ krs.

Attached to the custom-house tariff will be found the various regulations under which the transit duties are levied in the States of the Prussian Union.

The legislature of Prussia has generally made the transit of goods through her provinces a source of revenue; and it has not been wholly unproductive, as a large portion of Poland and southern Russia import and export through the Prussian ports in the Baltic. The difficulties which Russian legislation has always thrown in the way of transit may, perhaps, have had some influence on the councils of Prussia; in fact, the heavy transit-duty imposed on goods imported through the ports of the Baltic could hardly be maintained were the Prussian transit-system a wise and liberal one. The southern States of the union have, for the most part, endeavored to secure through their territories a cheap transit for commodities intended for other countries. The general principles of the transit law are, that, —

1. All articles admitted without duty shall transit without duty through the Zoll Verein.

2. All articles upon which the export and import duties, separate or together, do not amount to $\frac{1}{2}$ dol. or $52\frac{1}{2}$ kr. per cwt., are to pay the amount of the said duties.

3.* All articles upon which the export and import duties exceed $\frac{1}{2}$ dol., or $52\frac{1}{2}$ kr. per cwt., shall pay on transit $\frac{1}{2}$ dol. per cwt.

But there are many exceptions. The exceptional transit duties levied by the tariffs of the Zoll Verein are: On cotton and other goods, coming or going through Baltic ports, 4 dol. (12s.) per cwt.; through other roads, 2 dol. (6s.) per cwt.; on cotton twist and dyed woollen yarn, 2 dol.; on copper, coffee, etc., 1 dol. per cwt.; on raw sugar, 20 s. gr. (2s.)

But goods going from the Oder mouth on the left bank of the Oder, westward, towards the Rhine, and through the frontier between Neu-Benin, in Silesia, to Thorn, in Bavaria; or, entering the right bank of the Rhine again, to traverse the Rhine for export, cottons, woollens, and many other articles, 1 dol. (3s.) per cwt.

Goods conveyed by the left bank, or on the Rhine, or on the Moselle, and over the southern frontier between Hamburg and Freilassing, or over the northern frontier between the Rhine and the Elbe, 10 sq. (1s.) per cwt.

Goods conveyed over the southern frontier, or from the Rhine to the Danube, $4\frac{1}{2}$ sq. ($5\frac{1}{4}$d.) per cwt.

The details will be found in the Appendix (III.) attached to the Tariff.

The transit system of the Zoll Verein is somewhat complicated, and inconsistent with the general and simple character of the legislation. The tables in the Appendix (V., P. D. pp. 99–112) will exhibit the amount of goods passing through the various provinces of the League. One general transit duty, of low amount, would certainly be very favorable to the carrying trade of the union; nor are the reasons quite obvious why, in the recognition of a principle of equality, the conveyance of goods through certain States of the union should be loaded with much heavier fiscal charges than through others. It would seem more accordant with sound principles to encourage transit through the districts which geographically present the greatest facilities, rather than to give advantages, by lower duties, to districts less conveniently situated.

Perhaps the wisest course, in the common interest of the Zoll Verein, would be to completely disassociate all fiscal considerations from the question of transit, and to levy no other duty than is necessary for paying the expenses of collection and control. The prohibitory tariffs of Russia, Poland, and Austria, certainly require no new charge or impediment to be added by a heavy transit duty to the cost of the articles imported through the States of the League. And, even with the high rate of duty levied (or perhaps rather on account of the high rate of duty levied), the pecuniary interest to preserve the present system is small, — far too small to counterbalance the disadvantages and detriments which the system creates.

Another obvious inconvenience and loss accrues to the Zoll Verein from the motives which the lower transit dues of France, Holland, and Belgium create for transporting goods through the ports of those countries instead of the ports of Germany; added to which, a habit of forwarding articles by a particular line creates new interest and motives, which make it difficult to revert to a former state of things. When business has been forced out of its natural channel into a novel course it does not promptly resume its old direction, and the ground lost is often not again to be won.

The lowest transit duty levied in the Zoll Verein, with the exception of the road from Mayence to the southern frontier, is 4½ silver gr. (5½ d.) per cwt.; but on the main roads of Austria transit is free from charge, while in France the charge is less than half the amount of the *minimum* Prussian duty. At the same time, the advantages which the railroads of Belgium offer, and the free navigation of the principal rivers of Germany, as established by the Vienna Congress, would all seem to cooperate in showing how much it is for the interest of the League to facilitate *transit* by every possible means.[1] The attention which has been of late years so successfully given in Germany to the improvement of the roads, and all other means of communication, cannot receive a greater recompense than by encouragement given to the transit trade by a low rate of duty levied. The profits deposited by the transport of merchandise, are, from their diffusion, apt to escape attention ; but perhaps there are none which give a greater activity to agricultural industry, nor which are more intimately connected with the public prosperity and the general progress of improvement and civilization.

There is considerable difficulty in estimating the amount of the imports from Great Britain into the States of the Zoll Verein, as they penetrate through so many channels, — not only through German ports, but from the ports of Holland and Belgium and the Hanse Towns. From Hamburg and the Elbe especially a large part of the wants of the Verein are supplied; there are also large importations through Rotterdam and the Rhine, as well as through Bremen and the Weser. But, by a comparison of the returns of our imports from and exports to the various circumjacent countries, which have been prepared with his accustomed accuracy and diligence by Mr. Young (Appendix VI. to IX., P. D. pp. 113-139), with the very detailed statements given me by the Prussian government, all of which documents will be found in the Appendix (XI. to XVII., P. D. pp. 143-226), an approximative estimate of the general amount, and of the special details of our commercial intercourse, will be obtained.

Though the strong and irresistible tendency of an organization like that of the Commercial League is to blend the separate interests of its component parts into the common and paramount interests of the whole, and to give to the Union, as a body, an influence sufficiently powerful to predominate over the local and partial influences of the various elements of which that Union is composed, still much time and much judicious legislation will be required, in order that the Union may fairly represent the various interests which are comprehended in its action. Happily the greater interests are and must long continue intimately connected with the foreign trade of Germany — for though the

---

[1] Osiander, pp. 115-117.

manufacturing tendencies of a portion of the States of the Union, associated as such tendencies are with a restless activity — a spirit of association, a unity of purpose, a combined action, which give them more than their fair and full importance in the struggle for what is called "protective legislation," yet it cannot be denied that there is in Germany such a general diffusion of intelligence as will check the sinister interests in their demand for prohibitory duties on foreign manufacture. And at the present moment the agricultural interests, taking in the whole of the confederated states, represent a vastly greater amount of capital and labor than the manufacturing. The agricultural interest exists everywhere and in many extensive provinces of the Union without any counterbalancing manufacturing interest, while the manufacturing interest is to a great extent of modern growth, and confined to a limited portion of the field of production. And even that manufacturing interest can only safely rest upon a system of moderate duties; for as soon as it is able to supply the markets of Germany, it must, for its surplus produce be thrown into competition with the manufacturers of other lands, and can only compete successfully by *cheap* production, to which a protective and prohibitory system is in its very nature opposed; for its object and its essence are to promise and to secure high prices to the home manufacturer. And if the interest of Prussia for example be considered, Prussia, whose population comprises two-thirds of the whole population of the Commercial Union, it is certain that not only are her true interests hostile to any system which prohibits the introduction of foreign manufactures, her capital engaged in manufactures being inconsiderable; but the general conviction of the heads of departments in Prussia is opposed to a protecting legislation.

The financial necessities of Prussia have frequently been put forward as the reason for the high rate of duties established by the tariff of the Zoll Verein;[1] but it is clear that many of the rates are far too high to be productive; some of them are wholly prohibitory; and the revenue would certainly be benefited by a considerable reduction. The Zoll Verein, however, has never been regarded by the contracting States with a view solely to the financial question; its social and political consequences would reconcile many of its members even to considerable pecuniary sacrifices. . . . .

---

[1] Osiander.

LE ZOLLVEREIN.

(*Résumé Statistique.*)

FROM LEGOYT'S LA FRANCE ET L'ÉTRANGER, VOL. I., PP. 250-5.

LE *Zollverein* (des deux mots allemands *Zoll*, douane, et *Verein*, association), est le nom donné à l'association douanière qui existe aujourd'hui entre tous les membres de la Confédération germanique, moins l'Autriche, les trois villes Anséatiques (Brême, Hambourg et Lübeck), le Mecklembourg, les duchés de Holstein et du Lauenbourg, et la principauté de Lichtenstein. La Prusse y figure même pour ses provinces placées en dehors de la Confédération.

Le principe de cette association se trouve dans l'article 19 du traité qui a fondé la Confédération germanique et qui est ainsi conçu : "Ses membres se réservent, à la première réunion de leurs plénipotentiaires à Francfort, de délibérer sur un projet de douanes et de navigation pour toute l'Allemagne." Mais elle trouvait surtout sa raison d'être dans l'organisation territoriale et politique de l'Allemagne, composée de quarante États presque tous enclavés les uns dans les autres, ayant chacun ses barrières fiscales et son tarif. On a comté que, pour parvenir de la frontière au centre du pays, soit du nord au sud, soit de l'ouest à l'est, sur un espace de 370 à 445 kilomètres, les marchandises n'avaient pas moins de seize lignes de douanes à traverser, non compris les lignes intérieures appartenant à l'État, aux communes et même aux particuliers ! De là, des frais et des pertes de temps énormes, qui, en les grevant outre mesure, arrêtaient à la fois la production et la consommation.

La Prusse, dont les provinces orientales étaient séparées du reste de la monarchie par le Hanovre, le Brunswick et la Hesse-Cassel, et qui souffrait le plus, peut-être, de ce morcellement de son territoire, prit l'initiative des négociations qui devaient conduire au Zollverein actuel. Ses ouvertures furent d'abord accueillies par le Schwarzbourg-Sondershausen, l'une de ses enclaves ; puis, de 1819 à 1828, l'association naissante vit successivement venir à elle les principautés ou duchés de Hesse-Darmstadt, Schwarzbourg-Rudolstadt, Saxe-Weimar, Anhalt-Bernbourg,

Anhalt-Dessau, et Anhalt-Coethen, soit pour la totalité, soit pour une partie de leur territoire. Un certain nombre d'États du second ordre, ayant à leur tête la Bavière et le Wurtemberg, tentèrent d'enrayer ce mouvement dans lequel ils voyaient un agrandissement indirect de l'influence politique de la Prusse ; mais, convaincus de l'inutilité de leurs efforts pour constituer une ligne douanière de quelque importance, ils se réunirent au Zollverein, le 23 mars 1833. La Saxe suivit leur example, le 30 mars de la même année, et entraîna à sa suite les États de la Thuringe, la branche Ernestine de Saxe, Schwarzbourg et Reuss. Après de longues hésitations, Bade se déclara pour le Zollverein le 12 mai 1835 ; Nassau, le 10 décembre 1835 ; Francfort-sur-le-Mein, le 25 janvier 1836 ; la principauté de Lippe-Detmold, le 18 octobre ; le Brunswick, le 19 octobre ; la Hesse-Électorale et le comté de Schaumbourg, le 13 novembre ; le comté de Waldeck, le 11 décembre 1841 ; le duché de Luxembourg, le 8 février 1842 ; enfin, le 1er janvier 1854, les derniers États restés fidèles à l'association du *Stuerverein*, c'est-à-dire le Hanovre et le duché d'Oldenbourg.

D'après le recensement de décembre 1861, la population de chaque État associé s'élevait aux nombres ci-après : —

Prusse	18,867,061	Hanovre 1,908,631	Brunswick 257,624
Luxembourg	197,731	Wurtembourg 1,720,708	Oldenbourg 238,562
Bavière	4,695,424	Bade 1,365,732	Nassau 454,326
Saxe royale	2,225,244	Hesse-Cassel 710,680	Francfort 84,506
Thuringe	1,009,821	Hesse-Darmstadt 874,231	Total 34,670,277

Ces 34.6 millions d'habitants occupent une superficie de 502,260 kilomètres carrés.

Le Zollverein n'est pas resté commercialement isolé. Dès sa formation, il s'est efforcé d'agrandir ses débouchés par des traités avec les principaux États de l'ancien et du nouveau monde.

Ces traités de commerce se sont succédé dans l'ordre ci-après : avec la Hollande, les 21 janvier 1839 et 31 décembre 1851 ; avec la Porte, le 19/22 octobre 1840 ; avec l'Angleterre, les 2 mars 1841 et 11 novembre 1857 ; avec la Belgique, les 1er septembre 1844, 2 janvier 1851 et 18 février 1852 ; avec la Sardaigne, les 23 juin 1845, 20 mai 1851 et 28 octobre 1859 ; avec l'Autriche, le 19 février 1853 (d'abord avec la Prusse seulement, puis avec le Zollverein et plus tarde, aves les duchés de Parme et de Modène) ; avec le Mexique, le 30 juillet 1855 ; avec Brême, le 26 janvier 1856 ; avec la Sicile, le 10 août 1856 ; avec le Danemark, le 14 mars 1857; avec l'Autriche et la principauté de Lichtenstein (convention monétaire), le 24 janvier 1857; avec la Perse, le 25 juin 1857; avec la confédération Argentine, le 19 septembre 1857.

L'influence de ces traités sur le commerce du Zollverein est clairement indiquée par le tableau suivant, qui en fait connaître, de 1834 à 1860, la valeur moyenne annuelle absolue et par tête d'habitant. Pour la période 1834-1846, cette valeur a été *calculée* par M. O. Hübner (*Jahrbuch* pour 1860 et 1861[1]), d'après des prix invariables; pour les autres années, d'après les prix réels. Les sommes sont en millions de francs.

Périodes et années.	Importations.	Exportations.	Transit.	Importations et exportations réunies.	Population moyenne en millions.	Valeur par tête.
1834-1838 . . .	477.0	591.0	219.0	1,068.0	24.6	43.4
1839-1843 . . .	677.2	662.6	207.4	1,339.9	26.7	50.2
1844-1846 . . .	813.4	655.1	260.6	1,468.5	29.0	50.6
1850-1852 . . .	704.6	670.5	314.6	1,375.1	30.2	45.5
1853	764.6	942.7	395.6	1,707.3	32.5	52.5
1854	1,009.1	1,252.9	457.5	2,262.0	32.6	69.2
1855	1,184.2	1,157.2	626.2	2,341.4	32.7	71.5
1856	1,312.9	1,195.5	550.9	2,508.4	33.0	76.0
1857	1,327.5	1,324.1	541.5	2,651.6	33.2	79.9
1858	1,205.6	1,315.5	419.2	2,521.1	33.5	75.2

D'après ce tableau, l'histoire commerciale du Zollverein a eu trois phases très-distinctes. La première comprend la période 1834-1846; c'est peut-être la plus brillante. La seconde embrasse les années de crise 1847 à 1852. La troisième commencée en 1853, se continue en ce moment; 1857 en est le point culminant. Vient ensuite une réaction assez sensible, qui, quoique perdant chaque jour de son intensité, n'a pas encore fait place à une recrudescence bien caractérisée. — Les deux colonnes, *importations* et *exportations*, indiquent la corrélation intime qui existe toujours et partout entre ces deux éléments du commerce. Inférieures pendant assez longtemps aux premières, les secondes ne tardent pas à les égaler et même à les dépasser dans certaines années. C'est la preuve du rapide

---

[1] On sait que les droits de douane du Zollverein sont établis au poids. Les publications officielles ne font donc pas connaître la *valeur* du commerce de l'association.

développement manufacturier de l'association. Par suite de l'extension graduelle de son réseau de voies ferrées, de l'amélioration de ses voies navigables et de la réduction des droits de transit (aujourd'hui supprimés), son territoire est, en outre, emprunté par une valeur (calculée) sans cesse croissante de marchandises. Ne perdons pas de vue toutefois que la valeur, surtout la valeur *actuelle*, ne saurait donner, particulièrement dans ces dernières années où les prix ont été l'objet d'une hausse si soudaine et si rapide, la mesure exacte du mouvement des échanges et du transit du Zollverein. L'indication des quantités serait un document plus précis ; mais elle exigerait des développements qui ne sauraient trouver place ici.

Le tableau ci-après fait connaître la valeur des produits fabriqués que le Zollverein a importés et exportés en 1834, 1844, et 1857. Il n'a d'autre but que d'indiquer ceux de ces produits qui sont le plus habituellement consommés ou fabriqués dans les États de l'Union, les quantités ayant dû nécessairement s'élever avec le chiffre de la population. Cependant il fournit ce renseignement important et indépendant du mouvement de la population, que, tandis que les importations ne se sont accrues, de 1834 à 1857, que de 36 p. 100, les exportations ont plus que doublé. C'est, comme nous le disons plus haut, le signe certain des progrès remarquables de l'industrie manufacturière dans l'association.

LE ZOLLVEREIN.

DESIGNATION DES ARTICLES.	IMPORTATIONS.			EXPORTATIONS.		
	1834.	1844.	1857.	1834.	1844.	1857.
Toiles de fil	88.9	61.5	78.4	41.2	46.5	100.9
Soieries pures	34.1	8.6	16.9	88.1	57.0	55.5
Soieries mélangées	12.4	14.6	33.0	27.4	40.1	85.1
Lainages	2.6	8.2	7.1	7.9	13.5	18.0
Fourrures et pelleteries	4.9	13.1	22.5	67.1	96.0	158.6
Habits d'enfants	0.2	0.1	0.4	0.4	0.7	1.9
Objets en fer	0.1	0.3	0.2	0.7	1.5	1.9
Objets en cuivre et laiton	2.2	5.2	10.9	12.7	13.9	18.0
Objets en plomb	0.7	2.2	3.0	3.4	3.0	6.7
Objets en zinc	0.04	0.04	0.03	...	...	0.4
Objets en étain	...	...	0.1	0.04	0.1	6.0
Quincaillerie	0.1	0.1	0.1	0.1	0.1	0.4
Objets en pierre, marbre et autres minéraux	1.9	3.7	1.4	18.4	45.4	52.5
	0.4	0.4	0.03	0.3	1.1	0.3
Vaisselle et porcelaine	1.5	1.5	0.1	3.7	7.5	20.2
Verre et verrerie	2.6	5.6	7.1	6.0	3.7	18.0
Objets en bois	1.1	2.6	4.5	7.9	9.4	22.9
Objets en cuir	0.7	1.5	3.0	3.7	1.9	7.1
Brosserie et boissellerie	0.1	...	0.04	0.04	0.1	0.2
Objets en paille, en écorce, etc.	0.4	0.7	1.9	0.04	0.1	0.3
Papiers, jeux de cartes, papier de tenture, cartons	0.4	0.4	1.1	4.5	1.5	7.5
Produits chimiques	1.9	2.6	6.0	3.4	4.9	16.9
Poudre à tirer	...	...	...	0.1	0.1	0.4
Savons	0.1	0.2	0.1	0.1	0.04	0.2
Bougies et chandelles	0.1	0.1	0.1	0.1	0.1	1.9
Farines et produits farineux	0.1	0.1	4.9	1.5	1.1	13.5
Sucre raffiné	0.3	0.2	0.1	1.1	1.9	7.1
Eau-de-vie	0.3	30.4	2.2	1.1	1.9	35.2
Tabac	1.5	13.1	9.0	5.2	5.6	18.7
Livres	4.9	7.1	8.6	4.5	6.0	16.9
Instruments	0.4	0.4	1.1	1.5	6.7	5.7
Valeur totale	164.9	184.5	223.9	315.2	365.4	698.9

La signature récente d'un traité de commerce et de navigation entre la France et la Prusse, traité en ce moment soumis à l'examen des autres États de l'association, donne un intérêt particulier au tableau ci-après, relatif à nos relations commerciales avec le Zollverein. Il a été dressé d'après les documents français et indique les valeurs actuelles (en millions de francs). Il se rapporte au commerce spécial.

Années.	Importations en France.	Exportations de France.	Années.	Importations en France.	Exportations de France.
1847	52.7	46.2	1853	69.9	49.0
1848	23.0	29.6	1854	75.7	54.6
1849	32.3	38.0	1855	118.1	65.5
1850	36.2	44.7	1856	110.3	89.7
1851	38.1	44.1	1857	120.7	117.7
1852	43.3	42.3	1858	106.8	147.7

Les importations du Zollverein en France portent principalement sur des matières premières de l'industrie (laines, bestiaux, houille, coke, bois, peaux brutes, poils). Les soieries et les lainages y figurent cependant pour un chiffre assez élevé.

Les exportations de la France pour le Zollverein ont, au contraire, pour objets principaux des produits frabriqués, comme les soieries, les lainages, les vêtements et lingeries, les cotonnades imprimées; les peaux ouvrées, les fils de laine, les outils et instruments, etc. La France expédie en outre dans de Zollverein, quand la récolte est bonne, des quantités assez considérables de vins ordinaires.

S'il fallait juger, d'après le mouvement de la navigation dans les ports prussiens, de l'importance relative du commerce du Zollverein avec les divers États européens, c'est avec l'Angleterre qu'il entretiendrait le mouvement d'affaires le plus considérable. Viendraient ensuite, par ordre décroissant de trafic, les trois royaumes scandinaves, la Hollande, les portes anséatiques, la France, la Russie, etc. Mais il ne faut pas perdre de vue qu'en ce qui concerne la France, la plus grande partie de son commerce avec le Zollverein se fait par la voie de terre.

Les recettes des douanes du Zollverein ont oscillé ainsi qu'il suit de 1834 à 1859 (nombres en millions de francs).

Années.	Importation.	Exportation.	Transit.	Années.	Importation.	Exportation.	Transit.
1834	52.1	1.5	1.9	1847	100.9	3.0	1.5
1835	59.6	1.9	1.9	1848	85.5	1.5	1.1
1836	65.6	1.9	1.9	1849	88.9	1.5	1.9
1837	63.7	1.5	2.2	1850	86.2	1.1	1.9
1838	72.4	1.9	1.9	1851	87.0	1.1	1.5
1839	73.9	1.9	2.6	1852	91.1	1.1	1.5
1840	76.9	1.9	2.6	1853	82.5	1.1	1.9
1841	80.2	1.5	2.2	1854	86.2	0.7	1.5
1842	85.5	1.5	2.2	1855	97.5	0.7	2.2
1843	92.6	1.5	2.2	1856	98.6	0.7	1.5
1844	96.0	1.9	2.6	1857	99.0	0.7	1.5
1845	101.6	1.5	1.5	1858	106.1	0.7	1.5
1846	99.5	1.9	1.1	1859	88.1	0.7	1.5

Les faibles oscillations du produit des douanes depuis 1844 constituent le trait saillant de ce tableau. Toutefois, cet état à peu près stationnaire des recettes ne saurait être interprété, en présence des documents qui précèdent, comme le signe d'un mouvement d'affaires peu progressif. Il ne faut pas perdre de vue, d'ailleurs, que les plus grand nombre des matières premières

ont été, en 1851 et depuis, ou complétement affranchies ou considérablement dégrevées. Les droits de transit ont également été l'objet d'importantes réductions jusqu'au moment de leur suppression en 1861. . . . .
En 1858 et 1859, les recettes à l'importation (seulement), ramenées à 100,000, se sont réparties ainsi qu'il suit entre les États qui précèdent (Francfort-sur-le-Mein non compris) : —

	1858.	1859.
Prusse	50,920	54,021
Bavière	13,188	13,022
Hanovre	10,062	10,321
Saxe	5,194	5,980
Wurtemberg	4,843	4,769
Bade	3,808	4,759
Thuringe	2,975	2,941
Hesse (Grand-duché)	2,460	2,431
Hesse (Électorale)	2,058	1,972
Oldenbourg	1,268	1,310
Nassau	1,242	1,228
Brunswick	713	704
Luxembourg	549	542
Totaux	100,000	100,000

Voici quelle a été la répartition de la recette nette entre les divers États, de 1857 à 1859 (valeurs en millions de francs) : —

	1857.	1858.	1859.	Pour 100.
Prusse	45,330,221	49,468,492	39,776,546	50.77
Bavière	11,635,260	12,689,373	10,055,831	12.84
Hanovre	9,156,903	9,704,025	7,969,578	10.18
Saxe	5,282,801	5,762,655	4,677,101	5.97
Wurtemberg	4,273,155	4,667,726	3,679,368	4.70
Bade	3,359,430	3,070,278	2,902,875	3.71
États de Thuringe	2,657,085	2,898,435	2,300,415	2.94
Hesse (Grand Duché)	2,147,583	2,370,881	1,877,872	2.40
Hesse (Électorale)	1,815,843	1,983,858	1,522,751	1.94
Oldenbourg	1,154,006	1,223,058	1,011,798	1.29
Nassau	1,096,125	1,197,142	948,247	1.21
Francfort-sur-le-Mein	717,188	781,402	667,983	0.85
Brunswick	633,926	691,882	548,051	0.70
Luxembourg	484,833	529,695	418,218	0.50
Totaux	89,744,369	97,938,902	78,356,634	100.00

La colonne des rapports centésimaux des deux tableaux qui précèdent, appelle tout particulièrement l'attention en indiquant les États qui gagnent ou perdent à l'association. Ainsi, par exemple, la Prusse, qui encaisse 58.82 p. 100 des recettes totales, ne figure que pour 50.77 dans la répartition, tandis que, pour la Bavière, ces rapports sont respectivement de 5.15 à le recette et de 12.84 à la répartition. En résumé, les États gagnants sont les suivants : Bavière, Hanovre, Wurtemberg, les deux Hesses, la Thuringe, Oldenbourg et Nassau. La Prusse, le Luxembourg, la Saxe, Bade, Brunswick et Francfort-sur-le-Mein composent la série des perdants. Les parts du Zollverein sont ceux de la Prusse, du duché d'Oldenbourg et du Hanovre. Les documents qui suivent indiquent le mouvement de la navigation de ces ports de 1856 à 1859 (grand et petit cabotage non compris).

PORTS PRUSSIENS.

ANNÉES.	BÂTIMENTS.		TONNEAUX.[1]		BÂTIMENTS SUR LEST.[2]		TONNEAUX.	
	Entrés.	Sortis.	Entrés.	Sortis.	Entrés.	Sortis.	Entrés.	Sortis.
1859	9,116	9,197	1,471,522	1,414,602	2,668	1,743	452,846	319,458
1858	8,922	9,032	1,401,560	1,469,582	2,590	1,939	433,788	401,614
1857	8,533	8,441	1,584,622	1,564,384	3,052	1,229	561,130	254,432
1856	7,582	7,684	1,337,746	1,374,416	1,994	2,111	381,850	380,310

Dans le duché d'Oldenbourg, la navigation a été en 1859 : à l'entrée, de 933 navires chargés, jaugeant 78,484 lasts et de 11 sur lest, jaugeant 879 lasts ; à la sortie, de 311 navires chargés, jaugeant 38,295 lasts et de 502 sur lest avec 37,821 lasts.

PORTS HANOVRIENS.

		NAVIRES CHARGÉS.		NAVIRES SUR LEST.	
		Nombre.	Lasts.	Nombre.	Lasts.
1859	Entré	1,141	36,850	782	21,664
	Sortie	1,092	29,270	899	32,964
1858	Entré	3,016	112,931	592	21,858
	Sortie	1,194	36,459	2,470	100,281

Les avantages purement matériels du Zollverein pour les États

[1] Le tonneau de mer prussien = 968k.80.
[2] Compris dans les totaux précédents.

intéressées peuvent se résumer ainsi qu'il suit : 1° reduction des frais de perception et d'administration, par suite de la suppression des rayons de douanes entre les États associés ; 2° rapide developpement industriel, par suite de l'application d'un tarif modéré ; 3° élevation du chiffre primitif des recettes de douane, par suite de l'accroissement de consommation résultant de l'application de ce tarif ; 4° conclusion de traités de commerce avantageux avec l'étranger, plus disposé à faire des concessions à un État qui lui offre un débouché considérable qu'à des pays sans importance ; 5° usage gratuit ou à des conditions tres modérées des grandes voies de communication terrestres, fluviales ou maritimes, qui n'existaient auparavant qu'au profit d'un ou de quelques-uns d'entre eux ; 6° rapide essor de certaines industries indigènes, auxquelles la libre ouverture d'un marché intérieur de 33 millions d'habitants,[1] ainsi que l'usage en franchise de matières premières fournies par l'un ou l'autre des États associés et autrefois frappées de droits de douane, permettent de produire plus économiquement ; 7° création d'une forte marine marchande.

L'institution du Zollverein a eu des avantages correspondants pour le commerce étranger. Au lieu d'avoir á traverser 40 lignes douanières, défendues par des droits plus ou moins compliqués, plus ou moins élevés, et appliqués par des administrations plus ou moins tracassières, il s'est trouvé en face d'un pays unique, recevant ses produits à des conditions relativement modérées. Au lieu d'avoir à traiter avec des consommateurs peu aisés, restreignant leurs dépenses au plus strict nécessaire il a profité du developpement de la richesse publique dans le Zollverein devenu, aprés quelques années, un grand pays, non-seulement par le territoire et la population, mais encore par le bien-être croissant de sa population.

Le Zollverein n'est cependant pas, dans son organisation et ses résultats actuels, la formule la plus complète, la plus heureuse du principe de l'association commerciale. Le mode compliqué de ses délibérations ;[2] la difficulté, pour ses membres, d'arriver, sur les questions les plus graves, à une solution favorable aux intérêts souvent très-opposés qu'ils représentent ; les influences politiques qui s'agitent dans son sein et l'empêchent de discerner toujours

---
[1] D'aprés le dénombrement de 1861 dont les résultats officiels nous arrivent en ce moment, de 34,705,694 habitants.
[2] On sait que toutes les délibérations du Zollverein, pour être valables, doivent être prises à l'unanimité. Ainsi, dans ces délibérations, la Prusse ne pèse pas d'un plus grand poids que Francfort-sur-le Mein avec ses 80,000 habitants ! . . .

clairement la voie à suivre pour tirer de l'union les résultats économiques les plus considérables, telles sont les justes critiques dont il a souvent été l'objet. On peut encore lui reprocher de maintenir, malgré l'exemple de l'Angleterre et de la France, des droits qui, pour certains produits fabriqués, dépassent très-sensiblement, par le fait de la diminution considérable, depuis la formation du Zollverein, du prix des produits grevés, cette moyenne de 10 p. 100 de la valeur, destinée, d'après le programme de l'association, à son début à devenir la base de son tarif. Cette protection exagérée est une double faute, d'abord parce que les consommateurs de l'association, moins aisés que ceux des deux pays que nous venons de citer, sont moins en état de payer des prix élevés ; puis, parce que le Zollverein, par les perfectionnements introduits dans ses procédés de fabrication et le bas prix de la main-d'œuvre, est aujourd'hui tout à fait en mesure de lutter efficacement contre la concurrence étrangère. 1862.

IX.

THE CORN LAWS.

FROM LEVI'S HISTORY OF BRITISH COMMERCE, 2D ED.

PART III.—CHAP. 8.

THE corn laws had long been a bone of contention in England. Maintained for the interest of a class who clung to them as their anchor of safety, they had always been attacked as an obstacle to the well-being of the middle and lower classes. In the opinion of their advocates, protection was necessary in order to keep certain poor lands in cultivation, and to encourage the cultivation of as much land as possible in order to provide for the wants of the country. Let the cultivation of such lands cease, they said, and we shall be dependent on foreigners for a large portion of the people's food. Such dependence, moreover, may be fraught with immense danger, inasmuch as, in the event of war, the supplies may be stopped or our ports may be blockaded, the result of which may be famine, disease, or civil war. According to the defenders of protection it was the advantage gained by the corn laws that enabled landed proprietors and their tenants to encourage manufactures and trade. Abolish the corn laws and half the country shopkeepers will be ruined, mills and factories will be stopped, large numbers of the working-classes will be thrown out of work, disturbances will ensue, capital will be withdrawn, and no one dare venture to say what may be the fatal consequences.

In 1801 the price of wheat reached the high limit of 155s. a quarter, and we may well imagine what sufferings that price entailed among the people, at a time especially when trade and manufacture were so much paralysed by the Continental war. Happily, for two or three years afterwards, a succession of good harvests changed the condition of things, and in March, 1804, the price of wheat fell to 49s. 6d. per imperial quarter. But what was anxiously desired by the people was regarded a great disaster by the agricultural interest. They complained that with the high cost of production, in consequence of high wages, high rate of interest, and the heavy cost of implements of husbandry, they could not afford to sell at such prices. Meetings were held throughout the country to consider the case of the farmers. Mr. Western brought the state of agriculture before the House of Commons, and a committee was appointed on the subject. The farmers contended that at a time when all foreign supplies were shut out from our markets, and when we were more than ever depending on home production, it was the bounden duty of the legislature to pass laws which would encourage the production of grain at home, so that the nation might be as much as possible independent as regards the first necessaries of life. Unfortunately all the measures hitherto taken for the protection of the farmers resulted only in the aggravation of the sufferings of the people. It was easy by means of prohibitions and bounties to raise the price of corn and to give an artificial stimulus to agricultural prosperity, but the people were not able to buy bread at famine prices, especially at a time when taxes were so heavy. The report of the committee of the House of Commons, presented the same session in 1804, was to the effect that the price of corn from 1791 to the harvest of 1803 had been very irregular, but that upon an average it had increased in a great degree in consequence of the years of scarcity, and had in general yielded a fair profit to the grower. It appeared to the committee, moreover, that high prices had the effect of stimulating agricultural industry in bringing into cultivation large tracts of waste lands, and that this fact combined with the abundance of the two last productive seasons, and other causes, occasioned such a depression in the value of grain as would tend to the discouragement of agriculture, unless maintained by the support of Parliament. Nor was there much difficulty in persuading the legislature to give heed to such recommendations. Very soon after the presentation of the report a corn law was passed,[1] which imposed a duty of 24s. 3d. per quarter on wheat so long as the price of the home market should be under 63s.; of 2s. 6d. so long as the price should be at or above that rate, and under 66s.; and of 6d. a quarter when the price should be above that rate. It does not appear, however, that the fear entertained by the farmers and the agricultural interest had been very substantial, for in the same year the harvest was deficient in quantity and inferior in quality, and all appre-

---

[1] 44 Geo. III. c. 109.

hensions that bread might become too cheap were entirely out of the question. A proposal, indeed, was made to encourage the growth of corn in Great Britain, and yet to diminish the price thereof for the benefit of the people by exempting farmers from all direct taxes. But such a plan would have only transferred the burden from one class to another. The time had not yet arrived for acting on the "laissez-faire" principle. Artificial aid was sought for on all sides, and that always ended in disappointment.

At the conclusion of the French war, in 1815, precisely the same state of matters arose as in 1804. By the opening of the ports, wheat which hitherto averaged 5l. 10s. a quarter suddenly fell to 3l. 5s., and immediately the farmers raised a cry of distress. Again a committee of the House of Commons was appointed to inquire into the state of the law affecting the corn trade, and once more the legislature was engaged in framing a corn law,[1] which resulted in an act prohibiting the importation of wheat when the price was under 80s., and rendering it free when above 80s. Yet, serious misgivings existed as to the ultimate effect of the restrictive legislation respecting corn in the minds of many, and in the very House of Lords, which traditionally stood in bold defence of a protective policy, protests were lodged, which indicated the existence of a more enlightened opinion on the real bearings of the whole question. Lord Grenville and his compeers protested against this new corn law, because they were adverse in principle to all new restraints in commerce, deeming it most advantageous to public prosperity to leave uncontrolled the free current of national industry. In their opinion "the great practical rule of leaving all commerce unfettered, applied more peculiarly, and on still stronger grounds of justice as well as of policy, to the corn trade than to any other. Irresistible, indeed, must be that necessity which could, in their judgment, authorize the legislature to tamper with the sustenance of the people, and to impede the free purchase and sale of that article, on which depends the existence of so large a portion of the community. They thought that expectations of ultimate benefit from any corn law were founded on a delusive theory. They could not persuade themselves that such a law would ever contribute to produce plenty, cheapness, or steadiness

---

[1] 55 Geo. III. c. 26.

of price. So long as it operated at all, its effects must be the opposite of these. Monopoly is the parent of scarcity, dearness, and uncertainty. To cut off any of the sources of supply can only tend to lessen its abundance. To close against ourselves the cheapest market for any commodity, must enhance the price at which we purchase it. And to confine the consumer of corn to the produce of his own country, is to refuse ourselves the benefit of that provision which Providence itself has made for equalizing to man the variations of climate and of seasons. But, whatever might be the future consequences of that law, at some distant and uncertain period they were convinced that these hopes must be purchased at the expense of a great and present evil. To compel the consumer to purchase corn dearer at home than it might be imported from abroad was the immediate practical effect of the law just passed. In this way alone could it operate. Its present protection, its promised extension of agriculture must result (if at all) from the profits which it created by keeping up the price of corn to an artificial level. These future benefits were the consequences expected, though they confidently believed erroneously expected, from giving a bounty to the grower of corn by a tax levied on its consumers." Such were the reasons urged against the corn law of 1815, and certainly they do honor to those who recorded them in the journal of the House. But many a year was to pass ere the protests of the few did become the deliberate conviction of the entire community.

For twelve years nothing further occurred on the subject of the corn laws, except the emission of repeated cries of distress by the agricultural classes, especially in the House of Lords. The country was indeed learning by bitter experience how direct is the relation between dear bread and bad trade, and the time arrived when the working of the corn law was to be laid before the legislature. "The corn laws," said Mr. Whitmore, "have inflicted the greatest injury upon the general trade of the world that ever, perhaps, was produced by injudicious legislation. They have deranged its course, stagnated its current, and caused it to flow in new and far less beneficial channels than it formerly occupied. To the corn laws he attributed the great and ruinous fluctuation of prices, which is the inevitable result of a system of restriction. The more the basis from whence your supplies are drawn is widened, the greater the steadiness of prices; the more it is narrowed, the more constant and the more fatal is their effect on the fluctuations to which you are subject. In the early times, when there was a difficulty in the conveyance of bulky commodities from one part of the country to another, arising from want of roads, when there existed a prejudice as well as a legal penalty against what was called forestalling and regrating, the fluctuations in prices were immense. And the same holds good as regards other times and other countries." Lord Lauderdale himself, while entertaining considerable fear of foreign competition, clearly showed what are the solid and what are the fictitious ways to agricultural prosperity. " I will take upon myself," he said, " to assert, that, if there is any one proposition in political economy which may be affirmed, it is this, that the interests of landlords properly understood are absolutely identified with the general interests of the country. Landlords have no interest in high prices; high prices raise rents nominally and in appearance; and now and then, some temporary advantage may be obtained from them, for which landlords will always pay afterwards with more than compound interest; but rents can only be raised largely, permanently, and beneficially to landlords by one of two causes, both of which are equally conducive to the prosperity of all other classes; first, by improvements in agriculture, which leave a larger surplus produce after the expenses of cultivation are defrayed; and, secondly, by improved and extended markets. Now, all improvements of agriculture which increase the surplus produce of the country are obviously a direct addition to the public wealth. And how are markets improved and extended? By new communication, — roads, railways, canals, — but principally by the continual rise and increase of large towns within our own empire, rendered rich and prosperous by thriving manufactures, and by all the improvements in skill and machinery connected with such establishments. The best job for the landlord is the prosperity of trade in all its branches, as the best job for trade is a prosperous state of agriculture. There is nothing to make the inhabitant of the town and the cultivator of the soil jealous of each other; quite the contrary, for the more each produces, the more he will have to exchange for the other; and this is the foundation of the great internal trade which is worth one hundred times more than all the foreign commerce of the country put together."

Yet, notwithstanding the enunciation of these truths, the farmers clung tenaciously to protection; and it was not without a great struggle that they allowed the corn laws to be relaxed to a small extent. In the session of 1827 resolutions were passed in the House of Commons, to the effect that corn should be allowed to be imported free of duty, in order to be warehoused, and that it should be admissible for home consumption at a shilling per quarter duty when the price of wheat should be 70s., and at two shillings more for every shilling that the price fell below 70s. per quarter. These resolutions, however, made no progress, in consequence of the change of government. The following session the House of Commons passed other resolutions, to the effect of imposing a sliding scale from 23s. per quarter when the price of wheat should be 64s., and 16s. 8d. when the price should be 69s., to one shilling per quarter when the price should be at and above 73s. per quarter. And upon these bases a new corn law was passed,[1] which, like its predecessors, did not long remain in force.

It was ten years after the passing of this first sliding scale, or on March 15, 1838, that Mr. Villiers, seconded by Sir William Molesworth, first commenced his attack on the policy of the corn laws in the House of Commons, though with little effect. In those days political economists were simply allowed to speak and complain. Their opinions were received as mere speculative theories, their recommendations were deemed as far beyond the reach of practical statesmanship. There was only one minister present when Mr. Villiers' motion was made, and, as might have been expected, it was lost by an overwhelming majority. But about that time a lecture was advertised to be delivered at Bolton, the birthplace of Arkwright and Crompton, on the corn laws, by a person quite a stranger to the town. It was a new subject for a lecture, and, as the public mind was directed to the question, the lecture drew a fair number of hearers. The lecturer, however, found, only when it was too late, that it was not easy to deal with economic questions before a mixed audience, and he completely broke down. The audience, not prepared for the disappointment, became impatient and vociferous, and a riot was impending, when a youth, a medical student, rushed to the platform, and on the spur of the moment addressed the people on the subject in a vigorous and manly manner. The people were delighted at this turn, and Mr. Paulton won for himself enthusiastic admiration. On the

---

[1] 9 Geo. IV. c. 38.

news of such an event travelling to the neighboring towns, the volunteer lecturer was overwhelmed with invitations to redeliver his address, and everywhere he captivated the audience with his eloquent attacks on monopoly and monopolists.

As the interest in the question of the corn laws grew and extended, it became evident that a special and more popular agency was wanted for the purpose, and thus, in October of 1838, eight[1] men first united themselves with a view to establish an Anti-Corn Law Association. The list of the provisional committee was afterwards increased to thirty-seven, conspicuous among them being John Bright, George Wilson, and Richard Cobden. And the object of the association was declared to be to form a fund in order to diffuse information, by lectures or pamphlets, on the bearing of the corn laws, to defray the expense of petitioning, and, above all, to create an organization to bring numbers together in such force and with such energy of purpose, as to secure the great object, viz., the complete freedom of trade, by the destruction, not only of the corn monopoly, but of all the other monopolies bolstered up by this monster grievance. Small was the support at first obtained by this new association. Very few then appreciated its great moral importance. "For the first two or three years of our agitation," said Mr. Cobden, " it was a very hopeless matter, and there was no éclat nor applause. . . . We sat in a small room, and we had a dingy red curtain drawn across the room that we might not be chilled by the paucity of our numbers. Two or three were all that were here (Newall's Buildings) on one occasion, and I recollect saying to my friend Prentice, ' What a lucky thing it is the monopolists cannot draw aside that curtain and see how many of us there are, for, if they could, they would not be much frightened.'" It was not long, however, ere the small association began to manifest its power and influence, and when, aided by the powerful support of some, at least, of the leading journals, its voice resounded through the length and breadth of the land. Meetings and conferences then succeeded each other. From the manufacturing districts the movement spread to the metropolis, and with a clearly defined purpose in view, and with the highest economic authorities to appeal to in support of their principles, the Anti-Corn

---

[1] The original founders of the League were John Benjamin Smith, Archibald Prentice, Richard Cobden, Thomas Bazley, William Rawson, W. R. Callender, Henry and Edmund Ashworth. (See *Cobden and the League*, by Henry Ashworth, Esq.)

Law agitators made everywhere a profound and lasting impression.

On March 12, 1839, Mr. Villiers again brought the subject of the corn laws before the House of Commons, now, however, backed by a strong party both inside and outside the House. His motion was, "That this House resolve itself into a committee of the whole House, to take into consideration the act 9 George IV., regulating the importation of foreign grain." Mr. Villiers showed that the corn laws were not beneficial to the agricultural interest, and that neither the agricultural laborer nor the farmers reaped from them any benefit. He asserted that the community at large suffered a loss through the corn laws, equal to a poll tax of 8s. a head, or a tax of £2 on each family in the kingdom, and he demonstrated that commerce and shipping were greatly injured by them. Mr. Villiers' motion was seconded by Sir George Strickland, and on his side spoke Mr. Poulett Thomson, Sir William Molesworth, Mr. Grote, Mr. Clay, Lord Howich, Sir Henry Parnell, Mr. Ward, Lord John Russell, Mr. Hume, Mr. Fielden, and Mr. O'Connell; whilst against him were Sir James Graham, Sir Robert Peel, and a host of Conservatives. The discussion was animated and well sustained, and after five whole nights' debate the votes were taken and the motion was lost by 195 to 342. In the House of Lords, too, a discussion was commenced on the subject. On March 14 the Earl of Fitzwilliam moved, "That the act 9 George IV. c. 60, entitled 'An Act to amend the law relating to the importation of corn,' has failed to secure that steadiness in the price of grain which is essential to the best interests of the country;" but the motion was lost by 24 against 224. A day after Lord Brougham moved, "That this House do immediately resolve itself into a committee of the whole House, to take into consideration the importation of foreign corn." But the motion met a similar fate, only 7 having voted for it, and 61 against it. Slow is the progress of any measure in the House of Commons when any substantial reform is contemplated, but slower still is its advance in the House of Lords. Coming less in contact with the mass of the people, comparatively strangers to their feelings and wants, conservative by interest and hereditary policy, the peers of the realm are necessarily the last to admit the need of change, and the last to make concessions to the altered exigencies of the times. Nevertheless, there have never been wanting enlightened members in the upper House who sought the maintenance and preservation of their order from that same law of progress on which all the institutions of the realm depend, and who, far from regarding their interests as antagonistic to those of other classes of society, had the wisdom to discern that we are all subject to the same laws, influenced by the same circumstances, and alike bound to obey those laws of nature, which, more than any human contrivance, determine the progress and prosperity of states.

The result of Mr. Villiers' motion in the House of Commons was not likely to discourage the Anti-Corn Law Association. On the contrary, it imparted to it a new life and a fresh impulse. Determined to persevere till the end, the agitators saw in the strength of their opponents only an additional cause for more energetic labors. A meeting was accordingly organized in London, and the same voice which first gave strength and vivacity to the Manchester gathering, was now heard exclaiming, "We are the representatives of three millions of people, — a far greater number of constituents than the House ever could boast of. We well know that no great principle was ever indebted to Parliament for success; the victory must be gained out of doors. The great towns of Britain have extended the right hand of fellowship to each other, and their alliance will be a Hanseatic league against the feudal corn-law plunderers." The Anti-Corn Law League was never a political organization. For years its members went on lecturing, distributing tracts, and acting as a peripatetic university in instructing the people on the evil of commercial monopoly. Never did it allow itself to be tempted to other political topics. The League did not even wish to interfere with the system of taxation, further than extinguishing, at once and forever, the principle of maintaining taxes for the benefit of a particular class. "If it be asked," said Mr. Cobden, " why it is that we, professing to be free-traders in everything, should restrict the title of our association to that of the ' National Anti-Corn Law League,' I will explain the reason. We advocate the abolition of the corn law because we believe that to be the foster-parent of all other monopolies; and if we destroy that, — the parent, the monster monopoly, — it will save us the trouble of destroying all the rest."

PART IV.—CHAP. I.

The day arrived when the government of the country had to be confided to the great Conservative party in the House. For some time past the administration of Lord Melbourne had shown unmistakable signs of inherent weakness, and its opponents, counting among them such men as Sir Robert Peel, Lord Stanley, Mr. Gladstone, and Mr. Disraeli, were decidedly gaining strength and influence. The Conservative party has been charged with thwarting and opposing the liberal tendencies of the nation, and they certainly resisted the passing of the Reform Bill, the repeal of the Test and Corporation Acts, and the Emancipation of Roman Catholics. Yet a memorable Conservative administration is before us, which inaugurated an era of great prosperity, and one which, under the presiding genius of Sir Robert Peel, has ever since been held in grateful remembrance for the practical wisdom which it displayed, and the bold and vigorous commercial and financial policy it carried into effect. Sir Robert Peel had already gained for himself a high reputation as a statesman.[1] As a member of the Bullion Committee of 1810, as under-secretary for the colonies during the most trying years of the Continental War, as secretary for Ireland, in all these capacities he proved himself an able minister and an economist of much practical wisdom ; and it was a good omen for the country when, in September, 1841, at a time of much financial anxiety, Sir Robert Peel was called to take the helm of the State.

There was something novel and encouraging in the speech from the throne which opened the labors of the new administration. " Her Majesty is anxious that this object, viz., the increase of the public revenue, should be effected in the manner least burdensome to her people ; and it has appeared to Her Majesty, after full deliberation, that you may, at this juncture, properly direct your attention to the revision of duties affecting productions of foreign countries. It will be for you to consider, whether some of the duties are not so trifling in amount as to be unproductive to the revenue, while they are vexatious to com-

---

[1] Sir Robert Peel's first administration was a short one. He formed his Cabinet on December 9, 1834, and forthwith dissolved Parliament. A new Parliament was summoned to meet on February 19, 1835, but an amendment to the address was carried in the House of Commons on February 26, by a majority of 309 to 302. Other adverse divisions immediately thereafter took place, and Sir Robert Peel announced his resignation of the ministry on April 8.

merce. You may further examine whether the principle of prohibition, in which others of these duties are founded, be not carried to an extent injurious alike to the income of the state and the interest of the people. Her Majesty is desirous that you should consider the laws which regulate the trade in corn. It will be for you to determine whether those laws do not aggravate the natural fluctuation of supply, whether they do not embarrass trade, derange currency, and by their operation diminish the comfort and increase the privations of the great body of the community." Surely this was a programme more liberal than could have been expected from a Conservative ministry; but the temper of the people and the exigencies of the time demanded that and a great deal more. Gloom and discontent prevailed extensively throughout the manufacturing districts. The Anti-Corn-Law League had by this time become formidable. The demand was loud and imperious for cheap food, and the total repeal of the corn laws. And on the day fixed for the announcement of the ministerial measure some five hundred deputies from the Anti-Corn-Law Associations in the metropolis and provinces went in procession to the House of Commons, but were refused admittance. Yet with all this the government was not disconcerted, and with imperturbable gravity on February 9, 1842, Sir Robert Peel exposed the policy of the cabinet on the corn laws.

At first Sir Robert Peel did not attach much weight to the influence of these laws. In his speech in the House, he said that to his mind the question was not so much what was the price of food, as what was the command which the laboring classes of the population had of all that constituted the enjoyments of life. His belief and the belief of his colleagues was, that it was important for the country to take care that the main source of the supply of corn should be derived from domestic agriculture. And he contended that a certain amount of protection was absolutely required for that industry. But he made a most important avowal, one which no Protectionist ministry had ever made, that protection should not be retained for the special benefit of any particular class, but only for the advantage of the nation at large, and in so far only as was consistent with the general welfare of all classes of society. Sir Robert Peel then entered on the extent of such protection, and having taken 54s. to 58s. per quarter, as the price at which corn should range for a fair remuneration to the agriculturist, he asked, Shall the corn laws be based on a sliding scale, or on a fixed duty? Much might be said for the one and for the other. A sliding scale was introduced in France in 1819, one had been adopted in Belgium, the Netherlands, and other countries, and it seemed to have the advantage of adapting itself to every circumstance. But experience did not confirm the hopes entertained of its working. It did not hinder prices falling lower than was desirable in years of scarcity; and it had the same prejudicial effect as every corn law of causing the cultivation of land to be regulated, not by inherent capacity, but by the amount of forced stimulus given to it by the Legislature. Besides these radical defects the objections urged against the sliding scale were, that the reduction of duty was so rapid as to hold out temptation to fraud; that it operated as an inducement to retain corn, or combine for the purpose of influencing the averages; that the rapid decline of the duty was injurious to the consumer, the producer, the revenue, and the commerce of the country; that it was injurious to the consumer because, when corn was at a high price—say, between 66s. and 70s.—and just when it would be for the public advantage that corn should be liberated for the purpose of consumption, the joint operation of increased price and diminished duty induced the holders to keep it back, in the hope of realizing the price of upwards of 70s. and so paying only 1s. duty; that it operated injuriously to the agricultural interest, because it held out a temptation to keep back corn until it could be suddenly entered for consumption at the lowest amount of duty, when the agriculture lost the protection which the law intended it should possess; that it was injurious to the revenue, because, instead of corn being entered for home consumption when it arrived, it was retained until it could be introduced at 1s., the revenue losing the difference between 1s. and the amount of duty which would otherwise have been levied; that it was injurious to commerce, because, when corn was grown at a distance — in America for instance — the grower was subject to the disadvantage that before his cargo arrived in this country the sudden entries of wheat at 1s. duty from countries nearer England might have so diminished the price and increased the duty, as to cause his speculation to prove not only a failure but ruinous. These were formidable objections to any sliding scale, but between a gradual and a fixed rate of duty there was not a material difference. On the other hand, a fixed duty of 8s. per quarter was too low as a protection in time of abundance, and was in effect a prohibitory duty in time of scarcity. Nor was it possible to maintain more than a nominal duty when prices began to rise. It was indeed difficult to strike the balance of advantage and inconvenience between the sliding scale and the fixed duty. So, on the whole, Sir Robert Peel favored the principle of the sliding scale—that is, of making the duty upon corn vary inversely with the price in the home market, taking the average of the market prices from returns collected by excise officers. Having, therefore, decided on charging 20s. duty when the average price of wheat was 50s. and 51s. per quarter, he proposed to make the duty fall by a reduction of 1s. a quarter as the average price rose 1s. with some slight modifications, so that the duty should be only 1s. per quarter, when the price of wheat rose to 73s. a quarter and upwards, and a bill so framed he presented to the House of Commons. The House was not prepared at the time for a very liberal measure. Lord John Russell made a motion in favor of a fixed duty, but it was not popular, and, notwithstanding a few expressions of dissatisfaction, the Government proposal was well received. Lord John Russell's amendment was lost by 226 to 349, and Sir Robert Peel's bill passed into law.[1] But the country was not satisfied. Meetings continued to be held in the manufacturing districts, and Mr. Villiers, stimulated by the representations and efforts of the Anti-Corn-Law League, again brought forward his motion for the total repeal of the corn laws, which was again lost by the enormous majority of 90 to 393. The battle of the corn laws had by this time become violent, both in and out of Parliament, and Mr. Villiers was not likely to be dispirited by the result of this division.

It is not, however, by the vain attempt to render a corn law acceptable that the commercial administration of Sir Robert Peel will be remembered. That was, at best, a temporary and transitory measure. It is when we consider his financial policy as a whole, and more especially the plan which he devised for improving the state of the finances, and imparting new life to commerce and industry, that we recognize the breadth of view, the sound wisdom, and practical knowledge which Sir Robert Peel possessed. For years past the finances of the country had fallen into complete disorder. An annual deficiency of one or two millions had become a chronic evil, and no means of escape presented it-

---

[1] 5 & 6 Vict. c. 14. [Table omitted.]

self.[1] With a disaffected people, and frequent riots in the manufacturing districts, with a paralysed trade, and wages reduced to a very low scale, any idea of imposing new taxes, or making those existing heavier, was out of the question. A temporary and casual deficiency might have been met by an issue of exchequer bills; but what would have been the use of resorting to such expedient when there was no ground whatever for expecting any immediate improvement? On the other hand, to have recourse to loans in times of peace in order to balance the revenue and expenditure, was equally inadmissible. Sir Robert Peel knew that a timely and moderate reduction of taxes is favorable rather than injurious to the revenue. He knew that, though for the moment such a reduction might show a loss, nevertheless, by the stimulus it affords to increasing consumption, the revenue would soon recover itself, and probably exceed the amount previously produced. Yet, unfortunately, the few precedents he had for such an operation, attempted in times not very prosperous, were not encouraging. In 1825 the revenue from wine amounted to £2,153,000. The duty was then reduced from 9s. 1¼d. to 4s. 2¾d. per gallon; and what was the result? The year after the revenue was £1,400,000; it afterwards increased to £1,700,000, but it fell again to £1,400,000. The duty on tobacco had been reduced from 4s. to 3s. per lb. Before the reduction the revenue was £3,378,000; immediately after it fell to £2,600,000; and, though it rose somewhat from that point, it did not reach the previous amount. Of course the consumption of articles of luxury, such as wine and tobacco, is not so affected by a reduction of duty, as that of tea, sugar, and other necessaries of life. Moreover, the resources of the country were, at that time, comparatively undeveloped to admit of any large increase of consumption. Still, such experience did not warrant the expectation that a reduction of taxes would have the effect of filling the exchequer.

But the circumstances of trade required instant relief, and the tariff needed a thorough reform and simplification. Two years before, in 1840, on the motion of Mr. Hume, a committee of the House of Commons was appointed to inquire into the duties levied on imports, and to determine how far they were imposed for pur-

---

[1] The deficiency in the year ended April 5, 1841, was £1,157,601; in the year ended April 5, 1842, £117,627; and 1843, £2,704,510.

THE CORN LAWS.

poses of revenue ; and in their report the committee said : " The tariff of the United Kingdom presents neither congruity nor unity of purpose ; no general principles seem to have been applied. The tariff often aims at incompatible ends ; the duties are sometimes meant to be both productive of revenue and for protection, objects which are frequently inconsistent with each other. Hence they sometimes operate to the complete exclusion of foreign produce, and, in so far, no revenue can of course be received ; and sometimes, when the duty is inordinately high, the amount of revenue is, in consequence, trifling. They do not make the receipt of revenue the main consideration, but allow that primary object of fiscal regulations to be thwarted by the attempt to protect a great variety of particular interests at the expense of revenue, and of the commercial intercourse with other countries. Whilst the tariff has been made subordinate to many small-producing interests at home by the sacrifice of revenue, in order to support their interest, the same principle of interference is largely applied, by the various discriminating duties, to the produce of our colonies, by which exclusive advantages are given to the colonial interests at the expense of the mother country." Such were the general features of the tariff, the result of years of careless legislation on the subject. The fact was indeed too evident that it was necessary to prune the over-burdened tariff, and to liberate a large variety of articles from the needless trammels of legislation.

But how to accomplish this without a handsome surplus revenue? Fortunately Sir Robert Peel, undeterred by the state of the revenue, determined to do what was necessary for trade. And he acted wisely. Untrammel industry from the bonds of legal restrictions, open the avenue to wealth and prosperity : that is the right policy. Pursue this course, and there is no fear but the revenue will set itself speedily right. Some slight reductions he made in 1841, but on March 11, 1842, in his famous financial statement, he proposed to reduce considerably all the duties on the raw materials of manufacture, all duties on goods partially or wholly manufactured, as well as the duties on timber, and all export duties, together producing £1,500,000 ; and to make up this loss, as well as the duties on timber and all export duties, together producing £1,500,000 ; and to make up this loss, and to provide for the original deficit in the revenue, amounting to £2,570,000, by an income and property tax of 7d. in the pound, which he expected would produce £3,700,000;[1] by the equalization of the stamp and spirit duties, which would give £400,000; and by a small tax on the exportation of coals, which would give £200,000, making in all £4,310,000. It was a very simple plan; yet there was profound wisdom in Sir Robert Peel's budget. The value of the reductions proposed far exceeded the amount of relief in taxation they each and collectively afforded. The removal of the taxes on raw materials was a great boon, inasmuch as they had the effect of putting our manufactures in a disadvantageous position in the markets of the world, and restricting the field for the employment of capital and labor. As was said in the discussion on the budget, suppose 50,000 head of cattle were to be annually imported in consequence of such remissions, such importation would produce but a small effect on the price of meat, but it would create an import trade to the amount of half a million of money, a trade which, in its nature, would tend to produce an export trade, in return, of an equal amount. Our export trade is measured and limited by our import trade. If an individual merchant cannot afford to send his goods to other countries without obtaining any return, neither can all merchants collectively, and the country as a whole, afford to export commodities to foreign countries, if in some shape or other imports are not received from those countries in return. Reduce the duties on imports, and you thereby promote the export of our produce and manufactures. Remove those taxes which burden our manufactures, and you promote the importation of those articles which are necessary to the comfort and welfare of the nation. The income tax might be odious, "inquisitorial, intolerable," yet it was at that time the only means by which the necessary reforms in the tariff could be attempted. And the nation, having balanced the evil and the good of the proposal, and being convinced that the advantages preponderated, cheerfully accepted the government proposal, and gave to the proposal its hearty consent.

The commercial policy thus inaugurated by Sir Robert Peel, being in perfect accord with sound economic principles, could not fail to be successful. From 1841 to 1843, as we have seen, there was a yearly deficit in the budget. In the year ending April 5, 1844, Sir Robert Peel found himself in possession of a handsome

---

[1] The amount of duty assessed, in 1843, was £5,608,348. The amount of property assessed was: Schedule A, £95,284,497; Schedule B, £46,769,915; Schedule C, £27,909,793; Schedule D, £71,330,344; Schedule E, £9,718,454. Total, £251,013,003. [Additional note omitted.]

surplus of £2,600,000, which was exceeded in the following year, and continued at a high point for four consecutive years.[1] The exports of British produce, which in 1842 had fallen to £47,000,000, increased to £52,000,000 in 1843; to £58,000,000 in 1844; and £60,000,000 in 1845. The shipping entered and cleared increased from 9,000,000 tons in 1842 to 12,000,000 tons in 1845. In every way, financially and commercially, the results fully realized the anticipations formed, and Sir Robert was encouraged to advance still further in the same direction. Nothing important was attempted in the budget of 1843,[2] but in 1844 the duty on wool was abolished; the duties on currants and coffee were reduced, and a great change was made on the duties on marine insurance. And then, as we have seen in the previous chapter, the differential duties against foreign-grown sugar were relaxed, by permitting the importation of sugar, the growth of China, Java, or Manilla, or of any other countries which Her Majesty in council shall have declared to be admissible, at moderate rates. In 1845 another still more important series of reform was introduced. The duty on cotton wool, which, however slight and inappreciable on the coarser material, pressed rather heavily on the finer muslin, was abolished. The export duty on coals, which had been found vexatious and injurious, was removed. The timber duties were further reduced. The duty on glass was removed from the tariff, and also the duties on four hundred and thirty articles, which produced little or no revenue, including fibrous materials, such as silk, hemp, and flax, furniture, woods, cabinet-makers' materials, animal and vegetable oil, ores and minerals, etc. In 1846 the liberal policy was further extended. Hitherto our manufacturers had been benefited by the free access granted to the raw materials. It was right to ask of them to relinquish some, at least, of the protecting duties still in existence. And the duties on linen, woollen, and cotton manufactures were reduced from 20 to 10 per cent. The silk duties, then at 30 per cent., were also reduced to 15 per cent. A reduction was made on the duties on stained paper, on manufactures of metals, on earthenware, on carriages, and on manufactures of leather; and the duties on butter, cheese, and hops were further reduced.[3]

---

[1] The surplus in the year ended April 5, 1844, was £2,685,125; 1845, £3,027,615; 1846, £1,647,324; and in 1847, £2,823,762.

[2] [Foot-note on " Taxes Reduced or Repealed," omitted.]

[3] In 1842 there were 1,050 articles and subdivisions of articles charged with distinct rates of import duty in the Customs Tariff. In 1846 the number was reduced to 424.

But was it right to effect all these reforms without asking for reciprocity on the part of foreign countries? For years past it was known that Her Majesty's government had used every effort to enter into treaties with several states, such as Brazil, Portugal, Spain, and France, with a view to enter into a system of mutual concessions. In 1843 and 1844 Mr. Ricardo brought the subject before the House of Commons, and moved for an address to Her Majesty, praying that Her Majesty be pleased to give directions to her servants not to enter into any negotiations with foreign powers which would make any contemplated alterations of the tariff of the United Kingdom contingent on the alterations of the tariff of other countries; and expressing to Her Majesty the opinion of the House, that the great object of relieving the commercial intercourse between this country and foreign nations from all injurious restrictions, would be best promoted by regulating our own customs duties, as might be most suitable to the financial and commercial interests of this country, without reference to the amount of duties which foreign powers might think it expedient for their own interest to levy on British goods. But the government opposed the motion, and Mr. Ricardo was defeated. Mr. Gladstone especially defended the policy of endeavoring to obtain such treaties. He did not wish, he said, "to be trammelled by an abstract proposition, and unless Mr. Ricardo could show that there were no possible circumstances in which a commercial treaty could be aught other than evil, he had no right to call upon the House to affirm his resolution." The government, however, now practically acted on the policy advocated by Mr. Ricardo, and Sir Robert Peel avowed it frankly.

"I have no guarantee," he said,[1] "to give you that other countries will immediately follow our example. I give you that advantage in the argument. Wearied with our long and unavailing efforts to enter into satisfactory commercial treaties with other nations, we have resolved at length to consult our interests, and not to punish other countries for the wrong they do us in continuing their high duties upon the importation of our products and manufactures, by continuing high duties ourselves, encouraging unlawful trade. We have had no communication with any foreign government upon the subject of these reductions. We cannot promise that France will immediately make a corresponding

---

[1] Hansard's *Debates*, Jan. 27, 1846.

reduction in her tariff. I cannot promise that Russia will prove her gratitude to us for our reduction of duty on her tallow by any diminution of her duties. You may, therefore, say, in opposition to the present plan, 'What is this superfluous liberality that you are going to do away with all these duties, and yet you expect nothing in return?' I may, perhaps, be told that many foreign countries, since the former relaxation of duties on our part — and that would be perfectly consistent with the fact — foreign countries, which have benefited by our relaxations, have not followed our example: nay, have not only not followed our example, but have actually applied to the importation of British goods higher rates of duties than formerly. I quite admit it. I give you all the benefit of that argument. I rely upon that fact as conclusive proof of the policy of the course we are pursuing. It is a fact, that other countries have not followed our example, and have levied higher duties in some cases upon our goods. But what has been the result upon the amount of your exports? You have defied the regulations of these countries. Your export trade is greatly increased. Now, why is that so? Partly because of your acting without wishing to avail yourselves of their assistance; partly because of the smuggler, not engaged by you, in so many continental countries, whom the strict regulations and the triple duties which are to prevent the ingress of foreign goods have raised up; and partly, perhaps, because these very precautions against the ingress of your commodities are a burden, and the taxation increasing the cost of production, disqualify the foreigner from competing with you. But your exports, whatever be the tariff of other countries, or however apparent the ingratitude with which they have treated you, your export trade has been constantly increasing. By the remission of your duties upon the raw material, by inciting your skill and industry, by competition with foreign goods, you have defied your competitors in foreign markets, and you have been enabled to exclude them. Nothwithstanding their hostile tariffs the declared value of British exports has increased above £10,000,000 during the period which has elapsed since the relaxation of duties on your part. I say, therefore, to you, that these hostile tariffs, so far from being an objection to continuing your policy, are an argument in its favor. But, depend upon it, your example will ultimately prevail. When your example could be quoted in favor of restriction, it was quoted largely. When your example can be quoted in favor of relaxation as conducive to your interest, it may, perhaps, excite at first in foreign governments, in foreign boards of trade, but little interest or feeling; but the sense of the people of the great body of consumers will prevail; and in spite of the desire of government and boards of trade to raise revenue by restrictive duties, reason and common sense will induce relaxation of high duties. That is my firm belief." . . . .

PART IV.—CHAP. 4.

The Anti-Corn Law agitation was one of those movements which, being founded on right principles, and in harmony with the interest of the masses, was sure to gather fresh strength by any event affecting the supply of food. It was popular to attempt to reverse a policy which aimed almost exclusively to benefit one class of society. It was well known that the League wanted to outset an economic fallacy, and that they wished to relieve the people from a great burden. And as time elapsed and the soundness of the principles propounded by the League at their public meetings was more and more appreciated, their triumph became certain, and Her Majesty's government itself began to see that it was no longer possible to treat the agitation either by a silent passiveness, or by expressed contempt. The economic theorists had the mass of the people with them. Their gatherings were becoming more and more enthusiastic. And even amidst conservative landowners there were not a few enlightened and liberal minds who had already, silently at least, espoused the new ideas. No change certainly could be expected so long as bread was cheap, and labor abundant. But when a deficient harvest and a blight in the potato-crop crippled the resources of the people and raised grain to famine prices, the voice of the League acquired greater power and influence. Hitherto they had received hundreds of pounds. Now, thousands were sent in to support the agitation. A quarter of a million was readily contributed. Nor were the contributors. Lancashire mill-owners exclusively. Among them were merchants and bankers, men of heart and men of mind, the poor laborer, and the peer of the realm. The fervid oratory of Bright, the demonstrative and argumentative reasoning of Cobden, the more popular appeals of Fox, Rawlins, and other platform speakers, filled the newspaper press, and were eagerly read. And when Parliament dissolved in

August, 1845, even Sir Robert Peel showed some slight symptoms of a conviction that the days of the corn laws were numbered. Every day, in truth, brought home to his mind a stronger need for action, and as the ravages of the potato disease progressed he saw that all further resistance would be absolutely dangerous.

A cabinet council was held on October 31 of that year, to consult as to what was to be done, and at an adjourned meeting on November 5, Sir Robert Peel intimated his intention to issue an order in council remitting the duty on grain in bond to one shilling, and opening the ports for the admission of all species of grain at a smaller rate of duty, until a day to be named in the order; to call Parliament together on the 27th inst., in order to ask for an indemnity, and a sanction of the order by law; and to submit to Parliament, immediately after the recess, a modification of the existing law, including the admission at a nominal duty, of Indian corn and of British colonial corn. A serious difference of opinion, however, was found to exist in the cabinet, on the question brought before them; the only ministers supporting such measures being the Earl of Aberdeen, Sir James Graham, and Mr. Sidney Herbert. Nor was it easy to induce the other members to listen to reason. And though, at a subsequent meeting, held on November 28, Sir Robert Peel so far secured a majority in his favor, it was evident that the cabinet was too divided to justify him in bringing forward his measures, and he decided upon resigning office.

His resolution to that effect having been communicated to the Queen, Her Majesty summoned Lord John Russell to form a cabinet; and, to smooth his path, Sir Robert Peel, with characteristic frankness, sent a memorandum to Her Majesty, embodying a promise to give him his support. But Lord John Russell failed in his efforts, and the Queen had no alternative but to recall Sir Robert Peel, and give him full power to carry out his measures. It was under such circumstances that Parliament was called for January 22, 1846, and on January 27 the government plan was propounded before a crowded house. It was not an immediate repeal of the corn laws that Sir Robert Peel recommended. He proposed a temporary protection for three years, till February 1, 1849, imposing a scale during that time ranging from 4s., when the price of wheat should be 50s. per quarter and upward, and 10s. when the price should be under 48s. per quarter, and that after that period all grain should be admitted at the uniform duty of 1s. per quarter. The measure, as might have been expected, was received in a very different manner by the political parties in both houses of Parliament. There was treason in the conservative camp, and keen and bitter was the opposition they offered to the chief of their party. For twelve nights speaker after speaker indulged in personal recriminations. They recalled to Sir Robert Peel's memory the speeches he had made in defence of the corn laws. And as to his assertion that he had changed his mind they denied his right to do so. Mr. Colquhoun " wondered that Sir Robert could say, ' I have changed my opinion, and there is an end of it.' But there was not an end of it. His right hon. friend must not forget the laws by which the words of men of genius — whether orators or poets — are bound up with them. His right hon. friend's words could not thus pass away. They were winged shafts that pierced many minds. They remained after the occasion which produced them passed away. His right hon. friend must remember that the words which he had used adhered to the memory, moulded men's sentiments, guided public opinion. He must recollect that the armor of proof which he had laid aside, and the lance which he had wielded, and with which he had pierced many an encumbered opponent, remained weighty and entire. Greatly did he wish that his right hon. friend were again on this side to wield them — that he were here to lead their ranks and guide them by his prowess. But if not, they retained at least his arms; these lay at their feet, strewed all around them, an arsenal of power." Petulant remonstrances like these were of course of little avail. Sir Robert Peel and Mr. Cobden were ready to meet every challenge, and to refute every argument with their unanswerable logic of facts. And when the opposition endeavored to throw all the responsibility of a measure of such a character on the prime minister, Mr. Cobden besought them to turn from the will of one individual to those laws economic and divine which seemed to impose the duty of laying wide open the door for the importation of food. " Oh, then, divest the future prime minister of this country of that odious task of having to reconcile rival interests; divest the office, if ever you would have a sagacious man in power as prime minister, divest it of the responsibility of having to find food for the people! May you never find a prime minister again to undertake that awful responsibility! That responsibility belongs to the law of nature: as Burke said, ' it belongs to God alone to

THE CORN LAWS. 185

regulate the supply of the food of nations.' . . . We have set an example to the world in all ages; we have given them the representative system. The very rules and regulations of this House have been taken as the model for every representative assembly throughout the whole civilized world; and having besides given them the example of a free press, and civil and religious freedom, and every institution that belongs to freedom and civilization, we are now about giving a still greater example; we are going to set the example of making industry free—to set the example of giving the whole world every advantage of clime and latitude and situation, relying ourselves on the freedom of our industry. Yes, we are going to teach the world that other lesson. Don't think there is anything selfish in this, or anything at all discordant with Christian principles. I can prove that we advocate nothing but what is agreeable to the highest behests of Christianity. To buy in the cheapest market and sell in the dearest. What is the meaning of the maxim? It means that you take the article which you have in the greatest abundance, and with it obtain from others that of which they have the most to spare, so giving to mankind the means of enjoying the fullest abundance of earth's goods, and in doing so carrying out to the fullest extent the Christian doctrine of 'Do ye to all men as ye would they should do unto you.'" The passing of the measure was, however, more than certain, and after a debate of twelve nights' duration on Mr. Miles' amendment, the government obtained a majority of 97; 337 having voted for the motion and 240 against it. And from that evening the corn law may be said to have expired.[1] Not a day too soon, certainly, when we consider the straitened resources of the country as regards the first article of food, caused not only by the bad crop of grain, but by the serious loss of the potato crop, especially in Ireland.

Ireland had often grievously suffered from social and political wrongs, from absenteeism and repeal cries, from Protestant and Roman Catholic bigotry, from Orangeism and Ribbonism, from threatening notices and mid-day assassinations, but seldom has her cup of adversity been so brimful as in 1845 and 1846, from the failure of the potato crop. Though comparatively of recent introduction,—the first potato root having been imported by Sir Walter Raleigh in 1610,—potatoes had for years constituted a large propor-

---

[1] 9 and 10 Vict. c. 22, suspended by 10 and 11 Vict. c. 1.

tion of the food of the people of Ireland. A considerable acreage of land was devoted to that culture, and an acre of potatoes would feed more than double the number of individuals that can be fed from an acre of wheat. Such cultivation was, moreover, very attractive to small holders of land. It cost little labor. It entailed scarcely any expense, and little or no care was bestowed on it, since the people were quite satisfied with the coarsest and most prolific kind, called lumpers or horse potatoes. Nor was it the food of the people only in Ireland. Pigs and poultry shared the potatoes with the peasant's family, and often became the inmates of his cabin also. One great evil connected with potato culture is, that whilst the crop is precarious and uncertain, it cannot be stored up. The surplus of one abundant year is quite unfit to use in the next, and owing to its great bulk it cannot even be transported from place to place. Moreover, once used to a description of food so extremely cheap, no retrenchment is possible, and when blight comes and the crop is destroyed the people seem doomed to absolute starvation. This, unfortunately, was the case in 1822 and 1831. In those years public subscriptions were got up, king's letters issued, balls and bazaars held, and public money granted. But in 1845 and 1846 the calamity was greater than any previously experienced.

The potato disease first manifested itself in 1845. The early crop, dug in September and October, which consists of one-sixth of the whole, nearly escaped; but the whole of the late crop, the people's crop, dug in December and January, was tainted before arriving at maturity. In that year there was a full average crop of wheat. Oats and barley were abundant, and turnips, carrots, and greens, including hay, were sufficient. Yet on the continent the rye crop failed, and the potato disease appeared in Belgium, Holland, France, and the west of Germany. On the whole the supply of grain was fair during the year 1845, and prices ruled moderately high. In 1846, however, blight attacked the potatoes with even greater fury and suddenness in the month of July, and it attacked both the early crop and the people's crop, at the same time that the wheat crop proved under an average. Barley and oats were also deficient, and the rye crop again failed on the continent. In the previous year some counties in Ireland escaped the potato disease, but this year the whole country suffered alike. The loss was indeed very great. Probably £13,000,000 was a low estimate, and from 4,000,000 to 5,000,000 quarters of grain at least would be required to replace it. As might be expected the news of such a disaster had a fearful effect throughout the country, and the utter helplessness of many millions of our fellow-subjects became a subject of the greatest anxiety.

As soon as the potato disease appeared in 1845, government took the step of appointing Professors Kane, Lindley, and Playfair to inquire into the nature of the disease, and to suggest means for preserving the stock, but this was of little avail. Urged by necessity, the government even stepped out of its province, and sent orders to the United States for the purchase of £100,000 worth of Indian corn, established dépôts in different parts, and formed relief committees. But this was nothing compared with what became necessary to be done in 1846. Public works were then commenced on a large scale, giving employment to some five hundred thousand persons. The poor law was put in action with unparalleled vigor, so that in July, 1847, as many as three millions of persons were actually receiving separate rations. A loan of £8,000,000 was contracted by government, expressly to supply such wants, and every step was taken by two successive administrations — Sir Robert Peel's and Lord John Russell's — to alleviate the sufferings of the people. Nor was private benevolence lacking. The Society of Friends, always ready in acts of charity and love, was foremost in the good work. A British Association was formed for the relief of Ireland, including Jones Loyd (Lord Overstone), Thomas Baring, and Baron Rothschild. A Queen's letter was issued. A day of general fast and humiliation was held, and subscriptions were received from almost every quarter of the world. The Queen's letter alone produced £171,533. The British Association collected £263,000; the Society of Friends, £43,000; and £168,000 more were intrusted to the Dublin Society of Friends. The Sultan of Turkey sent £1,000. The Queen gave £2,000, and £500 more to the British Ladies' clothing fund. Prince Albert gave £500. The National Club collected £17,930. America sent two ships of war, the "Jamestown" and "Macedonian," full of provisions; and the Irish residents in the United States sent upwards of £200,000 to their relatives to allow them to emigrate. But with all this, the people passed through a most eventful catastrophe. One-third of the people, at least, was reduced to destitution. A large number died by fever and pestilence. Such as could raise the requisite funds emigrated to America. Crowds of emaciated and famished people flocked by every available means to English ports. The rest were kept alive by employment on public works, by private local charity, by local subscriptions, by contributions from all parts of the world, and by the most extensive system of gratuitous distribution of food which history affords any record of.

The price of wheat and other grain did not rise much at first. Indeed, for a lengthened time but faint conception was entertained of any want of foreign grain. The potato failure was comparatively a new thing, and few imagined that it would act powerfully on the consumption of grain. In 1845 the average price of wheat was no more than 50s. 11d. per imperial quarter, it having risen from a minimum of 45s. 3d. in March to 58s. 10d. in November; whilst the average price of barley was 31s. 8d., and of oats 22s. 6d. In 1846, also, the average price of wheat was 54s. 8d., the price having ruled first 55s. 6d., falling to 46s. 3d. in August, and rising to 60s. 7d. in November, whilst the average price of barley was 32s. 8d., and of oats 23s. 8d. But in 1847 a sudden great rise took place. The price of wheat rose from an average of 69s. 11d. in January to an average of 92s. 10d. in June; the price of barley was 50s. 2d. in January, 53s. 5d. in February, and 52s. 11d. in May and June; and oats, commencing at 29s. 6d. in January rose to 34s. 2d. in June. In July, however, a sudden change took place by the concurrent action of large importations and excellent prospects of the approaching harvest. From June to December wheat fell from 92s. 10d. to 52s. 3d.; barley from 52s. 11d. to 30s. 9d.; and oats from 34s. 2d. to 21s. 10d. per imperial quarter. The importation of grain had never been so large as in this year. In former years 1,000,000 or 2,000,000 quarters was the maximum, but in 1846 the imports amounted to 4,752,174 quarters of grain and meal, and in 1847 to as much as 11,912,864 quarters, the greatest increase having taken place from Russia and America. Then, indeed, the nation realized that the corn law could not be maintained any longer. Our dependence on foreign grain became very great, and thankful indeed we were that, by the wisdom and foresight of our legislators, the last corn law and the navigation law were alike suspended, and our ports were opened to the supply of food from any quarter of the globe. . . .

X.

THE NEW GOLD.

FROM CAIRNES' ESSAYS IN POLITICAL ECONOMY.

ESSAY II.—THE COURSE OF DEPRECIATION.

No one, I think, who has attended to the discussions occasioned by the recent gold discoveries, can have failed to observe, on the part of a large number of those who engage in them, a strange unwillingness to recognize, amongst the inevitable consequences of those events, a fall in the value of money. I say, a strange unwillingness, because we do not find similar doubts to exist in any corresponding case. With respect to all other commodities, it is not denied that whatever facilitates production promotes cheapness; that less will be given for objects when they can be attained with less trouble and sacrifice: it is not denied, *e.g.*, that the steam-engine, the spinning-jenny, and the mule have lowered the value of our manufactures; that railways and steamships have lessened the expense of travelling, or that the superior agricultural resources of foreign countries, made available through free-trade, keep down the price of our agricultural products. It is only in the case of the precious metals that it is supposed that a diminution of cost has no tendency to lower value, and that, however rapidly supply may be increased, a given quantity will continue to command the same quantity of other things as before.

Amongst persons unacquainted with economic science, the prevalence of this opinion is doubtless principally due to those ambiguities of language, and consequent confusion of ideas, with which our monetary phraseology, unfortunately, abounds, many of which tend to encourage the notion of some peculiar and constant stability in the value of the precious metals. Thus, the expression "a fixed price of gold" has led some people to imagine that the possibility of a depreciation of this metal is precluded by our mint regulations. The double sense, again, of the phrase, "value of money," has countenanced the same error; for people, perceiving the rate of interest (which is the measure of the value of money, in one sense of the phrase) remaining high, while the supply of gold was rapidly increasing, — perceiving money still scarce according to this criterion, notwithstanding the increase in its production, — have asked whether this did not afford a presumption that its value would be permanently preserved from depreciation; a bank rate of discount at 6, 8, or 10 per cent., as they remarked, affording small indication of money becoming too abundant.

It appears to me, however, that misconceptions respecting the influence of an increased supply of gold upon its value, and upon general prices, are by no means confined to the class who could be misled by such fallacies, but that even among economists (at least among economists in this country) we may observe the same indisposition to believe in an actual and progressive depreciation of this metal. It is not, indeed, denied — at least, I presume it is not denied — by any one pretending to economic knowledge, that the enlarged production of gold now taking place has a tendency to lower its value; but it seems to be very generally supposed that the same cause — the increased gold production — has the effect, through its influence on trade, of calling into operation so many tendencies of a contrary nature, that, on the whole, the depreciation must proceed with extreme slowness, the results being dispersed over a period so great as to take from them any practical importance, and that, at all events, up to the present time no sensible effect upon prices proceeding from this cause has become perceptible.

The existence of this opinion among economists is, I apprehend, to be attributed in some degree to the circumstance that so few have taken the pains to compare the actual prices of the present time with those of the period previous to the gold discoveries, but much more to the fact that the character of the new agency and the mode of its operation are not, in general, correctly conceived. I believe the most general opinion with reference to the action of an increased supply of money upon its value is, that it is uniform, takes place, that is to say, in the same degree in relation to all commodities and services, and that therefore prices, so far as they are influenced by an increase of money, must exhibit a uniform advance;[1] and, no such uniformity being observed in the actual

---

[1] " In relation to the influence of the gold discoveries on the prices of agricultural produce, it is plain that it could be only the same upon them as upon those of any other class of commodities. *If it has caused a rise of 20 per cent. in their favor, it must have caused a rise of 20 per cent. in everything else.*" *Times* City article, August 6, 1852. And the same assumption, either expressed or implied, runs through most of the reasoning which I have seen on this question.

movement of prices, the inference has not unnaturally been drawn that such enhancement as has taken place is not due to this cause; that it is not money which has fallen, but commodities which have risen in value.

Now I am quite prepared to admit that an increase of money tends ultimately, where the conditions of production remain in other respects the same, to affect the prices of all commodities and services in an equal degree; but before this result is attained a period of time, longer or shorter according to the amount of the augmentation and the general circumstances of commerce, must elapse. In the present instance the additions which are being made to the monetary systems of the world are upon an enormous scale, and the disturbance effected in the relation of prices is proportionally great. Under such circumstances it is very possible that the inequalities resulting may not find their correction throughout the whole period of progressive depreciation; a period which, even with our present facilities of production and distribution, may easily extend over some thirty or forty years. During this transitionary term the action of the new gold will not be uniform, but partial. Certain classes of commodities and services will be affected much more powerfully than others. Prices generally will rise, but with unequal steps. Nevertheless there will be in these apparent irregularities nothing either capricious or abnormal. The movement will be governed throughout its course by economic laws; and it is the purpose of the present inquiry to ascertain the nature of these laws and the mode of their operation.

The process by which an increased production of gold operates in depreciating the value of the metal and raising general prices appears to be twofold: it acts, first, *directly* through the medium of an enlarged money demand, and secondly, *indirectly* through a contraction of supply.[1]

When an increased amount of money comes into existence, there is, of course, an increased expenditure on the part of those into whose possession it comes, the immediate effect of which is to raise the prices of all commodities which fall under its influence. It is obvious, however, that the advance in price which

---

[1] According to Mr. Newmarch ("History of Prices," vol. vi., pp. 224-225) the depreciation of money may occur by a process which is neither of these, when money operates upon prices neither through demand nor yet through supply, but " by reason of augmented quantity." I must confess myself wholly unable to conceive the process here indicated.

thus occurs will be, in its full extent, temporary only; since it is immediately followed by an extension of production to meet the increased demand, and this must again lead to a fall in price. Some writers who have treated this question, observing this effect, have somewhat hastily concluded that under the operation of this principle the level of prices would never permanently be altered, since, as they have urged, each addition to the circulating medium forming the basis of a corresponding increase of demand, gives a corresponding impetus to production; every increase of money thus calls into existence an equivalent augmentation in the quantity of things to be circulated; and the proportion between the two not being ultimately disturbed, prices, it may be presumed, will return to their original level.[1] The least reflection, however, will show that this doctrine has been suggested by a very superficial view of the phenomena.

For — not to press the obvious *reductio ad absurdum* to which this argument is liable — how is this extension of production to be carried out? In the last resort it is only possible through a more extended employment of labor. But, when once all the hands in a community are employed, the effect of a further competition for labor can only be to raise wages; and, wages once being generally raised, it is plain (supposing all other things to remain the same) that profits can only be maintained by a corresponding elevation of prices. When, therefore, the influence of the new money has once reached wages, it is evident that there will be no motive to continue production to that point which would bring prices to their former level, and that consequently an elevation of price must, at this stage of the proceeding, be permanently established.

So far as regards articles which fall *directly* under the action of the new money. With respect to those which do not happen to come within the range of the new demand, price is, I conceive, in their case raised by an indirect action of the new money in curtailing supply.

---

[1] [It may be worth while to preserve a specimen of the sort of Political Economy that was talked and written on this subject some fifteen years ago. A leading article in the *Examiner* (December 13, 1856) contains the following: "The additional supply of the precious metals has stimulated the industry of the world, and in fact produced an amount of wealth in representing which they have been themselves, as it were, absorbed." . . . "But the produce of the Australian and Californian gold, as well as that of silver which has accompanied it, is likely to go on; and it may be asked if this must not in course of time produce depreciation. We think it certainly is not likely to do so; . . . on the contrary, it will surely be absorbed by increasing wealth and population as fast as it is produced."]

We have seen that the effect of the efforts to extend production in the directions indicated by the new expenditure must be to raise wages; but it is plainly impossible that wages should continue to advance in any of the principal departments of industry without affecting their rates in the rest; whence it will happen that, under the operation of the new monetary influence, some departments of industry will experience a rise of wages before any advance takes place in the prices of the new commodities produced by the laborers whose wages have risen. It is evident that in all departments of industry which may be thus affected — in which prices will not have shared the advance which has affected wages — profits will fall below the general average; the effect of which must be to discourage production until, by a contraction in the supply of the articles thus furnished, the price shall be raised up to that point which will place the producers on the same footing of advantage as those in other walks of industry.

An increased supply of money thus tends, by one mode of its operation, to raise prices in advance of wages, and thus to stimulate production; by another, to raise wages in advance of prices, and thus to check it; in both, however, to raise wages, and thus ultimately to render necessary, in order to the maintenance of profits, a general and permanent elevation of price.[1]

This being the process by which increased supplies of money operate in raising prices, in order to ascertain the laws of their advance we must attend, first, to the direction of the new expenditure; secondly, to the facilities for extending the supply of different kinds of commodities; and, thirdly, to the facilities for contracting it.

With regard to the first point, — the direction of the new expenditure, — this will naturally be determined by the habits and tastes of the persons into whose possession the new money comes. These persons are the inhabitants of the gold countries, and, after them, those in other countries who can best supply their wants. Speaking broadly, we may say that the persons who will chiefly

---

[1] It must not be supposed that this is inconsistent with the fundamental doctrine maintained by Ricardo, that "high wages do not make high prices." That doctrine assumes the value of money to be constant. Ricardo was quite aware of the exception to the general principle, and points it out in the following passage: —
"Money, being a variable commodity, the rise of money wages will be frequently occasioned by a fall in the value of money. A rise of wages *from this cause* will, indeed, be invariably accompanied by a rise in the price of commodities; but in such cases it will be found that labor and all commodities have not varied in regard to each other, and that the variation has been confined to money." — RICARDO's *Works* (Second Edition), p. 31.

benefit by the gold discoveries belong to the middle and lower ranks of society; in a large degree to the lowest rank, the class of unskilled laborers. The direction of the new expenditure will consequently be that indicated by the habits and tastes of these classes, and the commodities which will be most affected by it will be those which fall most largely within their consumption.

With respect, secondly, to facilities for extending supply, these will be found to depend principally upon two circumstances: first, on the extent to which machinery is employed in production; and, secondly, on the degree in which the process of production is independent of natural agencies which require time for accomplishing their ends. The distinction marked by these two conditions, it will be found, corresponds pretty accurately with two other distinctions, — with the distinction, namely, between raw and manufactured products; and, amongst raw products, with that between those derived from the animal and those derived from the vegetable kingdom. An article of finished manufacture, in the production of which machinery bears a principal part, and which is independent, or nearly so, of natural processes, may after a short notice be rapidly multiplied to meet any probable extension of demand. An article of raw produce, being in a less degree under the dominion of machinery, and depending more upon natural processes which require time for their accomplishment, cannot be increased with the same facility; and production will consequently, in this case, be comparatively slow in overtaking an extension of demand. But of raw products, those derived from the animal are still less under the dominion of machinery than those derived from the vegetable kingdom, and still more dependent on the slow processes of nature, and, consequently, production must, in their case, be still more tardy in overtaking demand. Supposing, then, the extension of demand to be in all three cases the same, the immediate rise of price will, *cæteris paribus*, be in all the same; but in the case of articles of finished manufacture, this rise will be quickly corrected by the facilities available for increased production, while in raw vegetable products the correction will take place more slowly, and in raw animal products more slowly still.[1]

---

[1] The following passage occurs in the "History of Prices," vol. vi., p. 170: "The groups of commodities which exhibit the most important instances of a rise of price are the raw materials most extensively used in manufactures, and the production of which does not

But, thirdly, I said that the progress of prices under the influence of the gold supplies would be governed by the facility with which supply can be contracted. Every one who has practical experience of manufacturing operations is aware that, when capital has once been embarked in any branch of production, it cannot at once be removed to a different one the moment the needs of society may require a change; whence it happens that, on any sudden change taking place in the direction of a nation's expenditure, or when from miscalculation production has been extended beyond existing wants, producers frequently choose to continue their business at diminished profits or even at a positive loss, rather than incur still greater damage by suffering their capital to lie idle, or by attempting to transfer it suddenly into some new branch of production. The supply of a commodity is not therefore always, or generally, at once contracted on the demand for it falling off, or on its production becoming less profitable, and, where this is so, it is evident that prices must at times continue depressed below the normal level; the duration of the depression depending on the length of time required to effect a transference of the unproductive capital to some more lucrative investment. Now, the difficulty of accomplishing this will generally be in direct proportion to the amount of fixed capital employed; and the principal form in which fixed capital exists is that of machinery. It is, therefore, in articles in the production of which machinery is extensively employed — that is to say, in the more highly finished manufactures — that the contraction of supply will be most difficult; and this, it will be observed, is also the kind of commodities for extending the supply of which the facilities are greatest. While, therefore, manufactured articles

---

admit of rapid extension; and, second, the groups of commodities in which there is little, if any, rise of price in 1857, as compared with 1851, are articles of colonial and tropical produce, the supply of which, drawn from a variety of sources, does admit of being considerably and expeditiously enlarged." The *fact* of the rise of price in raw materials is here admitted, though, in ascribing that rise, as by implication the passage does, to the paucity of the sources of supply, the explanation is, as I conceive, erroneous. The sources, *e.g.*, from which tea and sugar are drawn are not more various than, nor indeed so various as, those from which beef and mutton, butter and provisions, timber, tallow, and leather are drawn; yet all these latter articles have very considerably advanced in price. Again, amongst colonial and tropical produce Mr. Newmarch includes rum and tobacco, and he might also have included cotton; yet these articles, though falling within the class which he says admits of being expeditiously enlarged, and which, therefore, according to his theory, should *not* have risen in price, *have in fact risen* in a very marked manner. It appears to me that these phenomena can only be understood by reference to the principle which I have endeavored to explain further on—namely, the efficacy of the currency of different countries in determining local prices.

can never be very long in advance of the general movement of prices, they may, of all commodities, be the longest in arrear of it.

The operation of this principle will be shown chiefly in that class of articles which feels the effect of the new gold only through its indirect action — that is to say, through its action upon wages. With respect to such articles there is no extension of demand, and the price consequently can only be raised through a contraction of supply. It is evident that of all commodities this is the class in which the rise of price must proceed most slowly.

From the foregoing considerations, then, I arrive at the following general conclusions: —

First. — That the commodities, the price of which may be expected first to rise under the influence of the new money, are those which fall most extensively within the consumption of the productive classes, but more particularly within the consumption of the laboring and artisan section of these.

Secondly. — That of such commodities, that portion which consists of finished manufactures, though their price may in the first instance be rapidly raised, cannot continue long in advance of the general movement, owing to the facilities available for rapidly extending the supply; whereas, should the production, from over-estimation of the increasing requirements, be once carried to excess, their prices, in consequence of the difficulty of contracting supply, may be kept for some considerable time below the normal level.

Thirdly. — That such raw products as fall within the consumption of the classes indicated, not being susceptible of the same rapid extension as manufactures, may continue for some time in advance of the general movement, and that, among raw products, the effects will be more marked in those derived from the animal than in those derived from the vegetable kingdom.

Fourthly. — That the commodities last to feel the effects of the new money, and which may be expected to rise most slowly under its influence, are those articles of finished manufacture which do not happen to fall within the range of the new expenditure; such articles being affected only by its indirect action, and this action being in their case obstructed by impediments to the contraction of supply.

This is one class of laws by which I conceive the ascending movement in prices will be governed; and up to this point I have the satisfaction of finding my conclusions very fully corroborated by the independent investigations of a French economist, M. Levasseur, who, in some articles lately contributed by him to the *Journal des Économistes*, has, by an entirely different line of investigation from that which I have followed, — namely, by generalizing on the statistics of prices in France during the period of 1847 to 1856, — arrived at conclusions in the main points identical with those which I have now advanced.[1]

There is, however, another principle to which I venture to call attention, which has not, so far as I know, been noticed by any of the economists who have treated this question, but which, it appears to me, must exercise a powerful influence on the course of the movement. The principle to which I refer is that efficacy which resides in the currency of each country, into which any portion of the new money may be received, for determining the effect of this infusion on the range of local prices.

It is evident that the quantity of metallic money necessary to support any required advance of prices throughout a given range of business will vary with the character of the currency into which it is received; that the quantity required will be greater in proportion as the metallic element of the currency is greater; and, on the other hand, less in proportion as the credit element prevails. If the currency of a country be purely metallic, a given addition of coin will increase the aggregate medium of exchange in that country only by the same amount; if, on the other hand, the currency consists largely of credit contrivances, each addition to its coin becomes the basis of a new superstructure of credit in the form of bank-notes and credits, bills of exchange, checks, etc., and the aggregate circulation is increased, not simply by the amount of the added coin, but by the extent of the new fabric of credit of which this coin is made the foundation. Applying this principle to the different countries of the world, it follows that a given addition to the metallic stock of Great Britain or the United States, in whose monetary systems credit is very efficacious, will cause a greater expansion of the total circulation, and therefore will support a greater advance in general prices, than the same addition to the currency of countries like France, in which credit is less active; and that, again, the effect in countries like France will be greater than in countries

---

[1] See Cairnes, Appendix, p. 360, for a summary of M. Levasseur's conclusions.

like India or China, in which the currencies are almost purely metallic, and where credit is comparatively little used.

Now, this being so, if we consider further that the countries which receive in the first instance the largest share of the new money — namely, England and the United States — are also those in which, from the character of their currencies, a given amount of coin will produce the greatest effect; and, on the other hand, that Asiatic communities, in which, from the weakness of the credit element, the currencies are least expansible, receive but a small portion of their share of the new money direct from the gold countries;[1] being compelled to wait for the remainder till it has flowed through the principal markets of Europe and America, affecting prices in its transit; — if, I say, we consider these facts in connection with the principle to which I have adverted, I think we must recognize in that principle — in the influence of the currency of each country on the range of its local prices — an agency which must modify in no small degree the general character of the movement which is now in progress.

In speaking of the influence of the currency of a country on the range of its local prices, I should explain that I use the words "local prices" in a somewhat restricted sense; namely, with reference to the locality in which commodities are *produced*, not to that in which they are sold, their price in the latter place being always determined by their price in the former. Thus, when I speak of Australian, English, or Indian prices, I shall be understood to mean the prices of their several products in Australia, England, or India.

Understanding the words, then, in this sense, let us see how far local prices are likely to be affected by the cause to which I have adverted.

In the first place, then, let it be observed that a very remarkable divergence of local prices from the range previously obtaining in

---

[1] [From statistics recently furnished by the *Economist*, I learn that the facts have not been as I here assumed, at least since 1858 (the date from which full returns of specie imports have been published by the Board of Trade); and it is probable I was mistaken in my supposition with regard to what had occurred before that time. Since 1858, of £90,000,000 of gold received and retained by India and the East, some £49,000,000, more than a half of the whole, appear to have gone there *directly* from Australia, the remainder only having come through Europe. This error as to matter of fact will, no doubt, affect to some extent the conclusion contended for. The causes tending to a divergence of European from Asiatic prices have not been, it seems, as powerful as I had supposed; and, in point of fact, this feature in the movement has been less marked than I sketched it; but for this, other causes besides that noticed here have been responsible (1873). See Introductory Chapter, p. 12.]

the international scale has already taken place.[1] The prices of all articles *produced* in Australia and California are at present on an average from two to three times higher than those which prevailed previous to the gold discoveries; these rates have now been maintained for several years, and are likely to continue; but, while this advance has taken place in the gold countries, in no part of the world external to those regions have prices advanced by so much as one-third. The possibility of a divergence of local prices is thus, as a matter of fact, established; and the explanation of the phenomenon I take to be this. The sudden cheapening of gold in Australia and California quickly led, through the action of competition amongst the different departments of industry, to a corresponding advance in the prices of everything produced in those countries; *this advance being in their case possible*, because, from the limited extent of the transactions, the local circulation was quickly raised to the point sufficient to sustain a double or triple elevation; but it was impossible that the currencies of all countries should be expanded in the same proportions in the same time; and, consequently, prices in other countries have not risen with the same rapidity. The cause, therefore, of this divergence of local prices — the circumstance which keeps general prices in arrear of that elevation which they have attained in Australia and California — is the difficulty of expanding the currencies of the world to those dimensions which such an advance would require. This expansion, however, is being gradually effected by the process we are now witnessing, — the increased production of the precious metals, and their diffusion throughout the world. But, as I have said, the diffusion is not uniform over the various currencies, nor are the currencies receiving the new supplies of uniform susceptibility; and the inequalities are such as to aggravate each other; the currencies which are the most sensitive to an increase of the precious metals receiving in the first instance nearly the whole of the new gold; while the least sensitive currencies are the last to receive their share. And these, it appears to me, are grounds for expecting amongst other countries further examples of that phenomenon of local divergence, of which one has already been afforded by the gold countries.

To judge, however, of the extent to which such local variations

---

[1] See Cairnes, pp. 24, 25.

of price can be carried, we must advert to the corrective influences which the play of international dealings calls into action; and these appear to me to resolve themselves into the two following: namely, first, the corrective, which is supplied by the competition of different nations, producers of the same commodities, in neutral markets; and, secondly, that which exists in the reciprocal demand of the different commercial countries for each other's productions.

The first form of the corrective is obviously the most powerful, and must, so far as its operation extends, at once impose a check upon any serious divergence. Thus it is evident that prices in England and the United States could not proceed very much in advance of prices on the continent of Europe, since the certain effect of such an occurrence would be to send consumers from the dearer to the cheaper markets, and thus to divert the tide of gold from the currencies of England and America to the currencies of France, Germany, and other continental states, — a process which would be continued until prices were restored to nearly the same relative level as before. But it is only amongst nations which are competitors in the same description of commodities that this equalizing process comes into operation: as between countries like England and America on the one hand, and India and China on the other, — in which the climate, soil, and general physical conditions differ widely, in which, consequently, the staple industries are different, and whose productions do not, therefore, come into competition in the markets of the world, — this corrective influence would be felt slightly or not at all. The only check which could be counted on in this case would be that far weaker one which is furnished by the action of reciprocal demand in international dealings. Thus, supposing prices to rise more rapidly in England than in India, this must lead, on the one hand, to an increased expenditure in England on Indian commodities, and, on the other, to a diminished expenditure in India on English commodities, with this result, — a steady efflux of the precious metals from the former to the latter country. Such an efflux, as commercial men are well aware, has long been a normal phenomenon in our Eastern trade, but it has lately assumed dimensions which constitute it a new fact needing a special explanation. I believe that explanation is to be found in the circumstances to which I am calling attention.

English and American prices, and with them money incomes

in England and America, have, under the action of the new gold, been advancing more rapidly than prices and incomes in Oriental countries ; and the result has been a change in the relative indebtedness of those two parts of the world, leading to a transfer to the creditor country of corresponding amounts of that material which forms the universal equivalent of commerce. It is true, indeed, that other causes have also contributed to this result, and in particular I may mention the failure of the silk crop in Europe, which has largely thrown us upon China, as a means of supplementing our deficient supplies. But the main cause of the phenomenon in its present proportions is, I conceive, to be found, not in any such mere temporary disturbances, but in the natural overflowing (consequent upon the increase of the precious metals) of the redundant currencies of Europe and America into the more absorbent and impassive systems of Asia.[1] This, then, I say, is the only substantial corrective afforded to the advance of prices in Europe and America beyond their former and normal level in relation to prices in the East; and the question is, will this corrective be sufficient to neutralize the tendency to a divergence? Will the flow of the precious metals from West to East suffice to keep prices in England and America within the range prescribed by the inelastic metallic systems of Asia? I do not conceive that the corrective will be adequate to this end, and I rest this conclusion upon the facts and principles which I have stated,— the vast proportion of the whole gold production which finds its way in the first instance into the markets of England and America, the comparatively small portion which goes direct to the markets of Asia,[2] the highly elastic and expansible currencies of the former countries, and the extremely impassive and inexpansible currencies of the latter.

We find, therefore, two sets of laws by which the progress of prices, or (which comes to the same thing) the depreciation of

---

[1] Accordingly we find that the drain which, during the revulsion of trade following on the commercial crisis of 1857, had for a while ceased, has, with the revival of trade, recommenced. As a proof how little mere practical sagacity is to be trusted in a question of this kind, it may be worth while to mention that, only three months since, mercantile writers were confidently predicting *the turning of the tide of silver from the East to England*. The following is from a circular of Messrs. Ellisen & Co., quoted in the *Times* City article, July 28, 1858, apparently with the editor's approval: "The time is rapidly approaching when silver will also be shipped from here [China] to England." So far from this being the case, the drain to the East has again set in, and gives every indication of assuming its former dimensions. Every mail to India during the present month (November, 1858) has taken out large amounts of silver.

[2] See *ante*, p. 198, note.

gold under the action of an increased supply, is regulated: first, those which I explained in the earlier portion of this paper, which depend chiefly on the facility with which the supply of commodities can be adjusted to such changes in demand as the new money expenditure may occasion; and, secondly, those which result from the action of the new money on the currencies into which it is received. According to the former principle, the rise in price follows the nature of the commodity affected; thus it will in general be greater in animal than in vegetable productions — in raw produce than in finished manufactures. According to the latter principle, the advance follows the economic conditions of the locality in which the commodity is produced. Thus the rise in price has been most rapid in commodities produced in the gold countries; having in these at a single bound reached its utmost limit, — the limit set by the cost of procuring gold. After commodities produced in the gold regions, the advance I conceive will proceed most rapidly in the productions of England and the United States; after these, at no great interval, in the productions of the continent of Europe; while the commodities the last to feel the effects of the new money, and which will advance most slowly under its influence, are the productions of India and China, and, I may add, of tropical countries generally, so far as these share, as regards their economic conditions, the general character of the former countries.

Such appear to be the general principles according to which a depreciation of the precious metals, under the action of an increased supply, tends to establish itself. With a view to ascertain how far, in the progress of prices up to the present time (1858), any trace of their operation can be discerned, I have drawn up some statistical tables;[1] and although, from the imperfect nature of the materials which I have been able to collect, I cannot claim for the result a complete verification of the theoretic conclusions which I have ventured to advance, I think they are such as to justify me in placing some confidence in the general soundness of those views. Before, however, stating the results of the tables, two or three remarks must be premised.

First, I would crave attention to this fact, that the present time [1858] is one singularly free from disturbing influences, and that such as do exist are of a kind rather to conceal than exaggerate

---

[1] See Cairnes, Appendix.

the effects of depreciation. Thus, we have had three harvests in succession of, I believe, more than average productiveness (the last year of deficiency being 1855); and this cause of abundance has been assisted by free-trade, which has opened our ports to the produce of all quarters of the world. Again, although in the period under review we have passed through a European war, yet we have now enjoyed two years and a half of peace, during which, I think, the economic influences of the war may be taken to have exhausted themselves. It is true, indeed, that we have an Indian revolt still on our hands, besides having but just concluded some hostile operations in China. But these disturbances have not been of a kind to interfere seriously with the general course of trade, except in some few Oriental commodities in which their effects are slightly apparent.

But what renders the present time peculiarly important as a point of comparison with former periods, is its being in immediate sequence to a severe commercial crisis. The effect of the crisis of last winter has been effectually to eliminate one great disturbing element from those causes to which a rise of price might be attributed, — the element of credit. Trade is now suffering depression in almost all its branches; and prices, after a period of undue inflation, have, through an ordeal of bankruptcy, been brought to the test of real value. In the fluctuations of commerce we have reached the lowest point of the wave; whatever, therefore, be the range of prices at the present time, we may at least be sure that no commercial convulsion is likely to lower it.

We have further to remember that in an age like the present, in which science and its applications to the arts are in all civilized countries making rapid strides, there exists in most articles of general consumption (but more particularly in the more finished manufactures) a constant tendency to a decline of price, through the employment of more efficient machinery and improved processes of production. Now, taking all these circumstances together, — the propitiousness of the seasons, the action of free-trade, the absence of war, the contraction of credit, and the general tendency to a reduction of cost proceeding from the progress of knowledge, — it appears to me that, were there no other cause in operation, we should have reason to look for a very considerable fall of prices at the present time, as compared with, say, eight or ten years ago. Prices, however, as the following tables will show, have not fallen; they have, on the contrary, very decidedly risen, and the advance has, moreover, as the same tables will also show, on the whole proceeded in conformity with the principles which I have in this paper endeavored to establish. And this is my ground for asserting that the depreciation of our standard money is already, under the action of the new gold, an accomplished fact.

ESSAY III. — INTERNATIONAL RESULTS.[1]

In a former essay[2] it was attempted, from a review of the industrial history of Australia since the late discovery of gold, to make some general deductions respecting the character of that event, and of its influence upon national interests. Among other conclusions it was maintained that the tendency of the gold discoveries, or, to speak with more precision, the tendency of the increased production of gold, was rather to alter the distribution of real wealth in the world than to increase its amount; the benefit derived by some countries and classes from the event being for the most part obtained at the expense of others. It was shown, for example, that the gain to Australia and California from their gold-fields accrued to them exclusively through their foreign trade, — their cheap gold enabling them to command on easier terms than formerly all foreign productions; while, on the other hand, the only result to foreign nations of the traffic thence arising was an increase in their stock of money,— a result rendered necessary indeed by the new conditions of raising gold introduced by the gold discoveries, but in itself destitute of any real utility. It was shown, in short, that, as regards commercial nations, the effect of the gold discoveries was to place them under the necessity of enlarging their currencies, compelling them to pay for the requisite increase by an increased export of their productions.

To this conclusion I was led by direct inference from the facts presented in the gold countries. In the present paper it is proposed to follow up the inquiry, with a view to a more particular ascertainment of the consequences formerly described; the object being to discover in what manner the loss arising from the gold movement is likely to be distributed among commercial nations, and how far this loss may in particular cases be neutralized or compensated by other influences which the same movement may develop.

---

[1] *Fraser's Magazine*, January, 1860.   [2] Essay I. of this Series.

In the discussions which have hitherto taken place upon this question, the inquiry into the consequences of the gold discoveries has been confined almost exclusively to that aspect of the event in which it is regarded as affecting fixed contracts through a depreciation of the monetary standard.[1] As soon as the probability of depreciation is settled, and the effects of this upon the different classes of society, according as they happen to be debtors or creditors under fixed contracts, explained, the subject for the most part is considered as exhausted. I venture, however, to think that this mode of treatment is very far from exhausting the question. It seems to me that, independently altogether of the existence of fixed contracts, independently even of gold being a standard of value, the increased production of this metal which is now taking place will be attended — indeed has already been attended — with very important results. Let us observe for a moment the movement which is now in progress. Australia and California have, during the last eight or ten years, sent into general circulation some two hundred millions sterling of gold. Of this vast sum portions have penetrated to the most remote quarters of the world; but the bulk of it has been received into the currencies of Europe and the United States, from which it has largely displaced the silver formerly circulating; the latter metal, as it has become free,. flowing off into Asia, where it is permanently absorbed. Viewing the effect as it occurs in the mass of the two metals combined, it may be said that the stream which rises in the gold regions of Australia and California flows through the currencies of the United States and Europe, and, after saturating the trade of these countries, finally loses itself in the hoards of China and Hindostan. The tide which comes to light in the sands and rocks of the auriferous regions disappears in the accumulations of the East. In conjunction, however, with this movement, there has been a counter one. With every advance in the metallic tide, a stream of commodities has set in in the opposite direction along the same course, — a stream which, issuing from the ports of Europe, America, and Asia, and depositing as it proceeds a portion of the wealth with which it is charged, finds its termination in the

---

[1] See Stirling's "Gold Discoveries and their probable Consequences;" Chevalier "On the Probable Fall in the Value of Gold;" Levasseur's contributions to the *Journal des Économistes*, 1858; M'Culloch's article "Precious Metals," in the "Encyclopædia Britannica." In all these, and in many other minor productions on the same subject, almost the only consequences of the gold discoveries which are taken account of are those which occur in fixed contracts through a depreciation of the standard.

markets of the gold countries. Here, then, we find a vast disturbance in the conditions of national wealth,—a disturbance originating in the gold discoveries, and resulting in a transfer, on an enormous scale, of consumable goods,—the means of well-being—from one side of the globe to the other. This disturbance, it is evident, is entirely independent of the accident that gold happens to be in some countries a standard of value, as well as of the existence of fixed money-contracts; for it includes within the range of its influence countries in which gold is not, no less than those in which it is, the monetary standard; and it affects alike persons whose bargains are made from day to day, and those who engage in contracts extending over centuries. The fact is, the movement in question is the result not of gold's being a standard of value, but of its being a source of purchasing power; and the influence of the gold discoveries having been hitherto regarded almost exclusively with reference to the former function, the vast effects which they are producing through the action of the latter—that is to say, by altering the distribution of purchasing power in the world—have been almost wholly overlooked. It has indeed been perceived that a great influx of the precious metals is taking place, accompanied with certain consequences on the trade of the world; but so far as I know, beyond some general phrases respecting the stimulus given to production by an increase of money, and the great development of commerce which it is causing, no attempt has yet been made to state the principles by which the movement is governed, or the effects which may flow from it. It is to these questions, then, that I would now solicit the reader's attention, and towards their solution the following remarks are offered as a contribution.

Those who have followed the course of this controversy are aware that, by most persons who have taken part in it, it has been assumed, almost as an axiom, that no depreciation of gold in consequence of the gold discoveries has, up to the present time, taken place.[1] As a matter of fact, however, we know that the gold prices of all commodities produced in Australia and California

---

[1] The principal exceptions to this statement are M. Levasseur (who, in an article in the *Journal des Économistes*, March, 1858, estimates the rise of prices in France since 1847 at 20 per cent. on all commodities), and Dr. Soetbeer, of Hamburg, who, in his table of prices given in his " Contributions to the Statistics of Prices in Hamburg," arrives at a similar result (see Appendix). Many other writers, indeed, acknowledge that prices have risen, but the rise is always attributed to causes distinct from the increased production of gold.

have risen in at least a twofold proportion;[1] while we have seen that (so long as the conditions of producing gold remain as at present) this rise must be permanent. To express the same thing differently: — in the purchase of every commodity raised in the gold countries two sovereigns are now required, and (the above conditions being fulfilled) will continue to be required, where one was formerly sufficient; and if this does not amount to a fall in the value of gold, I must confess myself unable to understand the meaning of that expression. It is not to be supposed that so remarkable a fact as this should have escaped the attention of those who have written on this question; it seems to me rather that the ignoring of it in the discussion is to be attributed to a want of definite ideas respecting value in the precious metals, as well as respecting the mode in which changes in their value are accomplished. The language which is commonly used on the subject would seem to imply that gold and silver possess throughout the world a uniform value, and that all changes therein proceed in a uniform manner, showing themselves at the same time in all countries, and in respect to all commodities. But nothing can be further from the truth than such a notion. Gold and silver, like all other things which are the subjects of international exchange, possess local values;[2] and it is by a succession of operations on the local values of gold of an unequal and fluctuating character, that its depreciation is being effected, and that (the conditions of production remaining as at present) its value will continue to decline. The twofold rise of prices in the gold countries forms the first step in this progress; and it will be through a series of similar partial advances in other countries, and not by any general movement, that the depreciation of the metal throughout the world will be accomplished, if that consummation is indeed to take place. With the question of depreciation, however, I am at present no further concerned than may be necessary to show the bearing of these changes in the local values of gold upon the movements of trade, and, through these, upon national interests.

There is no need here to resort to argument to prove that a general rise or a general fall of prices, provided it be simultaneous and uniform, can be attended — always excluding the case of

---

[1] See Cairnes, p. 24.
[2] See on the subject of the local values of the precious metals, Ricardo's " Works," pp. 77-86, and Mill's " Principles of Political Economy," Book iii., chaps. xix. and xxi.

fixed incomes and contracts already entered into — with no important consequences either to nations or to individuals. It is evident that such a change would merely alter the terms in which transactions are carried on, not the transactions themselves. But when the rise or fall of prices is not general, — in other words, when the change in the values of the precious metals is merely local, — it will be seen that important consequences must result. Supposing, *e.g.*, the prices of all commodities produced in England to be doubled, while prices throughout the rest of the world remained unchanged, it is evident that half the commodities exported from England would, under these circumstances, be sufficient to discharge our foreign debts. With half the capital and labor now employed in producing goods for the foreign markets, we should attain the same result as at present, — the procuring of our imports; while the remaining half would be set free to be applied to other purposes, — to the further augmentation of our wealth and well-being. England would, therefore, in the case we have supposed, be benefited in all her foreign dealings to the full extent of the rise in price. On the other hand, foreign countries would, in exchange for the commodities which they send us, receive in return of our commodities but half their present supply. Their labor and capital would go but half as far as at present in commanding our productions, and they would be losers in proportion. It is evident, therefore, that while nations have not, any more than individuals, any interest in the positive height which prices may attain, every nation, as well as every individual trader, is interested in raising, *in relation to others*, the price of its own productions. The lower the local value, therefore, of the precious metals in any country, the greater will be the advantage to that country in foreign markets.

This being the manner in which nations are interested in changes in the value of gold, let us now observe the effect which the gold discoveries are producing in this respect. As has been already stated, the local value of gold in Australia and California has fallen to one-half, — the prices of their productions having risen in a twofold proportion;[1] and prices in other parts of the

---

[1] This statement is not given as strictly accurate. On the whole, the advance of local prices in the gold countries is at present (1859) considerably more than this, some leading articles, as house-rent, meat, etc., having risen in a fourfold proportion and upwards. I adopt the proportion of two to one, because money wages have risen in about this ratio, and money wages, under a depreciation of the precious metals, ultimately govern money prices.

world having undergone no corresponding change, these countries realize the position which we have just been considering in our hypothetical case. A given quantity of their capital and labor goes twice as far as formerly in commanding foreign productions, while a given quantity of foreign labor and capital goes only one-half as far in commanding theirs. The world has thus, through the gold discoveries, been placed in its dealings with California and Australia at a commercial disadvantage; and from this disadvantage it can only escape (always supposing the present conditions of producing gold to continue) by raising the prices of its productions in a corresponding degree. Every country, therefore, is interested in raising as rapidly as possible the prices of its productions, — in other words, in the most rapid possible depreciation in the local value of its gold.[1] The sooner this is effected, the sooner will the country be restored to its natural commercial footing in relation to Australia and California; while in relation to countries where prices do not rise with the same rapidity, it will possess the same kind of advantage which is now enjoyed by the gold countries.

This conclusion, I find, is directly at variance with the opinion of some economists of eminence. Mr. M'Culloch, for example, in his recent contribution to the "Encyclopædia Britannica,"[2] maintains "that the mischievous influence resulting from a fall in the value of the precious metals depends in a great measure on the rapidity with which it is brought about." But I apprehend the difference between Mr. M'Culloch and myself arises from his attending exclusively to a single class of consequences, — those, namely, which result, in the case of fixed contracts, from a depreciation of the standard. With respect to this class of effects, it is quite true that the evils which they involve will be increased by the rapidity of the depreciation; but as I have shown, the new gold is producing effects quite independently of its operation upon fixed contracts; and it is to those other effects that the statement I have just made is intended to apply. The distinction which I have in view will be best exemplified by recurring to the experience of the gold countries. In these the value of gold fell by more than 50 per cent. in a single year, the depreciation involving a

---

[1] For the general ground of this assertion the reader is referred to Mr. Mill's chapters on International Values, and on Money as an Imported Commodity, in his "Principles of Political Economy;" also to Mr. Senior's Essay "On the Cost of Obtaining Money."
[2] Article "Precious Metals."

proportional loss to creditors with a corresponding gain to debtors, and entailing in addition those numerous incidental evils which always result from a sudden disturbance of social relations. No one, however, on this account, will say that the sudden depreciation of gold in Australia and California was not for these countries a great gain. The nature and extent of that gain I endeavored on a former occasion to estimate.[1] It consisted, as I showed, in the increased command conferred by the cheapness of their gold over markets in which gold prices had not proportionally risen. With every rise in the price of Australian and Californian products, or, what comes to the same thing, with every fall in the local value of their gold, their power of purchase in foreign markets increased, — an increase of purchasing power which, as we know, was immediately followed by a sudden and extraordinary influx of foreign goods. Now, precisely the same principle applies in the case of other countries. A fall in the value of gold will, where gold is the standard, lead to a disturbance in fixed contracts, with the concomitant evils; but it will at the same time, as in the case just considered, place the countries in which it occurs in a better position commercially in the markets of the world. Supposing, *e.g.*, a rise in prices to take place in all commercial countries equivalent to that which has occurred in California and Australia, the consequence would be what I endeavored to explain in the paper just referred to; the export of gold from California and Australia, at least on its present scale, would at once cease, and the world would receive instead an increased supply of agricultural and pastoral products, and of other commodities which those countries are fitted to produce, — a result which, I ventured to think, would be a gain for the world. On the other hand, supposing the rise in price to be confined to a single country, — say to England, — then England would at once be placed on a footing of commercial equality with California and Australia, while as regards other countries she would occupy the same vantage-ground which California and Australia now possess. She would, in short, obtain her gold at half its present cost (for she would receive twice as much as at present in return for the same expenditure of labor and capital), while the gold thus obtained would be expended on foreign commodities of which, according to the hypothesis, the prices had not risen. Notwith-

---

[1] See Cairnes, p. 39.

standing, therefore, the evils which undoubtedly attend variations in the standard of value, more especially in an old and highly artificial community like ours, it is nevertheless, I maintain, for the interest of every country, that, a fall in the cost of gold having been effected, the progress of depreciation should *in it* be as rapid as possible. Until, by a depreciation of gold corresponding to that which has occurred in California and Australia, the value of that metal is brought into harmony with its cost, we must continue to receive from those countries little more than a barren addition to our stock of money. But with each successive step in the progress of depreciation, there will be for the nation in which it occurs, a nearer approach to the footing of commercial equality with the gold countries from which it has been temporarily displaced; while in its dealings with other places where the decline has been less rapid, the nation so circumstanced will, during the period of transition, enjoy a commercial superiority. As a general conclusion, therefore, we may say, that in proportion as in any country the local depreciation of gold is more or less rapid than the average rate elsewhere, the effect of the monetary disturbance will be for that country beneficial or injurious.

This conclusion, I may in passing remark, throws light upon a practical question of some interest at the present time, — I mean the question of introducing a gold currency into India. The measure has been advocated by Mr. M'Culloch, on the ground that, by providing a new market for the increased supplies of gold, its effect would be to " counteract that fall in its value which is so generally apprehended."[1] There can be no doubt that the effect of the measure would be what Mr. M'Culloch describes ; but, if the above reasoning be sound, this circumstance, instead of being a reason for introducing gold into the currency of India, affords (*so far as the interests of India are concerned*) a strong reason against the adoption of this course. Mr. M'Culloch does not state whether the effect which he anticipates upon the value of gold would be general or local; whether extending over the whole commercial world, or confined to the markets of India, — a point of vital importance in determining the character of the result. If the effect were general — if, while counteracting depreciation in India, it influenced the value of gold *proportionately* in other parts of the world — then it must be conceded that the result

---

[1] " Encyclopædia Britannica," article " Precious Metals," p. 473.

would be entirely beneficial. The evils incident to a disturbance of fixed contracts would be avoided, and no others would be incurred. But this is just the point which I venture to deny. The adoption of gold as the monetary standard of India would certainly not affect the local value of gold in Australia and California; for, as I proved on a former occasion, the value of gold in these countries is determined by its cost, and its cost depends on the productiveness of the gold-fields. Nor, for reasons which will be hereafter stated, would it influence more than in a slight degree the range of gold-prices in England and the United States. The operation, therefore, of the measure would be to depress gold-prices in India, or, at least, to prevent them from rising in that quarter as rapidly as they otherwise would; while in California and Australia, in England and the United States, it left their course substantially unaffected. Now, this result would tend undoubtedly to the advantage of California and Australia, of England and the United States, but, as it seems to me, would as clearly be injurious to India. The purchasing power of the former countries over the markets of India would, through the relative superiority of their prices, be increased, but the purchasing power of India over *their* markets would, for the opposite reason, be diminished. An English or American merchant, instead of discharging his debts, as at present, through the medium of silver which he has to purchase with gold at 62d. per ounce (and may soon have to purchase at a higher rate), might discharge the same debts with gold directly; and gold being by hypothesis more valuable in India than before, the same amount would of course go farther. But an Indian purchaser of English or American commodities would have the same sum in gold to pay as if no change had taken place in the currency of India; while the gold prices of his native productions being lower, his ability to pay would of course be less. It seems to me, therefore (and the considerations here adduced are entirely independent of the reasons which exist on the score of good faith — the Indian debt having been contracted in a silver currency), that, viewing the matter from the side of Indian interests, the introduction of a gold currency into India must be regarded as a measure decidedly detrimental.[1]

---

[1] Referring to the adoption of a silver standard by Holland in 1851, Mr. M'Culloch characterizes it as a measure "in opposition to all sound principles." I confess I am at a loss to conjecture what sound principle was violated in preferring as the standard of value that metal, the value of which there was every reason to believe would be the steadier of the

Returning once more to the general question, we may consider the following conclusions as established : 1st, that the effect of the cheapening of gold upon commercial countries being to compel them to enlarge their metallic currencies, for which enlargement they must pay by an export of their productions, each country will endure a loss upon this head to the extent of the additional sum which may be requisite for each ; and, 2dly, that while there will be a general loss from this cause, yet the progress of depreciation over the world not being uniform or simultaneous, the primary loss may, through the disturbance in international values thence arising, in particular cases, be compensated, or even converted into a positive gain ; the loss or gain upon the disturbance being determined according as the rise of prices in any country is in advance or in arrear of the general average. To ascertain, therefore, the effect of the movement upon any particular nation, we must consider the manner in which, in its case, these two principles will operate.

With respect to the first, I am aware that, in speaking of the loss imposed on a country by the necessity of enlarging its currency, — by the necessity of receiving and keeping increased supplies of gold and silver, — I am using language which, notwithstanding what was said on a former occasion in its justification, and notwithstanding that it is merely in strict conformity with the most elementary principles of economic science, will still appear paradoxical to many. I would, therefore, before proceeding farther with this branch of the argument, ask the reader to consider the case of a private merchant who is compelled to increase the stock of cash with which he carries on his business. The metallic circulation of a country performs in relation to the community functions precisely analogous to those which are discharged for a merchant by his cash reserve. If a merchant can safely dispense with a portion of his ready cash, he is enabled, with the money

---

two. [I may say now (1872) that I am disposed to assign much less importance to this question of a change in the monetary standard of India than I did when the above passage was written. The reasoning assumes the possibility of a serious divergence in the relative values of gold and silver; but I now believe that such a divergence is practically out of the question, the grounds for which opinion will be found farther on (*post*, p. 141). This circumstance, however, does not affect the theoretic point argued with Mr. M'Culloch. *If* the exchange of the existing silver for a gold standard in India were calculated to produce the effects Mr. M'Culloch expected from it, the measure, it still seems to me, would be open to the objections I have urged against it. But I do not believe that the effects in question would result; and I can well conceive that, having regard to the general convenience of commerce, the change might, on the whole, be advantageous.]

thus liberated, either to add to his productive capital, or to increase his private expenditure. On the other hand, if he finds it necessary to increase his reserve of cash, his productive capital must be proportionally encroached upon, or his private expenditure proportionally curtailed. And precisely the same may be said of the currency of a nation. Where a country does not itself yield gold or silver,[1] every increase of its metallic circulation must be obtained—can only be obtained—by parting with certain elements of real wealth,—elements which, but for this necessity, might be made conducive to its well-being. It is in enabling a nation to reduce within the narrowest limits this unproductive portion of its stock that the chief advantage of a good banking system consists; and if the augmentation of the metallic currency of a country be not an evil, then it is difficult to see in what way the institution of banks is a good. In regarding, therefore, the necessity imposed upon commercial countries of enlarging their metallic currencies as injurious to their interests, I make no assumption which is not in perfect keeping with the best known and most generally recognized facts of commercial experience.

An increase in the metallic currency of a country, then, being an evil, let us consider what the circumstances are by which the augmentation rendered necessary by the gold discoveries will be determined. This, it is evident, will principally depend—the amount of business to be carried on being given—on the extent to which substitutes for metallic money are in use; in other words, on the degree of perfection which the banking system of each country has attained. To illustrate this, let us suppose a given sum of metallic money—say a million sterling—to be introduced into two countries in which the currencies are differently constituted,—*e.g.*, into England and India. In India coin is the principal medium of circulation[2]—in many parts the only one,

---

[1] Even where it does yield these metals, the necessity of augmenting the currency is not the less an evil, since the operation will occupy, with no result but that of avoiding an inconvenience, a portion of the labor and capital of the country, which, but for this, might have contributed to its positive welfare.

[2] [The reader will bear in mind that this was written in 1859. The state of the Indian currency at that time may be gathered from the following extracts from a paper on " The Trade and Commerce of India," read before the British Association in 1859.] "Intimately connected with Indian trade and commerce is a sound system of banking. At present there are only three banks of importance in India,—the banks of Bengal, Bombay, and Madras. These have no branches, the absence of which constitutes one of the main defects of the system. The few other banks in India do not issue notes, and employ their capital in making advances on bills of lading, in exchange operations, and in some instances in loans to members of the Service, at high rates of interest; but afford no banking facilities for con-

and consequently a million sterling introduced into the currency of India would represent only an equal, or little more than an equal, addition to its total medium of circulation — to the whole monetary machinery by which the exchange of commodities is effected and prices maintained. But in England, where the currency is differently constituted, the result would be different. The great bulk of the circulating medium of this country consists of certain forms of credit; and the amount of these credit media standing in a certain large proportion to the coin in the country, the effect of introducing a million sterling into our currency would be to increase the medium of circulation by an amount very much greater than that of the added coin. Let us consider for a moment what becomes of a sum of coin or bullion received into England. I do not now speak of that moving mass of metal which passes (so to speak) *through* the currency of the country, — which, received to-day into the vaults of the Bank of England, is withdrawn to-morrow for foreign remittance, — but of gold, which is permanently retained to meet our genuine monetary requirements. Of such gold a portion — greater or less, according to circumstances — will always find its way into the channels of retail trade; and so far as it follows this course, its effect in augmenting the circulation will be, as in India, only to the extent of its actual amount. But a portion will also be received into the banks of the country, where, either in the form of coin, or of notes issued against coin, it will constitute an addition to their cash reserves. The disposable cash of the banks being thus in-

---

ducting the internal trade of the country." The writer then refers to a table, showing the state of the three leading banks (Bengal, Bombay, and Madras) in the preceding June, from which it appears that the bullion at that time in the coffers of the banks was *in excess* of the notes in circulation, the amount of these latter being, for the whole of India, £2,241,471, or about one-tenth of the amount issued by the Bank of England alone; while the total amount of "accounts current" was only £1,855,000, — about one-sixth of those held by some of the private banks of London, and not one-fifteenth of those of the Bank of England. The total amount of commercial bills discounted in these three leading banks of India is set down at £278,906! "And this," it is observed, "in a country where the gross annual revenue is £34,000,000; the export trade, on an average of the last five years, £24,000,000; the import trade, on the same average, £23,000,000, with an internal trade to an extent almost impossible to estimate." ("The Trade and Commerce of India," by J. T. Mackenzie, read before the British Association, 1859, pp. 15, 16.) In the evidence taken before the late Committee "On Colonization and Settlement in India," Mr. Alexander Forbes, when questioned with reference to the large absorption of silver in India, expressed his opinion that the silver was all required for current coin. "It has often been said that the natives hoard silver. Now my experience is that they do not hoard silver; they hoard gold; and that the silver is actually required for the commerce of the country." And this he traces (Answers 2,222, 2,223, 2,372–80) to the want of banking accommodation and the imperfect means of communication generally in the country. See also the evidence of Mr. Mangles (Answers 1,625–1,633).

creased, an increase of credit operations throughout the country would in due time follow. The new coin would become the foundation of new credit advances, against which new checks would be drawn, and new bills of exchange put in circulation, and the result would be an expansion of the whole circulating medium greatly in excess of the sum of coin by which the new media were supported. Now, credit, whatever be the form which it assumes, so long as it is *credit*, will operate in purchases, and affect prices in precisely the same way as if it were actually the coin which it represents. So far forth, therefore, as the new money enables the country to support an increase of such credit media, — to support them, I mean, by cash payments, — so far it extends the means of sustaining gold-prices in the country; and this extension of the circulating medium being much greater than in proportion to the amount of added coin, the means of sustaining gold-prices will be in the same degree increased. Thus, supposing the ratio of the credit to the coin circulation of the country to be as four to one (and the proportion is greatly in excess of this), the addition of one million sterling of coin would be equivalent to an increase in the aggregate circulation of four millions sterling,[1] and one million sterling of gold would consequently, in England, for a given extent of business, support the same advance in gold-prices as four times that amount in India. It follows from these considerations, that, in order to raise prices throughout a given range of transactions to any required level, the quantity of metallic money which will be necessary will vary in different countries, according to the constitution of their currencies; the requirements of each increasing generally in an inverse ratio with the efficiency of its banking institutions.

We may thus see how very unequal will be the operation of the gold discoveries with respect to commercial communities. The reduction in the cost of gold to which they have led has, as we have seen, produced in the gold countries a twofold rise of gold-prices; and supposing the present conditions of raising gold to

---

[1] Strictly speaking, this conclusion would not follow on the above supposition, the efficiency of different forms of credit in performing the work of circulation being (as pointed out by Mr. Mill, " Principles of Political Economy," vol. ii., pp. 58–61) different, and only some of them being in this respect equal to coin. But such distinctions do not affect the general truth of the principle contended for in the text, that the necessity for coin varies inversely with the use of credit. Besides, as I intimated, the proportion of credit to coin in our circulation is much greater than I have assumed; and a million of coin taken into our currency would really be equivalent to more than four millions added to a purely metallic one.

continue, the same cause must ultimately lead to the same result throughout the world: imposing upon each country the necessity of so enlarging its currency as to admit of this advance. But we have seen that the quantity requisite for this purpose varies according to the monetary status of the country for which it is required; and inasmuch as the new money must be paid for by commodities, the abstraction of commodities, and therefore the loss of the means of well-being, to which each country must submit, will vary with the same circumstance. On the supposition, therefore, on which we are arguing, the quantity of new money which England would require would be, when compared with the extent of her business, extremely small, and her loss of real wealth small proportionally. The same would be true of the United States, where credit institutions have also attained a high degree of efficiency, and whose paper consequently forms a large proportion of the whole circulation. In France, the use of credit being more restricted, the requirements for coin would be greater, and consequently also the loss of consumable commodities; while in India and China, and indeed in Asiatic communities generally, the circulating medium being almost purely metallic, the requirements for coin would, in proportion to the business in which it was employed, attain their maximum, with a corresponding maximum of loss in the elements of well-being.[1]

The operation of this principle is indeed, in the actual circumstances of the world, in some degree concealed by the complex conditions under which it comes into play. Thus Great Britain and the United States, instead of obtaining the smallest shares, receive in the first instance nearly the whole of the new gold. On the other hand, the quantity which goes to India and China from the gold countries is comparatively trifling;[2] and although a large

---

[1] It is curious to observe the contradictions in which persons are involved who, still under the influence of the mercantile theory of wealth (and there are few even among professed economists who are free from its influence), are nevertheless sensible from experience of the advantages of a system with which it is incompatible. Thus several witnesses before the late Committee on Indian Colonization refer to the large influx of silver into India in recent years as a sure indication of the increasing prosperity of that country; yet, almost in the same breath, they speak of the deficiency of banking accommodation as among its most pressing wants. Now, it is certain that, just in proportion as banking accommodation is extended, the absorption of silver by India will decline; whence it would follow, if the reasoning of the witnesses be sound, that the effect of the extension of banks would be to check the growing prosperity of the country. See "Minutes of Evidence," Questions 1,625-1,633, 2,221-2,223.

[2] This order in the diffusion of the new gold has not been sustained. See *ante*, p. 198, note.

drain of treasure has set in thither from Europe, yet this consists chiefly of silver. If, however, passing by the accidents of the movement, we attend to its essentials, we shall find that the results are entirely conformable to the principle I have endeavored to describe. For though the bulk of the new gold comes in the first instance to England and the United States, — determined thither by the course of international demand, — yet England and the United States do not form its ultimate destination. The monetary requirements of these countries being easily satisfied, the mass of the metal, on reaching these markets, becomes immediately disposable for foreign purchases; by which means the United States and England are enabled to transfer to other countries this unprofitable stock, the commodities with which in the first instance they parted being replaced by others which they more require. So also, although the metallic drain to the East is composed principally of silver, the efflux — at least in its present proportions — is not the less certainly the consequence of the increased production of gold; for the silver of which it consists has been displaced from the currencies of Europe and America by the gold of Australia and California; and the drain to the East is only not a golden one, because silver alone is in that region the recognized standard. As the final result of the whole movement, we find that, while the metallic systems of England and the United States are receiving but small permanent accessions, those of India and China are absorbing enormous supplies. The former countries, though the first recipients of the treasure, yet, not requiring it for domestic purposes, are enabled to shift the burden to others, whose real wealth they command in exchange; while the latter, requiring what they receive, are compelled to retain it. Having parted with their commodities for the new money, they are unable afterwards to replace them. As their stock of coin increases, their means of well-being decline, and they become the permanent victims of the monetary disturbance.

But, secondly, we conclude that the loss of real wealth resulting from the augmentation of their currencies would in particular countries be compensated, and might in some be even converted into positive gain, by the disturbance which, during the period of transition, would take place in international values. As has been already remarked, a general rise of prices in all countries, if simultaneous and uniform,—since it leaves the proportions in which commodities are exchanged undisturbed, — leads to no change in international values, and produces no effect upon national interests. But where prices rise unequally, international values, and through these, national interests, are affected. We have therefore to consider how far, in the actual circumstances of the world, a rise of prices in particular countries, unaccompanied by a corresponding advance in others, is possible, and, in so far as it is possible, in what order the several changes may be expected to occur.

As regards the question of possibility, this is placed beyond controversy by the example of California and Australia. It is a matter of fact that prices in those regions have advanced in a twofold proportion, while no corresponding rise of prices has occurred throughout the world. The circumstances, however, of the gold countries will probably be thought of too exceptional a character to form the basis of any general conclusion; and it will therefore be desirable to advert for a moment to the causes which produced in California and Australia that local elevation of price, with a view to consider how far the same conditions are capable of being realized elsewhere.

These causes, as was formerly shown,[1] were the special facilities for producing gold enjoyed by California and Australia, combined with the limited range of their domestic transactions. The sudden cheapening of gold, involving a corresponding increase in money earnings, placed an extraordinary premium on the production of the metal, while the limited range of their domestic trade rendered the necessary enlargement of their monetary systems an easy task. On the other hand, the immense extent of the aggregate commerce of the world required, in order to secure a similar advance, a proportional increase in its aggregate stock of money, an augmentation which could only be accomplished after the lapse of a considerable time. Prices therefore rose rapidly in the gold countries, while over the area of general commerce the rise had been but slow.

Such being the circumstances which produced the local divergence of prices to which I have called attention, it will at once be seen that of the two conditions which I have stated, the latter — the necessary enlargement of the local currency — may in most countries, though not in all at the same time, be fulfilled, if not with the same rapidity as in Australia and California, still after

---

[1] See Cairnes, pp. 25, 26.

no very long delay. It has been computed,[1] for example, that the total quantity of gold coin circulating in Great Britain amounts to £75,000,000 sterling. Assuming this to be correct, it would follow (all other conditions being supposed identical) that an addition of £75,000,000 would be sufficient to effect an elevation of our local prices equivalent to that which has occurred in Australia. Now, at the present rate of production, the quantity of gold which arrives annually in Great Britain cannot fall much short of £30,000,000 sterling;[2] so that were we merely to retain all that we receive, we should at the end of two years and a half be in a position, so far as the augmentation of our currency is concerned, to maintain the same advance in price as has occurred in the gold countries. If, then, prices in Great Britain have not risen in the same degree, the result, it is evident, cannot be due to the difficulty of procuring the supply of gold necessary for the enlargement of our currency. It remains, therefore, to be considered how far those special facilities for procuring gold which have operated in the gold countries may come into play in other parts of the world.

The extraordinary facilities for procuring gold enjoyed by Australia and California depend, of course, on the possession of their gold mines; and this being so, it might seem as if all countries, not being like them auriferous, were by the nature of the case precluded from fulfilling this condition of the problem; but this by no means necessarily follows, as will be evident if we reflect that there are other modes of obtaining gold than by direct production, of which modes the efficiency enjoyed by different countries differs almost as much as the degrees of fertility in different gold mines. Where countries do not themselves produce gold, the mode by which they obtain it is through their foreign trade. Now, it is a fact well known to economists[3] that, with reference to the cost of commodities, the terms on which foreign trade is carried on differ greatly in different countries, the labor of

---

[1] "History of Prices," vol. vi., App. xxii. This also is Mr. M'Culloch's estimate: "Encyclopædia Britannica," article "Precious Metals," p. 465. [It will be borne in mind that these estimates apply to the period immediately preceding the first publication of these Essays (1859-60).]

[2] [£20,000,000 would have been nearer the mark, but at the time this paper was written no trustworthy statistics of gold imports existed. Either amount, however, answers equally well the purpose of the argument (1873).]

[3] See Ricardo's "Works," chap. vii., on Foreign Trade. Mill's "Principles of Political Economy," chaps. xvii., xix. Also, Senior's Essay, "On the Cost of Obtaining Money."

some going much farther in commanding foreign productions than that of others. According, however, to the conditions on which foreign productions generally are obtainable, will be those on which gold may be obtained. If a country possess special facilities for supplying markets where gold can be given in exchange, it will obtain its gold more cheaply — at a less sacrifice of labor and capital — than countries which do not share these facilities, and amongst such countries it will therefore occupy precisely the same position as an auriferous country whose mines are of more than the usual richness among the countries which yield gold. It is thus possible for a non-auriferous, no less than for an auriferous country to possess exceptional facilities in the means of procuring gold, and therefore to fulfil the second of the conditions by which a divergence of local prices from the ordinary level of the world may be effected.

Now, it appears to me there are two countries which possess in an eminent degree the qualifications requisite for attaining this result — I mean Great Britain and the United States: the former, as being *par excellence* the great manufacturer among civilized nations, — the manufacturer more particularly of descriptions of goods, — as cotton, woollen, linen, and iron, which enter largely into the consumption of the classes by whom chiefly the gold countries are peopled; and the latter, as the principal producer of raw material, as well as of certain commodities — as grain, tobacco, sugar, and rice — which are also largely consumed by the same classes. In these circumstances, Great Britain and the United States enjoy peculiar advantages in the markets of the gold-countries, and these advantages are extended and confirmed by other important incidents of their position. Thus they possess the greatest mercantile marine in the world, by which they are enabled to give the fullest scope to their manufacturing and agricultural superiority, while by race, language, and religion they are intimately connected with the producers of the new gold, — a connection from which spring ties, moral, social, and political, to strengthen and secure those which commerce creates. Great Britain and the United States thus possess in their foreign trade a rich mine,[1] worked by their manufacturers, planters, and farmers, tended by their mercantile marine, and protected by their naval

---

[1] "The mine worked by England is the general market of the world; the miners are those who produce those commodities by the exportation of which the precious metals are obtained." — SENIOR's *Essay " On the Cost of Obtaining Money,"* p. 15.

power, — a mine by means of which they are enabled to obtain their gold on terms more favorable than other nations. The effect of this, in ordinary times, is shown by a scale of money rates, wages, salaries, and incomes, permanently higher than that which elsewhere prevails; but in times of monetary disturbance like the present, when the cost of gold having been reduced its value is falling, these advantages, it seems to me, must tell, as analogous advantages have told in the gold countries, in a more rapid realization of the results which are in store, — in a quicker ascent towards that higher level of prices and incomes which the cheapened cost of gold is destined ultimately to produce.

There is reason, therefore, on considerations of theory, to expect a repetition in England and America of that phenomenon which has been already exhibited in Australia and California, — a divergence of local money-rates from the average level of surrounding countries. On a future occasion I shall endeavor to ascertain how far, in the case of Great Britain, these *à priori* conclusions are supported by facts, — how far prices and incomes have here, under the influence of the gold discoveries, outstripped the corresponding movement in other countries.[1] Having settled this point, we shall be in a position to form a general estimate of the benefit which may thence accrue to us. Meanwhile, however, I may, in conclusion, point out the mode in which the advantages incident to the monetary position we shall occupy are likely to be realized.

And here it may be well to call the reader's attention to the distinction, sometimes overlooked, between a fall in the value of gold and a rise in the price of commodities. A rise in the price of commodities, if general, implies commonly a fall in the value of money; but, according to the ordinary use of language, alike by economists and common speech, money would, I apprehend, in certain circumstances, be said to have fallen in value, even though the prices of large classes of commodities remain unaffected. For example, supposing improvements to have been effected in some branch of production resulting in a diminished cost of the commodity, the value of money remaining the same, prices would fall; if under such circum-

---

[1] [Some evidence on the point will be found in the Appendix; but the inquiry here contemplated was never carried into effect. A very interesting and carefully prepared paper on the subject, however, was read some years later by my friend Professor Jevons, before the London Statistical Society, when I had the satisfaction to find that the results of his entirely independent investigations to a very large extent corroborated the conclusions at which I had arrived, mainly by way of deduction from the general principles of the science.]

stances prices did not fall, that could only be because money had not remained the same, but had fallen in value. The continuance of prices unaltered would, therefore, under such circumstances, amount to proof of a fall in the value of gold. Now, when, in connection with this consideration, we take account of the fact that over the greater portion of the field of British industry improvement is constantly taking place, it is obvious that the mere movements of prices here, taken without reference to the conditions of production, are no sure criterion of changes in the value of gold.

The truth is, in a large class of commodities, — in all those to which mechanical or chemical inventions are extensively applicable, — even on the supposition of a very great depreciation of gold, no considerable advance in price is probable. Gold, for example, might have fallen since the beginning of the present century to the extent of 75 per cent., — that is to say, four sovereigns now might be equal to no more than one sovereign at the commencement of the period, — and yet in a large class of manufactured goods no advance in price would be apparent, the reduction in the cost of production being in more than an equal proportion. In ordinary times, agricultural operations escape in a great degree the influence of industrial progress; but within the last ten years — that is to say, since the repeal of the Corn Laws, which nearly synchronized with the gold discoveries — the spirit of improvement has been as busy in agriculture as in any other department of industry, and, in conjunction with importations from foreign countries, has acted, and must for some time at least continue to act, powerfully upon the price of raw products in this country.

The depreciation of gold, therefore, may be realized either in a corresponding advance of prices, or in the neutralization of a fall which, in the absence of depreciation, would have occurred; but in whatever form it may come to us, our gain or loss as a nation will be the same, and will depend upon the condition I have stated, — the more or less rapid depreciation of our currency as compared with the currencies (convertible, like ours, into gold) of other countries. Whether, the conditions of production remaining unaltered, the depreciation be indicated by a corresponding advance of prices, or, those conditions undergoing improvement, the fall in the value of gold merely operates in neutralizing, as regards price, the effects of the cheapened cost of commodities, —

in either case *the gold price of the products of English labor and abstinence will rise.* A given exertion of English industry will reap a larger *gold* reward than before; and foreign commodities not rising in price in the same degree, the larger gold reward will indicate, *over so much of our expenditure as is directed to foreign productions,* a real augmentation of well-being. As regards that portion of our expenditure which falls upon the products of our own industry, individuals and classes will, according to circumstances,[1] be benefited or injured by the change; but as a nation, we shall neither gain nor lose, since here the increased cheapness of gold will be exactly neutralized, either by a corresponding advance in price, or by the prevention in the same degree of a fall which would otherwise have taken place. It is in this way,— by the increased command which she obtains over foreign markets by her cheap gold,— and not, as is commonly supposed, by finding an outlet for her wares in California and Australia, that England will benefit by the gold discoveries. That outlet for her productions, — were the movement to stop here, — however it might benefit individuals, would for the country at large be an injury and not a boon; it would deprive her of that which might conduce to her comfort and happiness, and would give her a "breed of barren metal" in exchange. But the movement does not stop here. The money which she obtains from the gold countries, instead of absorbing, like India or China, she employs in purchasing the goods of other nations. It is in the enlarged command which she acquires over such goods that her gain consists, and it is thus that she indemnifies herself, though at the expense of the nations who ultimately retain the new gold, for the loss — the indubitable loss — which she is called on in the first instance to sustain.

---

[1] On this point see Cairnes, p. 147, *et seq.*

XI.

FRANCE SOUS LE SECOND EMPIRE.

From Levasseur's Histoire des Classes Ouvrières. Vol. II, pp. 307-321.

Crédit et Échanges.

Depuis quinze ans, trois grand faits économiques ont exercé en France une influence considérable sur la production manufacturière ; le développement du crédit, la multiplication des chemins de fer et la réforme douanière.

Il entrait dans les vues du gouvernement de provoquer l'esprit d'entreprise. L'année 1852 vit se former deux établissements d'une nature très-diverse, mais qui tous deux devaient concourir au même but, celui de fournir des capitaux au travail, le Crédit foncier et le Crédit mobilier.

Le premier, depuis longtemps réclamé par M. Wolowski, se proposait de venir en aide à l'agriculture en avançant sur première hypothèque à la propriété foncière des sommes remboursables par annuités ; en réalité, les prêts agricoles, qui augmentent aujourd'hui, ont été les plus lents à se développer, et la nature de sa clientèle l'a fait servir plus à la construction des maisons et aux travaux publics dans les communes qu'à la culture proprement dite : à ce titre, il appartient à l'histoire de l'industrie. Le second, créé et dirigé par M. E. Péreire, est une puissante banque de commandite et de spéculation, non sans analogie avec celles que recommandait le saint-simonisme. Il était destiné par ses statuts à fonder ou à soutenir de grandes entreprises, et il a, en effet, donné naissance aux chemins de fer du Midi, à la compagnie immobilière de Paris, au gaz de Marseille, aux paquebots transatlantiques ; il devait être, en raison même de son caractère, très-vivement affecté par toutes les influences de hausse et de baisse, et sa fortune dépendait entièrement de l'habileté de ses directeurs.

La Banque de France, dont le gouvernement avait le droit de suspendre le privilége en 1855, fut affranchie de cette crainte et autorisée à faire des avances sur dépôt d'actions et d'obligations de chemin de fer :[1] la spéculation en usa largement. Quelques années après, la Banque obtenait par une loi la prorogation de son privilége jusqu'en 1897, au prix de 100 millions prêtés à l'État et fournis par une émission de nouvelle actions ; la Banque pouvait élever le taux de son escompte au-dessus de 6 pour 100, et le gouvernement pouvait exiger, dix ans après la promulgation de la loi, qu'elle eût au moins une succursale par département.[2]

"Les opérations de la Banque se sont considérablement améliorées, disait le gouverneur en parlant de la situation en 1852, le commerce et l'industrie ont repres leur essor." En effet, le montant des opérations s'était élevé d'un milliard et demi, chiffre de 1851, à deux milliards et demi. Le produit des impôts indirects s'était notablement accru ; la rente avait dépassé le pair ; toutes les valeurs de bourse avaient été emportées dans le même mouvement, et les marchandises, sous la triple impulsion de l'abondance de l'or, d'une consommation plus active et d'une spéculation audacieuse, enchérissaient chaque jour.

Ce fut l'âge d'or de la Bourse. Londres, qui avait été depuis le commencement du siècle le principal marché des capitaux et des grandes entreprises en Europe, céda le pas à Paris. L'élan était tel qu'il permit au commerce de franchir le choléra, la disette, la guerre d'Orient, et à l'État d'emprunter un milliard et demi sans briser le ressort du crédit. Les capitaux, à peine formés, étaient absorbés ; les travaux publics, les emprunts, la disette elle-même, tout y contribuait ; on spéculait à la hausse, et les cours s'élevaient.

Cependant les affaires étaient devenues plus difficiles en 1856 : le gouvernement crut utile d'enrayer lui-même la spéculation[3] et de faire une loi restrictive sur les sociétés en commandite par actions.[4] La langueur continua cependant en 1857, et l'abondance de la récolte rendait inevitable éclata avec violence aux États-Unis. Elle se communiqua rapidement à Londres, à Hambourg, à Paris. Quoique moins rudement éprouvée que ses voisines, la France vit, comme elles, les sources du crédit tarir ; la spéculation dut liquider, et l'année 1858 fut marquée par une baisse générale des marchandises[5] et par un ralentissement des transactions.

---

[1] Décret du 28 mars 1852.   [2] Loi du 9 juin 1857.
[3] *Voir* au *Mon.*, la note du 9 mars 1856.
[4] Loi du 17 juillet 1856. Il s'était formé, en 1852, 21 sociétés de ce genre ; en 1853, 25 ; en 1854, 36 ; en 1855, 18 ; en 1856, 17. Il s'en forma, en 1857, 6 ; 13 en 1858, et 12 en 1859.
[5] *Voir*, sur cette crise, la *Question de l'or*, par E. Levasseur.

La guerre d'Italie qui survint l'année suivante, et ses conséquences qui se firent sentir jusqu'en 1862, empêchèrent les affaires de reprendre leur essor jusqu'au jour où le combat d'Aspromonte fit croire à la consolidation du trône de Victor-Emmanuel. Les cours se relevèrent alors, et l'esprit d'entreprise se ranima. Mais une autre cause de malaise pesait déjà sur le marché : la guerre d'Amérique privait l'Europe de coton et réduisait à la misère les districts manufacturiers de l'Angleterre et de la France. Une crise monétaire s'ensuivit ; en 1864, l'escompte de la Banque de France monta à 8 pour 100,[1] et le gouvernement, sollicité par une pétition de trois cents négociants et par une contrepétition de la Banque, ordonna une enquête sur le régime du crédit. Cette crise s'apaisait à son tour, lorsque éclata la guerre du Danemark, puis la guerre d'Allemagne. Les agitations de la politique, dans le vieux et dans le nouveau monde, contrarient fréquemment, depuis dix ans, le déploiement pacifique des forces du travail marchant à la conquête de la matière.

Une ville a particulièrement souffert, et souffre aujourd'hui plus que les autres, de la langueur des affaires dont se plaint le commerce. C'est Lyon, dont la nombreuse population ouvrière, dépendant presque tout entière, pour sa subsistance, d'une seule industrie de luxe, est toujours la première à s'affaisser sous le coup des crises et la dernière à se relever. Elle avait développé ses relations extérieures ; la guerre d'Amérique lui a été funeste ; de 84 millions en 1865.[2] Le meilleur remède pour elle serait, à côté de son industrie de luxe, soumise aux caprices de la mode et aux variations de la fortune, la création d'une industrie commune ayant un large débouché.

Néanmoins, malgré les obstacles, le travail a brillamment déployé ses forces.[3] La Banque de France dont les escomptes, à Paris, avaient une seule fois atteint 1,329 millions, sous le règne de Louis-Philippe, atteignit de nouveau et dépassa ce chiffre en 1856 ; en 1865, elle faisait 2,458 millions. Elle était alors devenue la seule banque d'émission et la regulatrice souveraine du crédit en France ; les opérations de ses succursales, jointes au chiffre des affaires de Paris, formaient, à la même époque, un total de

---

[1] Au mois de mai.
[2] Lettre de M. Arlès Dufour à l'*Opinion nationale* du 18 octobre 1866.
[3] Le progrès des impôts indirects, qui a continué en 1866, est, avec le progrès du commerce extérieur, une preuve que la situation, considérée dans son ensemble, n'a pas empiré depuis un an, malgré la langueur des affaires dans diverses industries.

7,422 millions, tandis qu'en 1847 les banques départementales et la Banque de France n'atteignaient que 2,075 millions. Dans le même temps, sans que le commerce des banques privées parût diminuer,[1] se fondaient d'autres grands établissements, comme la Société générale de credit industriel et commercial,[2] la Société de dépôts et de comptes courants,[3] la Société générale pour favoriser le commerce et l'industrie en France.[4] L'usage des chèques, autrement dit l'habitude déposer en banque ses fonds de caisse et de faire ses paiements en mandats, commence, quoique trop lentement, à se naturaliser en France et à mettre une plus grande masse de capitaux à la disposition du crédit.

Parmi les entreprises qui devaient obtenir la faveur, les chemins de fer étaient au premier rang. On avait souvent reproché à la France de s'être laissé devancer par ses voisins, et l'activité imprimée aux constructions durant la seconde moitié du règne de Louis-Philippe par la loi de 1842, s'était amortie sous la République. Le nouveau gouvernement la ranima.[5] Les capitaux étaient confiants. On en profita pour inaugurer un autre mode de concession. A la construction de la voie par l'État, on substitua la construction par les compagnies que l'on encouragea par une longue jouissance; les baux, avec les nouvelles compagnies et même avec les anciennes, furent la plupart passés ou revisés pour quatre-vingt-dix-neuf ans.[6] On engageait sans doute un plus lointain avenir; mais on faisait immediatement peser toute la charge sur les capitaux appelés à recueillir les bénéfices les plus directs de l'entreprise; la combinaison était évidemment préférable. Elle n'eût pas été possible dix ans plus tôt.

Les concessions multiples, créant des intérêts divers et parfois hostiles sur un même parcours, étaient un obstacle à la circulation. On les réunit, de manière à former de vastes compagnies qui se partagèrent le domaine du réseau français: ce ne fut pas sans quelques tâtonnements qui fournirent des armes à la spéculation.[7] Mais dans l'espace de la première année, 3,000 kilomè-

---

[1] On prétend toutefois qu'il n'augmente pas. [2] 7 mai 1859.
[3] 6 juillet 1863. [4] 4 mai 1864.
[5] Le chemin de ceinture avait été décrété dès le 11 décembre 1851. Dans la seule année 1852, 46 décrets furent rendus relativement aux chemins de fer, et 267 kilom. furent livrés à la circulation.

[6] Les concessions étaient faites pour 99 ans, avec garantie, pour le capital engagé par les Compagnies, d'un minimum d'intérêt de 4% pendant la moitié de ce temps. Quelques concessions furent même faites sans garatie. Cette granantie fut d'ailleurs supprimée pour le premier réseau, lorsque la loi du 11 juin 1859 accorda une garantie particulière au second réseau.
[7] Décrets du 17 janvier, 19 février, 20, 27 mars 1852.

tres trouvaient des concessionnaires ; et, à la fin de la quatrième année, sur une longuer d'environ 5,000 kilomètres, les trains circulaient.

Les grandes artères étaient dessinées et allaient se terminer en peu d'années. Le gouvernement résolut hardiment d'aborder la construction des lignes secondaires et de faire pénétrer la vie commerciale dans tout le corps de la nation, comme les petits vaisseaux font pénétrer le sang jusque dans les chairs de l'homme. Cette fois, le profit ne semblait pas pouvoir de longtemps rémunérer la dépense et d'ailleurs la crise de 1857 avait rendu plus timides les entreprises. Le gouvernement intervint, et, par deux lois successives,[1] donna des subventions ou garantit aux capitaux du second réseau, lesquels devaient être fournis par des obligations, un intérêt de 4 pour 100 et l'amortissement en cinquante ans.

C'est ainsi qu'à la fin de l'année 1866, la longueur totale des concessions définitives atteignait 21,050 kilom., et celle des lignes exploitées, 14,506 ; la dépense faite s'élevait à près de 7 milliards.[2]

Les canaux, quoique relégués au second plan, ont été terminés sur plusieurs points, entrepris sur quelques autres,[3] et sont rentrés, pour la plupart, dans le domaine de l'État,[4] qui s'est empressé d'abaisser presque partout les droits au niveau des frais d'entretien. La navigation des rivières a été améliorée.[5] Les grandes routes, parallèles aux voies de fer, se trouvaient délaissées ; mais les routes transversales, emportant ou apportant voyageurs et marchandises, que les trains recueillent ou sèment sur leur route, s'animaient.[6] On a en conséquence redoublé de zèle dans l'application de la loi de 1836 sur les chemins vicinaux,[7] et une loi nouvelle a encouragé les conseils généraux à construire, aux mêmes conditions, des chemins de fer,

---

[1] Lois du 11 juin 1859 et du 11 juin 1863.
[2] On se rappelle qu'à la fin du règne de Louis-Philippe, la dépense effectuée était d'environ 1 milliard ½, et le nombre de kilomètres exploités de 1830.
[3] La France possédait 4,200 kilom. de canaux en 1848, en 1866, 4,500 ; de plus, 6,900 kil. de rivières navigables. De grands travaux ont été poursuivis. Voir *Exp. de la sit. de l'Emp.*, 1867, *Mon.*, p. 450 et 451.
[4] Décret du janvier 1852 et loi du 28 juillet 1860.
[5] *Voir*, entre autres, la loi du 14 juillet 1861.
[6] De 1848 à 1866 exclusivement, l'État a dépensé pour routes, canaux, ponts, phares, etc., 627 millions.
[7] Relativement aux chemins de fer, routes, canaux, etc. M. P. Boiteau. Voir *Fortune publique et finances de la France*, t. I. Le chemins vicinaux ont coûté en 1866, 120 millions, dont un tiers en prestations, en nature.

qui, à l'exemple de ceux de l'Alsace, formeront un troisième reseau.[1]

La télégraphie électrique, qui était à ses débuts en 1851, a commencé à envelopper de son réseau la France, à la suite du décret du 6 janvier 1852 ; elle couvre aujourd'hui l'Europe ;[2] elle fait communiquer les deux mondes et transmet, en France seulement, près de trois millions de dépêches pour le compte des particuliers.[3] La poste, dont le service a reçu à diverses reprises de notables améliorations, transportait trois fois plus de lettres ou d'imprimés, en 1865 qu'en 1847 ;[4] de nombreuses conventions postales et des conventions monétaires ont été signées avec les pays voisins.[5] Les régions lointaines de l'Asie et de l'Amérique ont été mises en relations régulières avec nos ports par la Compagnie des messageries impériales, qui s'est habilement transformée devant la concurrence des chemins de fer, et par la Compagnie des paquebots transatlantiques dont, vingt ans auparavant, un ministre aurait déjà voulu doter la France.[6]

Les hommes, leurs pensées et leurs produits circulent aujourd'hui en beaucoup plus grande nombre,[7] avec plus de rapidité et à moins de frais : cette mobilité qui a sensiblement modifié l'éco nomie de la vie privée, et qui modifie les rapports des nations restera, un des caractères distinctifs de la seconde moitié du dix neuvième siècle.

Avec de pareilles conditions, le commerce extérieur ne pouvait manquer de s'accroître. En 1850, époque à laquelle il avait à peu près retrouvé le niveau de l'année la plus prospère du règne

---

[1] C'est en 1859 et 1860 que le conseil général du Bas-Rhin, M. Migneret, étant préfet, classa les premiers chemin de ce genre. — La loi rendue sur la matière et du 12 juillet 1865, Deux départements (Eure, Saône, et Loire), indépendamment du Haut et du Bas-Rhin ont déjà entrepris des chemins de ce genre 29 autres départements ont décidé en principe des créations du même genre.

[2] Grâce à la convention télégraphique du 17 mai 1865, " le reseau télégraphique du continent européen est aujourd'hui dans toutes ses parties sans exception, soumis à des principes et à des règles uniformes." *Exp. de la sit. de l'Emp.*, 1867.

[3] 2,367,991 dépêches dans les 10 premiers mois de 1866, ce qui suppose environ 2,480,000 pour l'année. Au 1er déc. 1866, il y avait 2,091 bureaux télégraphiques. Des lignes souterraines ont été établies dans quelques grandes villes et des fils d'un diamètre supérieur sur les principales lignes pour prévenir les interruptions de service.

[4] En 1847, 216 millions ; en 1865, 590 millions.

[5] La convention monétaire du 23 déc. 1865 a établi une monnaie uniforme (mais critiquable à certain égard) entre la France, la Belgique, la Suisse, l'Italie et commence à constituer ce que M. de Parieu nomme le *Münzverein latin*.

[6] Plusieurs autres services ont été établis, *Exp. de la sit. de l'Emp*, 1867.

[7] Le nombre des voyageur des chemins de fer était de 37 millions en 1857, de 84 millions en 1866. Dans cette dernière année, les 84 millions de voyageurs ont fait 3,361 millions de kilomètres, et 34 millions de tonnes ont fait 5,171 millions de kil. Le produit brut a été de 184 millions de francs pour les voyageurs et de 314 millions pour les marchandises. Depuis 1855, le prix moyen kilométrique du transport de la tonne a baissé de 0 fr. 1,117.

de Louis-Philippe, il était de 2,555 millions. En 1864, il s'élevait à 7,329 millions, c'est-à-dire qu'il a presque triplé dans l'espace de quinze ans.

Si l'on prend la moyenne de chacun des trois lustres qui composent cette période, on constate, non-seulement un progrès, mais une progression constante, à n'envisager que les marchandises importées ou exportées au commerce special. La moyenne de 1850–1854 est de 2,294 millions ; celle de 1855–1859, de 3,626 millions, et celle de 1860–1864, période pendant laquelle l'abaissement des tarifs français a provoqué la concurrence étrangère, de 4,701 millions et le progrès continué.[1]

Il a été plus rapide qu'aux deux époques précédentes de notre histoire contemporaine. Durant les quinze années de la Restauration, notre commerce extérieur avait à peu près doublé ; durant les dix-sept années du règne de Louis-Philippe, il avait fait un peu plus que doubler.[2]

Ce progrès tient à des causes générales et n'est pas un privilegé particulier à la France. Dans les établissements de crédit c'est elle qui a donné des exemples à une partie de l'Europe, mais elle n'a fait que suivre à distance l'Angleterre ; dans la construction des chemins de fer, elle avait été devancée par plusieuas États. Cependant aucune nation, la Belgique exceptée,[3] n'a, depuis quinze ans, plus largement que la France, étendu ses relations extérieures. Pendant qu'elle en triplait le chiffre, la plupart des pays commerçants, et l'Angleterre en particulier, doublaient seulement le leur ; il est juste de noter toutefois que ce doublement, en Angleterre, portait son chiffre à 11 milliards.[4]

---

[1] Ces chiffres, il est vrai, sont ceux des valeurs actuelles, c'est-à-dire des prix du marché, et, comme la valeur de l'argent a diminué, ils ne représentent pas une quantité triple de marchandises. L'année 1865, dont on ne connaît encore que le commerce spécial, a produit 5,981 millions, l'année 1866 produira environ 6,360 millions (a produit 5,308 millions pour les 10 premiers mois) ; le commerce spécial de 1864 était de 5,452 millions. La navigation s'est accrue comme le reste; 12,531,504 tonnes en 1854 ; 17,638,900 tonnes en 1866. La principale augmentation a été pour les ports de Marseille, du Havre et de Bordeux.

[2] En 1815 (très-mauvaise année d'ailleurs), 621 millions, en 1830, 1,211 millions; en 1847, 2,437 millions.

[3] Belgique, en 1835, 358 millions de francs, et, en 1847, 584; en 1850, 618 millions et, en 1864, 2,432 millions ; ce qui fait environ 500 fr. par habitant. En France, la proportion n'est pas tout à fait à 200 fr. par habitant. Elle est en Angleterre de 366 fr.

[4] En 1854 (première année où la statistique ait donné les valeurs), 268 millions de livres sterling, et, en 1864, 435 millions, (soit environ 10 milliards, 900 millions). En 1830, une statistique anglaise (*voir* les *Annales du commerce extérieur*) donnait 120 millions: il y aurait donc eu à peu près doublement de 1830 à 1850. Pays-Bas, en 1832, 471 millions de francs; en 1850, 1,079 ; en 1864, 1,904. Russie, en 1850, 192 millions de roubles; en 1863, 306 millions. États-Unis, en 1831, environ 184 millions de dollars; en 1851, 412 millions; en 1860, 762 millions.

Il reste à dire quelles lois ont favorisé cette extension du commerce et régissent aujourd'hui le travail.

LES TRAITÉS DE COMMERCE.

Quelques jours après la proclamation de l'Empire, le sénatus-consulte du 25 décembre 1852 interprétait et étendait les prérogatives du souverain en matière de traités de commerce, en déclarent qu'ils auraient " force de loi pour les modifications de tarif qui y sont stipulées," e'est-à-dire que le Corps législatif n'aurait plus le droit de les ratifier ou de les annuler par son vote. Ce pouvoir, remis au chef de l'État, pouvait, en dehors des considérations politiques, inquiéter certains intérêts ; le président du Sénat, dans son rapport, s'appliqua à les rassurer en se prononçant contre les théories de la liberté commerciale.

Cependant la récolte de 1853 fut mauvaise. L'importation seule pouvait combler le déficit. Le gouvernement, pour l'encourager, n'hésita pas à abaisser toutes les barrières de la douane ; il décréta la suspension de l'echelle mobile,[1] l'exemption du droit de tonnage et de la surtaxe de pavillon pour les navires chargés de substances alimentaires,[2] l'abaissement du droit sur les bestiaux.[3] Ce n'étaient que des mesures temporaires ; mais elles semblaient indiquer un esprit nouveau.

Dans les deux camps opposés on s'émut M. Jean Dollfus entreprit une campagne contre la prohibition des fils de coton. Le début fut porté successivement devant la Société industrielle de Mulhouse, devant le Conseil supérieur du commerce et dans le cabinet de l'Empereur : M. Dollfus attaqua, M.M. Feray d'Essonne et Seillière défendirent le système protecteur. Le tarif des cotons ne subit qu'une modification légère ;[4] mais déjà un décret, plus significatif, changeait les zones d'entrée pour la houille et diminuait, de moitié environ, le droit sur les fers.[5] Deux ans après, nouvelle réduction, et, comme conséquence, abaissement du droit sur le fer-blanc, le fil de fer, la vieille ferraille et les machines.[6] L'année 1855 était marquée, en outre, par le retranchement de

---

[1] Décret du 18 août 1853. Cette réforme était alors demandée par le conseil municipal de Marseille et par le conseil général de l'Hérault que présidait M. Michel Chevalier.
[2] Déc. du 8 août 1853.
[3] Déc. du 14 septembre 1853. — Les droits sur bœufs et taureaux étaient reduits de 50 fr. à 3 fr.
[4] Voir le décret du 28 décembre 1853.
[5] Déc. du 22 novembre 1853. — La diminution sur l'acier fondu était même beaucoup plus forte : de 132 fr. à 3 fr.
[6] Déc. du 7 septembre 1855.

près de 200 articles sans importance, tels que les yeux d'ecrevisse ou le gui de chêne, qui allongeaient le tarif sans profit pour le Trésor,[1] et par une diminution importante du droit sur les laines et les peaux brutes.[2] La tendance du gouvernement s'accusait avec plus de netteté.

L'Exposition universelle de Paris venait d'avoir lieu et l'industrie française y avait brillé au premier rang parmi les nations. Dans le but d'épargner aux exposants étrangers là la coûteuse nécessité de remporter leurs produits, et peut-être aussi de tenter une expérience, le prince Napoléon, président de la Commission, avait fait décider que tous les objets exposés, qu'ils fussent prohibés ou non, pourraient être vendus et admis exceptionnellement en France en payant un droit de 22 p. 100.[3] Or, sur un total d'environ 22 millions de richesses étrangères, qui avaient été, pendant plusieurs mois, étalées sous les yeux d'un public si nombreux, 2 millions ½ seulement avaient trouvé des acheteurs français.[4] L'industrie française n'était donc pas aussi incapable de lutter contre la concurrence du dehors que le proclamaient les parties intéressées.

"L'observation qui m'a frappé tout d'abord, disait le prince Napoléon dans son rapport, c'est que de ces grands concours jaillit une fois de plus la preuve que les sociétés modernes marchent vers la liberté"; déjà le gouvernement, désireux de développer "les relations internationales qui préparent le progrès de la civilisation," avait présenté au Corps législatif "un projet levant toutes les prohibitions." Pour la première fois peut-être, il avait rencontré une résistance qui l'avait d'autant plus étonné qu'elle était plus rare et qu'elle cherchait à prendre son point d'appui, hors de l'assemblée, dans l'agitation des villes manufacturières. Il retira le projet, en annonçant qu'une nouvelle loi était mise à l'étude, et que la levée des prohibitions n'aurait lieu qu'à partir du 1er. juillet 1861. "L'industrie française, prévenue des intentions bien arrêtées du gouvernement, ajoutait le *Moniteur*, aura tout le temps nécessaire pour se préparer à un nouveau régime commercial.[5]

Durant trois ans, le silence se fit sur cette grave question.[6] D'ailleurs vers la fin de 1857, une crise terrible avait désarçonné la

---

[1] Déc. du 16 juillet 1855.
[2] Déc. du 6 avril 1854.
[3] *Moniteur* du 17 octobre 1856.
[4] Déc. du 17 janvier et du 10 décembre 1855.
[4] Voir *Journ. des Écon.*, 2e série, t. xi, p. 471.
[6] Cependant plusieurs décrets importants furent rendus.

spéculation et fait momentanément refluer en baisse le prix, sans cesse montant depuis 1852, des denrées, des matières premières, et, par suite, des objets manufacturés ; la reprise des travaux avait été suspendue, en 1859 par la guerre d'Italie.

Le commerce commençait à peine à retrouver son équilibre, lorsque, le 15 janvier 1860, le *Moniteur* publia la lettre que l'Empereur avait, quelques jours auparavant, écrite à son ministre des finances.[1] C'était un vaste programme économique dont le but était "d'imprimer un grand essor aux diverses branches de la richesse nationale," et que son auteur résumait en ces termes.

" Suppression des droits sur la laine et les cotons ;

" Réduction successive sur les sucres et les cafés ;

" Amélioration énergiquement poursuivie des voies de communication.

" Réduction des droits sur les canaux, et, par suite, abaissement général des frais de transport ;

" Prêts à l'agriculture et à l'industrie ;

" Suppression des prohibitions ;

" Traité de commerce avec les puissances étrangères."

" Par ces mesures, ajoutait l'Empereur, l'agriculture trouvera l'écoulement de ses produits ; l'industrie, affranchie d'entraves extérieures, aidée par le gouvernement, stimulée par la concurrence, luttera avantageusement avec les produits étrangers et notre commerce, au lieu languir, prendra un nouvel essor."

La pensée du gouvernement, sur ce point, se relevait tout entière. Il était impossible qu'issu du suffrage universel et dégagé des liens qui avaient arrêté ses prédécesseurs, il consentît à maintenir dans son intégrité le système prohibitif que les gouvernements précédents eux-mêmes n'avaient créé ou conservé aussi rigoureux que par la nécessité de compter avec de puissantes influences ; mais il eût pu se faire qu'un autre souverain embrassât moins résolûment un moins vaste ensemble. Quoi qu'il en soit, depuis le décret de Berlin, aucun fait aussi considérable ne s'était produit dans l'histoire de notre législation douanière.

Déja étaient arrêtés les articles du plus important traité de commerce que pût signer la France, de celui qui devait la lier à sa rivale la plus redoutée. Le héros de la ligue anglaise, Richard Cobden et M. Michel Chevalier, qui, depuis 1852, faisait à chaque session du Conseil général de l'Hérault, voter un manifeste en

---

[1] Lettre du 5 Janvier 1860.

faveur de la liberté commerciale, en avaient eu les premiers la pensée, et avaient trouvé des dispositions favorables dans le ministère anglais et à la cour des Tuileries. Au lendemain de la paix de Villafranca et à la veille du traité de Turin, l'Empereur, désireux de serrer les nœuds pacifiques de la France et de l'Angleterre, approuva un projet qui répondait aux besoins de sa politique extérieure comme à ses vues de réformes économiques, et dès la fin de novembre 1859, les négociations préliminaires, conduites avec le plus grand secret par M. Rouher, ministre du commerce, et par les deux économistes, étaient terminées. Ce fut par la lettre du 5 janvier que la France apprit qu'elle entrait dans une nouvelle ère industrielle. Le 23 du même mois, le traité était signé.

Les prohibitions étaient supprimées. Les marchandises anglaises entreraient en France en payant un droit *ad valorem*, qui serait bientôt converti en droit spécifique, et qui n'excéderait pas 30 pour 100 au début, 25 pour 100 à partir de l'année 1864. La Grande-Bretagne, de son côté, admettait en pleine franchise nos produits, qui payaient encore pour la plupart un droit de 10 pour 100, et ne prélevait plus qu'une taxe variable de 1 à 2 schellings sur nos vins, et de 8 schellings 5 pence sur nos eaux-de-vie.[1]

Le traité du 23 janvier était un type sur lequel on se proposait de réformer toute notre législation douanière, et de régler les rapports commerciaux de la France avec ses voisins. Des négociations furent presque aussitôt entamées ; elles ont amené la conclusion de plusieurs traités, d'abord avec la Belgique,[2] puis avec la Prusse et le Zollverein,[3] puis avec l'Italie et la Suisse,[4] enfin, en 1865 et 1866 avec les Pays-Bas, les villes hanséatiques, le Mecklembourg, la Suède, l'Espagne, le Portugal, le Pérou, l'Autriche.[5]

Le Corps législatif ne fut saisi de ces réformes qu'après le fait accompli.[6] Cet usage des droits conférés au souverain par le sénatus-consulte du 25–30 décembre 1852, eut le regrettable effet

---

[1] Le traité portait 8 sch. 2 pence ; mais le taux fut trouvé insuffisant en Angleterre et porté à 8 sch. 5 p. par un art. addit. du 20 février.

[2] 10 mai 1861. [3] 24 mars et 2 août 1862, 10 mai 1865.

[4] 17 janvier 1864, et 30 juin 1864.

[5] 7 juin 1865, 11 mars 1865, 9 juin 1865, 4 et 30 juin, 18 juin 1865, 11 juillet 1866 ; 2 déc., 11 déc. 1866. Voir M. Boiteau, *Les Traités de commerce* et *Exposé de la sit. de l'Empire*. (*Mon.* de janv. 1866 et de fév. 1867.)

[6] La discussion sur les modifications de tarif du traité du 23 janvier recommença au Corps législatif que le 28 avril.

de donner à une transformation libérale l'apparence d'une coup d'État commercial, et prêta aux partisans de la protection leur plus solide argument. Le gouvernement tint bon. Dans les discussions successives qu'ont amenées les traités, il s'est appliqué constamment à établir des droits de plus en plus modérés, afin de rendre toujours plus faciles les relations internationales,[1] et quoique la politique ait rendu vaine durant plusieurs années la Convention avec le Zollverein, la France communique aujourd'hui avec toutes les nations limitrophes de son territoire, sans rencontrer l'obstacle insurmontable de la prohibition, et sans avoir, dans la majorité des cas, à payer autre chose qu'un simple droit de consommation, assez léger en fait, et légitime en principe.

Ces traités avaient fait disparaître les prohibitions. Le système protecteur qu'elles étayaient, et dans lequel de si larges brèches étaient ouvertes, devait nécessairement crouler. Il ne restait au Corps législatif qu'à déblayer le terrain et à rétablir l'harmonie dans les diverses parties de notre Code douanier, en votant les projets que lui présentait le gouvernement. . . .

---

[1] Ainsi, par exemple, les modérations de droits portées dans le traité avec l'Italie, ont été, par décret du 20 janvier 1864, appliquées à la Belgique et à l'Angléterre.

XII.

THE FRENCH INDEMNITY.

THE PAYMENT OF THE FIVE MILLIARDS.

BLACKWOOD'S EDINBURGH MAGAZINE, FEB., 1875, PP. 172-187.

As soon as it became known, five years ago, that France had to hand over £200,000,000 to Germany, it was generally predicted that the financial equilibrium of Europe would be upset by the tranfer of so vast a sum from one country to another, and that the whole system of international monetary relationship would be thrown into confusion. Apprehensions of an analogous nature were abundantly expressed when the two French loans successively came out. Wise bankers shook their heads in Frankfort, London, Amsterdam, and Brussels, and assured their listeners that, though the money would probably be subscribed, it could not possibly be paid up under five years at least. And yet the whole of this vast transaction was carried out between 1st June, 1871, and 5th September, 1873; twenty-seven months sufficed for its completion; and not one single serious dfficulty or disorder was produced by it. The fact was that the commercial world had no idea of its own power; it thought itself much smaller than it really is; it failed altogether to suspect that its own current operations were already so enormous that even the remittance of five milliards from France to Germany could be grafted on to them without entailing any material perturbation. Such, however, has turned out to be the case; and of all the lessons furnished by the war, no other is more practical or more strange. The story of it is told, in detail, in a special report which has recently been addressed by M. Léon Say to the Commission of the Budget in the French Chamber. It is so curious and instructive that it is well worth while to analyze it. It may, however, be mentioned, that the order of exposition adopted by M. Say is not followed here. To render the tale clear to Enlish readers, the form of it is changed.

But before explaining the processes by which the war indemnity was paid, it will be useful to recall the principal features of the position in which France was placed by her defeat. It is now computed that the entire cost of the campaign amounted, directly and indirectly, to about £416,000,000; and this outlay may be divided into five sections, — the first three of which were declared officially by the Minister of Finance in his report of 28th October, 1873, while the two others have been arrived at by a comparison of various private calculations. They are composed as follows: —

1. *Sums paid by France for her own military operations* —
   War expenses to the end of 1872 . . £76,480,000
   Food bought for Paris before the siege . 6,781,000
   Assistance to families of soldiers, etc. . 2,000,000
   Balance of war expenses payable out of the
      Liquidation Account 21,942,000

   Total of French expenses proper, £107,203,000

2. *Sums paid to Germany* —
   Indemnity £200,000,000
   Interest on unpaid instalments of indemnity 12,065,000
   Maintenance of German army of occupation 9,945,000
   Taxes levied by the Germans . . . 2,468,000

   Total paid to Germany . . . £224,478,000

3. *Collateral expenses* —
   Cost of issue of the various war loans, rebates of interest, exchange, and cost of remitting the indemnity . . . £25,247,000
   Loss or diminution of taxes and revenue in consequence of the war . . . 14,567,000

   Total of collateral expenses . . £39,814,000

4. *Requisitions in cash or objects* —
   Supplied by towns or individuals, including the £8,000,000 paid by Paris — estimated at £15,000,000

5. *Loss of profits consequent upon the suspension of trade* —
   Estimated at £30,000,000

RÉSUMÉ.

1.	. . . .	£107,203,000
2.	. . . .	224,478,000
3.	. . . .	39,814,000
4.	. . . .	15,000,000
5.	. . . .	30,000,000
General Total	.	£416,495,000

Now, what has France to show against this? Her annual gains before the war were put by M. Maurice Block ("Europe, Politique et Sociale," p. 317) at £900,000,000; unfortunately he does not tell us how much of this she spends, and how much she lays by; but there is a prevalent impression in France that her annual savings amount to £80,000,000. We shall mention presently a calculation which seems to indicate that, during the later period of the Empire, they must have amounted to a considerably larger sum than this; but if we admit it, for the moment, as correct, it would follow that the cost of the war, in capital, represented five years' accumulation of the net profits of the country. It is not, however, in that form that a proportion can be established between liabilities and resources; the measurement must be made, not in capital, but in interest, for it is, of course, in the latter form alone — that is to say, in new taxation to pay interest on loans — that France now feels the pressure. That new taxation, when completed (it is not all voted yet), will amount to about £26,000,000 a year; and that is the real sum which is to be deducted from the annual profits of the country in consequence of the war. Now, if those profits were only £80,000,000, and if they are not progressing, but standing still at their previous rate, this deduction would absorb almost a third of them, but as they are continually advancing — as every branch of trade in France is active— as foreign commerce, which is generally accepted as a safe test of national prosperity, was one-fifth larger in 1873 than in 1869—it may fairly be supposed that, after paying the £26,000,000 of war taxes, France is effectively laying by as much as she did in the best years before the war, whatever that really was.

After this rough indication of the situation, we shall better understand the story of the five milliards. It is scarcely possible to disassociate it from the general attendant circumstances of the position as a whole; the two should be kept in view together.

The payment of the indemnity, and the detailed conditions under which that payment was to be made, were stipulated in the three treaties or conventions signed successively at Versailles, Ferrières, and Frankfort, in January, March, and May, 1871. It was determined by the last-named treaty that " payments can be made only in the principal commercial towns of Germany, and shall be effected in gold or silver, in English, Prussian, Dutch, or Belgian bank-notes, or in commercial bills of the first class." The rates of exchange on coin were fixed at 3f. 75c. per thaler, or at 2f. 15c. per Frankfort florin; and it was agreed that the instalments should be paid as follows:—

30 days after the suppression of the Commune	£20,000,000
During 1871	40,000,000
1st May, 1872	20,000,000
2d March, 1874	120,000,000
Total	£200,000,000

The last £120,000,000 were to bear interest at 5 per cent.

It must be particularly observed that no currency was to be "liberative" excepting coin, German thalers or German florins. The other forms of money which the German Government consented to accept, did not constitute a definite payment; it was not until those other forms were converted into their equivalent value in thalers or in florins that the payment became "liberative." This was the essential basis of the bargain.

Furthermore, it was declared that the instalments must be paid at the precise dates fixed, neither before nor afterwards; and that no payments on account should be allowed. It was not till July, 1872, that leave was given to make partial payments, but only then with the express reservation that such partial payments should never be for less than £4,000,000 at a time, and that one month's notice of them should be given on each occasion. Under no circumstances, from first to last, was any payment permitted on account.

Two main conditions, therefore, governed the operation: the first, that all payments made in anything but coin or a proper German form were to be converted into a German form at the expense of France; the second, that the proceeds of all bills or securities which fell due prior to the date fixed for an instalment, were to be held over until that date. The dates themselves were ultimately changed — the last payment was advanced six months; but, with two special exceptions, those conditions were rigorously enforced throughout the entire business.

As the annexation of Alsace-Lorraine to the German Empire obliged the Eastern Railway Company of France to abandon all its lines within those provinces, it was agreed that Germany should pay for them, that the price should be £13,000,000, and that this sum should be deducted from the indemnity. This was the first exception. The second was, that Germany consented, as a favor, to accept £5,000,000 in French bank-notes. By these two means the £200,000,000 were reduced to £182,000,000. But thereto must be added £12,065,000 for interest which accrued successively during the transaction, and which carried the total for payment in coin or German money to £194,065,000. And even this was not quite all, for France had to furnish a further sum of about £580,000 for exchange, and for expenses in the conversion of foreign securities into German value. This last amount does not appear to be finally agreed between the two Governments — there is a dispute about it; but as the difference extends only to a few thousand pounds, the final sum remitted may be taken at about £194,645,000, or at £199,645,000, if we include the £5,000,000 of French bank-notes. The £13,000,000 credited for the railways carried the entire total of the indemnity, with interest and expenses, to £212,645,000.

The first payment (in French bank-notes) was made on 1st June, 1871. As the first loan was not brought out until the end of the same month, £5,000,000 were taken for the purpose from the Bank of France; but with that exception and subject to temporary advances (as will be seen hereafter), the funds for the entire outgoing were provided by the two great loans; the interest was, however, charged separately to the budget. Consequently, the money was derived successively from the following sources: —

The value of the Alsace-Lorraine railways	£13,000,000
Loan from the Bank of France	5,000,000
Out of the first loan for two milliards	62,478,000
Out of the second loan for three milliards	120,102,000
Out of the budgets of 1872 and 1873 (interest),	12,065,000
Total	£212,645,000

It is not necessary to go into the details of the dealings with the Bank of France, of the subscription of the loans, or of the dates and proportions of the payments made upon them; it will suffice to observe, as regards those elements of the subject, that though the payments on the loans came in, nominally, before the dates fixed for the delivery of the corresponding instalments to Germany, they, practically, were not always available in time. The reason was, that though the actual handing over to Berlin took place at fixed periods, the remittances themselves were necessarily both anterior and continuous, their proceeds being accumulated by French agents until wanted. The result was that the French Ministry of Finance was under the necessity of making almost constant advances on account of those remittances. Each time a payment was coming due, the means of effecting it had to be arranged long beforehand. It is not possible to collect or carry £20,000,000 at a week's notice; so the Treasury was of course obliged to keep on buying bills as fast as it could get them, in order to have a stock in hand for future needs. That stock fluctuated a good deal, and there is some contradiction in M. Léon Say's report as to its amount; but it appears, at one period, to have ranged for months as high as £30,000,000, part of the cash to pay for it being provided temporarily, until the loan moneys came in, either by Exchequer bills, or by the Bank of France in notes.

There was, moreover, towards the end of the operation, an advance made specially in gold by the Bank of France; and, as the circumstances under which it was effected present a certain interest, it will be worth while to state them. In May, 1873, the French Treasury had before it the obligation of providing £40,000,000 between 5th June and 5th September; £24,000,000 of bills were in hand for the purpose, and about £10,000,000 of instalments were coming due on the loan; but there was, at the best, a clear deficit of about £6,000,000 in the resources available. The Bank of France agreed to supply that sum; but as, at that very moment, the circulation of its notes had reached £112,000,000, and as it had, consequently, only a margin of £16,000,000 between that figure and its total authorized issue of £128,000,000, it seemed dangerous to withdraw £6,000,000 of that margin in notes, and it was decided to effect the loan, by preference, in gold. It is worth remarking that this is probably the first example, in the history of national banks, of a bank electing to make

THE FRENCH INDEMNITY. 243

an advance in gold, as being less " dangerous " than the delivery of its own notes. The French Treasury was, of course, well pleased to obtain bullion, which was immediately "liberative," instead of notes, which would have had to be converted into bills at various dates. But, after all, this aid did not suffice; the incomings from the loan did not arrive, practically, in time for use, and the Treasury had to supply a further final balance of £9,760,000 to enable the concluding payment to Germany to be regularly effected.

Finally, it may be noted that there were thirty-three deliveries to Germany, the component parts of each of which were so scrupulously verified by the representatives of the Berlin Finance Department that several days were occupied by the counting, on each occasion. Indeed, when thalers had to be told up, the maximum got through in a day never exceeded £32,000.

After these preliminary explanations we can now begin to show the means by which the transfer was performed. We will divide them, in the first instance, into four categories: —

1. German bank-notes and money collected in France after the war	£4,201,000
2. French gold and silver	20,492,000
3. French bank-notes	5,000,000
4. Bills	169,952,000
Total	£199,645,000

The first observation to be made here is, that the German money found in France amounts to a singularly large sum; indeed, if this proof of its importance had not been furnished, no one could possibly have suspected that the invaders, for their personal and private necessities, had spent anything like so much. Their wants, as soldiers, were supplied, during the war, either by stores sent from Germany, or by requisitions levied in France; until peace was signed they paid for no objects of public or official need: all this cash represented, therefore, individual expenditure. And, manifestly, the real total must have been still larger. It cannot be supposed that the whole of the German money spent in France was reserved, by its French proprietors, for sale to their own Government; it may be taken for granted that a considerable portion of it went back straight to Germany through ordinary channels; and it may be guessed that the entire sum expended by the conquerors, out of their individual resources, in German money, was at least a half more than the amount here shown, and that it consequently attained £6,000,000. The question is curious, and this is the first time that any official information bearing on it has been published. It remains to add, as regards this element of the payment, that, as might have been expected, the German money was included, almost entirely, in the earlier instalments, and that scarcely any of it appeared in the later remittances.

The £20,492,000 of French money was composed of £10,920,000 in gold and £9,572,000 in silver. But it should be said at once that these figures express only the amounts transmitted by the French Government officially, and do not comprise the quantities of French gold bought by Germany or forwarded by private bankers to cover their own bills; these other quantities will be referred to presently. £6,000,000 of the Government gold were supplied by the Bank of France; the rest was bought from dealers or furnished by the Treasury. Of the silver, £5,840,000 were obtained in France, and £3,732,000 were drawn, in bars, from Hamburg, and coined in Paris.

But these direct remittances of German and French cash represented, after all, only about one-eighth of the entire payment; the other seven-eighths were transferred by bills, and it is in this section of the matter that its great interest lies. It will at once be seen that, as no remittance in paper became "liberative" until it was converted into an equivalent value in thalers or in florins, the French Treasury could obtain no receipt for an instalment until all its various elements had been so converted; its object, therefore, was to obtain the largest possible amount of bills on Germany, so that, at their maturity, their proceeds might be at once available in the prescribed form. But, at the same time, it was quite impossible to collect in France alone, within the time allowed, anything approaching to the quantity of German bills required. The result was, that it was found necessary not only to hand in a large amount of bills on other countries, which had to be converted into German values at the cost of France, but also, as regards the purchase of direct bills on Germany, to effect it frequently in two stages. In the first stage, bills were bought in Paris, as they offered, on England, Belgium, or Holland; in the second, a portion of the proceeds of those bills was reinvested, in those countries, in other bills on Germany itself. Of course the French Government was very anxious to employ every sort of means to increase the quantity of German bills, and to avoid leaving to the German Treasury the right of converting foreign paper into German value at French expense. At the origin of the operation the importance of this element of it was not fully realized; but by degrees the French minister discovered that it was far more advantageous to effect his conversions himself than to leave them to be carried out anyhow at Berlin. The result of this discovery was, that while £454,000 were paid to Germany for the cost of conversion on the first two milliards, only £11,000 were paid to her under the same head on the remaining three milliards; after the experience of the first twelve months, France sought for bills on Germany wherever she could get them, all over Europe ; and it may be added that she was somewhat aided in the effort by the special position of Germany, who, at the moment, was in debt considerably to England not only for the war loans she had issued there, but also on commercial account as well. But, as has just been mentioned, a good many of these bills were substitutions for each other, and, consequently, the amount of paper shown as bought is considerably larger than the real sum paid to Germany, the reason being that a good deal of it appears in the account twice over. The following table gives the composition of the total quantity of bills bought by France : —

Bills on Germany, bought direct, in thalers	£62,550,000
Do. do. in florins	9,548,000
Do. bought, in thalers, with the proceeds of other bills	42,218,000
Do. in reichsmarcs	3,172,000
Do. England, in sterling	61,780,000
Do. Hamburg, in marcs-banco	21,432,000
Do. Belgium, in francs	20,856,000
Do. Holland, in florins	12,952,000
Total	£234,508,000

These bills were paid for, mainly, in French bank-notes ; and the average rates of exchange at which they were bought came out as follows, for the entire operation : —

	Francs.
Thalers	3.7910
Pounds sterling	25.4943
Marcs-banco	1.9089
Belgian francs	1.0061
Dutch florins	2.1500
Frankfort florins	2.1637
Reichsmarcs	1.2528

Every one at all acquainted with exchanges will recognize how low, under such circumstances, these prices are; and will ask, with wonder, how they can have been kept down to such averages on so large an undertaking.

But though the foregoing table shows the quantities of bills, of each kind, that were bought by the French Government as vehicles of transmission, it in no way indicates the form in which the money was in reality handed over to the German Treasury. Most of the above figures were largely modified by conversions and substitutions; and when all the bills had been cashed — when the whole payment had been effected — it appeared that the real totals of each sort of currency which had been finally delivered to Germany were as follows : —

French bank-notes	£5,000,000
French gold	10,920,000
French silver	9,572,000
German notes and cash	4,201,000
Bills — Thalers	99,412,000
Do. — Frankfort florins	9,404,000
Do. — Marcs-banco	10,608,000
Do. — Reichsmarcs	3,190,000
Do. — Dutch florins	10,020,000
Do. — (and in silver) — Belgian francs	11,828,000
Do. — Pounds sterling	25,490,000
Total	£199,645,000

This catalogue shows, at last, in what shape the bills were really utilized and made "liberative," either in German money direct, or by the equivalent of foreign value in thalers or florins. The differences of composition between this definitive list and that of the bills originally bought, are only partially explained by M. Léon Say; it is not, however, necessary, nor would it be interesting, to follow out precisely the various conversions which took place;—we will only mention, as an illustration, that, out of the £61,780,000 of original bills in England, £31,687,000 were converted here into other bills on Germany, that £25,490,000 were sent to Berlin in sterling bill, and that the balance remains unexplained. As regards the direct delivery, by France herself, of English, Belgian, or Dutch bullion, the report says nothing; it is only stated, incidentally, that £720,000 of Belgian francs were sent to Berlin in metal, and that the London agency of the French Treasury bought £1,132,000 here in gold and silver, which, probably, was also shipped to Berlin; but these are the sole allusions to the subject. It is probable, as indeed has always been supposed, that the bullion which was withdrawn, during the operation, from London, Brussels, and Amsterdam, was not taken for French account, but by Germany, out of the sums at her disposal in each place after the bills on that place had matured.

We have now before us, in a condensed form, the main elements of this prodigious operation; we see now what were the conditions which regulated it, where the money came from to realize it, how that money was successively employed, and in what shapes the payments were at last effected.

We recognize that France herself provided, in
her own notes and coin . . £25,492,000
" that German money and bills on
Germany produced . . . 126,815,000
" and that bills on England, Belgium, and Holland contributed 47,338,000

Total £199,645,000

Here, however, we must repeat that the Paris bankers who sold drafts on Germany were obliged, to some extent, to remit cash to meet them. On this point M. Léon Say goes into calculations which we will mention presently; for the moment it will suf-. fice to say that, according to his view, the effective transmission of bullion from France to Germany, through private hands, from 1871 to 1873, did not exceed £8,000,000 for the purposes in view here. He acknowledges, as will be seen, that the entire exportation of French gold during the three years reached (probably) £40,000,000; but still he expresses the opinion that £8,000,000 were all that was required, as a balance, to cover the French bills on Berlin. Of course this is a question which nobody can decide; but, to lookers on, it does seem somewhat contrary to the probabilities of such a case that this sum can have been sufficient. It may, perhaps, have been enough, as M. Say says, to balance accounts in the long-run, but it is difficult to believe that it was not considerably exceeded while the operation was under execution. Furthermore, M. Léon Say makes a mistakes of £10,000,000 in his account, as we shall show; and, for that reason, we believe that £18,000,000 instead of £8,000,000 were required, so putting the whole total of French bullion temporarily used, including the £20,000,000 of the Government, at about. £38,000,000, or a little more than one-sixth of the entire sum to pay. As this is certainly a maximum, it follows that France got out of this great debt with a payment of only 18 per cent. of it, at the outside, in her own money. And there is good reason to suppose that all the gold exported by her has come back, and that her reserves of bullion are reconstituted at present as they were before the war.

And now we can approach the most important and interesting point in the whole transaction. How came it that £170,000,000 of bills could be got at all? We have given a general answer to the question at the commencement of this article; we will now consider it more in detail, partly with the aid of M. Léon Say's report, partly by reference to other sources of information. It appears, as might have been expected, that various measures were employed by the French Government in order to render possible the collection of such a huge mass of paper. In the first place, particular facilities and temptations were offered to foreigners to induce them to subscribe to the two loans; commissions varying from ¼ to 1 per cent. were offered to them, — the object being to acquire the power of drawing on them for the amount of their instalments. Secondly, everything was done to encourage anticipated payments of those instalments, so as to hasten the dates at which they could be drawn for. Thirdly, as some fear was felt that the second loan might possibly not be eagerly subscribed, coming, as it did, so immediately after a previous issue which was not quite paid up, it was thought desirable to get a portion of it guaranteed by bankers. But, in order not to risk giving to those bankers a large commission for nothing, it was stipulated with them, as a part of the arrangement, that they should supply the Treasury with a fixed quantity of foreign bills. By the two former plans of action the immense amount of £70,920,000 of drafts on other countries was obtained, £15,960,000 of which were on account of the first loan, and £54,960,000 on account of the second; and it may be remarked at once, before we proceed, that though this figure supplies decisive evidence of the fact that at least one-third of the two great loans was paid up by foreign subscribers, it is certain that nearly the entire amount has been bought back since, and that almost the whole of the new stocks is, at the present moment, in French hands. By the third plan, the bankers who formed the syndicate — and it may be mentioned that fifty-five of the first houses in Europe were associated for the purpose — engaged to supply £28,000,000 of paper. Consequently, by these admirably devised schemes, £98,920,000 of drafts were successively procured, and the exact quantity to be bought in the open market was reduced to £71,032,000.

It must, however, be observed, that though we can regard these drafts on foreign countries for loan instalments as a special product of the occasion, and are therefore justified in counting them apart, the same cannot anyhow be said of the £28,000,000 of bills furnished by the syndicate of bankers. The latter were evidently composed of ordinary commercial paper, and consequently must be added to the total which had to be supplied from commercial sources proper, so putting that total at £99,032,000. Now, bills of this sort necessarily imply an effective counter-value of some kind; so, as we have already seen that at the outside only £18,000,000 of that counter-value was supplied in bullion, there remained at least £81,032,-000 of bills which must necessarily have been based on ordinary trading or financial operations. What were those operations? Very often the general character of a bill is indicated on its face; but in this case a test of that kind could not be applied, not only because there were so many bills to handle that a serious examination of their nature was impracticable (there were, in all, one hundred and twenty thousand of them, of every conceivable amount from £40 to £200,000), but also because every possible kind of business transaction must have been represented in that accumulation of securities from all parts of the world. Bank credits, circulation bills, settlements for goods delivered, remittances on account of future purchases, drafts against the coupons of shares and stocks, special paper created for the occasion, — all these forms, and many others, too, were, according to M. Léon Say, included in the collection. It was not possible to seek out in detail the origins and meanings of such a varied mass; but we may take M. Say's general description of it to be true, not only because it corresponds with probabilities and experience, but also because he was himself Minister of Finance during a part of the operation, and has therefore a personal knowledge of its main circumstances. Researches, however, which could not be attempted with the bills themselves, may be practically and usefully pursued if they are directed towards the general signs and symptoms of the financial state of France. It is probable that a relatively small amount of bills was created specially to be sold to the French Government. We may, indeed, take the supposed £18,000,000 of exported bullion as indicating the approximate extent of uncovered or manufactured paper; all the rest was evidently based on mercantile transactions. Now, we know that mercantile transactions imply the delivery of property of some kind, and that the two main forms of property, commercially, are merchandise and stocks. It is therefore necessary, in order to arrive at an idea upon the question, to glance at the actual position of France in her dealings with other nations in these two values.

We have already alluded to the development of French trade, and to the general influence of that development on the payment of the war indemnity as a whole; but we must go into a few figures here in order to make the bearings of the subject clear. The value of the foreign commerce of France — importations and exportations together — was £257,000,000 in 1871, £293,000,000 in 1872, and £301,000,000 in 1873. Now, it will be at once recognized that the amount of bills necessitated by this quantity of commerce supplied a solid foundation for carrying the additional paper whose origin we are now seeking to discover. M. Say is of opinion that scarcely any part of the indemnity bills was furnished by the current commercial trade of the country; but, as we have just seen that the quantity required from trading sources was £81,000,000, or about £40,000,000 per annum, it does seem to be possible, notwithstanding his contrary impression, that some portion of that relatively reduced quantity may have been found in the ordinary commercial movement. For instance, it may reasonably be argued — as indeed M. Say himself admits — that bills drawn against French exports to Germany or England would be included, to some extent, amongst those which were offered to the Government. There seems to be no reason why this should not have been so.

But if M. Say considers that the habitual commercial paper of France has not been of much service to the Treasury in its conduct of this operation, he holds a totally different opinion with reference to the influence of the foreign investments of the French people. What he says on this subject is new and curious, and is well worth repeating.

He begins by stating, with an appearance of much truth and reason, that for many years before the war, French capital was being continuously invested in foreign securities; that the sums so placed have been estimated by different economists at from £30,000,000 to £60,000,000 a year. Here, however, before we follow out his argument, we must open a parenthesis, and observe that if even the smaller of these figures is exact, the computation of £80,000,000 of annual savings, which was alluded to at the commencement of this article, must be altogether wrong. It is manifestly inadmissible that France can have been investing in foreign countries three-eighths of her whole net yearly profits. Consequently, we may legitimately suppose that the popular impression about the £80,000,000 is a delusion, and that France is in reality laying by a vast deal more than that. If so, the ease and speed with which she has recovered from the war would be comprehensibly explained. M. Léon Say goes on to tell us that French investments in foreign stocks amounted in 1870 to so large a total, that the dividends on them represented, at that date, about £25,000,000 a year, for which sum drafts on other countries were of course put into circulation by its French proprietors. Furthermore, the revenues of the strangers who live in France come to them principally from their own country ; and it is estimated that, before the war, £10,000,000 or £12,000,000 of such incomes were drawn for annually in the same way. Consequently, on this showing, it would appear that somewhere about £35,000,000 or

£40,000,000 of French drafts on foreign countries were created every year from those two sources. It is, however, certain that this quantity has diminished since the war, by the departure of some of the strangers who used to live in France, and also by the sale, in order to provide funds for subscription to the two new loans, of some of the foreign securities held in France. But M. Léon Say considers that the annual diminution, on both heads together, does not exceed £4,000,000, and that at least £30,000,000 of paper, representing cash due to France on account of incomes from abroad, irrespective of commerce properly so called, were drawn in 1871 and 1872. In support of these considerations, he mentions, amongst other facts, that in 1868 and 1869 the coupons paid in Paris on Italian stock alone amounted to £3,400,000; while in 1872 and 1873 they fell to £2,400,000. On this one security, therefore, — which is, however, probably held in France in larger proportions than any other foreign stock, — the diminution of income since the war amounts to £1,000,000. With these figures and probabilities before him, he concludes by expressing the confident opinion that, as French purchases of foreign stocks have ceased, to a great extent at least, since 1870, and as remittances of French money to pay for such purchases have consequently ceased as well, the drafts on other countries for coupons and revenues became entirely disposable for transmission to Berlin, and that it is here that the main explanation lies of the facility with which the bills were found. This theory is ingenious, and it is probably, in great part, true.

The movement of the precious metals forms a separate element of the subject, and one that is not easy to trace out; for in France, as in most other countries, the public returns of the international trade in specie are very incomplete. We know how much gold and silver are raised from mines, and how much thereof is coined by each country; but we are very ill informed as to what becomes of them when once they have issued from the mint. On this head also, however, M. Léon Say has collected some valuable facts. The Custom-house Reports inform us that during the three years from 1871 to 1873, £53,400,000 of bullion were exported, and £50,480,000 were imported; on this showing, therefore, the loss of bullion was only £2,920,000. But as private information gave good reason to believe that the amounts must have been in reality considerably larger, calculations have been made in order to arrive at a more correct conclusion. It appears, from official publications, that the stock of gold and silver in the Christian world is supposed to have increased by £371,000,000 from 1849 to 1867; but the augmentation has not occurred in both the metals — it has taken place in gold only; the quantity of gold is greater by £428,000,000, while, in consequence of exportations to Asia, the quantity of silver has diminished by £57,000,000. Now, out of this £428,000,000 of new gold, France alone, in the first instance, received more than half; at least we are justified in supposing so, from the fact that, during the same period, the Paris mint converted £230,000,000 of bar gold into French coin. Of course this quantity of gold did not remain permanently in France; its whole value was not added in reality to the general French stock of metal; as gold arrived in France silver went away; indeed it is imagined that, out of the £200,000,000 of silver which have been coined in France since the year 1800, only £40,000,000 remained in the country in 1869. It is, however, calculated that the £100,000,000 of hard cash, gold and silver together, which were said to really belong to France in 1848, have doubled since; and M. Wolowski, who is regarded as an authority on such questions, declared in the French Chamber, on 4th February last, that, in his opinion, the national stock now ranges between £200,000,000 and £250,000,000.

But whatever be the interest of these computations, and useful as it may be to count up the amount of bullion which has come into France, we must look elsewhere for information as to the quantity of it which the consequences of the war took out. We know that the German mint melted down, for its own coinage, £33,880,000 of French napoleons. It is also known, says M. Léon Say, that the Bank of England bought nearly £8,000,000 of the same sort of money between 1870 and 1873. Here, therefore, we can trace the passage out of France, since the war, of nearly £42,000,000 of her gold. But, as Germany drew from London £1,680,000 of the napoleons which she put into the furnace, it may be that that sum was included in the £8,000,000 of the Bank of England, and is therefore counted twice. For this reason the amount really sent to Germany and England may be put at £40,000,000. M. Léon Say adds, that the Bank of Amsterdam bought a further £3,600,000 of French gold; but, as he fancies that this may not have come direct from France, he does not add it to the total, and he holds to £40,000,000 as representing probably the effective loss of gold which France had to support after the war. Of this sum, £10,920,000 were exported to Berlin, as we have already shown, by the French Government itself; the other £29,080,000 were consequently carried out by private firms for transmission to Berlin, and for various other purposes. Silver, however, arrived in considerable quantities to replace the gold. £9,500,000 of silver were coined in Paris between 1870 and 1873; and the Custom-house returns, which are almost always below the truth, show an importation of £12,160,000 of it. From all this, M. Say concludes that £40,000,000 of gold left France; that £12,000,000 of silver came to her; and that the £28,000,000 of difference between the two represents the real total loss of bullion which the war entailed.

But in making this calculation M. Léon Say commits a most wonderful mistake; he entirely omits to take account of the £9,572,000 of silver which the French Government sent to Berlin, and which must, of course, be added to the outgoing. When this strange error is corrected, the loss becomes, not £28,000,000, but £38,000,000, of which the Government exported £20,000,000, — leaving, apparently, £18,000,000, instead of £8,000,000, as the sum contributed by private bankers. This difference of £10,000,000 in the issue of the calculation gives some value to another computation which M. Léon Say has made, but which would have had no foundation if this error had not existed. He says — probably with some truth — that the quantity of money in circulation in a country remains usually at the same general total, during the same period, whatever be the nature of the various elements which compose it. He then goes on to argue that as the issue of French bank-notes was £44,000,000 higher in September, 1873, than in June, 1870, that increase ought to approximately indicate the amount of metal withdrawn in the interval from circulation, and replaced by notes. But, according to his theory, that amount of metal did not exceed £28,000,000, leaving an excess of £16,000,000 of notes, which excess he explains by saying that it represents an equal sum in gold which the French people had hidden away! Now, everybody knows that the lower classes of the French people do hide money — do " thesaurise," as they say; but such an explanation of the missing £16,000,000 is so purely imaginary that it cannot merit any serious credit. The theory assumes, however, a very different form when the error of the £10,000,000 is corrected. In that case we have an extra issue of £44,000,000 in bank-notes, corresponding to a loss of

£38,000,000 in gold and silver; and there the two figures get sufficiently close to each other for it to be possible that there really is some relationship between them, without being forced to resort to the possible but improbable solution of thesaurising.

Consequently, with all these various considerations before us, it seems reasonable to suppose that the natures of the bills employed to pay the war indemnity were of three main classes, and were grouped approximately in the following proportions: —

Drafts for foreign subscriptions to the loans	£70,920,000
Bills against French bullion specially exported,	18,000,000
Commercial bills and drafts for dividends and revenues from abroad	81,032,000
General total of bills	£169,952,000

Before we proceed to sum up the case, and to try to draw from it the teaching it contains, there is one more detail which is worth explaining.

We have alluded to the coining in Paris of a certain quantity of Hamburg silver. To make the story of it clear, it is necessary to remind our readers that, according to the constitution of the Bank of Hamburg, — which dates from 1619, — accounts were kept by it in a money called marc-banco, and credits were opened by it in that money on the deposit of silver, — coined or uncoined, — the value of that silver being calculated pure. By degrees the marc-banco, though only an imaginary money, grew to be the universal denominator employed in the home and foreign business of Hamburg; it acquired an importance greater than that of the effective money of many German states. But when the Empire was established, and it was decided to introduce a gold standard into Germany, it became essential to suppress the marc-banco, for it had the double defect of representing silver and of forming a separate value outside German monetary unity. So it was abolished by law and ordered to disappear, — the plan adopted being that the Bank of Hamburg should liquidate its deposits by paying off, in pure silver, the marcs-banco in circulation. It was, however, stipulated that this right should cease on 15th February, 1873, and that, after that day, all persons who held securities in marcs-banco should lose the old right of receiving pure silver, and should only be entitled to half a thaler for each marc-banco, that being the value of the silver represented by the latter. Now, the French Treasury had bought, as we have seen, £21,000,000 of bills in marcs-banco, and, consequently, possessed the right of claiming silver for such of them as fell due before 15th February, 1873, while all the rest, from that date, were payable in thalers. The thaler was "liberative," while the marc-banco was not; but the pure silver which the marc-banco represented could be coined into five-franc pieces, and be delivered to the German Government at the rate of 3 francs 75 centimes per thaler. The result was, that being by far the largest holder of marcs-banco paper, the French Treasury was able for a time to control the Hamburg market, and it naturally used for its own advantage the power which this position gave it. The Hamburg Bank was utterly unable to deliver the quantity of silver for which France held acceptances in marcs-banco; it was absolutely in the hands of the French Minister of Finance; that functionary appears, however, to have acted very fairly, — to have only asked for silver in moderation, and to have profited by his power solely to obtain conversions into thalers on good conditions. The result was, as we have said, that £3,732,000 of Hamburg silver came to the Paris mint, partly through Government importations on marcs-banco bills, partly through private speculators, who followed the example of the Treasury, and pressed the Hamburg Bank for metal.

Such are, in a condensed form, the essential features of the history of this extraordinary operation; and now that we have completed the account, we need no longer delay the expression of our admiration of the consummate ability with which it was conducted. Its success may be said to have been, in every point, complete; we cannot detect one sign of a grave hitch or of a serious error in it. It does the highest honor to the officials of the French Treasury, and proves that they possess a perfect knowledge of exchange and banking, both in their minutest details and in their largest applications.

When we look back upon the subject as a whole, three great facts strike us in it. The first, that France is vastly rich; the second, that the trade of Europe has attained such a magnitude that figures are ceasing to convey its measure; the third, that the aggregate commercial action of nations is a lever which can lift any financial load whatever. As we see the transaction now, with these explanations of its composition before us, we cannot fail to recognize that it has been rather European than purely French. All purses helped to provide funds for it; all trades supplied bills for it. In every previous state of the world's commerce such an operation would have been impossible; fifty, thirty, twenty years ago, it would have ruined France and have disordered Europe; in our time it has come and gone without seriously disturbing any of the economic conditions under which we live. France, out of her own stores, has quietly transported to Berlin a quantity of bullion larger than the whole ordinary stock of the Bank of England; and yet she shows no sign of having lost a sovereign. She has paid, in her bank-notes, for £170,000,000 of transmission paper, and yet the quantity of her bank-notes in circulation is now steadily diminishing. Such realities as these would be altogether inconceivable if we did not see their cause behind them: that cause is simple, natural, indisputable; its name is the present situation of the world's trade. The vastness of that trade explains the mystery.

But yet, with these advantages to help it, the operation had, in addition to its enormous size, certain special difficulties to contend with. As one example it may be mentioned that, amongst the elements of perturbation and of consequent impediments to remittance, the French Government had to keep in view the fact that, at the very moment when it needed all the monetary facilities it could obtain, the German Government was locking up gold in its cellars, in order to provide metal for the new coinage it was preparing. This was a most unlucky coincidence; but it existed, and it had to be met. The German plan was to hold back the issue of the new money until £30,000,000 of it were ready to be exchanged for the old silver currency; consequently, no silver could be expected to leave Germany until some months after the date at which the gold had been brought in there; and, during the interval, France knew that she must suffer from the withdrawal of so much bullion from the general market. But she found assistance in an unexpected way; silver did flow back to her at once from Germany, without waiting for the issue of the new gold currency. France paid Germany £9,572,000 in French silver; but this was of no use to the latter; on the contrary, it was an embarrassment to her; for she was on the point of exporting a quantity of her own silver, which would become superfluous as soon as the new gold got into circulation. So, for this reason, a considerable portion of the French five-franc pieces came back immediately to France, and helped to reconstitute her store.

And all the other difficulties were, more or less, like this one. At first sight they looked grave and durable, but they diminished or disappeared as soon as they were seriously attacked; the whole thing turned out to be an astonishing example of obstacles overrated. The unsuspected wealth of France, assisted by an extent of general commercial dealings which was more unsuspected still, managed to get the better of all the stumbling-blocks and impossibilities which seemed to bar the road. France has lost £400,000,000, one-half of which she has delivered to her enemy, and yet she is going on prospering materially as if nothing at all had happened. But it is now quite clear that she never could have managed all this alone; she could have found the money, but never could she, single-handed, have carried it to Germany. It is there, far more than in subscriptions to her loans, that the world has really helped her; she has bought back the stock that foreigners subscribed for her, but she could not do so without the bills they sold her. If she had been left to her own resources for the transport of the indemnity to Berlin, she would probably have been forced to send two-thirds of it in bullion, and to empty her people's pockets for the purpose; the vastness of the world's trade and the unity of interests which commerce has produced, permitted her to use other nations' means of action instead of her own.

Viewed in this light, the payment of the five milliards becomes an enormous piece of admirably well-arranged international banking, in which nearly all the counting-houses of Northern Europe took a share. That definition of it is worth knowing, and we may be glad that the information given in M. Say's report has enabled us to arrive at it.

THE FRENCH INDEMNITY.

APPLICATION OF THE INDEMNITY.

FROM KOLB'S THE CONDITION OF NATIONS (TRANS.), PP. 296-299.

When the North German Confederacy was formed, notwithstanding the transfer of the proceeds of the customs and of other indirect imposts to the Confederacy, and in spite of considerable contributions by the different States, the revenues did not suffice to cover the expenditure, especially that of the establishment of a larger sea force. A deficit was the result, and loans had to be raised.

In the year 1868 the debt of the Confederacy amounted
to £540,000
In 1869 to 1,312,338
And in 1870 it rose to 1,735,743
While in 1871 it was 1,988,882

The war made the contraction of a further debt unavoidable, both for the States of the North German Confederacy as well as for those of South Germany. The sum immediately expended on the war must have amounted to about £51,000,000. The result of the war led to a complete revolution in the condition of finance. We extract the following data from the memorandum, which was laid before the Diet by the Imperial Chancellor on February 18, 1874, with regard to the application of the French war contribution:—

The *Receipts* amounted to —

1. War contribution by France	£200,000,000
2. Interest upon this till the payment of the debt,	12,047,678
Total	£212,047,678
3. Added to this, contribution of the City of Paris	8,025,879
4. Customs levied in France and local contributions, less cost of collection, so far as these sums were not employed for special military purposes, about	2,609,133
Total receipts	£222,682,690

Of this sum, £12,999,999 must be deducted for the acquisition of railways belonging to a private company in Alsace-Lorraine, the remainder being, therefore, £209,682,691.

Expenditures.

1st. Expenses for which fixed sums were granted by Imperial decrees, viz. : —

For the Imperial Invalid Fund	£28,050,000
For the completion of German fortresses	10,800,000
For fortresses in Alsace-Lorraine	6,037,642
For railroads in the Imperial Dominions, particularly the Wilhelm-Luxembourg line	8,210,883
For Imperial war treasures, to be kept in the Julius tower of the fortress of Spandau	6,000,000
Compensation for the decrease in the revenue caused by alterations in the management of the customs and taxes	2,968,907
Imperial Treasury fund, for the administration of the marine, and for unredeemable advances for the management of the Imperial army	1,503,000
For gratuities to generals for distinguished services,	600,000
For aid to Germans banished from France	300,000
For exercise ground for the Artillery-trial Commission	206,250
Expenditure for general purposes defrayed by the Imperial Treasury in 1870 and 1871, and the additional outlay for troops garrisoned in Alsace-Lorraine till the end of 1872	1,249,500

Lastly, £6,195,181 granted by an Imperial decree of July 8, 1873. For marine, £4,206,783. Buildings for the Diet, £1,200,-000. Supplemental expenses of war, including various other grants, making total of £72,116,704.

To this must be added those outlays, the amount of which depends on the sum required for the attainment of the object in view. They may be estimated as follows : —

1. Compensation for damages by war and for war	£5,655.000
2. Compensation to German ship-owners	840,000

THE FRENCH INDEMNITY. 261

3. For war medals £45,000
4. Invalid pensions in consequence of the war of
   1870, 1871, and 1872 1,513,466
5. Additional for payment of invalid pensions, payable out of the Imperial Invalid Fund during the time that that fund was not perfectly established 897,000
6. War expenses connected with the French War costs indemnification, which, according to Art. 5 of the decree of July 8, 1872, are to be treated as common charges, viz. : —

(a) For arming and disarming of fortresses . £1,477,078
(b) For siege material 1,409,223
(c) For marine administration 1,402,876
(d) For temporary arrangements for coast defence, etc. 148,121
(e) For laying down and repairing railroads, etc., necessary for prosecuting the war . . 718,797
(f) For the establishment and working of telegraphs outside the limit of the telegraph system 30,418
(g) For temporary civil administration in France, especially for management of railways in Alsace-Lorraine, till the end of 1871 . 563,057

Further for services which from July 1, 1871, were in connection with the war, viz. : —

(h) Management of the post £33,750
(i) Management of telegraphs 88,500
(k) Increased expenditure in the management of the army, over and above that in time of peace, consequent upon the occupation of French territory 3,150,000
(l) Further estimates for general expenses to be defrayed by the Imperial Treasury, about, 37,500

The total amount of expenditure fund to be deducted from the revenue amounts therefore to £90,125,544, leaving a remainder of £119,057,197 to be divided. It is, however, desirable to retain a moderate reserve for possible deficiencies in the estimated receipts, in expectation of greater requirements in the expenditure.

The sum to be divided may, therefore, be estimated in round numbers at £118,900,000. Three-fourths of this were, in accordance with Article 6 of the Statute of the 8th of July, 1873, set apart for military purposes, in the proportion specified in the above Article 6, and one-fourth to be divided according to a fixed standard of 1871. The sum for division is shared as follows:—

1. Bavaria	£13,380,061
2. Würtemburg	4,275,130
3. North German Confederation	79,517,407
4. Baden	5,019,977
4. Hesse	1,400,051
For the payment of expenses	{ 917,850
	{ 16,289,521

About £22,500,000 of the entire war contribution were, in obedience to Imperial decrees, applied to civil objects, the rest for purposes of war. The sums which fell to the separate States in the division were also mostly expended in defraying the costs of war, and the repayment of loans for war.

According to the Statute of 2d of July, 1873, £16,027,021 of the sum to be divided were set apart for restoring the army to a war-footing and increasing its general efficiency.

We find from a report of the Commission on the State Debt, under date April, 1874, that the Imperial Invalid Fund possessed paper of nominal value in thalers £23,081,742
In South German guldens 933,187
In Dutch guldens 213,333
In English £ sterling 918,760
In dollars 3,556,800
And in banks 393

The fortress building fund possessed at the same time a nominal value of £5,229,795 in effects, and a capital of £2,789,913 in the Prussian bank. . . .

XIII.

THE RECENT PROGRESS OF ITALY.

FROM WILSON'S THE RESOURCES OF MODERN COUNTRIES,
VOL. II., CHAP. IX.

1877.

THE rapidity with which the new Italian kingdom has grown out of a congeries of petty States and subject Provinces is a good augury for its future. Unless we must yet look forward to a time of social revolutions, — to struggles between priestcraft and popular liberties, — of which there are at present few seriously disturbing signs, there is little to hinder modern Italy from advancing to the position of one of the most thriving nations of the Old World.

There is, indeed, something very attractive in the progress which Italy is making. It is a progress dashed with errors, and not without dangers, of course; but it has for all that been great and admirable. We have but to glance for a moment at the picture which the dismembered kingdom presented before she began to stir for her freedom in 1848. The first stirrings were indeed earlier than that; for Italy, bound hand and foot at the feet of Austria, as she was by the Congress of Vienna, which restored and solaced exiled and effete dynasties in all Western and Central Europe, — Italy never quite forgot the liberal ideas which the republican armies of the young citizen Bonaparte had carried with them out of France. The dull brutal rule of Austria in Venetia and Lombardy, and the more than Asiatic ruthlessness of the Bourbons of Naples, gave the Italians small chance to forget their dreams of a bright deliverance. Accordingly, there had been risings before 1848; and, besides the risings, many an effort to persuade the people to stand up like men for their rights, that had seemingly led to nothing. But it was not till 1848 that Italy could be said seriously to bend herself to the task of wrenching her shackles off. That year sent a quiver of dread through the heart of every king and kinglet in Europe. Again the impulse came from France, that country so full of striking ideals in its modern political history, — ideals which have been made the pretext of tremendous crimes; but dismembered Italy could have made no headway at all against either Bourbon or Hapsburg, except for the resolution of Charles Albert, the King of Sardinia, to become the champion of national unity and independence. The new generation of to-day forgets these things; but middle-aged men remember the excitement, the hopes, at first even stimulated by the sovereign Pontiff, destined to so cruel a disappointment. Italy was beaten back apparently into slavery, in this her first grand dash for freedom, and the dreams of Mazzini and Cavour seemed to be gone as dreams all go. The weak-kneed Pope had turned traitor to the nation, in his greed of temporal ascendency, and had given it his curse. Powers too strong for them were arrayed against the people, the Sardinian armies were defeated, and Italy seemed by 1850 to have lost everything. It was not, however, so to be. The defeat gave a keenness to the national feeling all over the land, such as it had not attained to before. Neapolitan and Lombard began to recognize themselves as men of the same nationality. The repression of the foreigners had thus to do its final work in welding the nation, and the conquerors endeavored to do it effectually, to their own ultimate overthrow.

Louis Napoleon also did something, no doubt, for the liberation of Italy, in a *grandiose*, histrionic, morally contemptible way, urged as he was by the necessity of justifying his rather despicable existence in the eyes of France; but, whether he had interfered or not, the power of Austria was destined to fall before the rising forces of Prussia, and with it that of the Bourbons of Sicily, Naples, and Tuscany, most corrupt of all the corrupt creatures whom England had propped up again for a brief space, to play the part of tyrants and oppressors in mundane affairs. It is not my purpose to follow the history of the Italian struggle for independence, through its Napoleonic and other phases; suffice it that we call to mind some of the cardinal facts. Before 1848 Italy, all except Piedmont, seemed hopelessly crushed. Austria, the Pope, and the Bourbons held her in their grasp. Even the comparatively native sovereign of Tuscany had turned oppressor, and all Italy groaned like a man in the grasp of the torturer. Commerce languished, divergent fiscal laws and arbitrary raids on private wealth choked up the channels of intercourse between one part of the kingdom and another; without shipping, without manufacturers or foreign trade of a solid kind, possessed of no political security, Italy was, thirty years ago, more insignificant in the eyes of neighboring nations than Greece or Spain is now. But, once free, her consolidation was almost as rapid as that of the still newer German Empire ; and to-day Italy is a power to be reckoned with in the councils of nations, and possesses a trade that begins to be a distinct element in European prosperity, — a trade that we in England cannot too carefully give heed to. The bitter bondage which the country has long lain under has ended in making its mixed population, in a hopeful degree, a nation ; and, prudently ruled, new Italy may yet have a remarkable career before it.

Naturally enough, all this progress has not been made without great cost, and it is our duty to look at both sides of the picture ; nor should the political and commercial success blind us to the fact that the young kingdom is not free from serious economic and social dangers on more sides than one. The very transition from a collection of petty States to a single power entailed enormous waste of resources and almost irremediable administrative confusion. Jealousies were also engendered between province and province, which it will take some time to heal ; so that this transition stage cannot by any means be considered at an end in Italy. Nor need we wonder when we remember that it is barely seven years ago since the crowning act of Italian unity was performed, and Victor Emmanuel entered Rome as King of all Italy, to the disgust of Pio Nono and the corrupt creatures around him.

I must leave the historical part of the subject, however, and trace some of the financial characteristics of this period of transition, before examining the trading capacity and mercantile development which Italy exhibits. These financial characteristics are again so intimately bound up with the administrative machinery of the State, that in noticing the one we must notice the other. Indeed, the first things that strike the observer are the concurrent facts that the government of Italy has, throughout, been impecunious, and, throughout, comparative feeble and irresolute, while yet the nation has grown and consolidated. No statesman has succeeded to the seat of Count Cavour ; and, either because the men were feebler, or because the constitutional powers, donned suddenly like a garment, fitted but ill, the remedial measures which society and the State required on all hands have been but tentatively and tardily applied, amid not a little bungling. The new kingdom succeeded to all the debts of the petty States it absorbed, and it also succeeded to their corrupt administrations. The debts made a most serious burden to begin with; and, when added to the cost of the wars of independence, so handicapped Italy that few people would have been surprised if she had pulled up short and proclaimed herself bankrupt. In a most valuable report on the financial system of the kingdom, recently made to our foreign office by Mr. Herries, Legation Secretary at Rome,[1] we are enabled to trace very clearly the stages of this financial malady; and many of the statements I shall make here will be drawn from this source. Quoting Mr. Pasini, for instance, he gives the total debt of the petty States of Italy, just before the consolidation of the kingdom in 1871, at £90,000,000, or 2,241,270,000 lira.[2] The debt was growing rapidly then, as the expenditure in all cases exceeded the income; but, after the new kingdom was fairly started, the deficits grew worse and worse. In the words of Mr. Pasini it is stated that during this disastrous period the receipts were diminished by £1,280,000, while the expenditure was increased by £2,280,000 and the public debt by £30,360,000. Only in the old provinces forming the kingdom of Sardinia was there any elasticity of revenue; in all other provinces the ousting of the old government and the setting up of the new involved almost hopeless fiscal confusion and loss. Income fell off and expenditure increased until the budget deficits, which had nominally been but £520,000 in 1859 for the various States composing Italy, rose to over £4,000,000, the greater part of which was due to the Neapolitan provinces and Sicily. Taxes of an odious character imposed by the old tyrannical governments had to be taken off and reduced before any regular system of substitutes could be framed to take their place; so that, as pointed out in the report of a finance committee, also quoted by Mr. Herries, and which gives, it would seem, a different estimate from that of Pasini, the income of the States forming United Italy fell from over £200,000,000, at the time of the breaking out of the war, to £18,500,000, the following year, and the

---

[1] *Embassy and Legation Reports*, part iv., 1876.
[2] Martin, in his *Statesman's Year-book*, states the debt of Italy in 1860, the year before the emancipation, at £97,500,000, but does not give his authority. It is possible he may be right, however, because the debts being reckoned in different currencies, some of which were of fluctuating values, the best statement which could be given was partly only an estimate.

expenditure exceeded that diminished income by £7,200,000. This deficit, however, as others similar, refers mostly, if not exclusively, to the ordinary income and expenditure, and does not include the special outlay incident to the war, which is partially at least represented by the increase of the public debt. In 1860 and 1861, no less than some £370,000,000 nominal appears to have been raised by loans, issues of inconvertible paper, or sales of stocks, only part of which have since been redeemed.[1] There were six separate budgets for the various parts of Italy in 1860, and it was not till 1862 that the government was able to present a single budget for the united nation; but that was only the initial stage of the task which Italian financiers had before them. A cumbersome method of account-keeping had to be swept away, which under the old system entailed the mischief of several distinct statements of accounts running alongside each other. The budget passed through no less than seven different stages before it could be considered a finished account, and it was not till 1869 that this was swept away. Now the financial account runs even with each year, and comprises within it only the actual receipts and payments of the year. Further reforms as to the administration of the various departments of the State had still to be carried out, and it was only the other year that Italy could be said to have her finances completely under parliamentary control. A far more formidable difficulty remains to be noticed, — the ref-

[1] I find great divergencies in the estimates given in various works of the present debt of Italy. For example, Kolb, whom I am disposed to place first as a compiler of statistics of this kind, gives the debt, funded and floating, at the end of 1872, as 10,060,000,000 lira, the interest of which is 460,445,614 lira. In other words, the capital of the debt was £400,000,- 000 odd, and the interest-charge just under £18,500,000. Martin, on the other hand, in the new issue of his *Statesman's Year-book*, places the capital of the debt at about £380,000,- 000, at the end of 1873, including of course the paper money, and the interest-charge at just over £15,500,000. Again, the *Investor's Monthly Manual*, a publication usually accurate, and with figures to a more recent date than either Martin or Kolb, places the capital of the debt at only £357,000,000, and the interest and other charges thereon at £15,300,000. This last estimate appears to me to be an obvious error, because for one thing the deficits on the annual budget have not yet ceased, and these alone for the past four years have amounted to an aggregate of £28,000,000, which has necessarily added to the debt in some form. If we take Kolb to be correct, therefore, the debt at the end of last year cannot have been less than £430,000,000 all told. This is, it need hardly be said, a very serious burden for so young a nation to carry, and it has been further heavily augmented since by the Italian government taking over the Italian portion of the old Lombardo-Venetian Railways, as it contracted with the Rothschilds last year to do. This bargain will involve an addition to the debt of at least £30,000,000, including the extra payments, and should the yearly deficits go on, and the railways not pay, — both likely contingencies, — the taxation of Italy will have to be seriously increased. By 1880 we may expect to see the funded and floating debt raised to the amount of £470,000,000 to £500,000,000, and the chances of a redemption of the paper currency almost as remote as ever.

ormation of the taxes, — and that cannot yet be said to be anything like completed, for Italy is still too poor to have a consistent fiscal system. There was a too radical cutting down of obnoxious imposts in the first moment of liberty and unity, when men's hearts overflowed, and ever since the government has had to struggle painfully to make ends meet. One of the best sources of national income, the property and the land tax, has also been most difficult of administration, through the absence of anything like a sound basis of assessment, and it now only yields something like £9,300,000, including provincial and communal surtaxes. In 1874 this was levied upon 5,130,146 proprietors, and the average impost per proprietor for imperial purposes only, was almost exactly £1. The amount of this tax which actually goes to the State is thus only about £5,000,000, the rest being devoted to local purposes under the law which permits provinces and communes to levy certain imposts for themselves. The figures as regards the number of people assessed cannot, however, be depended upon, any more than the cadastral basis of the tax; and there is no reform more urgently needed than the one which shall distribute the burden fairly over the landowners and metayers. At present the tax falls too lightly on some parts of the country, and on the tenant classes, and far too heavily on others, and altogether does not yield probably within millions of what it ought to do. Another considerable source of revenue is the income tax, which is not however to be taken as similar in character to the English tax of that name, being a complex and irritating impost which includes licenses of various kinds, and which presses very heavily on small incomes.[1] It seems to vary in character, too, in different parts of this kingdom. The grist-tax should also be mentioned as an old and most oppressive impost on the grinding of corn, which was withdrawn at the Revolution, and reimposed afterwards under pressure of the necessities of

---

[1] Mr. Herries makes the following comparison between the burden of this tax on the Italians and of the English income tax. His figures were compiled before the date of Sir Stafford Northcote's budget last year, which relieved small incomes up to £300, while imposing an additional penny on all beyond that; but they are sufficiently close to the facts, and illustrate the peculiar irritation of the Italian tax. "An Englishman having an income of exactly £100 pays nothing. An Italian pays on its equivalent, if in Category A, £13 4s.; if in Category B, £9 18s.; if in Category C, £5 5s. A so-called 'professional man' in London, with an income of just £300, pays on that amount, minus £80, a tax of £1 16s. 8d. If he establishes himself at Rome, he will soon find his means of subsistence diminished by a charge of £24 15s.; the sum which in England would be due from a commercial house making a clear profit of £2,970 a year."

the State. In its new form it is vexatious, and that it should be required at all is a proof both of the poverty which Italy still labors under and of the imperfect manner in which the fiscal reforms have yet been carried out. It gives a gross return of about £3,500,000.

We might pursue this subject further, and find it very interesting; but my object is only to indicate the broad fact that Italy is reforming; is, though slowly, growing solidly together; that she has, to all appearance, heartily adopted constitutional forms, and is shaping her destiny to good purpose, in spite of the many drawbacks to which she is subject. By means of the changes which have been introduced, the peace and security that have prevailed, and the consequent increase in wealth, the gross income of the kingdom has slowly recovered itself, until in 1875 it amounted to £55,480,000. In 1876 it was rather less, being only £54,800,000, owing to the insufficient harvest, rather than to any weakness in the country. In 1877 the fiscal estimate of ordinary income was about £51,000,000, but the total receipts, ordinary and extraordinary, were placed at about £56,000,000. There are still deficits, of course, but they are growing on the whole less alarming; that for 1875 having been only £1,124,000, that for last year £1,160,000, and the estimate for the present year showing a surplus, which will, however, in all possibility prove delusive. There is, perhaps, some reason to hope that deficits may really disappear before long, unless unforeseen events check the gradual development of the community, or unless the imprudent commitments of the government to railway purchases and administration lead to unexpected loss. I should not be surprised, however, were this to prove the case; and, if so, the small deficits of the last year or two may again increase for a time, but only for a time. Italy has but to push forward her social reformation, to steadily reorganize her finances and her provincial administrations, and there can be no fear that the wealth of the country will not be found in time sufficient to furnish all the government requires. The only serious elements of financial danger are the funded and floating debt, and the wasteful expenditure of the municipal and district governments; some of the Italian cities, such as Florence, Naples, and Genoa, being, for example, almost as spendthrift as New York. These, therefore, constitute grave dangers, which Italian statesmen cannot too deeply recognize. Not only should every effort be made to keep down the national and local expenditure, so that there should be no further increase in its amount, but every effort should be made to reduce the debt also. This is especially necessary with regard to the paper currency, which now forms such an intolerable drag upon the commerce of the people. In amount it seems light beside that of France, being only some £40,000,000; but then the population of Italy and the trade of Italy are both much less. The imports and exports together are under £100,000,000, or less than a third of those of France. Moreover, Italy has little or no metallic reserve, so that her paper currency is of necessity bound to fluctuate with every adverse movement of the exchanges. As the imports of the country have been stimulated for many years by the issue of such paper, and by other loans, so that they uniformly exceed the exports, it follows, of course, that exchanges are often adversely affected. Add to this the fact that a good deal of Italian *rente* is held abroad, in France, Holland, and England, and we have abundant materials for a very troublesome state of mercantile credit. The premium on gold is rarely less than 10 per cent., and it rises sometimes to 12 and 15, or even to 20. During one year the fluctuation is not unfrequently as much as from 5 to 7 per cent., so that the difficulty of adjusting prices, so as to avoid ruinous losses, becomes most serious. A premium on gold becomes, as I have said before, a universal tax, because no commodity, sold or bought, can be made exempt from its influences. Of late, however, there has been less tendency to violent movement in this gold premium, and the average is lower now than it was in the years immediately succeeding the national independence. Should the funded debt be kept well within bounds, therefore, it might be worth the consideration of Italian statesmen whether the government should not make an approach towards a resumption of specie payments, by means of an issue of bonds for the purpose of redeeming the currency debt. A measure of the kind, were it accompanied by the exemption of the foreign creditors of the State from an income tax, which is not fairly justifiable when imposed on loans which were raised abroad, would do a great deal to elevate the commerce of Italy out of its fifth-rate position, and to make it solidly prosperous.

There are, as we see, drawbacks in the situation of the country; but for all that I shall miss my aim grievously, if, in this rapid sketch, giving the outlines of both sides of the subject, I do not show that Italy has made, and is making, steady progress. She is not standing still, nor going back in either her political organization or her finances. The nation has vitality as a nation, and through all the drawbacks and difficulties one can discern the possibility of a new future for the peninsula which once ruled the world. Splendidly situated for doing at all events a continental trade with Asia and the far East, it is possible that the tide of commerce will partially roll backwards to her long-deserted shores. We must try, then, to find out what Italy is doing in the way of developing her trade — what her capacities are, and what hindrances there may be in her way other than the merely financial or administrative.

In the first place, it may be at once admitted that Italy is not a manufacturing country now, nor very likely speedily to become one. The races which inhabit southern Italy are ill adapted for the hard incessant labor to which " factory hands " and " foundry hands " have to submit in any country, but most of all in a country striving to establish a business for itself at the expense of rivals. In northern Italy there is much more raw capacity for industry; and the hardy Lombards or Piedmontese — even the Venetians and Tuscans — might, if it depended upon mere labor alone, rise with some rapidity into the position of competitors with other nations for certain kinds of manufactured staples. But, granting everything to be favorable in the character of the people, Italy does not possess the raw materials necessary to a great manufacturing nation in sufficient quantities, or in a form so readily accessible as to make it possible for her to become great in this way. The only industry in which she can be said to possess some advantage over her neighbors is silk-weaving, and in this, I believe, some progress was made up to the time when a change of fashion, and failure in the Italian silk crop, gave the entire industry a severe blow; but as a producer of textile fabrics generally, Italy does not promise to take a strong position. Her exports of silk, raw and manufactured, averaged in value about £15,000,000 in the years 1870 to 1874, according to tables given by Mr. Herries. This was balanced to some extent by imports of the average value of £5,500,000. Besides silk, Italy grows a certain amount of cotton, but not nearly enough to supply her own wants; and although she has an export trade to Austria in cotton tissue, it is more of a transit trade, I believe, than the result of the competition of Italian spinners and weavers. Her industries are, indeed, all, except that of silk, small and of quite local importance. Italy is in nothing more provincial, in fact, than in the isolated condition of her cotton, linen, and woollen manufactures. But, although insignificant, they still increase in a measure, and may well grow very much bigger without interfering in the least with the purchasing power of Italy in other countries, or competing very seriously in foreign markets. With her immediate neighbors, Switzerland, Austria, and France, it is in the nature of things that her trade should grow larger, and that where competition is possible Italian products should in some directions beat ours; but there is yet certainly nothing alarming in the situation, and we have no cause to be envious of her prosperity. At present the total export and import trade of Italy is, as I have said, well under £100,000,000, and the bulk of the exports — silk, oil, wine, marble, and glass — are of a kind which do not come much within our competing range. As far as the direct trade with Great Britain is concerned, it is not on the whole steady and profitable, and amounts to about an eighth part of her entire commerce; Italy buying from us much more largely than we do from her, although the discrepancy is less now than it has been, owing in part, I fear it must be said, to the more effectual competition of French manufacturers. The consumption of Indian and Egyptian raw cotton is also steadily increasing in Italian mills, although these are in great part still of a primitive kind. Some progress has been made in the establishment of small iron-works, and one work at Venice, belonging to an Englishman named Nevill, has attained to some local celebrity. Italy possesses few iron mines, however, and, as far as we know, has no rich contiguous stores of iron and coal, such as are essential to a country destined to lead in almost any branch of skilled production.[1] We must, therefore, after making all allowance for the signs of local activity which are to be met with in the country, come to the conclusion that Italy is not in a position to become a great manufacturing centre. Her people are by preference pastoral; and as in France, although the tenure of the land is not the same, large tracts of the soil are parcelled out

---

[1] In Kolb's *Vergleichende Statistik* it is stated that the average annual value of the production of iron in Italy in the years 1867-70 was just over £800,000, the product of 11,100 workpeople; that of copper, £53,000, won by the labor of 2,500 workmen. Coal and petroleum together represented the insignificant value of £126,000 and gave employment to 3,450 workmen. Lead was considerably more valuable than copper, but it only gave an average of about £330,000, a quantity clearly not sufficient for home consumption. Italy is, in fact, a steady consumer to England for the metals of manufacture and for coal.

amongst small holders, whose position is nearly as secure, if not so independent, as that of the French peasant proprietor, and the attractions of the workshops are not sufficient to draw a comparatively comfortable and by no means crowded population from their fields.[1]

But, though not a great manufacturing nation, Italy is, as we have seen, advancing in several respects as a producer of articles meant for home use, and her tariff is, like that of other countries

---

[1] According to the return published in 1861, the latest which seems to be available, about 8,000,000 of the population of 22,000,000 then comprising Italy were employed in agricultural pursuits, and a nearly equal number were returned as " without calling." The number engaged in mineral production was less than 60,000, and there were devoted to manufactures about 3,100,000. In this latter would of course be included all the local tradesmen, the shoemakers, smiths, carpenters, masons, and clockmakers, which go to make up the population of the villages, so that the numbers engaged actually in what we should in this country call manufactures would probably not reach half that figure. These figures are not of so much value now, however, for Italy has been changed and opened up greatly since then, and, in some of the northern provinces, manufactures and agriculture overlap each other, so that the same people ought to be classed in both; not only so, but the addition to the population, both by natural increment and through the incorporation of fresh provinces, has materially added to the proportions of certain classes. Instead of 22,000,000, Italy has now a population of 27,500,000, of which, according to Behm and Wagner's last Annual, on the population of the earth, issued in Petermann's *Mittheilungen*, 6,900,000, or 25.7 per cent., form the scattered population, the remainder being gathered in the cities, towns, and agricultural villages of the land. I am unable to say, however, what proportion of the entire population may now be actually employed in, or directly dependent upon, the labor of the agriculturist. From an official report lately issued on the state of the Italian agriculture in the years 1870-74, of which copious analyses have been appearing both in the *Economista d'Italia* and in the *Economiste Français*, I learn that 11,600,000 acres of land are devoted to wheat, and yield about 142,420,000, bushels, or, roughly, a little more than twelve bushels to the acre, — a very small yield for so rich a country, and the best commentary we could have upon the exceeding backwardness of agriculture. Of maize, rice, barley, and oats the yield was rather better, as the following table will show: —

	Acres.	Total yield in Bushels.	Yield per Acre.
Maize	4,242,000	85,959,000	20.3
Rice	582,000	27,000,000	46.4
Barley and rye	1,162,000	18,417,000	15.8
Oats	798,000	20,471,000	25.6

Allowing for the difference of grains, this table still shows great variableness in the yield. At the worst, however, Italy compares very favorably with such a country as Russia, where the yield per acre of wheat is estimated in the latest returns at only five and a half bushels per acre. The total yield of wheat in Italy is indeed within 15,000,000 bushels of that of Russia, and leaves a considerable margin for export. Besides these grains and root crops, olives, cotton, and flax, a large acreage is devoted to the vine, no less, according to the table from which I quote, than 4,700,000 acres, the yield upon which was 597,000,000 gallons of wine. Altogether, the agricultural land in Italy included in the official returns extends to 68,000,000 acres. The tendency would seem to be to extend the pasture lands, a good trade offering to Italy in cattle with Austria, Switzerland, and France, which the vegetarian habits of the agricultural population enables it to turn to better account than the mere enumeration of the flocks would lead one to suppose. In horses particularly Italy is poor, and she stands numerically in all kinds of animals behind Austria and Hungary, but for all that she can export to them.

we have mentioned, acting as a strong bulwark to protect the home producer against competition. One would imagine, for example, that in the matter of silk the Italian manufacturer would require little or nothing in the shape of protection, seeing that he could set up his mills in the heart of a silk-growing country, and yet Italy levies a duty on all kinds of silk tissues imported, which, though small, is, like the Indian duties on cotton goods, sufficient to debar foreign imports to a considerable extent, and to raise prices at home. Woollen, cotton, and linen fabrics are more heavily taxed still, as will be seen in the note which I append;[1] and, speaking generally of the Italian tariff, we may say that, instead of being now light and liberal, as Count Cavour wished it to be, when compared with that of other European countries, it is essentially the tariff of a country devoted to protectionist

---

[1] The import duty charged at Italian ports on silk tissues is 5 per cent. *ad valorem*, or 1s. 1d. per lb.; ribbons pay from 1s. 10d. to 2s. 11d. per lb. if of silk alone, and 10 per cent. *ad valorem* if mixed. Only silk twist is admitted free. Cotton yarn, on the other hand, pays according to fineness, and to whether it is bleached and dyed or unbleached, a duty varying from 6s. 1d. to 14s. 1d. per cwt., the twists and double yarns and bleached and dyed ditto paying respectively 11s. 9d. and 14s. 1d. On cotton tissues the duty is very heavy, varying from 26s. 5d. on unbleached cotton to 47s. on cotton prints per cwt., while cotton embroidery pays £4 14s. 3d. per cwt. Woollen yarn comes off worse still, undyed paying 18s. 9d. and dyed 28s. 3d. per cwt., while woollen cloths pay substantially about the same nominal duties per cwt. as cotton. Blankets and carpets, for example, are charged 23s. 6d. to 32s. 6d., according to quality, per cwt.; tapes and lace of pure wool, or mixed, £4 13s. 6d. Ordinary woollen tissues or cloths pay, however, either a 10 per cent. *ad valorem* duty, or £3 5s. per cwt. What the incidence of much of this taxation is according to the values of the articles taxed, it is of course impossible for any but exporters to tell; but it must vary considerably, and in some instances, when the cloth is of a cheap kind, represent something like 20 to 30 per cent. of its value, or more. The same may be said of linen, hempen, and jute fabrics, all of which pay heavy duties, which, if nominally less in amount than those levied by France or Russia, are by their rough and ready mode of adjustment probably practically as prohibitory. Measured by the wealth of Italy, compared with France, they must be more so. As to iron and steel, the tariff of Italy is, if anything, more foolish than that of any other country we have had under review, because in this instance there is nothing to be protected worth speaking of. There are no blown-up hectic home industries in iron to pamper and to fine the people for the maintenance of, as in the United States; and therefore these duties have here not even the irrational excuse which the States, France, Austria, and Germany may plausibly advance. Italy charges, for all that, a duty of some sort on every kind of iron except pig-iron and broken scraps. In some cases, as, for example, rails, the duty is relatively low, only some 5½d. per cwt., or 9s. 2d. per ton; but in others it is very high, — steel wire paying 9s. 5d.; rolled and -bar steel, 5s. 7d.; plates, 6s. 1d.; fine iron wire, 3s. 3½d.; tools for mechanics or agriculturists, 3s. 9d.; knives of ordinary kinds, 20s. 4d.; and with fine handles, 40s. 8d. per cwt. Steam-engine boilers and machinery of all sorts also pay duties ranging from 1s. 7½d. to 4s. 10½d. per cwt.; agricultural machines being admitted at the lowest scale. All this indicates an extreme short-sighted policy, because it is hampering the progress of the community, without doing any class in it even a temporary benefit, or bringing the government much profit. And these are by no means all. Italy taxes the import of food grains, of meats, of sugar (which pays from 8s. 5d. to 11s. 9d. per cwt., according to fineness), and chemicals (such as the alkalies so valuable in agriculture), and yet with it all the gross income from the customs barely reaches £4,000,000 a year.

ideas. Driven by stress of poverty, Italian statesmen not possessed of the political sagacity of Count Cavour have reimposed some very obnoxious custom duties, and increased their burden, without, however, adding materially to the yield, while certainly hindering the development of the trade of the nation. Compared with the fragmentary tariffs in force in 1858, the duties are, however, still very low, and Italy should get credit here also, for at all events not slipping back into the slough from which she emerged. Still, the present tariff is higher, in a good many instances, than that in force in 1863 and 1864,[1] which alarmed the short-sighted economists of the country by the smallness of its yield; and it is apparently further beset by vexatious provisions and excessive charges which aggravate importers and cumber business, without yielding any adequate return. We may hope then that, when the time comes for a fresh revision of the general and special customs tariffs of the kingdom, — as come it speedily must, — a step forward will be taken, and that England will be admitted within the inner circle, if Italy cannot find it in her heart to open her gates to all alike. But at present it must be candidly admitted that the signs are the other way. From year to year Italy has been going to revise her general tariff, but hitherto the revision has been postponed. A fragmentary tariff between Italy and France was, however, signed in the middle of July last, and it indicates rather an increase of fiscal obstructiveness than the reverse. Sundry duties on articles specially affecting the two countries, such as wine and silk, have been arranged mostly for the worse, and Italy has distinguished herself in particular by large additions to her list of export duties. Altogether this treaty augurs ill for free trade, and ill for the reciprocal business of Italy and France, which has lately been flourishing apace. We may rest patiently, therefore, under the present burdens imposed on our trade, lest a worse evil befall us. A few years' further experience of the mischiefs in the present system may lead to change in the direction of freedom, which Italy is clearly unprepared for now.

Yet it would be decidedly the interest of Italy to revise her tariff in a free-trade sense, were it for no other reason than that her wealth is neither mineral nor industrial in the English sense of the terms, but agricultural. How decidedly Italy is a pastoral

---

[1] See table in Mr. Herries' *Report*, pp. 597-599.

country is seen best by her actual foreign trade; the staple exports of Italy, beyond her silk and her small amount of silk manufactures, being oil and wine, fruits and seeds, cereals and hides, timber, animals, hemp, and flax, some sorts of provisions, and a little wool. She is inevitably, in spite of the development of her local industries and manufactures, much dependent on foreign supply for many necessary articles of clothing, for much of her machinery used in mills, on farms, on railways, and in steamboats. Italy is, in consequence, and in spite of herself, therefore, a customer of growing importance, either to Great Britain or to industrial countries such as France or Germany, and she ought to recognize the fact so as to make the benefits as much as possible mutual. For example, she took from us alone, in 1875, about £2,600,000 worth of cotton yarn and piece goods, besides what may have reached her indirectly, and a considerable amount of iron and iron manufactures, as well as woollen goods and coal. The character of her trade with us is very decidedly fixed by the tariff, however, and we discover here, as in the case of France, a tendency to take from us raw or half-manufactured articles in increasing quantities, rather than the finished goods. It is not satisfactory, for instance, from our point of view, to find that the value of cotton yarn entered for Italy was, in 1875, almost as large as the value of the cotton cloths. It shows us that, however unfitted Italy may be by nature and circumstances to become a great manufacturing country, she can at least secure the temporary advantage of being, in a considerable measure, her own provider. Still less satisfactory is it to find that for some years France has been gaining steadily where we have been losing, and that although our general trade with Italy gives few signs of weakness, but rather the reverse, our cotton manufacturers are being decidedly elbowed out of her market.

The following tables given by Mr. Malet in his report to the Foreign Office on the trade of Italy for 1875, will show the position most clearly : —

THE RECENT PROGRESS OF ITALY.

Table showing the Value of Imports from England and France to Italy of Tissues of Hemp or Flax of less than nine threads of Warp in the space of five Millimetres, whether Raw or Bleached, during the five years ending December 31, 1875.

	1871.	1872.	1873.	1874.	1875.
	FR.	FR.	FR.	FR.	FR.
England	1,473,000	1,287,000	1,035,000	978,000	1,145,000
France	798,000	717,000	1,031,000	674,000	1,338,000

Table showing the Value of Imports from England and France to Italy of Cotton Tissues, also mixed with Thread and Wool, Colored, Dyed, or Printed, during the five years ending December 31, 1875.

	1871.	1872.	1873.	1874.	1875.
England:—	FR.	FR.	FR.	FR.	FR.
Cotton or dyed	6,732,000	6,458,000	6,339,000	4,267,000	5,529,000
Printed	17,778,000	14,020,000	14,475,000	10,633,000	12,696,000
	24,510,000	22,478,000	22,814,000	14,900,000	18,225,000
France:—					
Cotton or dyed	2,620,000	3,727,000	4,497,000	5,566,000	6,649,000
Printed	5,311,000	6,326,000	7,748,000	7,166,000	8,472,000
	7,931,000	10,053,000	12,245,000	12,732,000	15,123,000

Table showing the Value of Imports from England and France into Italy of Tissues of Wool or Hair, also mixed with Cotton or Thread, during the five years ending December 31, 1875.

	1871.	1872.	1873.	1874.	1875.
England:—	FR.	FR.	FR.	FR.	FR.
Paying *ad valorem* duties,	16,542,000	15,734,000	12,485,000	9,521,000	10,873,000
Paying by weight	3,170,000	3,103,000	3,533,000	3,204,000	2,074,000
	19,712,000	18,837,000	16,018,000	12,725,000	12,947,000
France:—					
Paying *ad valorem* duties,	7,231,000	9,225,000	10,500,000	11,015,000	14,471,000
Paying by weight	4,918,000	6,653,000	6,926,000	7,812,000	6,831,000
	12,149,000	15,878,000	17,462,000	18,827,000	21,302,000

Embassy and Legation Reports, Part II., 1877, p. 137.

These figures are of a sufficiently startling kind, and would seem to make good the contention of Mr. Malet, that French manufacturers have now the advantage of us. There is no reason to be alarmed at that fact, even supposing it true, and least of all as regards Italy, which is France's next door neighbor; but I am disposed to think that the importance of this growth of the French trade in tissues might be easily exaggerated, and that were trade to be made free, we should regain a considerable part of the ground we have lost. At present both tariff and freight are against us, and the freight probably turns the scale as compared with France, more than anything else. And these figures at least tend to confirm the statement that Italy is dependent on foreign supply in most important branches of manufacture. Her tariff may give a certain forced prosperity to some of her endeavors to become a rival of England and France, but she has no other advantage than her tariff gives, for living is not much cheaper for the working classes in Italy than here, and, as a rule, they are less capable, more ignorant, and more disposed to " scamp " work than our own, so that, with wages nominally on a lower scale, the real cost of production in Italy is probably higher than here. I have not, indeed, attempted to discuss in any adequate way the " labor element " or the " wages element," in dealing with the competing capacities of other countries in contrast with our own, because, in my judgment, they are of comparatively secondary importance to the primary forces of reserves of capital, of habit, and, above all, of geographical and physical adaptabilities. Against the enormous advantage which England still possesses over almost all other countries in most respects, were she free of the markets of the world as the world is free to hers, the labor and wages elements have, in my opinion, little force. It is not labor itself so much as the facilities for applying labor in all departments of manufacture in the most economic manner possible which determines the battle, and in these facilities no country in the world can hope for some time to rival us. So far, therefore, as the policy of Italy tends to fight against this superiority, I hold it to be mistaken; but it is a policy which we cannot immediately hope to see departed from there or elsewhere; and we cannot therefore expect that the present reaction, partly the result of over-speculation, partly artificial, will soon end even in increased demand from Italy for our woven fabrics, although in regard to our general trade with that country we have good reason to be hopeful.

Left unforced, the course which Italy might pursue with most advantage to herself and to the world, as a commercial nation, is very clearly marked out by her poverty, her physical peculiarities, and her geographical situation. To the first we shall refer again presently. As to the second we need only say that the highly favored climate and rich soil of Italy render her admirably adapted for the production of wine, oil, sugar, maize, and choice fruits, for which she would find, and does find, a ready market, not in Europe only, but also in the East, and in America, North and South. Already a considerable trade is established with the United States, for instance, and the large flow of Italian emigration to that region, as to Brazil and the River Plate, tends to extend this kind of commerce. But for the backward character of Italian agriculture, which, except in Piedmont and perhaps part of Lombardy, is hardly worthy the name of tillage at all, Italy might to-day be much more prominent as a rival of France in the supply of luxurious nations with dainties, and of physically ill-conditioned countries with cheap food. With Italy, as with France, it is the fruits of the earth which must form the solid basis of all her trade. To much of the rest of the world these fruits are, or might become, delicacies of the most precious kind; and, therefore, whatever Italy does to develop agriculture is better than the establishment of a dozen unhealthy factories. In some measure the Italian government may be said to see this, inasmuch as they devote a considerable amount of attention to agricultural education, establish depots of agricultural implements in various districts for the purpose of educating the people, and so forth; but that is only toying with the great reforms needed, which must include a wide remodelling of the fiscal burdens, a new cadastral survey, followed by a revised land tax, and the protection of the tillers of the soil alike from the extortions of their do-nothing landlords and the robberies of the brigand. Recent letters from Italy have shown the Italians to be morbidly sensitive to this last subject; and the curious vanity which they have displayed about their rights and liberties is not pleasant. For certainly this brigand question is more vital to the true settlement and prosperity of southern Italy than almost any other. Until the nefarious robbers are extirpated, and the so-called upper classes of the towns — the remnant of a debased and corrupt nobility — prevented from aiding and abetting them in their depredations, Italy cannot advance as an agricultural nation. Her peasantry, unable to cultivate the vine, the olive, and the citron in peace, must remain, over almost half the land, degraded, stupid, and wasteful. Instead of strutting about, talking of national dignity, therefore, Italian statesmen would do well quietly to set about the task of making each man's life and property secure through the length and breadth of the land. Unless they do so, their work may one day be partially undone, and the country, ill-taxed and overtaxed, poor and vexed by thieves and priests, may see itself outstripped on every hand. In vine-growing now it cannot for a moment compete with France or Spain, hardly with Greece; indeed, but for the dishonest trade with France in bad wines, used for adulteration, the export wine trade of the mainland would be of hardly any value at all, and no Italian wine is known widely in England except the Sicilian Marsala. If she does not take care her silk trade will be in like danger from the competition of our Australian colonies, as well as from that of China and Japan. Italy has done much; but what she has done only brings into most startling relief all that she has to do. And, latterly, not the tariff only, but several acts of internal administration, show signs of retrogression rather than progress, which the best friends of Italy must lament over. Her apathetic deputies are far too disposed to shirk their duties, and would do better to display the fire and hot-headedness of the French Assembly than the selfish absenteeism now so common, which make the Sardinian again begin to think that he has nothing to do with the affairs of Lombardy; the Lombard indifferent to what interests Venice; and all the North together agree in looking with something like cold dislike on the troubles of Sicily and the South. Ministers, aided by such a Parliament, are hardly to be blamed if they sometimes go backwards in their attempt to keep the State solvent; and not the least unsatisfactory feature is the little help they get from the king, who, but for his family, might ere now have ruined all the fair prospect.

Reverting to the position of Italy as preëminently an agricultural country, I may enumerate a few of the clogs which prevent her progress in this direction. The reëstablishment of the grist tax was, for example, a distinctly retrograde movement. It costs the nation, directly and indirectly, perhaps five times as much as it yields. The mere irritation to which the millers who grind the corn and those who own it are alike subject must be very dispiriting, and check agricultural progress. Again, Italy copies

French fashions a good deal in the manner of her taxation; and we find all the array of succession duties, mortmain dues, stamps, taxes on locomotion, licenses, and such like, in full sway. Some of them are wise and fair enough, and might bear increasing, were their incidence fairly distributed; but many of them are obstructive and injurious to the prosperous growth of the national wealth. Italy also has her tobacco monopoly, on the security of which she raised a loan for £9,500,000 in 1868, and who shall say that it is not hurtful to her true interests? But of wider scope for evil, almost unproductive as they are, we must characterize the export duties now levied on many articles of vital importance to Italy. These duties have, like those on imports, been increased in recent years under the plea of necessity, and now act as a serious barrier on free export. A low customs duty on exports may do more harm than a higher one on imports, because it cripples the nation in competition directly, and, as it were, at the sources of its life; and no country is so exclusively possessed of advantages in the production of any particular article as to be safe under such hindrances. The liberal Sardinian customs law of 1854 was much inveighed against at the time it came into force,[1] and when its benefits were spread partially over the rest of the kingdom of Italy the manufacturing classes looked as usual for ruin. Of course no such ruin took place. On the contrary, Sardinia prospered then, and Italy has prospered always in proportion to the liberality of her commercial policy; and if many branches of her agricultural industry stagnate now, it is because, apart from general causes affecting all trade, she has gone backwards in her fiscal laws. Her small manufactures have ever been benefited by the lowering of her tariff. After the passing of the liberal import tariff, the import of raw cotton rose from an average of about 6,500.000 lbs., to over 17,000,000 lbs., and in other respects home industries such as these were benefited. What has thus, as always, proved true in the case of imports holds good with still greater force in regard to exports, because a tax on production is of all taxes the most wasteful. Make bread dear and you make life hard; and in like manner put a barrier between the tiller of the soil and a free market in any raw produce, and you strike at the root of the entire national prosperity. This is, unfortunately, what Italy has in no small measure done

---

[1] Mr. Herries' *Report*, p. 589, *et seq.*

by her grain taxes, her grist tax, and her vexatious, barren export duties, to which she has, in her special treaty with France, lately made large additions. Let her take a lesson from the policy of her greatest statesman and repeal these, and she will have done more to stimulate agriculture than all her schools and exhibitions ever can do. On the whole, agriculture may be pronounced now more burdened than manufactures, since the recent tinkering at the general tariff has, in various ways, increased the pressure on this, the all-important source of her prosperity. I will give below Mr. Herries' figures, comparing the present export duties charged on a few of the principal articles, with those in force in 1863 and 1864, which was the period when the tariff was lowest.[1] Hard necessity may be pleaded for this backward movement, as for that in the import duties; but no such plea can be admitted for a moment, inasmuch as taxation of this kind tends to keep agriculture, and all that depends on it, primitive and unproductive. Therefore this policy does also, and necessarily, lessen the tax-paying power of the community and the coherence of the young State. The whole fiscal system of Italy thus requires to be re-modelled, special favoritism in tariffs done away with, and the duties which cannot be dispensed with, levied with as little irksomeness as possible on the articles that can bear a tax with the least injury to the country. Till this is done the trade of Italy will not grow as it ought to do now in the directions which nature has marked out for it, and I will even say that the con-

[1] ITALIAN EXPORT DUTIES.

	On August 1, 1863.		1877.	
	Lira.	Cents.	Lira.	Cents.
Lime, per hectolitre	free.		1	10
Lime, per bottle	"		0	06
Olive oil, per 100 kilog.	0	33	1	10
Volatile oil, per 100 kilog.	free.		2	20
Lemon juice, per 100 kilog.	"		0 / 1	17 / 10
Extract of aloes, per 100 kilog.	"		3	30
Oranges and lemons, per 100 kilog.	"		0	25
Meat, fresh or salted, per 100 kilog.	"		2	20
Cheese, per 100 kilog.	"		4	40
Bulls and oxen, per head	"		5	50
Hides and skins, per 100 kilog.	"		2	20
Wool, per 100 kilog.	"		6	60
Silk, raw, per 100 kilog.	"		38	50
Silk, waste, per 100 kilog.	"		8	50
Unspecified dried fruits, per 100 kilog.	"		1	10
Almonds, per 100 kilog.	"		1 / 1	65 / 30

Report, p. 599.

solidation of the races which inhabit the peninsula cannot be held assured while their free development is in this manner forbidden.

We may, then, I think, put aside all fear both that Italy will become a rival to England in any of her important branches of manufacture, and that, once unfettered, she will cease to be a progressive customer. The character of the trade between the two countries may vary in some measure, and the competition of other countries may grow, in certain directions, more effective; but I do not think that these will cause our Italian trade to grow less in bulk or value, and a liberal well-organized and classified tariff in Italy would, I am sure, make it year by year greater, to the benefit of both countries.

But there is another direction in which I think Italy may not only rival us, but become in a great degree, and within well-defined limits, a monopolist, if she goes on as she has done these last dozen years. Her geographical position peculiarly fits her to become again the distributing and carrying maritime nation for Central Europe and the Levant. I do not dream of a revived Venice. Venice may indeed flourish again in a modest way, but not as a great port and mart for the civilized world. I mean, rather, that the sea-borne trade of Italy and of the neighbors of Italy along the Greek archipelago, in Egypt and Syria, and possibly even in the Black Sea and the Danube, seems likely to be carried on more and more in Italian ships, and that her merchant marine may in time come to be no mean rival of that of England in those regions of the South and East. The progress of Italian shipping since the establishment of the kingdom is evidence that in this direction she has already taken considerable strides. Italian vessels not only nearly monopolize the coasting trade of the Adriatic and Mediterranean ports near her borders, but the Rubattino line of ocean steamers, sailing from Genoa and other ports, compete successfully with the Austrian Lloyd's and the French Messagerie Maritime lines in the Eastern seas, while two other important lines, the Florio and the Pierano, are fast sweeping into Italian hands the heaviest share of the trade of the Mediterranean and the Levant. Moreover, the fact that our own mail company, the once unrivalled Peninsular and Oriental, is compelled to make a depot at Brindisi, is itself a sign of change in the position of the Eastern trade. As yet, this depot may be said to exist only for the convenience of overland passengers and fast mails, but goods will be sure to follow in time this overland route to some extent, and a certain portion of the carrying trade of England become diverted to Italy. The Suez Canal has hitherto been almost an English water-way, and will, no doubt, long continue to be used in a predominating degree by English ships; but it obviously makes competition by a country situated as Italy is much easier than it was before, and that competition is now felt, fostered as it is by the postal subsidies which the Italian government, in imitation of our own, gives to the Rubattino company. Looking at the map, we see that the harbors of Italy are, as it were, placed directly in the way of ships coming westward through the Canal, and the Asiatic trade which the discovery of the Cape passage threw into the hands of the Dutch, the Portuguese, and the English, to the ruin of Venice and Genoa, may not unlikely tend now to revert in some measure to its old channels. Steam, no doubt, neutralizes the altered circumstances somewhat, but not altogether. Once let Central Europe get consolidated into peaceful communities, Turkey become pacified or obliterated as a separate State, to be replaced by, at worst, less devastating governing agencies, and we may expect the trade of Italy as a common carrier on the seas to be greatly extended in that quarter. The cotton mills which she possesses, or that may exist in Austria, Hungary, and Bavaria, are likely to draw their supplies of Indian cotton direct from the ports of shipment, or by Italian ships, almost direct, instead, as heretofore, through England. Marts for the raw produce of India and China are thus not unlikely to spring up in Genoa and Leghorn, if not in Venice and Naples, just as a wool mart is now rising into importance at Antwerp; and London will then no longer occupy the exclusive position which the wars and follies of her neighbors have maintained her in for so long.

Nor need Italy halt with the Eastern trade. Her connections with the Brazils and South America, as well as with the United States and the islands in the Spanish Main, are extending, though comparatively insignificant now, and, unless emigration from her shores ceases, are likely to extend, for a large Italian population is now scattered over the fairest regions of South America.

Therefore, although I do not think that, as manufacturers, we have much cause to look on Italy with any dread, as a competitor for a portion of the European carrying trade, which has been so long in our hands, in all its most valuable departments, I think we have good reason to have misgivings. Italy is, in my opinion, destined to make a more marked impression on our monopoly in her own immediate neighborhood than almost any other European nation, and may yet become a far-reaching rival. Even at present Italy stands forward amongst the nations of the world as a great ship-owning nation. The only European country that is ahead of her besides ourselves is Norway, which has always been prominent with its seafaring population, who have much of the carrying trade of Germany, Russia, and Denmark in their hands. Year by year, until the last two years, when depressed trade has produced some slackening, the tonnage of foreign vessels entering our ports has been on the increase, and of this increase Italy bears its full share.

We must accept Italian competition on the sea as a factor of growing importance, therefore, and, instead of being jealous of it, seek to utilize it where it can serve our ends, just as we allow other countries to use our shipping for theirs. There must be free trade in ship freights as in everything else, and in the meantime we need have no fear that Italy will, for a long time to come, drive us from the markets for our manufactures, if ever she does it. While her budgets show an annual deficit, while her paper currency is always at a discount which seldom sinks much below ten per cent., while her population remains pastoral, and while her internal administration is but half organized, and her taxation oppressive, she cannot run far in the race with us, or with any manufacturing country; and for ourselves, free trade is, after all, our great stronghold. When we recognize how far behind us in this respect all other nations yet are, we may be easy in our minds, provided always, of course, we continue to work as heretofore. Free trade will do nothing for a nation of sloths. At present, I see no signs anywhere that other countries are in the least likely to be more diligent than we are. Italy, at all events, gives no such indication, and against her competition we can not only pit superior and freer industry, but a higher order of agriculture, a system of internal taxation, on the whole, less oppressive, and natural and acquired advantages, such as it takes generations to bring into play. For the rest, if on the high seas her ships should threaten to rival our own, we can only hope that the trade of the world will become large enough to afford them plenty to do without lessening the employment of ours.

XIV.

THE UNITED STATES IN 1880.

THE INCREASE OF POPULATION FROM 1790 TO 1880.

FROM WALKER AND GANNETT'S REPORT ON THE PROGRESS OF THE NATION. TENTH CENSUS, VOL. I., PP. XII-XX.

1790.

THE First Census of the United States, taken as of the first Monday in August, 1790, under the provisions of the second section of the first article of the Constitution, showed the population of the thirteen States then existing and of the unorganized territory, to be, in the aggregate, 3,929,214.

This population was distributed almost entirely on the Atlantic seaboard, extending from the eastern boundary of Maine nearly to Florida, and in the region known as the Atlantic plain. Only a very small proportion of the inhabitants of the United States, not, indeed, more than five per cent., was then to be found west of the system of the Appalachian mountains. The average depth of settlement, in a direction at right angles to the coast, was 255 miles. The densest settlement was found in Eastern Massachusetts, Rhode Island, and Connecticut, and about New York City, whence population had extended northward up the Hudson, and was already quite dense as far as Albany. The settlements in Pennsylvania, which had started from Philadelphia, on the Delaware, had extended northeastward, and formed a solid body of occupation from New York, through Philadelphia, down to the upper part of Delaware.

The Atlantic Coast, as far back as the limits of tide-water, was well settled at that time from Casco Bay southward to the northern border of North Carolina. In what was then the District of Maine, sparse settlement extended along the whole seaboard. The southern two-thirds of New Hampshire and nearly all of Vermont were covered by population. In New York, branching off from the Hudson at the mouth of the Mohawk, the line of population followed up a broad gap between the Adirondacks and the Catskills, and even reached beyond the centre of the State, occupying the whole of the Mohawk valley and the country about the interior New York lakes. In Pennsylvania population had spread northwestward, occupying not only the Atlantic plain, but, with sparse settlements, the region traversed by the numerous parallel ridges of the eastern portion of the Appalachians. The general limit of settlement was, at that time, the southeastern edge of the Allegheny plateau, but beyond this, at the junction of the Allegheny and Monongahela rivers, a point early occupied for military purposes, considerable settlements had been established prior to the War of the Revolution. In Virginia settlements had extended westward beyond the Blue Ridge, and into what is now West Virginia, on the western slope of the Allegheny mountains, though very sparsely. From Virginia, also, a narrow tongue of settlement had penetrated down to the head of the Tennessee river, in the great Appalachian valley. In North Carolina the settlements were abruptly limited by the base of the Appalachians. The State was occupied with remarkable uniformity, except in its southern and central portion, where population was comparatively sparse. In South Carolina, on the other hand, there was evidence of much natural selection, apparently with reference to the character of soils. Charleston was then a city of considerable magnitude, and about it was grouped a comparatively dense population; but all along a belt running southwestward across the State, near its central part, the settlement was very sparse. This area of sparse settlement joined with that of Central North Carolina, and ran eastward to the coast, near the junction of the two States. Further westward, in the "up country" of South Carolina, the density of settlement was noticeably due to the improvement in soil. At this date settlements were almost entirely agricultural, and the causes for variation in their density were general ones. The movements of population at this epoch may be traced in almost every case to the character of the soil, and to facility of transportation to the seaboard; and, as the inhabitants were then dependent mainly upon water transportation, we find the settlements also conforming themselves very largely to the navigable streams.

Outside the area of continuous settlement, which we have attempted to sketch, were found, in 1790, a number of smaller settlements of greater or less extent. The principal of these lay in Northern Kentucky, bordering upon the Ohio river, comprising an area of 10,900 square miles. Another, in Western Virginia, lay upon the Ohio and Kanawha rivers, and comprised 750 square miles. A third, in Tennessee, upon the Cumberland river, embraced 1,200 square miles.

In addition to these, there were a score or more of small posts, or incipient settlements, scattered over what was then an almost untrodden wilderness, such as Detroit, Vincennes, Kaskaskia, Prairie du Chien, Mackinac, and Green Bay, besides the humble beginnings of Elmira and Binghampton, in New York, which, even at that time, lay outside the body of continuous settlement.

Following the line which limits this great body of settlement in all its undulations, we find its length to be 3,200 miles. In this measurement no account has been made of slight irregularities, such as those in the ordinary meanderings of a river which forms the boundary line of population; but we have traced all the ins and outs of this frontier line, which seem to indicate a distinct change in the settlement of the country for any cause, whether of progression or of retrogression. The area of settlement, thus, is the area embraced between the frontier line and the coast, diminished by such unsettled areas as may lie within it, and increased by such as lie without it. These are not susceptible of very accurate determination, owing to the fact that our best maps are, to a certain extent, incorrect in boundaries and areas; but all the accuracy required for our present purpose can be secured. The settled area of 1790, as indicated by the line traced, is 226,085 square miles. The entire body of continuously settled area lay between 31° and 45° north latitude and 67° and 83° west longitude.

Outside of this body of continuous settlement are the smaller areas mentioned above, which, added to the main body of settled area, give as a total 239,935 square miles, the aggregate population being 3,929,214, and the average density of settlement 16.4 to the square mile.

In 1790 the District of Maine belonged to Massachusetts. Georgia comprised not only the present State of that name, but nearly all of what are now the States of Alabama and Mississippi. The States of Kentucky and Tennessee were then known as the " Territory south of the Ohio river," and the present States of Ohio, Indiana, Illinois, Michigan, Wisconsin, and part of Minnesota, as the " Territory northwest of the Ohio river." Spain claimed possession of what is now Florida, with a strip along the southern border of Alabama, Mississippi, and all of the region west of the Mississippi river.

An inspection of the maps relating to the earlier census years will show that the progress of population westward across the Appalachian system has taken place, in the main, along four lines. The northernmost of these, which was the first to be developed, runs through Central New York, following up, generally, the Mohawk river. This line has, throughout our history, been one of the principal courses of population in its westward flow. The second crosses Southern Pennsylvania, Western Maryland, and Northern Virginia, parallel to and along the course of the Upper Potomac. The third runs through Virginia, passing southwestward down the great Appalachian valley, crossing thence over into Kentucky and Tennessee. South of this, the principal movement westward has been around the end of the Appalachian chain, through Georgia and Alabama.

1800.

At the Second Census, that of 1800, the frontier line, as it appears on the map, has been rectified, so that while it embraces 282,208 square miles, it describes a course, when measured in the same manner as that of 1790, of only 2,800 lineal miles. The advancement of this line has taken place in every direction, though in some parts of the country much more markedly than in others.

In Maine and New Hampshire there is apparent only a slight northward movement of settlement; in Vermont, on the other hand, while the settled area has not decidedly increased, its density has become greater. Massachusetts shows but little change, but in Connecticut the settlements along the lower course of the Connecticut river have appreciably increased.

In New York settlement has poured up the Hudson to the mouth of the Mohawk, and thence, through the great natural roadway, westward. The narrow tongue which before extended out beyond the middle of the State has now widened until it spreads from the southern border of the State to lake Ontario. A narrow belt of settlement even stretches down the St. Lawrence, and along all the northern border of the State, to Lake Champlain, completely sourrounding what may be characteristically defined as the Adirondack region.

In Pennsylvania settlements have extended up the Susquehanna and joined the New York groups, leaving, as yet, an unsettled space in the north-east corner of the State, which comprises a body of rugged mountain country. With the exception of a little strip along the western border of Pennsylvania, the northern part of the State, west of the Susquehanna, is as yet entirely without inhabitants. Population has streamed across the southern half of the State, and settled in a dense body about the forks of the Ohio river, at the present site of 'Pittsburgh, and thence extended slightly into the State of Ohio.

In Virginia we note but little change, although there is a general extension of settlement, with an increase in density, especially along the coast. North Carolina is now almost entirely covered with population; the mountain region has, generally speaking, been nearly all reclaimed to the service of man. In South Carolina there is a general increase in density of settlement, while the southwestern border has been carried down, until now the Altamaha river is its limit. The incipient settlements in Northern Kentucky have spread southward across the State, and even into Tennessee, forming a junction with the little settlement, noted at the date of the last census, on the Cumberland river. The group thus formed has extended down the Ohio, nearly to its junction with the Tennessee and the Cumberland, and across the Ohio river into the present State of Ohio, where we note the beginning of Cincinnati. Other infant settlements appear at this date. On the east side of the Mississippi river, in the present State of Mississippi, is a strip of settlement along the bluffs below the Yazoo bottom. Besides the settlement on the present site of St. Louis, not at this time within the United States, is an adjacent settlement in what is now Illinois, while all the pioneer settlements previously noted have grown to a greater or less extent.

From the region embraced between the frontier line and the Atlantic must be deducted the Adirondack tract, in Northern New York, and the unsettled region in Northern Pennsylvania, already referred to; so that the actual area of settlement, bounded by a continuous line, is to be taken at 271,908 square miles. All this lies between 30° 45' and 45° 15' north latitude, and 67° and 88° west longitude.

To this should be added the aggregate extent of all settlements lying outside of the frontier line, which collectively amount to

U. S. POPULATION, 1810. 291

33,800 square miles, making a total area of settlement of 305,-708 square miles. As the aggregate population is 5,308,483, the average density of settlement is 17.4.

The infant settlements of this period have been much retarded at many points by the opposition of the Indian tribes; but in the neighborhood of the more densely settled portions of the northern part of the country these obstacles have been of less magnitude than farther south. In Georgia, especially, the large and powerful tribes of Creeks and Cherokees have stubbornly opposed the progress of population.

During the decade just past Vermont, formed from a part of New York, has been admitted to the Union; also Kentucky and Tennessee, formed from the " Territory south of the river Ohio ; " Mississippi Territory, having, however, very different boundaries from the present State of that name, has been organized; while the " Territory northwest of the river Ohio " has been divided and Indiana Territory organized from the western portion.

1810.

At 1810 we note great changes, especially the extension of the sparse settlements of the interior. The hills of Western New York have become almost entirely covered with population, which has spread along the south shore of Lake Erie well over into Ohio, and has effected a junction with the previously existing body of population about the forks of the Ohio river, leaving unsettled an included heart-shaped area in Northern Pennsylvania, which comprises the rugged country of the Appalachian plateau. The occupation of the Ohio river has now become complete, from its head to its mouth, with the exception of small gaps below the mouth of the Tennessee. Spreading in every direction from the " dark and bloody ground " of Kentucky, settlement covers almost the entire State, while the southern border line has been extended to the Tennessee river, in Northern Alabama. In Georgia settlements are still held back by the Creek and the Cherokee Indians, although in 1802 a treaty with the former tribe relieved the southwestern portion of the State of their presence, and left the ground open for occupancy by the whites. In Ohio settlements, starting from the Ohio river and from southwestern Pennsylvania, have worked northward and westward, until they cover two-thirds of the area of the State. Michigan and Indiana are still virgin territory, with the exception of a little strip about Detroit, in the former State, and a small area in the southwestern part of the latter. St. Louis, from a fur-trading post, has become an important centre of settlement, population having spread northward above the mouth of the Missouri and southward along the Mississippi to the mouth of the Ohio. At the mouth of the Arkansas, in what is now the State of Arkansas, is a similar body of settlement. The transfer of the Territory of Louisiana to our jurisdiction, which was effected in 1803, has brought into the country a large body of population, which stretches along the Mississippi river from its mouth nearly up to the present northern limit of the State of Louisiana, up the Red river and the St. Francis, in general occupying the alluvial regions. The incipient settlements noted on the last map in Mississippi have effected a junction with those of Louisiana, while in Lower Alabama and Mississippi a similar patch appears upon the Mobile and the Pearl rivers.

In this decade large additions have been made to the territory of the United States, and many changes have been effected in the lines of interior division. The purchase of Louisiana has added 1,124,685 square miles, an empire in itself, to the United States, and has given to us absolute control of the Mississippi and its navigable branches. Georgia, during the same period, has ceded to the United States the portion of its territory which now constitutes the larger part of the States of Alabama and Mississippi. The State of Ohio has been formed from a portion of what previously was known as the "Territory north of the Ohio river." Michigan Territory has been erected, comprising what is now the lower peninsula of Michigan; Indiana Territory has been restricted to the present limits of the State of that name; Illinois Territory comprises all of the present State of Illinois, with that of Wisconsin, and a part of Minnesota; while from the Louisiana purchase has been carved, under the name of the "Territory of Orleans," all that part of the present State of Louisiana which lies west of the Mississippi river, the remainder of the great territory so cheaply acquired from France being known by the name of the "Louisiana Territory."

At this date the frontier line is 2,900 miles long, and includes between itself and the Atlantic 408,895 square miles. From this must be deducted several large areas of unsettled land: first, the area in Northern New York, now somewhat smaller than ten years before, but still by no means inconsiderable in extent; second, the heart-shaped area in Northwestern Pennsylvania, embracing part of the Allegheny plateau, in size about equal to the unsettled area in New York; third, a strip along the central part of what is now West Virginia, extending from the Potomac southward, taking in what is now a part of Eastern Kentucky and Southwestern Virginia, and extending nearly to the border line of Tennessee; fourth, a comparatively small area in Northern Tennessee, upon the Cumberland plateau. These tracts together comprise 26,050 square miles, making the actual area of settlement included within the frontier line 382,845 square miles. All this lies between latitude 29° 30' and 45° 15' north, and between the meridians of 67° and 88° 30' west.

Beyond the frontier there are, in addition to the steadily increasing number of outposts and minor settlements, several considerable bodies of population, which have been above noted. The aggregate extent of these, and of the numerous small patches of population scattered over the West and South, may be estimated at 25,100 square miles, making the total area of settlement in 1810, 407,945 square miles; the aggregate population being 7,239,881, and the average density of settlement 17.7 to the square mile.

Between 1800 and 1810 the principal territorial changes have been as follows: Ohio has been admitted, and the Territories of Illinois and Michigan have been formed from parts of Indiana Territory.

1820.

The decade from 1810 to 1820 has witnessed several territorial changes. Florida at this date (1820) is a blank upon the map. The treaty with Spain, which gives her to us, is signed, but the delivery has not yet taken place. Alabama and Mississippi, made from the Mississippi Territory, have been organized and admitted as States. Indiana and Illinois appear as States, with their present limits. The Territory of Louisiana has been admitted as a State. The District of Maine has also been erected into a State. Arkansas Territory has been cut from the southern portion of the Territory of Louisiana. The Indian Territory has been constituted to serve as a reservation for the Indian tribes. Michigan Territory has been extended to include all of the present States of Michigan, Wisconsin, and part of Minnesota. That part of the old Louisiana Territory remaining, after cutting out Arkansas and Indian Territory, has received the name of "Missouri Territory."

Again, in 1820, we note a great change in regard to the frontier line. It has become vastly more involved and complex, extending from Southeastern Michigan, on lake St. Clair, southwestward into what is now Missouri; thence, making a great semicircle to the eastward, it sweeps west again around a body of population in Louisiana, and ends on the Gulf coast in that State. The area included by it has immensely increased, but much of this increase is balanced by the great extent of unsettled land included within it.

Taking up the changes in detail, we note, first, the great increase in the population of Central New York, a belt of increased settlement having swept up the Mohawk valley to Lake Ontario, and along its shore nearly to the Niagara river. A similar increase is seen about the forks of the Ohio river, while in Northern Pennsylvania the unsettled region on the Appalachian plateau has sensibly decreased in size. The unsettled area in Western Virginia and Eastern Kentucky has very greatly diminished, population having extended almost entirely over the Allegheny region in these States. The little settlements about Detroit have extended and spread along the shore of Lake Erie, until they have joined those in Ohio. The frontier line in Ohio has crept northward and westward, leaving only the northwestern corner of the State unoccupied. Population has spread northward from Kentucky and westward from Ohio into Southern Indiana, covering sparsely the lower third of that State. The groups of population around St. Louis, which at the time of the previous census were enjoying a rapid growth, have extended widely, making a junction with the settlements of Kentucky and Tennessee, along a broad belt in Southern Illinois; following the main watercourses, population has gone many scores of miles up the Mississippi and the Missouri rivers. The settlements in Alabama, which up to this time had been very much retarded by the Creeks, were rapidly reënforced and extended, in consequence of the victory of General Jackson over this tribe and the subsequent cession of portions of this territory. Immigration to Alabama has already become considerable, and in a short time the whole central portion of the State, embracing a large part of the region drained by the Mobile river and its branches, will be covered by settlements, to extend northward and effect a junction with the Kentucky and

Tennessee settlements, and westward across the lower part of Mississippi, until they meet the Louisiana settlements. In Georgia the Cherokees and the Creeks still hold settlement back along the line of the Altamaha river. There are, however, scattered bodies of population in various parts of the State, though of small extent. In Louisiana we note a gradual increase of the extent of redeemed territory, which appears to have been limited almost exactly by the borders of the alluvial region. In Arkansas the settlements, which we saw at 1810 at the mouth of the Arkansas river, have extended up the bottom lands of that river and of the Mississippi, forming a body of population of considerable size. Besides these, a small body is found in the southern central part of the State, at the southeastern base of the hill region, and another in the prairie region in the northern part.

The frontier line now has a length of 4,100 miles, embracing an area, after taking out all the unsettled regions included between it, the Atlantic, and the Gulf, of 504,517 square miles, all lying between 29° 30′ and 45° 30′ north latitude, and between 67° and 93° 45′ west longitude. Outside the frontier line are some bodies of population on the Arkansas, White, and Washita rivers, in Arkansas, as before noted, as well as some small bodies in the Northwest. Computing these at 4,200 square miles in the aggregate, we have a total settled area of 508,717 square miles; the aggregate population being 9,633,822, and the average density of settlement 18.9 to the square mile.

1830.

In the decade from 1820 to 1830 other territorial changes have occurred. In the early part of the decade the final transfer of Florida and Spanish jurisdiction was effected, and it became a Territory of the United States. Missouri has been carved from the southeastern part of the old Missouri Territory, and admitted as a State. Otherwise the States and Territories have remained nearly as before. Settlement during the decade has again spread greatly. The westward extension of the frontier does not appear to have been so great as in some former periods, the energies of the people being mainly given to filling up the included areas. In other words, the decade from 1810 to 1820 seems to have been one rather of blocking out work which the succeeding decade has been largely occupied in completing.

During this period the Indians, especially in the South, have still delayed settlement to a great extent. The Creeks and the Cherokees in Georgia and Alabama, and the Choctaws and the Chickasaws in Mississippi, occupy large areas of the best portions of those States, and successfully resist encroachment upon their territory. Georgia, however, has witnessed a large increase in settlement during the decade. The settlements which have heretofore been staid on the line of the Altamaha spread westward across the central portion of the State to its western boundary, where they have struck against the barrier of the Creek territory. Stopped at this point, they have moved southward down into the southwest corner, and over into Florida, extending even to the Gulf coast. Westward they have stretched across the southern part of Alabama, and joined that body of settlement which was previously formed in the drainage-basin of the Mobile river. The Louisiana settlements have but slightly increased, and no great change appears to have taken place in Mississippi, owing largely to the cause above noted, viz., the occupancy of the soil by Indians. In Arkansas the spread of settlement has been in a strange and fragmentary way. A line reaches from Louisiana up the Arkansas river to the State line, where it is stopped abruptly by the boundary of the Indian Territory. It extends up the Mississippi, and joins the great body of population in Tennessee. A branch extends northeastward from near Little Rock to the northern portion of the State. All these settlements within Arkansas Territory are as yet very sparse. In Missouri the principal extension of settlement has been in a broad belt up the Missouri river, reaching to the present site of Kansas City, at the mouth of the Kansas river, where quite a dense body of population appears. Settlement has progressed in Illinois, from the Mississippi river eastward and northward, covering more than half the State. In Indiana it has followed up the Wabash river, and thence has spread until it reaches nearly to the north line of the State. But little of Ohio remains unsettled. The sparse settlements about Detroit, in Michigan Territory, have broadened out, extending into the interior of the State, while isolated patches have appeared in various other localities.

Turning to the more densely settled parts of the country, we find that settlement is slowly making its way northward in Maine, although discouraged by the poverty of the soil and the severity of the climate. The unsettled tract in Northern New York is decreasing, but very slowly, as is also the case with the unsettled area in Northern Pennsylvania. In Western Virginia the unsettled tracts are reduced to almost nothing, while the vacant region in Eastern Tennessee, on the Cumberland plateau, is rapidly diminishing.

At this date, 1830, the frontier line has a length of 5,300 miles, and the aggregate area now embraced between the ocean, the Gulf, and the frontier line is 725,406 square miles. Of this, however, not less than 97,389 square miles are comprised within the included vacant tracts, leaving only 628,017 square miles as the settled area within the frontier line, all of which lies between latitude 29° 15' and 46° 15' north, and between longitude 67° and 95° west.

Outside the body of continuous settlement are no longer found large groups, but several small patches of population appear in Ohio, Indiana, Illinois, Michigan, and Wisconsin, aggregating 4,700 square miles, making a total settled area, in 1830, of 632,717 square miles. As the aggregate population is 12,866,020, the average density of settlement is 20.3 to the square mile.

1840.

During the decade ending in 1840 the State of Michigan has been created with its present limits, the remainder of the old territory being known as Wisconsin Territory. Iowa Territory has been created from a portion of Missouri Territory, embracing the present State of Iowa and the western part of Minnesota, and Arkansas has been admitted to the Union.

In 1840 we find, by examining the map of population, that the process of filling up and completing the work blocked out between 1810 and 1820 has been carried still farther. From Georgia, Alabama, and Mississippi the Cherokee, Creek, Choctaw, and Chickasaw Indians, who, at the time of the previous census, occupied large areas in these States, and formed a very serious obstacle to settlement, have been removed to the Indian Territory, and their country has been opened up to settlement. Within the two or three years which have elapsed since the removal of these Indians the lands relinquished by them have been entirely taken up, and the country has been covered with a comparatively dense settlement. In Northern Illinois, the Sac and Fox and Pottawotomie tribes having been removed to the Indian Territory, their country has been promptly taken up, and we find now settlements carried over the whole extent of Indiana, Illinois, and across Michigan and Wisconsin as far north as the forty-third parallel. Population has crossed the Mississippi river into Iowa Territory, and occupies a broad belt up and down that stream. In Missouri the settlements have spread northward from the Missouri river nearly to the boundary of the State, and southward till they cover most of the southern portion, and make connection in two places with the settlements of Arkansas. The unsettled area found in Southern Missouri, together with that in Northwestern Arkansas, is due to the hilly and rugged nature of the country, and to the poverty of the soil, as compared with the rich prairie lands all around. In Arkansas the settlements remain sparse, and have spread widely away from the streams, covering much of the prairie parts of the State. There is, besides the area in Northwestern Arkansas just mentioned, a large area in the northeastern part of the State, comprised almost entirely within the alluvial regions of the St. Francis river, and also one in the southern portion, extending over into Northern Louisiana, which is entirely in the fertile prairie section. The fourth unsettled region lies in the southwest part of the State.

In the older States we note a gradual decrease in the unsettled areas, as in Maine and in New York. In Northern Pennsylvania the unsettled section has entirely disappeared. A small portion of the unsettled patch on the Cumberland plateau still remains. In southern Georgia the Okeefenokee swamp and the pine barrens adjacent have thus far repelled settlement, although population has increased in Florida, passing entirely around this area to the south. The greater part of Florida, however, including nearly all the peninsula and several large areas along the Gulf coast, still remains without settlement. This is doubtless due, in part, to the nature of the country, being alternately swamp and hummock, and in part to the hostility of the Seminole Indians, who still occupy nearly all of the peninsula.

The frontier line in 1840 has a length of 3,300 miles. This shrinking in its length is due to its rectification on the northwest and southwest, owing to the filling out of the entire interior. It encloses an area of 900,658 square miles, all lying between latitude 29° and 46° 30' north, and longitude 67° and 95° 30' west. The vacant tracts have, as noted above, decreased, although they are still quite considerable in Missouri and Arkansas. The total area of the vacant tracts is 95,516 square miles. The settled area outside the frontier line is notably small, and amounts, in the aggregate, to only 2,150 miles, making the entire settled area 807,292 square miles in 1840. The aggregate population being 17,069,453, the average density is 21.1 to the square mile.

1850.

Between 1840 and 1850 the limits of our country have been further extended by the annexation of the State of Texas and of territory acquired from Mexico by the treaty of Guadalupe Hidalgo. The States of Iowa, Wisconsin, and Florida have been admitted to the Union, and the Territories of Minnesota, Oregon, and New Mexico have been created. An examination of the maps shows that the frontier line has changed very little during this decade. At the western border of Arkansas the extension of settlement is peremptorily limited by the boundary of the Indian Territory; but, curiously enough also, the western boundary of Missouri puts almost a complete stop to all settlement, notwithstanding that some of the most densely populated portions of the State lie directly on that boundary.

In Iowa settlements have made some advance, moving up the Missouri, the Des Moines, and other rivers. The settlements in Minnesota at and about St. Paul, which appeared in 1840, are greatly extended up and down the Mississippi river, while other scattering bodies of population appear in Northern Wisconsin. In the southern part of the State settlement has made considerable advance, especially in a northeastern direction, towards Green Bay. In Michigan the change has been very slight.

Turning to the southwest we find Texas, for the first time on the map of the United States, with a considerable extent of settlement; in general, however, it is very sparse, most of it lying in the eastern part of the State, and being largely dependent upon the grazing industry.

The included unsettled areas now are very small and few in number. There still remains one in Southern Missouri, in the hilly country; a small one in Northeastern Arkansas, in the swampy and alluvial region; and one in the similar country in the Yazoo bottom-lands. Along the coast of Florida are found two patches of considerable size, which are confined to the swampy coast regions. The same is the case along the coast of

Louisiana. The sparse settlements of Texas are also interspersed with several patches devoid of settlement. In Southern Georgia the large vacant space heretofore noted, extending also into Northern Florida, has entirely disappeared, and the Florida settlements have already reached southward to a considerable distance in the peninsula, being now free to extend without fear of hostile Seminoles, the greater part of whom have been removed to the Indian Territory.

The frontier line, which now extends around a considerable part of Texas and issues on the Gulf coast at the mouth of the Nueces river, is 4,500 miles in length. The aggregate area included by it is 1,005,213 square miles, from which deduction is to be made for vacant spaces, in all, 64,339 square miles. The isolated settlements lying outside this body in the western part of the country amount to 4,775 square miles.

But it is no longer by a line drawn around from the St. Croix river to the Gulf of Mexico that we embrace all the population of the United States, excepting only a few outlying posts and small settlements. We may now, from the Pacific, run a line around 80,000 miners and adventurers, the pioneers of more than one State of the Union soon to arise on that coast. This body of settlement has been formed, in the main, since the acquisition of the territory by the United States, and, it might even be said, within the last year (1849–50), dating from the discovery of gold in California. These settlements may be computed rudely at 33,600 square miles, making a total area of settlement at that date of 979,249 square miles, the aggregate population being 23,191,876, and the average density of settlement 23.7 to the square mile.

1860.

Between 1850 and 1860 the territorial changes noted are as follows: The strip of Arizona and New Mexico south of the Gila river has been acquired from Mexico by the Gadsden purchase (1853); Minnesota Territory has been admitted as a State; Kansas and Nebraska Territories have been formed from parts of Missouri Territory; California and Oregon have been admitted as States, while, in the unsettled parts of the Cordilleran region, two new territories (Utah and Washington) have been formed out of parts of that *terra incognita* which we bought from France as a part of Louisiana, and of that which we acquired by conquest from Mexico. At this date we note the first extension of settlements beyond the line of the Missouri river. The march of settlement up the slope of the great plains has begun. In Kansas and Nebraska population is now found beyond the 97th meridian. Texas has filled up even more rapidly, its extreme settlements reaching to the 100th meridian, while the gaps noted at the date of the last census have all been filled by population. The incipient settlements about St. Paul, in Minnesota, have grown like Jonah's gourd, spreading in all directions, and forming a broad band of union with the main body of settlement down the line of the Mississippi river. In Iowa settlements have crept steadily northwestward along the course of the drainage, until the State is nearly covered. Following up the Missouri, population has reached out into the southeastern corner of the present area of Dakota. In Wisconsin the settlements have moved at least one degree farther north, while in the lower peninsula of Michigan they have spread up the lake shores, nearly encircling it on the side next Lake Michigan. On the upper peninsula the little settlements which appeared in 1850 in the copper region on Keeweenaw point have extended and increased greatly in density as that mining interest has developed in value. In Northern New York there is apparently no change in the unsettled area. In Northern Maine we note, for the first time, a decided movement towards the settlement of its unoccupied territory, in the extension of the settlements on its eastern and northern border up the St. John river. The unsettled regions in Southern Missouri, Northeastern Arkansas, and Northwestern Mississippi have become sparsely covered by population. Along the Gulf coast there is little or no change. There is to be noted a slight extension of settlement southward in the peninsula of Florida.

The frontier line now measures 5,300 miles, and embraces 1,126,518 square miles, lying between latitude 28° 30' and 47° 30' north, and between longitude 67° and 99° 30' west. From this deduction should be made on account of vacant spaces, amounting to 39,139 square miles, found mainly in New York and along the Gulf coast. The outlying settlements beyond the 100th meridian are now numerous. They include, among others, a strip extending far up the Rio Grande in Texas, embracing 7,475 square miles (a region given over to the raising of sheep), while the Pacific settlements, now comprising one sovereign State, are nearly three times as extensive as at 1850, embracing 99,900 square miles. The total area of settlement in 1860 is thus 1,194,754 square miles; the aggregate population is now 31,443,321, and the average density of settlement 26.3 to the square mile.

1870.

During the decade from 1860 to 1870 a number of territorial changes have been effected in the extreme West. Arizona, Colorado, Dakota, Idaho, Montana, Nevada, and Wyoming have been organized as Territories. Kansas, Nebraska, and Nevada have been admitted as States. West Virginia has been cut off from the mother Commonwealth and made a separate State.

In 1870 we note a gradual and steady extension of the frontier line westward over the great plains. The unsettled areas in Maine, New York, and Florida have not greatly diminished, but in Michigan the extension of the lumber interests northward and inward from the Lake Shore has reduced considerably the unsettled portion. On the upper peninsula the settlements have increased somewhat, owing to the discovery of the rich iron deposits destined to play so important a part in the manufacturing industry of the country.

Settlement has spread westward to the boundary of the State in Southern Minnesota, and up the Big Sioux river in Southeastern Dakota. Iowa is entirely reclaimed, excepting a small area of perhaps a thousand square miles in its northwestern corner. Through Kansas and Nebraska the frontier line has moved steadily westward, following in general the courses of the larger streams and of the newly constructed railroads. The frontier in Texas has changed but little, that little consisting of a general westward movement. In the Cordilleran region settlements have extended but slowly. Those upon the Pacific coast show little change, either in extent or in density. In short, we see everywhere the effects of the war in the partial stoppage of the progress of development.

The settlements in the West, beyond the frontier line, have arranged themselves mainly in three belts. The most eastern of these is located in Central Colorado, New Mexico, and Wyoming, along the eastern base of and among the Rocky mountains. To this region settlement was first attracted in 1859 and 1860 by the discovery of mineral deposits, and has been retained by the richness of the soil and by the abundance of water for irrigation, which have promoted the agricultural industry.

The second belt of settlement is that of Utah, settled in 1847 by the Mormons fleeing from Illinois. This community then differed, and still differs, radically from that of the Rocky mountains, being essentially agricultural, mining having been discountenanced from the first by the church authorities, as tending to fill the "Promised Land" with Gentile adventurers, and thereby imperil Mormon institutions. The settlements of this group, as seen on the map for 1870, extend from Southern Idaho southward through Central Utah, and along the eastern base of the Wahsatch range into Northern Arizona. They consist mainly of scattered hamlets and small towns, about which are grouped the farms of the communities.

The third strip is that in the Pacific States and Territories, extending from Washington Territory southward to Southern California and eastward to the system of "sinks," in Western Nevada. This group of population owes its existence to the mining industry, the moving cause in nearly all westward migrations. Originated in 1849 by a "stampede" the like of which the world had never before seen, it has grown by successive impulses as new fields for rapid money-getting have been developed. Latterly, however, the value of this region to the agriculturist has been recognized, and the character of the occupations of the people is undergoing a marked change.

These three great Western groups comprise nine-tenths of the population west of the frontier line. The remainder is scattered about in the valleys and the mountains of Montana, Idaho, and Arizona, at military posts, isolated mining camps, and on cattle ranches.

The frontier line in 1870 embraces 1,178,068 square miles, all between 27° 15' and 47° 30' north latitude, and between 67° and 99° 45' west longitude. From this, however, deduction is to be made of 37,739 square miles, on account of interior spaces containing no population. To what remains we must add 11,810 square miles on account of settled tracts east of the 100th meridian, lying outside of the frontier line, and 120,100 square miles on account of settlements in the Cordilleran region and on the Pacific coast, making the total area of settlement for 1870 not less than 1,272,239 square miles, the aggregate population being

38,558,371, and the average density of settlement 30.3 to the square mile.

1880.

In tracing the history of the settlement of our country we are now brought down to the latest census, that of 1880. During the decade just past Colorado has been added to the sisterhood of States. The first point that strikes us in examining the map showing the areas of settlement at this date, as compared with previous ones, is the great extent of territory which has been brought under occupation during the past ten years. Not only has settlement spread westward over large areas in Dakota, Nebraska, Kansas, and Texas, thus moving the frontier line of the main body of settlement westward many scores of miles, but the isolated settlements of the Cordilleran region and of the Pacific coast show enormous accessions of occupied territory.

The migration of farming population to the northeastern part of Maine has widened the settled area to a marked extend, probably more than has been done during any previous decade. The vacant space in the Adirondack region of Northern New York has been lessened in size, and its limits reduced practically to the actual mountain tract. The most notable change, however, in New England and the Middle States, including Ohio and Indiana, has been the increase in density of population and the migration to cities, with the consequent increase of the urban population, as indicated by the number and the size of the spots representing these cities upon the map. Throughout the Southern States there is to be noted not only a general increase in the density of population and a decrease of unsettled areas, but a greater approach to uniformity of settlement throughout the whole region. The unsettled area of the peninsula of Florida has decreased decidedly, while the vacant spaces heretofore seen along the upper coast of Florida and Louisiana have entirely disappeared. Although the Appalachian mountain system is still distinctly outlined by its general lighter color on the map, its density of population more nearly approaches that of the country on the east and on the west. In Michigan there is seen a very decided increase of the settled region. Settlements have not only surrounded the head of the lower peninsula, but they leave only a very small body of unsettled country in the interior. In the upper peninsula the copper and the iron interests, and the railroads which subserve them, have peopled quite a large extent of territory. In Wisconsin the unsettled area is rapidly decreasing as railroads stretch their arms out over the vacant tracts. In Minnesota and in Eastern Dakota the building of railroads, and the development of the latent capabilities of this region in the cultivation of wheat, have caused a rapid flow of settlement, and now the frontier line of population, instead of returning to Lake Michigan, as it did ten years ago, meets the boundary line of the British possessions west of the 97th meridian. The settlements in Kansas and Nebraska have made great strides over the plains, reaching at several points the boundary of the humid region, so that their westward extension beyond this point is to be governed hereafter by the supply of water in the streams. As a natural result, we see settlements following these streams in long ribbons of population. In Nebraska these narrow belts have reached the western boundary of the State at two points: one upon the South Platte, and the other upon the Republican river. In Kansas, too, the settlements have followed the Kansas river and its branches and the Arkansas nearly to the western boundary of the State. Texas also has made great strides, both in the extension of the frontier line of settlement and in the increase in the density of population, due both to the building of railroads and to the development of the cattle, sheep, and agricultural interests. The heavy population in the prairie portions of the State is explained by the railroads which now traverse them. In Dakota, besides the agricultural region, in the eastern part of the Territory, we note the formation of a body of settlement in the Black Hills, in the southwest corner, which, in 1870, was a part of the reservation of the Sioux Indians. This settlement is the result of the discovery of valuable gold deposits. In Montana there appears a great extension of the settled area, which, as it is mainly due to agricultural interests, is found chiefly along the courses of the streams. Mining has, however, played not a small part in this increase in settlement. Idaho, too, shows a decided growth from the same causes. The small settlements which, in 1870, were located about Boisé City, and near the mouth of the Clearwater, have now extended their areas to many hundreds of square miles. The settlement in the southeastern corner of the territory is almost purely of Mormons, and has not made a marked increase.

Of all the States and Territories of the Cordilleran region

Colorado has made the greatest stride during the decade. From a narrow strip of settlement, extending along the immediate base of the Rocky Mountains, the belt has increased so that it comprises the whole mountain region, besides a great extension outward upon the plains. This increase is the result of the discovery of very extensive and very rich mineral deposits about Leadville, producing a "stampede" second only to that of '49 and '50 to California. Miners have spread over the whole mountain region, till every range and ridge swarms with them. New Mexico shows but little change, although the recent extension of railroads in the Territory and the opening up of mineral resources will, no doubt, in the near future, add largely to its population. Arizona, too, although its extent of settlement has increased somewhat, is but just commencing to enjoy a period of rapid development, owing to the extension of railroads and to the suppression of hostile Indians. Utah presents us with a case dissimilar to any other of the Territories, — a case of steady, regular growth, due almost entirely to its agricultural capabilities, as was noted above. This is due to the policy of the Mormon Church, which has steadily discountenanced mining and speculation in all forms, and has encouraged in every way agricultural pursuits. Nevada shows a slight extension of settlement, due mainly to the gradual increase in the agricultural interest. The mining industry is probably not more flourishing at present in this State than it was ten years ago, and the population dependent upon it is, if anything, less in number. In California, as the attention of the people has become devoted more and more to agricultural pursuits, at the expense of the mining and cattle industries, we note a tendency to a more even distribution of the inhabitants. The population in some of the mining regions has decreased, while over the area of the great valley, and in the fertile valleys of the Coast ranges, it has increased. In Oregon the increase has been mainly in the section east of the Cascade range, a region drained by the Des Chutes and the John Day rivers, and by the smaller tributaries of the Snake, — a region which, with the corresponding section in Washington Territory, is now coming to the front as a wheat-producing district. In most of the settled portions here spoken of irrigation is not necessary for the cultivation of crops, and consequently the possibilities of the region in the direction of agricultural development are very great. In Washington Territory, which in 1870 had been scarcely touched by immigration, we find the valley west of the Cascade Mountains tolerably well settled throughout, while the stream of settlement has poured up the Columbia into the valleys of the Walla Walla and the Snake rivers and the great plain of the Columbia, induced thither by the facilities for raising cattle and by the great profits of wheat cultivation.

The length of the frontier line in 1880 is 3,337 miles. The area included between the frontier line, the Atlantic and the Gulf coast, and the northern boundary is 1,398,945 square miles, lying between 26° and 49° north latitude and 67° and 102° west longitude. From this must be deducted, for unsettled areas, as follows: —

	Square Miles.
Maine	12,000
New York	2,200
Michigan	10,200
Wisconsin	10,200
Minnesota	34,000
Florida	20,800

making a total of 89,400 square miles, leaving 1,309,545 square miles.

To this must be added the isolated areas of settlement in the Cordilleran region and the extent of settlement on the Pacific coast, which amount, in the aggregate, to 260,025 square miles, making a total settled area of 1,569,570 square miles. The population is 50,155,783, and the average density of settlement 32 to the square mile.

THE FACTORY SYSTEM.

FROM WRIGHT'S REPORT ON THE FACTORY SYSTEM OF THE UNITED
STATES, TENTH CENSUS, VOL. II., PP. 537-541.

At the time of the agitation of their independence the desire to plant the mechanic arts in this country became almost a passion — certainly a feature of the patriotism of the day. Hon. Edward Everett, in an address on American manufactures, in New York, in 1831, stated : —

"The first measures of the patriots aimed to establish their independence on the basis of the productive industry and laborious arts of the country. They began with a non-importation agreement nearly two years before the Declaration of Independence. That agreement, . . . with the exception of the Address to the People of America and Great Britain, was the only positive act of the first Congress."

In this country, as well as in England, the germ of the textile factory existed in the fulling and carding mills; the former, dating earlier, being the mills for finishing the coarse cloths woven by hand in the homes of our ancestors; in the latter, the carding-mill, the wool was prepared for the hand-wheel. At the close of the Revolution the domestic system of manufactures prevailed throughout the States.

The first attempts to secure the spinning machinery which had come into use in England were made in Philadelphia early in the year 1775, when probably the first spinning-jenny ever seen in America was exhibited in that city. During the war the manufacturers of Philadelphia extended their enterprises, and even built and run mills which writers often call factories, but they can hardly be classed under that term. Similar efforts, all preliminary to the establishment of the factory system, were made in Worcester, Massachusetts, in 1780. In 1781 the British Parliament, determined that the textile machinery by which the manufactures of England were being rapidly extended, and which the continental producers were anxious to secure, should not be used by the people of America, reënacted and enlarged the scope of the Statute of 1774 against its exportation. By 21 George III., c. 37, it was provided that any person who packed or put on board, or caused to be brought to any place in order to be put on any vessel for exportation, any machine, engine, tool, press, paper, utensil, or implement, or any part thereof, which now is or hereafter may be used in the woollen, cotton, linen, or silk manufacture of the kingdom, or goods wherein wool, cotton, linen, or silk are used, or any model or plan of such machinery, tool, engine, press, utensil, or implement, should forfeit every such machine, etc., and all goods packed therewith, and £200, and suffer imprisonment for one year. In 1782 a law was enacted which prohibited, under penalty of £500, the exportation or the attempt to export "blocks, plates, engines, tools, or utensils used in or which are proper for the preparing or finishing of the calico, cotton, muslin, or linen printing manufactures, or any part thereof." The same act prohibited the transportation of tools employed in the iron and steel manufactures. Acts were also passed interdicting the emigration of artificers. All these laws were enforced with great vigilance, and were of course serious obstacles to the institution of the new system of manufacture in America.

The manufacturers of this country were thus compelled either to smuggle or to invent their machinery. Both methods were practised until most of the secrets of the manufacture of common goods were made available here.

The planting of the mechanic arts in this country became a necessity during the War of the Revolution, and afterwards the spirit of American enterprise demanded that New England and the Middle States should utilize the water-powers which they possessed, and by such utilization supply the people with home manufactures.

When the people of the States saw that the Treaty of Paris had not brought industrial independence, a new form of expression of patriotism took the place of military service; and associations were formed, the object of which was to discourage the use of British goods, and as the Articles of Confederation did not provide for the regulation of commerce, the Legislatures of the States were besought to protect home manufactures. The Constitution of 1789 remedied the defects of the articles in this respect, and gave Congress the power to legislate on commercial affairs. The Constitution was really the outcome of the industrial necessities of the people, because it was on account of the difficulties and the irritations growing out of the various commercial regulations of the individual States that a convention of commissioners from the various States was held at Annapolis in September, 1786, which convention recommended the one that framed the new or present Constitution of the United States.

Of course those industries whose products were called for by the necessities of the war were greatly stimulated, but with peace came reaction and the flooding of our markets with foreign goods.

The second act under the Constitution was passed July 4, 1789, with this preamble:—

"Whereas it is necessary for the support of the government, for the discharge of the debts of the United States, and for the encouragement and the protection of manufactures, that duties be laid on goods, wares, and merchandise imported;

"*Be it enacted*, etc."

Patriotism and statute law thus paved the way for the importation of the factory system of industry, and so its institution here, as well as in England, was the result of both moral and economical forces.

As early as 1786, before the adoption of the Constitution of the United States, the Legislature of Massachusetts offered encouragement for the introduction of machinery for carding and spinning by granting to Robert and Alexander Barr the sum of £200 to enable them to complete a roping-machine, and also to "construct such other machines as are necessary for the purpose of carding, roping, and spinning of sheep's wool, as well as of cotton wool." The next year these parties were granted six tickets in a land-lottery. Others engaged in the invention and construction of cotton-spinning machines at Bridgewater, being associated with the Barrs, who came to Massachusetts from Scotland at the invitation of Hon. Hugh Orr, of Bridgewater, and for the purpose of constructing spinning-machines. There is no doubt that the machinery built by them was the first in this country which included the Arkwright devices; the first factory, however, in America expressly for the manufacture of cotton goods was erected at Beverly, Massachusetts, in 1787. This enterprise was aided by the Legislature. The factory at Beverly was built of brick, was driven by horse-power, and was continued in operation for several years, but its career as a cotton-mill was brief, and no great success attended it. About the same time other attempts had been made in Rhode Island, New York, and Pennsylvania, but principally in Rhode Island and that part of Massachusetts contiguous to Rhode Island.

U. S. FACTORY SYSTEM. 311

The honor of the introduction of power-spinning machines in this country, and of their early use here, is shared by these last-named States; for while Massachusetts claims to have made the first experiments in embodying the principles of Arkwright's inventions and the first cotton factory in America, Rhode Island claims the first factory in which perfected machinery, made after the English models, was practically employed. This was the factory built by Samuel Slater, in 1790, in Pawtucket, Rhode Island, which still stands in the rear of Mill street in that city, and the hum of cotton machinery can still be heard within its walls. Previous to 1790 the common jenny and stock-card had been in operation upon a small scale in various parts of the United States, but principally in Pennsylvania, New York, Rhode Island, and Massachusetts; but every endeavor to introduce the system of spinning known as water-frame spinning, or Arkwright's method, had failed. The introduction of this system was the work of Slater, whom President Jackson designated "The father of American manufactures." Samuel Slater was born in Belper, Derbyshire, England, June 9, 1768, and at fourteen years of age was bound as an apprentice to Jedediah Strutt, Esq., a manufacturer of cotton machinery at Milford, near Belper. Strutt was for several years a partner of Sir Richard Arkwright in the cotton-spinning business; so young Slater had every opportunity to master the details of the construction of the cotton machinery then in use in England, for during the last four or five years of his apprenticeship he served as general overseer, not only in making machinery, but in the manufacturing department of Strutt's factory. Near the close of his term his attention was drawn to the wants of the States by accidentally seeing a notice in an American paper of the efforts various States were making by way of offering bounties to parties for the production of cotton machinery. Slater knew well that under the laws of England he could carry neither machines nor models or plans of machines out of the country; so, after completing his full time with Mr. Strutt, he continued some time longer with him, superintending some new works Mr. Strutt was erecting. This he did that he might so perfect his knowledge of the business in every department that he could construct machinery from memory without taking plans, models, or specifications. With this knowledge Slater embarked at London, September 13, 1789, for New York, where he landed November 17, and at once sought parties interested in cotton manufactures. Finding the works of the New York Manufacturing Company, to whom he was introduced, unsatisfactory, he corresponded with Messrs. Brown & Almy, of Providence, who owned some crude spinning-machines, some of which came from the factory at Beverly, Massachusetts. In January, 1790, Slater made arrangements with Brown & Almy to construct machinery on the English plan. This he did at Pawtucket, making the machinery principally with his own hands, and on the 20th of December, 1790, he started three cards, drawing and roving, together with seventy-two spindles, working entirely on the Arkwright plan, and being the first of the kind ever operated in America.

It is generally supposed that the course of the progress of the manufacture of cotton goods in this country is quite clearly marked, yet a careful study of the subject seems rather to dissipate the line of advancement instead of bringing it into clearer view. Dr. Leander Bishop, in his exceedingly valuable work, "A History of American Manufactures," in speaking of the clothing manufacture, states that a correspondent of the "American Museum," writing from Charleston, South Carolina, in July, 1790, refers to a gentleman who "had completed, and had in operation on the High Hills of the Santee, near Statesburg, ginning, carding, and other machines driven by water, and also spinning-machines, with eighty-four spindles each, with every necessary article for manufacturing cotton. If this information be correct, the attempt to manufacture by machinery the cotton which they were then beginning to cultivate extensively was nearly as early as those of the Northern States."

Certainly this bit of history of attempts in Southern States, of the efforts of Samuel Wetherell, of Philadelphia, of the Beverly Company, in Massachusetts, of Moses Brown, at Providence, R.I., all before Slater's coming, to introduce spinning by power, illustrates the difficulty of locating the origin of an institution when a country of such proportions as our own constitutes the field. It is safe, historically, to start with Slater as the first to erect cotton machinery on the English plan, and to give the factory system 1790 as its birthday.

The progress of the system has been uninterrupted from 1790, save by temporary causes and for brief periods; but these interruptions only gave an increased impetus to its growth.

In 1792, by the invention of the cotton-gin, an American, Eli

Whitney, of Massachusetts, residing temporarily in Georgia, contributed as much toward the growth of the factory system as England had contributed by the splendid series of inventions which made the cotton-manufacturing machinery of the system.

The alarm of the people at the increase in the demand for foreign goods took shape again in 1794 and the decade following, and, by patriotic appeals to all classes, societies and clubs were formed pledged to wear only home-made goods. Congress was called upon to restrict importations. The result of all these efforts and influences stimulated the manufacture of cotton and other textiles. The water privileges of New England and the Middle States offered to enterprising men the inducement to build factories for the spinning of yarn for the household manufacture of cloth. At the close of 1809, according to a report made by Mr. Albert Gallatin, Secretary of the Treasury in 1810, eighty-seven cotton factories had been erected in the United States, which, when in operation, would employ 80,000 spindles.

The perfect factory, the scientific arrangement of parts for the successive processes necessary for the manipulation of the raw material till it came out finished goods, had not yet been constructed. As I have said, the power-loom did not come into use in England till about 1806, while in this country it was not used at all till after the war of 1812. In England, even, it had not been used in the same factory with the spinning-machines. In fact, for many years the custom of spinning the yarn under one management and weaving the cloth under another has prevailed in England.

In 1811, Mr. Francis C. Lowell, of Boston, visited England, and spent much time in inspecting cotton factories, for the purpose of obtaining all possible information relative to cotton manufacture, with a view to the introduction of improved machinery in the United States. The power-loom was being introduced in Great Britain at this time, but its construction was kept very secret, and public opinion was not very favorable to its success. Mr. Lowell learned all he could regarding the new machine, and determined to perfect it himself. He returned to the States in 1814, and at once began his experiments on Broad street, Boston. His first move was to secure the skill of Paul Moody, of Amesbury, Mass., a well-known mechanic. By and through the encouragement of Mr. Nathan Appleton, a company had been organized by Mr. Lowell and Mr. Patrick T. Jackson, with Mr. Appleton as one of its directors, for the establishment of a cotton manufactory, to be located in Waltham, Mass., on a water privilege they had purchased. This factory was completed in the autumn of 1814, and in it was placed the loom perfected by Mr. Lowell, which differed much from the English looms. Mr. Lowell had neither plans nor models for his factory and looms, but in the year named the company set up a full set of machinery for weaving and spinning, there being 1,700 spindles; and this factory at Waltham was the first in the world, so far as record shows, in which all the processes involved in the manufacture of goods, from the raw material to the finished product, were carried on in one establishment by successive steps, mathematically considered, under one harmonious system. Mr. Francis C. Lowell, aided by Mr. Jackson, is unquestionably entitled to the credit of arranging this admirable system, and it is remarkable how few changes have been made in the arrangements established by him in this factory at Waltham.

So America furnished the stone which completed the industrial arch of the factory system of manufactures.

The growth of the factory system [is well] illustrated by the cotton manufacture. After the success of the power-loom, the cotton manufacture took rapid strides, both in Europe and America. The hand-loom and the hand-weaver were rapidly displaced. Factories sprung up on all the streams of Yorkshire and Lancashire, in England, while in this country the activity of the promoters of the industry won them wealth, and won cities from barren pastures. They erected Lowell, Lawrence, Holyoke, Fall River, and many other thriving cities and towns, and now in this generation the industry is taking root upon the banks of Southern streams. The progressive steps of this great tradè are shown by the tables which follow. The facts for Great Britain for the year 1833 are taken from Baines' *History of Cotton Manufacture*, and have been corroborated as far as possible from other sources; they constitute the most reliable data obtainable for that period. For 1831, for the United States, we have the census returns and other sources, none of them very accurate, yet they give the best approximate figures.

It will be observed that the number of cotton factories in this country was 801 in 1831, 1,240 in 1840, 1,074 in 1850, and that since 1850 there has been a constant decrease in the number of establishments. This is the result of consolidation and the establishment of large works, the smaller factories being closed or united with the large ones.[1] While the number of factories has decreased, the consumption of cotton and the production of goods has steadily increased. Perhaps the best gauge for the progress of the industry is to be found in the quantity of cotton consumed per capita of the population. In Great Britain, in 1831, the home consumption of cotton per capita (excluding the proportion for the export trade) was 6.62 pounds; in 1881 it was 7.75 pounds; in the United States, for 1830, it was 5.9 pounds; in 1880 it was 13.91 pounds. That is, the clothing of the people of this country in 1830 required 5.9 pounds of cotton per annum, and now it requires 13.91 pounds.

If we take the per capita consumption of the factories, including exports and home consumption, the proportion for Great Britain in 1831 was 16.15 pounds; in 1881, 40.8 pounds; for the United States, in 1831, it was, on this basis, 6.1 pounds; in 1880 it had risen to 14.96 pounds. The ratios given as to spindles to persons employed, capital to spindles, product to spindles, capital to product, product to persons employed, while in some sense fallacious, and more valuable to the expert than to the general reader, yet are true for the time given and the existing circumstances, and certainly show the change of circumstances. The ratio of consumption to spindles is of course influenced largely by the number of the yarn produced, and many of the British mills spin finer numbers than do the mills of this country; but whatever may be the cause, the ratio stands as given, and shows that the attendant circumstances, either of machinery or kind of product, or of some other matter, vary as to the two countries.

---

[1] The number of cotton factories for 1880 should be increased by the number of mills engaged in working raw cotton, waste, or cotton yarn into hosiery, webbing, tapes, fancy fabrics, or mixed goods, or other fabrics which are not sold as specific manufactures of cotton or of wool; some of these work both fibres, but belong more in the class of cotton manufactures than in any other. These establishments, 249 in all, in 1880, have, without doubt, been included in the list of cotton-mills heretofore; so that now the total number, to correspond with the past, should be 1,005 cotton factories in the United States in 1880.

The following table shows the condition of the cotton manufactures of Great Britain and the United States in the years named:—

Countries and years.	Number of establishments.	Capital invested.	Number of spinning spindles.	Number of looms.	Number of employés, including children.	Value of product.	Pounds of cotton consumed.
Great Britain { 1833	1,151	$170,000,000	9,333,000	100,000	237,000	$156,693,465	262,700,000
Great Britain { 1878	2,671	374,720,500	39,577,920	514,911	482,993	474,916,358	1,439,393,000
United States { 1831	801	40,612,984	1,246,703	33,433	57,466	....	77,457,316
United States { 1880	756	208,280,346	10,653,435	225,759	172,544	192,950,110	750,343,981

The following table shows the condition of the cotton-spinning and weaving industry of Great Britain and the United States in the years named:—

Countries and years.	Ratio of spindles to persons employed.	Ratio of capital to spindles.	Ratio of product to spindles.	Ratio of capital to product.	Ratio of product to persons employed.	Years.	Total annual consumption of cotton.	Total average consumption of cotton per year per capita of total population.	Average consumption of cotton (exclusive of exports) per capita of total population.
							Pounds.	*Pounds.*	*Pounds.*
Great Britain { 1833	39 to 1	$18 21 to 1	$16 79 to 1	$1 00 to $0 92	$661 15 to 1	1831	262,700,000	16.15	6.20
Great Britain { 1878	82 to 1	9 48 to 1	12 01 to 1	1 00 to 1 27	983 46 to 1	1881	1,439,393,000	40.80	7.75
United States { 1831	22 to 1	32 58 to 1	....	....	....	1830	77,457,316	6.10	5.90
United States { 1880	62 to 1	19 55 to 1	18 03 to 1	1 00 to 0 92	1,113 28 to 1	1880	750,343,981	14.96	13.91

THE COTTON MANUFACTURES.

FROM ATKINSON'S REPORT ON THE COTTON MANUFACTURES, TENTH CENSUS, VOL. II., PP. 946-955.

The cotton manufacture of the United States may be now considered more firmly established than ever before. The method on which the business is conducted in the United States varies greatly from that of any other country; and this difference arises mainly from a difference not only in the habits and customs of the people, but also in their condition and intelligence.

The home market is the most important one, and may long continue to be so, although the export demand for our fabrics now takes from 7 to 8 per cent. of our annual product, and is likely to increase.

In contrast with the cotton manufacturer of Great Britain, our principal rival, we are therefore called upon to meet the demands of an intelligent class of customers living under substantially uniform conditions and varying but little in their requirements. Hence we are not called upon for the great variety of fabrics that must be supplied by Great Britain. In consequence of this demand for a great variety of fabrics the work of the cotton manufacturer of England is much more divided than with us. With the exception of a few large establishments, working mainly to supply the home market, few goods are known in England by the name of the factory in which they are made, nor are they sold under the name of the manufacturer; but to a very large extent the yarn is spun in one establishment, woven in another, and finished in a third. The gray cloth is sold to the warehouseman, or to the merchant, to be stamped and packed by him, or to be dyed, bleached, or printed under his direction. If English goods had been sold under the name and stamp of the manufacturer, as cotton goods are in the United States, perhaps the substitution of clay for cotton might not have been carried to so great an extent. In the United States cotton goods are spun and woven in the same factory, and, whether sold in the gray or bleached, they are almost all stamped and marketed under the name of the factory in which they are made. Each factory, therefore, has its reputation to sustain, and whether the fabric be coarse or fine it is the effort of every one to make it good of its kind.

The same rule applies to printed calicoes. These are marketed under the name of the works in which they have been printed, and the reputation and permanent existence of these works rest upon uniformity in quality, excellence in color and style, and constant progress in the art of design.

We may not claim to be more honest than our rivals, but it is a great error to suppose that it is permanently profitable to make an article that is not what it purports to be. A cotton fabric may be of a low grade, and may be intended to sell at a low price, but yet it is not profitable to substitute clay for cotton; the fabric, whatever it is, has its name and reputation, and must be true to them, or else the demand for it will sooner or later cease. Even goods that are made for linings, and that need to be starched and stiffened in order to be used, must have a uniform quality in the fabric itself to hold a permanent place in our market. Dyed goods that require to be woven on heavily-sized warps cannot, except by rule, be loaded with sizing. If an attempt is made to introduce an article in which clay has been added to make it heavier, it is immediately detected, because the use of sewing-machines is almost universal, and the clay in the fabric heats the needle and exposes the fraud.

In stating those conditions under which the manufacture of cotton is conducted in the United States for the home demand, it is not intended to imply that the use of a foreign substance to give additional weight to a cotton fabric is, of necessity, a fraud. For instance, there is a very large demand in China for materials for the grave-clothes of corpses, and for this use "earth to earth, and dust to dust" may be considered a legitimate rule, even if the earth is conveyed in the fabric which is nominally made of cotton. Some of the finest cotton fabrics yet made in the United States, which closely resemble silk, are used mainly for lining coffins.

The principal market for our own fabrics is found among the thrifty working-people, who constitute the great mass of our population.

It has therefore happened that, although we have not until recently undertaken the manufacture of very fine fabrics, the average quality of the fabrics that we do make is better than that of any other nation, with the possible exception of France. It is for the wants of the million that our cotton factories are mainly worked, and we have ceased to import staple goods, and shall never be likely to resume their import. On the other hand, we may for a long period continue to import the finer goods that depend mainly on fashion and style for their use, and that are purely articles of luxury. As has been stated, the substantial fabrics that constitute the main part of our cotton manufacture, and that are used by the masses of the people, are of the best of their kind, with the possible exception of those made in France. The French peasantry are a sagacious and truly economical race, and will not buy a poor fabric if they can get a good one ; hence the cotton fabrics for their use are of a very substantial kind, and are much more free from adulteration than those of any other country in Europe. The common cotton fabrics of England, Belgium, and Germany could hardly be sold in the United States at any price.

The finest printed calicoes of France and England may be the best of their kind ; but the printed calicoes for the use of the multitude, and which constitute the really important branch of this department of the manufacture, are of much better quality in the United States than in Europe, and are also of finer colors and of more varied styles.

In fact, one of the chief obstacles that it has been necessary to overcome in the introduction of unbleached American cotton fabrics in the English market, and in other markets heretofore supplied by England, has been their apparently open texture, owing to the absence of heavy sizing. In the United States the sizing used upon the warp, and which is necessary in order to weave it, is made from corn or potato starch, free from any substance intending to make it heavier. In the gray cloth the sizing, therefore, constitutes only $2\frac{1}{2}$ to 5 per cent. of the weight, and when the fabric is washed it shrinks more in measure than it loses in weight; hence a square yard washed and dried without stretching will be heavier than a square yard taken directly from the loom.

In England, on the other hand, even the pure sizing is made from wheat flour, which is very glutinous ; and the fabrics thus woven, even where no adulteration is intended, lose from 10 to 12 per cent. of their weight on the first washing. These pure goods are, however, made chiefly for the home consumption of the richer classes of England. The greater part of the English cotton fabrics, exported or used by the working-classes, are loaded with from 10 to 40 per cent. of clay and other substances. The art of sizing has been highly perfected in England, and has been made the subject of very numerous patents; and, as the use of clay and flour to the extent of 100 pounds to each 100 pounds of cotton-warp yarn involves great danger of mildew, many ingenious chemical applications have also been patented to serve as antiseptics, such as chloride of zinc, chloride of calcium, common salt, white vitriol, etc. These various antiseptics are compounded with flour, gypsum, soapstone, china clay, and other heavy substances in various ways. The English text-books upon the art of sizing are instructive and suggestive, especially in respect to the rules for the purchase of the most glutinous kinds of flour and for the detection of adulteration in flour, it being obvious that unless the flour is pure and well adapted to the purpose, it would be necessary to use cotton instead of clay to make up the weight of the fabric.

It will, of course, take a good deal of time to accustom buyers to the more open texture of cotton fabrics in which no clay is used; but as time passes American fabrics are being steadily substituted for those previously used by foreign nations, especially in China.

Since the year 1860 the cotton manufacture of the United States has been exposed to greater vicissitudes than any other important branch of the national industry, and the wonder is not that there should have been some disasters, but that it should have survived at all in the hands of its original owners. In 1860 the whole number of spindles in the United States was 5,235,000. From 1857 to 1860 the cost of constructing a spinning and weaving factory on the medium fabrics woven of No. 25 yarn was from $16 to $20 per spindle (the number designates the number of skeins of 840 yards of yarn each in one pound). The value of a bale of cotton of 480 pounds was from $40 to $50. Then came the combined effects of war, paper money, and scarcity of cotton. At one period more than two-thirds of the cotton machinery of the United States was stopped; the value of a bale of cotton rose to over $900, and the price of some kinds of goods was seven to eight times the present price. A little later new mills were constructed which cost from $30 to $40 per spindle.

At the date of the census the number of spindles operated in the specific manufacture of cotton fabrics was 10,653,435; but the spindle has changed in its productive power, and each spindle of 1880 was much more effective than that of 1860. The value of the bale of cotton was again from $40 to $50; the standard printing-cloth, which reached 33 cents a yard during the war, was worth 4 cents; the No. 25 mill for spinning and weaving could be built for from $14 to $18 per spindle; our export of cotton fabrics was more in value and much more in quantity than in 1860, and the only check to its steady and profitable increase was the renewal of the home demand. Such have been the changes and fluctuations; yet, despite them all, not one spindle in ten has passed from the ownership of the person, firm, or corporation in whose possession it was in 1860, except in the regular process of bequest or voluntary sale.

During the period of inflation or of great vicissitude, the attention of the managers of the property was of necessity devoted to other matters than the improvements and minute savings in which the profit of the business now consists; but during the last few years very great improvements have been made, and the lesson of economy and saving has been learned. The best example that can be cited may be found in the record of one great factory working upon coarse and substantial fabrics, and consuming more than 20,000 bales of cotton a year. Sixty per cent. of its products are sold for export to various parts of the world. The proportion of operatives to each 1,000 spindles has been decreased 43 per cent., or from 26½ to 15. The wages of women, who constitute more than two-thirds of the operatives, have been increased 33 per cent. The cost of making the cloth, aside from the material used, has been decreased 21 per cent.

In 1860 the average product of one operative, working one year, was 5,317 pounds; in 1880, 7,928 pounds of drill, such as is exported to China. Assuming 5 pounds, or about 16 yards, as the annual requirement of a Chinaman for dress, in 1860 one Lowell operative, working one year, clothed 1,063 Chinese; in 1880 one could supply 1,586. It will be obvious that no hand spinning and weaving can compete with this product of machinery; yet the machine-made fabrics of Europe and America combined, have as yet reached only six or eight in a hundred of the Chinese. How soon the rest will be clothed in cotton fabrics made by machinery from American cotton, therefore, depends but little on whether the wages of the Lowell factory girl be $4 or $6 per week, but rather on what exchangeable products the Chinese can produce better or cheaper than we can. The more tea, silk, sugar, and other commodities we buy from them, the more cotton fabrics and other products in which we excel will they buy from us.

It has been held that the cotton of America must be more and more used, both in America and elsewhere, and that, as time goes on, almost every other kind, with the exception of the cotton of Egypt, must give place to it. To what extent may the same preëminence be secured for the cotton fabrics of the United States in the markets of the world that we have secured in respect to the cotton fibre?

In the consideration of this branch of the subject, our attention must be given to the present condition of competition between the mills of the Middle and Eastern States with the mills of Great Britain.

In respect to the Eastern States the cotton factories of Lowell in Massachusetts, Manchester in New Hampshire, Biddeford and Lewiston in Maine, may be considered in their relation to the factories of Manchester, Stockport, Preston, and Bolton, in England. For the purposes of this comparison it may be assumed, that there can be no permanent advantage of one set of mills over the other in respect to the quality and perfection of the machinery. At any given time some advantage may be claimed and admitted on either side in some special department of the mill; but every invention or improvement will sooner or later be adopted on both sides, and the supremacy in the art of converting cotton into cloth must ultimately fall to that country or section which possesses the advantage in respect to the conditions offered to the operatives and in proximity to the source of the raw material.

The best conditions of life for the operatives, and the best prospects of improving their condition and that of their children, are of the gravest importance. The factors in this problem are education, shelter, subsistence, and opportunity for other kinds of work. In respect to education, the common-school system of the United States assures a thorough training free of cost, and in the principal towns and cities free education is carried to the point of preparing the pupil to enter a university.

In respect to subsistence, the factories of New England are 3,000 miles nearer the wheat-fields and grazing-grounds of the West than those of Lancashire; and, so long as Europe buys food of America, our own mills must have the advantage of proximity to the Western prairies. In respect to the rents of dwelling-houses there cannot long be any difference, if there is any at present, because the materials for construction are most abundant in America. Opportunity for other work than that of the factory must continue for many generations, and until this continent is peopled.

In comparing our power to compete with England we may claim advantages of one kind, and in comparing with the nations of continental Europe we may claim advantages of another kind, in some respects of a different order. In competition with England, it is often claimed that our chief advantage lies in a certain alleged versatility and power of adapting means to ends, and in great quickness of perception on the part of working-people in respect to the advantages to be gained by the adoption of new processes or inventions. If we have this advantage, there must be special causes for it in the influences that are brought to bear upon the operatives and artisans who do the work; for a very large proportion of them are foreign-born, or are the children of foreign immigrants. Why should they work with any more zeal or judgment here than in the countries whence they have come? Why are Irish and French-Canadian factory hands to be relied on for more steady work, larger product, better discipline, and more cleanly and wholesome conditions of life than the operatives of England, Belgium, and Germany? To me it appears evident that these advantages, so far as they exist, are due mainly to the following circumstances:—

First. Our system of common and purely secular schools, attended by the children of rich and poor alike.

Second. Manhood suffrage.

Third. The easy acquisition of land.

Fourth. The habit of saving small sums, induced by the establishment of savings-banks throughout the manufacturing States.

Fifth. The absence of a standing army, and the application of the revenue derived from taxes on the whole to useful purposes.

In respect to the first of these influences, the public-school system, the foreign observer generally takes notice only of the quality of the instruction given, and, though he may find something to praise, he finds also much to blame. He finds in many cases the instruction bad and the subjects often ill-chosen, and he wonders at the misdirection of a force that might be so much more wisely applied. What he fails to notice is that the school itself, entirely apart from its instruction, is the great educator of the children who attend it. The school is, first of all, no respecter of persons: the stupid son of a rich man, led in every class by the son of a mechanic, cannot in after-life look down on him as an inferior, whatever the conventional position of the two may be; or, if the rich man's son has brains as well as fortune, the poor man's son can never attribute to fortune only, the lead that he may take in after-life. The school is thoroughly democratic, and each pupil learns in it that it depends on himself alone what place he may take in after-life, and that, although society may be divided into planes, there is no system of caste and no barrier in the way of social success, except the want of character and ability to attain it. The associations of the common school utterly prevent anything like servility in the relation of classes in after-life; and although it is sometimes made a little too manifest that "one man is as good as another, and a little better," on the part of those who are more eager than discreet in their effort to rise, yet, on the whole, the relation of the various classes, which must in the nature of things always and everywhere exist, is that of mutual respect, and anything like the old-world distinctions of caste and rank would seem about as absurd to one as to the other. The common school is the solvent of race, creed, nationality, and condition.

In another way, the discipline of the school affects the processes of manufacture. In the schools, cleanliness, order, and regular habits are enforced, with deference to the teachers and respect for authority; and, in these later years, this is coupled with the teaching of music and drawing in all the principal towns and cities. When children thus trained are removed to the mill or the workshop, habits of order and cleanliness, with some æsthetic taste, are already established. Nothing strikes an American manufacturer with so much surprise, as the extreme untidiness of the large textile mills of England and the dreariness of the factory towns. In this respect, however, it must be confessed that the managers of the New England mills are greatly aided by the absence of smoke, the coal commonly used being anthracite. Much surprise is often expressed by our foreign visitors, at the amount of decoration permitted in the fitting of stationary and locomotive engines and in much of our machinery; but, bad as the taste displayed may sometimes be, it is nevertherless a fact that such engines or machines are better cared for and kept in better repair than where no individuality, so to speak, is permitted. On one of our great railways the attempt was not long since made to dispatch the locomotives as they happened to arrive at the central station, sometimes with one and sometimes with another engine-driver; but the immediate and great increase in the repair account caused the corporation to return very soon to the customary plan, of giving each driver a particular locomotive, with which he may be identified.

The instruction of the school also gives every pupil a superficial knowledge, if no more, of the geography and resources of the country, which the universal habit of reading newspapers keeps up. Hence comes the almost entire absence of any fixed character in the labor of the country: every boy believes that he can achieve success somewhere else, if not at home. No congestion of labor can last long. The war and the succeeding railway mania combined, concentrated population at certain points to a greater extent than ever happened before, and it has taken more than five years to overcome the difficulty; but within these five years a million or more new inhabitants in Texas, half a million or more in Kansas, and probably two or three millions added to the population of Nebraska, Colorado, Minnesota, and the far North-west, indicate that the evil has already found a remedy.

It is already apparent that a very slight increase in the demand for skilled workmen in certain branches of employment would not easily be met in the Eastern States, except by drawing upon England and Germany. During the years of depression, the cessation of railway building and the use of the excess of railway plant existing in 1873 has caused the dispersion of a large portion of the trained mechanics and artisans who then did the work of supplying this demand; but these are not the men who have crowded the Eastern cities and caused the apparent excess of laborers out of work. Such men have gone back to the land, or in the new States and Territories have found other ways in which to apply their skill and energy, and they will not return. It may be that the greatest danger to the manufacturers of England will not be in our competition in the sale of goods in neutral markets, but in our competition for the skilled workmen and artisans who make these goods, when we offer them equal or higher wages and better conditions of life in the work that will very soon need to be done to supply the increasing demand in our own country.

The patent system may here be cited also as a factor in our industrial system. It has been carried to an almost absurd extreme, so that it is not safe for any one to adopt a new method, machine, or part of a machine, and attempt to use it quietly and without taking out a patent, lest some sharp person, seeing it in use and not published, shall himself secure a patent and come back to the real inventor with a claim for royalty.

Manhood suffrage, subject as it is to great abuses, and difficult as it has made the problem of the self-government of great cities, where voters do not meet each other, as in the town-meeting, face to face, but where the powers of government are of necessity delegated to men of whom the voters can have little personal knowledge, yet works distinctly in the direction of the safety, stability, and order of the community. Outside of two or three of the very largest cities, where there are concentrated great masses of illiterate citizens, it would be difficult to find a case of serious abuse of the power of taxation, except in the South since the war, and even there the evil is now mainly abated.

The easy acquisition of land throughout the country, under simple forms of conveyance, registered in every county, gives a motive to economy, and induces habits of saving that are of supreme importance in their effect on society. In the town in which I live,— and in which I can remember the coming of the first Irishman who became a land-owner,— out of about one thousand owners of real estate, over two hundred are of Irish birth or extraction. The richest one among them came from Ireland in 1846, a steerage passenger. He now pays taxes on property of the value of $50,000, almost all in real estate. His son is superintendent of the repairs of highways, and is one of the most efficient members of the school committee.

During the last thirty years the factory population of New England has passed through three phases. First came the sons and daughters of the New England farmer; but as the sewing-machine and other inventions opened new demands for women's work, women of American birth passed out to easier or better-paid employment, while the men took up other branches requiring more individual skill. These places were taken mainly by Irish, with a few Germans and English. But as the Irish saved their earnings, and as the New England yeomen emigrated to the richer lands of the great West, they passed out of the mills to buy up the deserted farms of the poorer North-eastern States, where, by their persistent industry and manual labor, they achieved success and gained a position which satisfied them, but with which the native New Englander is no longer contented. Their places in the mills are now being more and more taken by the French Canadians, who, in their new conditions and surroundings, show little of the stolid and unprogressive character which has kept them so long contented on their little strips of land on the Saint Lawrence River. In the very air they breathe they seem to imbibe a new and restless energy, while the intelligence shown by their children in the schools augurs well for their future progress. On the whole the simplicity of our system of land tenure, and the ease with which small parcels may be obtained, must be rated among the most important factors in considering our possible advantage over other countries.

Next in our list comes the savings-bank. In 1875, out of the 1,652,000 inhabitants of Massachusetts, 720,000 were depositors in savings-banks to the amount of $238,000,000. During the late years of depression the deposit has decreased somewhat in amount, but the decrease has been chiefly owing to the withdrawal of money for other investment, especially in United States bonds. There have been some failures of banks and some losses, as might well have been expected, but they have been less than in any other branch of business; and the savings-bank system stands firmly based on well-earned confidence, and offers an easy means of saving the smallest sums to every man, woman, and child in the State. At the present time the deposits in the savings-banks of Massachusetts amount to about $240,000,000, owned by about 750,000 persons.

To these causes of quick adaptation to any conditions that may arise, or to any necessity for the application of new methods or devices, may be added the custom, which has almost the force of law, of an equal distribution of estates among the children of the testator. *Tools to him who can use them* is the unwritten law; and neither land nor capital can remain long in the possession of him who cannot direct or use them wisely. Liberty to distribute is esteemed as important a factor in our body-politic as liberty to accumulate, even though the liberty may sometimes lead to the apparent waste of great fortunes.

Finally, it must be held that our freedom from the blood-tax of a standing army, and the fact that the proceeds of taxation are, on the whole, usefully and productively expended, are among our greatest advantages; and this is asserted with confidence, notwithstanding the misgovernment of some great cities and of several of the Southern States. What are these failures but proofs of the general confidence of the people in local self-government? Great frauds and great abuses can only happen where integrity is the common rule; and where each man distrusts his neighbor, or each town, city, or State distrusts the next, the opportunity for fraud or breach of trust cannot occur. The use of inconvertible paper money during many years has not been without its necessary malign result upon the character of the people, and the newspapers are filled with the fraud and corruption that have come to light; but no newspaper has ever yet recorded one fact that offsets many frauds: In the great Boston fire, one of the Boston banks lost not only every book of account, but every security and note that was in its vaults, amounting to over $1,250,000. On the morning after the fire, its officers had no evidence or record by which any of the persons or corporators who owed it money could be held to their contracts; yet, within a very short time, duplicate notes were voluntarily brought in by its debtors, many of whom knew not whether they could ever pay them, because the fire had destroyed their own property, and the known ultimate loss of that bank from the burning of its books and securities was less than $10,000.

Our army is but a border police. Although its officers are held in honor and esteem, military life is not a career that very many seek, and as time goes on it will become an occupation less and less to be desired. Thus we are spared not only the tax for its support, but the worse tax of the withdrawal of its members from useful and productive pursuits. It is in this respect that we claim our greatest advantage over the nations of continental Europe. What have we to fear from the competition of Germany, if we really undertake to beat her in the neutral markets, which we can reach as readily as she can? For a little while, the better instruction of the merchants in her technical and commercial schools may give her advantage; but that can be overcome in a single generation, or as soon as the need is felt with us, as it is now beginning to be felt. After we shall have supplied our present want of technical education, the mere difference between the presence of a great army on her soil and its necessary support, and the absence of such a tax on us, will constitute the difference on which modern commerce turns. When the traffic of the world turns on half a cent a yard, a cent a bushel, or a half-penny a pound on the great staples, no nation can long succeed in holding a traffic that is handicapped with a standing army. The protection of Germany from our competition in neutral markets may be offset in our yet more dangerous competition for men. The German already knows Texas, and in the one block of 60,000 square miles of land by which the State of Texas exceeds the area of the German empire, we offer room and healthy conditions of life for millions of immigrants; and, if they come in sufficient numbers, they can raise on that single square of land as much cotton as is now raised in the whole South, that is to say, 5,000,000 bales; and as much wheat as is now raised in the whole North, that is to say, 400,000,000 bushels, and yet subsist themselves beside on what is left of this little patch that will not be needed for these two crops.

It will be obvious that even the least imaginative cannot but be moved by the influences that have been designated, and that versatility and readiness to adopt every labor-saving device will not only be promoted, but will be absolutely forced into action, when such vast areas are to be occupied, and when even the dullest boy is educated in the belief that he also is to be one of those who are to build up this nation to the full measure of its high calling. We may not dare to boast, in view of all we have passed through; but we know that slavery has been destroyed, and that the nation lives stronger, truer, and more vigorous than ever before. We know that it has been reserved for a democratic republic to be the first among nations that, having issued government notes and made them a legal tender, has resumed payment in coin without repudiation or reduction of the promise. We know that we have paid nearly a half of our great national debt already, and that the rest is now mainly held by our own citizens. We believe that within the lives of men of middle age now living, the nation will number one hundred millions, and that, in whatever else we may be found wanting, we cannot long be kept back in our career of material prosperity, which shall be shared with absolute certainty by every one who brings to the work health, integrity, and energy.

If there is any force in this reasoning, our competition with other manufacturing countries, in the supplying of neutral markets with manufactured goods, will not be compassed by the low rates of wages paid to our factory operatives or to the working-people engaged in our metal works and other occupations, but first by obtaining and keeping such an advanced position in the application and use of improved tools and machinery, as shall make high wages consistent with a low cost of production; secondly, by our ability to obtain the raw materials at low cost. Every employer knows that among employés who are paid by the piece, it is the operative that gains the largest earnings whose production costs the least, because under the control of such operatives the machinery is most effectively guided during working hours. As it is with single operatives, so it is with large masses; if well instructed, and working under the incentives to industry and frugality that have been named, their large product will earn for them ample wages, and yet result in a low cost of labor to the employer. Such workmen never have any "blue Monday." The workman who in this country habitually becomes intoxicated is soon discharged, and his place is filled by one who respects himself and values his place too much to risk his position in dissipation.

Competition with England in supplying the markets of Asia, Africa, and South America with cotton goods, is now perhaps the best criterion by which to gauge our ability to compete in other branches of manufacture. It has been often assumed in England, that the increasing shipments of cotton goods from this country have been forced by necessity, and merely consisted of lots sold below cost, as a means of obtaining ready money; but there is no ground whatever for this general assumption, even though some small shipments may have been made at first with this view. Our export of cotton fabrics amounts as yet to but 7 or 8 per cent. of our production, and is but a trifle compared to that of Great Britain; but it is not made at a loss, and it constitutes a most important element in the returning prosperity of our cotton-mills. The goods exported are mostly made by strong and prosperous corporations, paying regular dividends, and consist mainly of. coarse sheetings and drills, which are sold by the manufacturers to merchants, who send them to China, Africa, and South America in payment for tea, silk, ivory, sugar, gums, hides, and wool. They are not made by operatives who earn less than the recent or present rates of wages in England, but in most departments of the mills by those who earn equal wages, or even more. This competition had been fairly begun before the late war in this country, but it is now continued under better conditions. The mills of New England, owing to through connections by rail, are now relatively much nearer the cotton-fields than they were then. Prior to 1860 substantially all the cotton went to the seaports of the cotton States, and from there the cost of moving it to the North or to Liverpool varied but little; but at the present day a large and annually-increasing portion of the cotton used in the North is bought in the interior markets, and is carried in covered cars directly to the mills, where the bales are delivered clean, and much more free from damage and waste than those which are carried down the Southern rivers on boats and barges, dumped upon the wharves, and then compressed to the utmost for shipment by sea.

In proof that this advantage is an actual one, the following example may be cited: A contract has just been made for the transportation of a large quantity of cotton from Texas to Liverpool at the rate of $1.10 per 100 pounds, the proportion assigned to the land carriage being 70 cents, to transshipment in Boston and to the steamship 40 cents; the rate of marine insurance is three-eighths of 1 per cent., and the cost of handling in Liverpool, and transportation to Manchester, not less than a quarter of a cent per pound. Bargains may be made to bring cotton from the same point in Texas to the principal factory cities of New England at the rate assigned to the land carriage, namely 70 cents per 100 pounds. This cotton is brought from the interior towns of Texas to Boston, and cannot be carried to Liverpool by way of Galveston or New Orleans so cheaply, else it would not come this way. Assuming the bale to weigh 500 pounds, at 10 cents a pound, we have the following comparative cost: —

LOWELL.

	Per bale.	Per cwt.
Cost of cotton in Texas, 500 pounds, at 10 cents, including all local charges	$50 00	
Freight to Lowell in a covered locked car, in which the cotton is protected from rain, mud, and other causes of waste, at 70 cents per 100 pounds	3 50	
Total	$53 50	$10 70

LANCASHIRE.

500 pounds, at 10 cents, including all local charges	$50 00	
Freight from Texas to Liverpool, at $1.10 per 100 pounds	5 50	
Insurance at three-eighths of 1 per cent. on $56	21	
Transshipment in Liverpool, and freight to Lancashire, one-fourth of a cent	1 25	
Total	$56 96	11 39
Advantage of Lowell over Lancashire	$3 46	$0 69

There may be changes in the rates, but it does not seem probable that the relation of the land to the ocean rate can be much changed, and it would therefore appear that the New England manufacturer will have a permanent advantage in the price of American cotton of any given grade, varying from 6 to 8 per cent. as the price of cotton may vary from 12 to 9 cents per pound; and this advantage may be equal to 15 or 25 per cent. in ability to pay wages, as the cost of labor varies from a quarter to a third in the total cost of coarse and medium goods, such as constitute the chief part of the demand of the world.

It may be said that this proves too much, and that the cotton spinners of the Southern States will have the same relative advantage over New England. Let this be freely admitted: We are treating the question of the future supremacy of the United States in the manufacture as well as in the growth of cotton, and if the future changes in population, wealth, and condition of the different sections of this country shall, in the future, cause the increase of spindles, especially in coarse fabrics, to be planted in the healthy hill country of northern Georgia, eastern Tennessee, and the Carolinas, it will simply be the greater evidence that natural laws are paramount. If Georgia has twice the advantage over Lancashire that New England now possesses it will only be the fault of the people of Georgia if they do not reap the benefit of it.

It has been stated that our present rates of wages in our cotton factories are higher than they were in 1860, and with our increasing prosperity they will tend to advance; but at the same time the cost of the labor in the finished fabric *has been reduced by the greater productive power of the machinery.* The fabrics upon which by far the largest part of the spindles and looms of the country are operated, may be divided substantially into the following classes : —

1. The printing-cloth, 28 inches wide and 7 yards to the pound. The cost of mill labor in making this fabric, including the salaries, wages, or earnings of every one employed, is now less than one cent, or a half-penny, a yard.

2. The heavy sheeting, 36 inches wide, and the heavy drill, 30 inches wide, each weighing from 2¾ to 3 yards to the pound. The cost of mill labor in making these fabrics is about 1¼ cents per yard.

3. Shirtings and sheetings, 30 to 36 inches wide, Nos. 20 to 30 yarns, each weighing from 3 to 4 yards to the pound. The cost of mill labor in these goods is from 1½ to 2 cents per yard.

4. The fine sheeting or shirting, from 30 to 40 inches wide, Nos. 30 to 40 yarns, weighing from 3 to 4 yards to the pound. The cost of mill labor in these goods is from 1½ to 3 cents per yard.

5. Fabrics of a similar kind to the above, from 1 to 3 yards wide.

6. Heavy cotton duck, cotton grain-bags, cotton hose, and other special articles.

7. Blue denims, stripes, tickings, brown denims and duck, and other heavy colored goods, substantial ginghams, cottonades, and other fancy woven fabrics of medium or heavy weight.

These seven classes comprise more than 95 per cent. of our cotton fabrics in weight; to them are to be added lawns, woven fabric of light weight for dresses, and spool-cotton.

In respect of one-half of these fabrics, being those of the heavier grade, our proximity to the cotton-field, computed at not less than half a cent per pound, oftener three-quarters, will enable the New England manufacturer to pay from 15 to 20 per cent. higher wages and yet to make the goods, other things being equal, at the same cost as his competitor in Lancashire. On a large portion of the other kinds this advantage in the cost of cotton would be from 10 to 15 per cent.

The natural advantages cannot work immediate results; the ways and means of a great commerce cannot be improvised in a year, hardly in a generation. Much depends on the wisdom of our legislators in framing the acts under which our taxes are collected, whether customs or excise, and yet more upon our adherence to a specie basis in our currency; but in the long run the only reason why we shall not assume a constantly-increasing share in the cotton manufacture of the world will be the free choice that our country offers for other occupations of a more profitable or more desirable kind.

Reference has been made to the small proportion of fine spinning in the United States. Within the last few years great progress has been made in spinning and weaving fabrics of Nos. 60 to 100, such as lawns and fine dress goods, and also in spinning fine yarn for spool-cotton. In the latter direction yarns as fine as No. 120 are now spun on the ring spinning-frame, a machine invented in this country and more used than any other for warp spinning, and now being adopted in Europe. Yarns as fine as 550 are spun on mules for three-cord sewing-cotton, and for experiment much finer counts have been reached. It has often been alleged that fine yarns could not be as well spun in the United States, as in England, owing to the dry and electrical conditions of the atmosphere during a considerable part of the year. This difficulty has existed in some degree, although not so as to preclude fine work if it had been profitable to undertake it; but as far as this difficulty existed it has lately been entirely removed by the invention of a very simple and inexpensive apparatus for moistening the air with the finest spray of pure cold water, by which method the air of a spinning or weaving-room may be kept at any desired degree of humidity in the driest day, so that the adverse effect of electricity is entirely overcome.

Whenever the condition and extension of our market will warrant the undertaking, there is now no obstacle to our manufacturing any variety of cotton fabric that is in demand, either coarse or fine.

While it may not be worth while to give historical statistics in relation to the cotton manufacture of this country in the present report, a few words may well be devoted to changes in the work, which have conduced not only to the welfare of the people, but to the welfare of the operatives also.

When the cotton manufacture was first established in the United States water-power was considered essential to the work, and, as a rule, the location of mills was limited to narrow valleys, or places where there was room only for mills of several stories in height. The first mills built were very considerable structures for their time, but they were low-studded, badly lighted, and were heated by stoves; and in these mills the operatives were compelled to work under arduous conditions (owing to the imperfection of the machinery) thirteen to fourteen hours a day. These narrow structures were in some places built seven stories in height. All the plans were made with reference to this form of structure, whether the mill was to be operated by water-power or by steam, until quite a recent period. In 1860 the "normal" cotton-mill (so to speak) had become a factory four or five stories high, about 60 feet wide, varying in length according to the amount of machinery, high-studded, well lighted, thoroughly well ventilated, and heated by radiation from steam-pipes.

In 1866 the machine for sizing yarn, known as the "slasher," was first imported, displacing the machine known as the "dresser." In the use of the slasher one man and a boy working in a thoroughly well-ventilated room, at a moderate degree of heat, took the place of seven or eight men who had been previously employed in the same work in a room which was of necessity kept at over 100° F., the atmosphere saturated with sour starch. This change removed the only really objectionable kind of work from the cotton factory. In the earlier mills the apparatus for the removal of dust from the factory was very imperfect, but to-day every room, even including those in which the cotton is opened, is substantially free from dust; and it happens that the degree of heat and of humidity required for the best work of the cotton factory is one which conduces in great measure to the health of the operative, perhaps a little warmer than may be desirable.

At the present time another change is in progress. The use of water-power is becoming less, its development for the purpose of sale having never proved profitable. The power thus developed has been a valuable auxiliary in the working of the factory, but as a matter of investment the development of land and water-power together have almost without exception failed to be profitable.

The great progress in the construction of the steam-engine and in the economy of fuel is steadily working towards a change to steam as the principal motive-power for the cotton factory. An incidental advantage in this change is that the factory may be placed nearer to the principal markets, where it can be more conveniently supervised and more easily reached. The use of steam also renders a choice of location perfectly feasible; and the model factory, one or two stories high, may be placed upon a level plain, and can be more easily lighted and ventilated and more economically operated than when any other form of building is used. Under these new conditions better dwellings for the operatives, less crowded, can also be provided, and in every respect the work can be conducted under better conditions.

At the present time the hours of labor in New England, where most of the cotton manufacturing is done, vary from ten to eleven hours per day. This great change has been brought about by a gradual comprehension of the best conditions both for the laborer and for the capitalist, and without much regard to legislation. It is probable that ere long ten hours will be the limit of factory work throughout New England, either by process of legislation or through the conviction on the part of employers that any longer hours are not profitable,—a conclusion to which many have already come.

A great change has also in the progress of time been affected in the dwellings in which the factory operatives live, in part tending towards better conditions, in part to worse conditions. On the whole there has been less average progress in this direction than in the construction and operation of the mills themselves. The choice of position, however, which is now given by the greater use of steam, gives better opportunities for scattering the dwelling-houses over a wider area at little cost.

A more abundant supply and choice of food has been effected in this as in all other branches of work, to the great benefit of the operatives, by the consolidation and more effective service of railroads. The average work of a male operative over sixteen years of age in textile factory will earn enough in a day to pay for the transportation of meat and bread for one year, one thousand miles, or from Chicago to Lowell, Lawrence, or Fall River. So far as cost is concerned, the great fields of the West and the factories of the East are in closer proximity than if the factory depended for its food upon its own immediate neighborhood, when served only by wagon-roads. The same changes which have so greatly reduced the railway charges between East and West are now taking place between North and South. The charge for moving cotton is becoming less year by year, and it will soon matter little where the cotton factory is placed, so far as distance between the field and the factory is concerned. The choice may be made so as to secure the stimulus of a moderately cold climate, in which in-door labor is more to be desired than out-door, in which the humidity of the atmosphere is measurably uniform or is not subject to extremes, and where facilities for repairs on machinery are close at hand, and the population is sufficiently dense to assure an adequate and constant supply of operatives, — mills which are much isolated always working at a disadvantage.

Great changes of a beneficial kind can now be foreseen in the application of electricity to the lighting of the factory. The developments in this direction are also such, that, whatever the relative cost of the electric light as compared to gas may be, it is yet so beneficial in other respects, that no factory manager can well afford to dispense with it, not only because of the more perfect work which its use assures, but because the choice of the operative in selecting the place in which to work will render the use of the electric light almost a matter of necessity.

In conclusion, it may be said that the progress in the art of manufacturing cotton fabrics in the last forty years has been very great, distinctly sustaining the rule which affects all the arts to which modern machinery can be applied, namely, that, in proportion to the effectiveness of capital in the form of machinery and the freedom with which it may be applied, the cost of production is lessened and the consumer is served more cheaply; while, on the other hand, the wages of the operatives are increased, the conditions of work made better, and the identity of interests between labor and capital are established.

It may be said that in the absence of any artificial obstructions to traffic between States or nations, the truest guide to the place where the lowest cost of production is compassed may be found by ascertaining where the wages of labor are the highest, and the conditions of life the best; that at that point the lowest cost of production must be found, for this reason: both wages and profits are derived from the sale of the thing produced; hence it follows that where the natural conditions of production are best, the machinery most effective, and the labor the most intelligent and skilful, the product will be largest at the least effort to those who do the work, and when the division of this product is made under the conditions of absolutely free competition, the relative proportion which capital can secure to itself will be least, even though its absolute share be greater and greater as the years go on; but the share which the laborer will receive will increase year by year, both absolutely and relatively. As capital increases the absolute sum of profits is greater, but the relative share of the product secured by capital becomes less. The increase of capital and its effective use by skilled laborers assure a larger production, and the workman obtains a larger share of a larger product, measured in kind or in wages paid in money. In the cotton-mill, as well as in many other arts, special skill is required, but perhaps less general intelligence; therefore a lower grade of operatives may be employed from time to time as the machinery becomes more automatic, but at a steadily-increasing rate of wages. Invention may, therefore, be said to enable all conditions of men to attain a higher plane of material welfare, and as one class passes from the factory to other occupations which offer better conditions of life, new improvements enable those who could not do the factory work before, to undertake and carry it on. Thus it has been in the past, since the farmers' daughters of New England left the factory in which, with much longer hours of work, they earned only about one-half the wages now paid; but those who have succeeded them could not then have been capable of doing the work at all which they now so easily accomplish.

THE IRON AND STEEL INDUSTRIES.

FROM SWANK'S STATISTICS OF THE IRON AND STEEL PRODUCTION, TENTH CENSUS, VOL. II., PP. 886-890.

Important Uses of Iron and Steel.

The people of the United States are the largest *per capita* consumers of iron and steel in the world, and of all nations they are also the largest aggregate consumers of these products. Great Britain makes more iron than we do, but she exports about one-half of all that she makes. She exports more than one-half of the steel that she makes, and yet makes but little more than this country. No other European country equals Great Britain either in the *per capita* or aggregate consumption of iron and steel. This country is not now producing as much iron and steel as it consumes, but imports large quantities of both products, Great Britain being the principal source of our foreign supply. Our exports of iron and steel are only nominal.

A simple enumeration of some of the more important uses to which iron and steel are applied by our people will show how prominent is the part these metals play in the development of American civilization and in the advancement of our greatness and power as a nation.

We have built almost as many miles of railroad as the whole of Europe, and consequently have used in their construction almost as many rails, and now use almost as many railroad cars and locomotives. At the close of 1881 this country had 100,000 miles of railroad, Europe had about 106,000 miles, and all the rest of the world had about 45,000 miles. The United States had nineteen miles of railroad to every 10,000 of population, while Europe had a little more than three miles to the same population. Railroads, it is well known, annually consume more than one-half of the world's production of iron and steel, — rails, bridges, cars, and locomotives being impossible without these metals. The street railway is an American invention which also consumes large quantities of iron and steel, and we are far in advance of every other nation in its use. We were also the first nation in the world to introduce elevated railways especially to facilitate travel in large cities. In the construction of our New York elevated railways beauty of design, fitness of parts, and strength of materials have been so perfectly combined as to excite the admiration of all who behold them. We are the foremost of all nations in the use of iron and steel in bridge-building for railroads and ordinary highways, and the lightness and gracefulness of our bridges are nowhere equalled, while their strength and adaptability to the uses to which they are required are nowhere surpassed. In the use of iron for water-pipes and gas pipes we are probably in advance of every other nation. We make more iron stoves for heating halls and dwellings and for the purposes of the kitchen than all the rest of the world, and in the use of heaters and ranges we are behind no other nation. Our household stoves, both for heating and cooking, are works of real art as well as of utility. They are ornaments of American homes, instead of being conveniences simply. Our heating stoves are especially handsome, bright, cheerful, healthful, and clean. In all respects they form the best combination of desirable qualities yet devised for the heating of private dwellings. Cooking and other domestic utensils of iron have always, even in colonial days, been freely used in American households. We make liberal use of both cast and wrought iron in the construction of public and private buildings. Our use of iron for these purposes has in late years been quite marked, and in no respect more so than in the truly artistic effects which we give to this metal. We probably excel all nations in the use of iron for ornamental purposes in connection with masonry, brick-work, and wood-work. Fine illustrations of the artistic combination of iron with other materials may be seen in the interior of the new State Department building at Washington and in the interior of the new passenger depot of the Pennsylvania railroad at Philadelphia. We lead the world in the use of iron and steel wire for fencing purposes, and we have more miles of telegraph wire in use than any other country. Barbed-wire fencing is an American invention. We have made creditable progress in the construction of iron ships, and we would have made much greater progress if the same encouragement that has been given by other nations to their shipping interests had been given to ours. We use immense quantities of plate-iron in the storage, transportation, and refining of petroleum, in the production of which nature has given us almost a monopoly. The oil-wells themselves yearly require thousands of tons of iron pipes for tubing. We make liberal use of plate and sheet iron in the construction of the chimneys of steamboats on our lakes and rivers, and in the construction of factory, rolling-mill, and blast-furnace chimneys, and the stacks of blast-furnaces. American planished sheet-iron has almost entirely superseded Russia sheet-iron in our markets. We use it for locomotive jackets, in the manufacture of stoves and stove-pipe, and for many other purposes. We are the largest consumers of tin plates in the world, — Great Britain, their principal manufacturer, sending us annually more than one-half of her whole product. Portable and stationary engines consume large quantities of iron and steel. Our beautiful steam fire-engines are the product of American taste and skill, if they are not strictly an American invention, and we annually make large numbers of them for home use and for exportation. Anchors and chains, cotton-presses and cotton-ties, sugar-pans and salt-pans, and general foundry and machine work annually require large quantities of either iron or steel. We make our own cotton and woollen manufacturing machinery, and nearly all the other machinery that we use. The manufacture of the printing-presses of the country consumes immense quantities of iron and steel. No other country makes such free use of the printing-press as this country. We are the leading agricultural nation of the world, and hence are the largest consumers of agricultural implements; but we are also in advance of every other nation in the use of agricultural machinery. Our use of iron and steel in agriculture takes rank next to their use in the construction and maintenance of railroads. We lead all nations in the manufacture of cut-nails and spikes. Having a larger and more rapidly increasing population than any other country that is noted for its consumption of iron, we are consequently the largest consumers of nails and spikes in the construction of dwellings and public buildings, stores, warehouses, offices, and similar structures. Our extended and varied mining operations consume iron and steel in large quantities. So do our manufactures of scales and balances, letter-presses, burglar-proof and fire-proof safes, sewing-machines, and wagons and carriages. Sewing-machines are an American invention. Considerable quantities of iron or iron and steel are used for sewer and other gratings, street-crossings, iron pavements, lamp-posts, posts for awnings, all sorts of small hardware, horseshoes and horseshoe nails, wire-rope, iron hoops, iron cots and bedsteads, woven-wire mattresses, iron screens, iron railings, and fire-arms. In the manufacture of machine and hand tools and general cutlery we are excelled by no other nation, and in the use of machine tools we are in advance of every other nation. In general cutlery our saws and axes especially enjoy a world-wide reputation. Not the least important use to which iron and steel are put in this country is in the extension of the iron industry itself, — every blast-furnace, rolling-mill, or steel works that is erected first devouring large quantities of these products before contributing to their general supply.

In the substitution of steel for iron this country is rapidly progressing, especially in the construction and equipment of its railroads. During the past few years fully two-thirds of all the rails that have been laid on American railroads have been made of Bessemer steel, and at present a still larger proportion of steel rails is required by our railroad companies. On several American railroads the boilers of all new locomotives are now required to be made of steel, and the tendency is toward the exclusive use of steel for locomotive boilers, and its general use for stationary and marine boilers. The tires of American locomotives are now made exclusively of steel, and the fire-boxes of our locomotives are generally made of steel. The steel used in the construction of American locomotives is now chiefly produced by the open-hearth process. We have built a few steel bridges, but there is no marked tendency to substitute steel for iron in bridge-building. Steel is, however, largely used in the manufacture of wire, including wire-fencing, and for car and carriage axles, carriage tires, fire-arms, screws, and many other purposes. But little steel has yet been used in this country for nails and horse-shoes.

Mention has been made of the artistic finish of some of our iron-work; but the subject seems worthy of further notice. It is not only in stove-founding, in the graceful designs of bridges and elevated railways, and in the delicate combination of iron with other materials in the construction and ornamentation of buildings that American iron-workers have displayed an exquisite taste and a bold and dexterous touch. The fine arts themselves are being enriched by the achievements of our ironworking countrymen. An iron foundry at Chelsea, in Massachusetts, has recently reproduced, in iron castings, various works of art with all the fidelity and delicacy of Italian iron-founders. The most delicate antique patterns have been successfully copied. Shields representing mythological groups and classic events, medallions containing copies of celebrated portraits, panels containing flowers and animals, an imitation of a Japanese lacquer-tray one-sixteenth of an inch thick, and a triumphal procession represented on a large salver comprise some of the work of the Chelsea foundry. Some of the castings have been colored to represent bronze, and others to represent steel, while others again preserve the natural color of the iron. The bronzed castings resemble beaten work in copper. Only American iron is used. The ornamental uses to which art castings of iron may be put are many, and as they can be cheaply produced it may be assumed that a demand will ere long be created for them that will be in keeping with the artistic taste which has been so generally developed in our country during the past few years.

We conspicuously fall behind many other nations in the use of iron and steel for military purposes. We maintain only a small standing army and a small navy, and hence have but little use for iron or steel for the supply of either of these branches of the public service. We are also behind many other nations in the use of iron and steel sleepers for railway tracks. We yet have an abundance of timber for railway cross-ties, and hence do not need to substitute either iron or steel cross-ties. Except possibly as an experiment, there is not an iron or steel cross-tie in use in this country. It is a singular fact that we still import many blacksmith's anvils, their manufacture being a branch of the iron business to which we have not yet given adequate attention. Anvils of the best quality are, however, made in this country. A far more serious hiatus in our iron industry is found in the almost total absence of the manufacture of tin plates, the basis of which is sheet-iron, as is well known. As we can import the crude tin as easily as we import other commodities, our failure thus far to manufacture tin plates must be ascribed to the only true cause, — our inability to manufacture sheet-iron and coat it with tin as cheaply as is done by British manufacturers. It is not improbable that tin ore may yet be discovered in our own country in sufficiently large quantities to supply any domestic demand that may be created for its use.

CONCLUSION. — In reviewing the historical pages of this report the most striking fact that presents itself for consideration is the great stride made by the world's iron and steel industries in the last hundred years. In 1788 there were only eighty-five blast-furnaces in Great Britain, most of which were small, and their total production was only 68,300 tons of pig-iron. In 1880 Great Britain had 967 furnaces, many of which were very large, and their production was 7,749,233 tons. A hundred years ago there were no railroads in the world for the transportation of freight and passengers. Iron ships were unknown, and all the iron bridges in the world could be counted on the fingers of one hand. Without railroads and their cars and locomotives, and without iron ships and iron bridges, the world needed but little iron. Steel was still less a necessity, and such small quantities of it as were made were mainly used in the manufacture of tools with cutting edges.

The great progress made by the world's iron and steel industries in the last hundred years is as marked in the improvement of the processes of manufacture as in the increased demand for iron and steel products. A hundred years ago all bar-iron was laboriously shaped under the trip-hammer; none of it was rolled. Nor was iron of any kind refined at that time in the puddling furnace; it was all refined in forges, and much of it was made in primitive bloomary forges directly from the ore. Nearly all of the blast-furnaces of a hundred years ago were blown with leather or wooden bellows by water-power, and the fuel used in them was chiefly charcoal. Steam-power, cast-iron blowing cylinders, and the use of bituminous coal had just been introduced. Less than sixty years ago heated air had not been used in the blowing of blast-furnaces, and fifty years ago anthracite coal had not been used in them, except experimentally. Thirty years ago the Bessemer process for the manufacture of steel had not been heard of, and the open-hearth process for the manufacture of steel had not been made a practical success. Thirty years ago the regenerative gas furnace had not been invented. The nineteenth century has been the most prolific of all the centuries in inventions which have improved the methods of manufacturing iron and steel, and which have facilitated their production in large quantities.

The next most important fact that is presented in the historical chapters of this report is the astonishing progress which the iron and steel industries of the United States have made within the last twenty years. During this period we have not only utilized all contemporaneous improvements in the manufacture of iron and steel, but we have shown a special aptitude, or genius, for the use of such improvements as render possible the production of iron and steel in large quantities. Enterprising and courageous as the people of this country have always been in the manufacture of iron and steel, they have shown in the last twenty years that they have in all respects been fully alive to the iron and steel requirements of our surprising national development. If we had not applied immense blowing engines and the best hot-blast stoves to our blast-furnaces our present large production of pig-iron would have been impossible. If we had not built numerous large rolling-mills we could not have had a sufficient supply of plate-iron for locomotive and other boilers, the hulls of iron ships, oil-tanks, nails and spikes, and other important uses; nor of sheet-iron for stoves and domestic utensils; nor of tee, angle, and channel iron for bridge-building and general construction purposes; nor of iron rails for our railroads; nor of bar-iron and rod-iron for a thousand uses. If we had not promptly introduced the Bessemer process the railroads of the country could not have been supplied with steel rails, and without the four and a half million tons of American steel rails that have been laid down in the past twelve years our trunk railroads could not have carried their vast tonnage of agricultural and other products, for iron rails could not have endured the wear of this tonnage. If we had not established the manufacture of crucible steel and introduced the open-hearth process there would have been a scarcity of steel in this country for the manufacture of agricultural implements, springs for railway passenger cars, tires for locomotives, etc. Foreign countries could not in late years have supplied our extraordinary wants for pig-iron, rolled iron, iron and steel rails, and crucible and open-hearth steel, for, if there were no other reasons, the naturally conservative character of their people would have prevented them from realizing the magnitude of those wants. If our iron and steel industries had not been developed in the past twenty years as they have been it is clear that our railroad system could not have been so wonderfully extended and strengthened, and without this extension of our railroads we could not have produced our large annual surplus of agricultural products for exportation, nor could our population have been so largely increased by immigration as it has been.

We cannot fully comprehend the marvellous nature of the changes which have taken place in the iron and steel industries of this country in recent years, unless we compare the early history of those industries with their present development.

In Alexander Hamilton's celebrated "Report on the Subject of Manufactures," presented to Congress on the 5th of December, 1791, just ninety years ago, it was stated with evident satisfaction that "the United States already in a great measure supply themselves with nails and spikes," so undeveloped and primitive was her iron industry at that time. In the preceding year, 1790, "Morse's Geography" claimed, in a description of New Jersey, that "in the whole State it is supposed there is yearly made about 1,200 tons of bar-iron, 1,200 ditto of pigs, and 80 of nail rods;" and in 1802 it was boastingly declared in a memorial to Congress that there were then 150 forges in New Jersey, "which at a moderate calculation would produce twenty tons of bar-iron each annually, amounting to 3,000 tons." In 1880 there were several rolling-mills in New Jersey and several hundred in the United States which could each produce much more bar-iron in a year than all of the 150 forges of New Jersey would produce in 1802.

Less than fifty years ago the American blast-furnace which would make four tons of pig-iron in a day, or twenty-eight tons in a week, was doing good work. We had virtually made no progress in our blast-furnace practice since colonial days. In 1831 it was publicly proclaimed with some exultation that "one furnace erected in Pennsylvania in 1830 will in 1831 make 1,100 tons of pig-iron." But, as George Asmus has well said, "a time came when men were no longer satisfied with these little smelting-pots, into which a gentle stream of air was blown through one nozzle, which received its scanty supply from a leather bag, squeezed by some tired water-wheel." After 1840 our blast-furnace practice gradually improved, but it was not until about 1865 that any furnace in the country could produce 150 tons of pig-iron in a week. Ten years later, in 1875, we had several furnaces which could each make 700 tons of pig-iron in a week; in 1880 we had several which could each make 1,000 tons in a week; and in 1881 we had one furnace which made 224 tons in a day, 1,357 tons in a week, and 5,598 tons in a month.

In 1810, seventy years ago, we produced only 917 tons of steel, none of which was crucible steel. In 1831, fifty years ago, we produced only about 2,000 tons of steel, not one pound of which was crucible steel of the best quality. So imperfect were our attainments as steelmakers in 1831, that we considered it a cause of congratulation that "American competition had excluded the

U. S. IRON AND STEEL INDUSTRIES. 347

British common blister steel altogether." In 1880 we had virtually ceased to make even the best blister steel, better steel having taken its place, and in that year we produced 1,247,335 gross tons of steel of all kinds, 64,664 tons of which was crucible steel. Our production of Bessemer steel and Bessemer steel rails in 1880 was larger than that of Great Britain.

It was not until 1844 that we commenced to roll any other kind of rails than strap rails for our railroads, and not even in that year were we prepared to roll a single ton of T rails. In 1880 we rolled 1,305,212 gross tons of rails, nearly two-thirds of which were steel rails, and nearly all of which were T rails.

The growth of the iron and steel industries of the United States during the present century is perhaps best exemplified in the statistics of the production of our blast-furnaces at various periods. In 1810 we produced 53,908 gross tons of pig-iron and cast-iron; in 1840 we produced 315,000 gross tons; in 1860 we produced 821,223 gross tons; and in 1880 we produced 3,835,191 gross tons. Our production in 1881 will be about 4,500,000 gross tons.

The position of the United States among iron and steel producing countries in 1880 is correctly indicated in the following table of the world's production of pig-iron and steel of all kinds, which we have compiled from the latest and most reliable statistics that are accessible. This table places the world's production of pig-iron in 1880 at 17,688,596 gross tons, and the world's production of steel in the same year at 4,343,719 gross tons. The percentage of pig-iron produced by the United States was nearly 22, and its percentage of steel was nearly 29.

348 SELECTIONS.

Countries.	Pig-iron.		Unwrought steel.			
	Year.	Tons of 2,240 pounds.	Tons of 2,240 pounds.			
			Bessemer.	Open-hearth.	Crucible and other kinds.	Total.
Great Britain	1880	*7,749,233	*1,044,382	*251,000	†120,000	1,415,382
United States	1880	*3,835,191	*1,074,262	*100,851	*72,222	1,247,335
Germany, including the Grand Duchy of Luxemburg	1879	*2,397,848	*686,500	†50,000	†40,000	776,500
France	1880	*1,705,249	†300,000	†47,327	*31,118	378,445
Belgium	1880	386,051	†125,000	†5,000	†5,000	135,000
Austria and Hungary	1880	*448,197	*99,741	*27,194	†5,000	131,935
Russia	1879	*429,885	†153,636	†50,000	*7,368	211,004
Sweden	1879	*36,992	†20,400	†5,718	†2,000	28,118
Other countries	1880	†200,000	....	†15,000	†5,000	20,000
Total	....	17,688,596	3,503,921	552,090	287,708	4,343,719

* Official.   † Estimated.

Although this country cannot produce iron and steel as cheaply as European countries which possess the advantages of cheap labor and proximity of raw materials, it is not excelled by any other country in the skill which it displays or the mechanical and scientific economies which it practises in any branch of their manufacture, while in certain leading branches it has displayed superior skill and shown superior aptitude for economical improvements. Our blast-furnace practice is the best in the world, and it is so chiefly because we use powerful blowing-engines and the best hot-blast stoves, possess good fuel, and carefully select our ores. The excellent quality of our pig-iron is universally conceded. Our Bessemer steel practice is also the best in the world. We produce much more Bessemer steel and roll more Bessemer steel rails in a given time by a given amount of machinery, technically termed a "plant," than any of our European rivals. No controversy concerning the relative wearing qualities of European and American steel rails now exists, and no controversy concerning the quality of American Bessemer steel ever has existed. We experience no difficulty in the manufacture of open-hearth steel in the Siemens-Martin furnace, and our steel which is thus produced is rapidly coming into general use side by side with crucible steel. In the manufacture of crucible steel our achievements are in the highest degree creditable. In only one respect can it be said that in its manufacture we fall behind any other country; we have not paid that attention to the manufacture of fine cutlery steel which Great Britain has done. This is, however, owing to commercial and not to mechanical reasons. American crucible steel is now used, without prejudice, in the manufacture of all kinds of tools, and in the manufacture of carriage-springs and many other articles for which the best kinds of steel are required. In the quantity of open-hearth and crucible steel, produced in a given time by a given plant, we are certainly abreast of all rivals. The largest crucible steel-works in the world are those of Park, Brother & Co., at Pittsburg, Penn. Our rolling-mill practice is fully equal to the best in Europe, except in the rolling of heavy armor plates, for which there has been but little demand, and in the production of which we have, consequently, had but little experience. The quality of our rolled iron, including bar-iron, plate-iron, sheet-iron, iron hoops, and iron rails, is uniformly superior to that of foreign rolled iron. In the production of heavy forgings and castings, as well as all lighter products of the foundry and machine-shop, this country has shown all the skill of the most advanced iron-working countries in Europe. In the production of steel castings we have exhibited creditable skill and enterprise, and we are in advance of all countries in the regular use of the Bessemer converter for this purpose.

All of our leading iron and steel works, and, indeed, very many small works, are now supplied with systematic chemical investigations by their own chemists, who are often men of eminence in their profession. The managers of our blast-furnaces, rolling-mills, and steel-works are themselves frequently well-educated chemists, metallurgists, geologists, or mechanical engineers, and, sometimes, all of these combined. Our rapid progress in increasing our production of iron and steel is not merely the result of good fortune or the possession of unlimited natural resources, but is largely due to the possession of accurate technical knowledge by our iron-masters, and by those who are in charge of their works, combined with the characteristic American dash which all the world has learned to respect and admire. The "rule of thumb" no longer governs the operations of the iron and steel works of this country.

A feature of our iron and steel industries which has attended their marvellous productiveness in late years is the aggregation of a number of large producing establishments in districts, or "centres," in lieu of the earlier practice of erecting small furnaces and forges wherever sufficient water-power, iron-ore, and charcoal could be obtained. This tendency to concentration is, it is true, not confined to our iron and steel industries, but it is to-day one of the most powerful elements that influence their development. It had its beginning with the commencement of our distinctive rolling-mill era, about 1830. In colonial days and long after the Revolution our iron-making and steel-making establishments belonged to the class of manufacturing enterprises described by Zachariah Allen, in his "Science of Mechanics," in 1829. "The manufacturing operations in the United States are all carried on in little hamlets, which often appear to spring up in the bosom of some forest, gathered around the waterfall that serves to turn the mill-wheel. These villages are scattered over a vast extent of country, from Indiana to the Atlantic, and from Maine to North Carolina, instead of being collected together, as they are in England, in great manufacturing districts." While these primitive and picturesque, but unproductive, methods could not forever continue, it is greatly to be regretted that our manufactures of iron and steel and other staple products could not have grown to their present useful and necessary proportions unattended by the evils which usually accompany the collection of large manufacturing populations in small areas.

Upon the future prospects of iron and steel industries it is unnecessary for us to dwell. Our resources for the increased production of iron and steel for an indefinite period are ample, and all other essential conditions of continued growth are within our grasp. We are, to-day, the second iron-making and steel-making country in the world. In a little while we shall surpass even Great Britain in the production of steel of all kinds, as we have already surpassed her in the production of Bessemer steel and in the consumption of all iron and steel products. The year 1882 will probably witness this consummation. We are destined, also, to pass Great Britain in the production of pig-iron. These conditions and results are certainly gratifying to our national pride, for, of themselves, they assure the ultimate preëminence of the United States among all civilized countries. If it is true, as recorded in the second chapter of Daniel, that "iron breaketh in pieces and subdueth all things," the country which produces and consumes the most iron and steel must hold the first rank. When the United States takes the position which it is destined soon to take, as the leading iron and steel producing as well as consuming country, the saying of Bishop Berkeley, that "Westward the course of empire takes its way," will receive a new interpretation, for the iron industry, which had its beginning in Asia, and then passed successively to the countries along the Mediterranean, upon the Rhine, and in the north of Europe, will then have made the circuit of the world.

XV.

LES DETTES PUBLIQUES.

FROM NEYMARCK'S LES DETTES PUBLIQUES EUROPÉENNES, PP. 86-102.

I.—AUGMENTATION DES DETTES PUBLIQUES DEPUIS 1870.

DANS cette longue énumération de chiffres, ce qui frappe tout d'abord l'esprit, c'est, l'augmentation considérable de la dette publique des États Européens depuis 1870. Cette dette s'élevait à 75 milliards en 1870 environ ; elle atteint 115 milliards en 1886. L'augmentation n'est pas moindre de 40 milliards.[1]

Nous avons pris à dessein cette date de 1870 qui nous rappelle les plus grands malheurs que notre pays ait jamais supportés, les lourdes charges qui ont été la conséquence de la guerre, le fardeau qui pèse sur nous tous. La guerre de 1870 a coûté à la France plus de 10 milliards : sans elle nous ne serions pas grevés d'impôts écrasants et aucun peuple ne supporterait plus facilement que nous le poids de sa dette publique.

Aucun pays n'a, en effet, subi des désastres aussi grands que les nôtres ; aucun n'a eu une indemnité de 5 milliards à payer à l'étranger ; aucun n'a dû reconstituer sa puissance militaire, son matériel de guerre ; aucun n'a eu à refaire, pour ainsi dire, la patrie elle-même tout entière. Et cependant que voyons-nous ?

---

[1] D'après le journal de la *Société de statistique* (avril 1867), la dette publique d'Europe s'élevait, en 1865-1866, aux chiffres suivants : —

Dépenses totales des budgets	10 milliards	508 millions.
Capitalisation des dettes	66 "	013 "
Intérêt et amortissement	2 "	438 "

La population de l'Europe était évalué à 291,738,379 habitants ; la dette par habitant représentait 226 fr. 30.

M. Paul Boiteau, dans son article sur le budget général de l'État, inséré dans le Dictionnaire des finances de M. Léon Say, a réuni sous le titre de : " Budgets Européens " la plupart des budgets du continent, et pour en faciliter l'étude, il a placé en regard du montant des dépenses prévues pour l'exercice 1885, le montant des dettes consolidées et autres qui grèvent l'actif des différents États ainsi que le montant des dépenses militaires et celles du service de la Dette et de l'amortissement. Il obtient les chiffres suivants : —

Prévisions totales des dépenses budgétaires annuelles . .	18 milliards	843 millions.
Capitalisation des dettes consolidées, des dettes amortissables annuités diverses, etc.	108 "	431 "
Dépenses du service des dettes et de l'amortissement : .	4 "	864 "
Dépenses militaires, guerre et marine	4 "	439 "

On pourra comparer ces chiffres à ceux que nous donnons plus loin.

A l'exception de l'Angleterre qui, par suite de divers remboursements d'annuités, a pu diminuer sa dette de 1.350 millions ; à l'exception du Danemark qui, par suite de conversions heureusement effectuées, a pu réduire sa dette de 20 millions, tous les pays se sont endettés depuis 1870 dans des proportions énormes. Voici sur ce point quelques chiffres précis. Nous rangeons les États par ordre d'accroissement de leurs dettes depuis 1870.

AUGMENTATION DU CAPITAL NOMINAL DE PLUSIEURS DETTES PUBLIQUES DEPUIS 1870.

France	12 milliards.	
Russie [1]	11 "	
Prusse	3 "	217 millions.
Italie	3 "	132 "
Hongrie	2 "	249 "
Autriche	1 "	770 "
Espagne	1 "	300 "
Belgique	1 "	89 "
Roumanie		701 "
Allemagne		526 "
Saxe		388 "
Grèce		270 "
Serbie		244 "
Wurtemberg		194 "
Suède		181 "
Hambourg		24 "
Finlande		20 "

Cette augmentation du capital nominal des dettes publiques européennes qui atteint, depuis 1870, 40 milliards environ, a eu pour conséquence l'augmentation des intérêts et des amortissements annuels pour les emprunts contractés, l'accroissement des dépenses totales des budgets, une surcharge dans les impôts. Combien ne serions-nous pas allégés si nous n'avions pas à payer chaque année les lourds impôts qui grèvent notre commerce et notre industrie, et qui, s'ajoutant aux frais de production, ont rendu la concurrence à nos produits d'autant plus facile ? Toutes proportions gardées, les pays d'Europe souffrent, comme nous, de ces lourdes charges qui, dans tous les pays, obèrent les contribuables. C'est la guerre, toujours la guerre, qui redoit aux budgets. Depuis seize ans, les budgets de la guerre et de la marine ont coûté à la France plus de 11 milliards, c'est-à-dire plus de 700 millions par an ; l'Allemagne et la Russie n'ont pas

---

[1] Augmentation depuis 1866.

dépensé moins de 10 milliards chacun pendant la même période, l'Autriche et l'Italie presque le même chiffre. Voilà donc cinq grands pays qui, en vue d'une guerre probable, dépensent tous les ans, de 500 à 900 millions, depuis seize ans. Que coûterait donc la guerre elle-même ?

Les États européens paient annuellement pour leurs dépenses de la guerre et de la marine à peu près les mêmes sommes que pour l'intérêt et l'amortissement de leurs dettes. D'après les derniers budgets, ainsi que le prouvent les chiffres que nous publions plus loin, la guerre et la marine coûtent à l'Europe 4 milliards 528 millions, alors que l'intérêt et l'amortissement des dettes publiques réclament 5 milliards 343 millions. En voici le relevé :

II.— DÉPENSES DE LA GUERRE, DE LA MARINE, CAPITAL NOMINAL ET INTÉRÊTS DES DETTES.

Etats.	Exercices financiers.	Capital nominal de la dette. Milliards-Millions.	Intérêts et amort. ann. Millions.	Dépenses ann. Guerre et marine. Millions.
Prusse	1er avril 1886.	4.814	220	539.1
Allemagne	31 déc. 1886.	526	20.1	
Autriche	31 déc. 1884.	9.288	389.9	342
Hongrie	" " "	3.178	205.8	
Wurtemberg	31 déc. 1885.	525	21.5	
Saxe	" " "	800	33.2	
Hambourg	31 déc. 1883.	178	8.7	
Bavière	1er avril 1886.	1.790	61.1	
Bade	31 déc. 1885.	53	2.1	
États allemands	" " "	268	11	
Italie	" " "	11.131	532	342.5
Suède	" " "	345	16.4	35.5
Norwège	30 juin 1885.	151	6	18.3
Danemarck	31 déc. 1885.	274	12.4	23
Pays-Bas	" " "	2.260	69.5	69.5
Belgique	" " "	1.771	86.5	45.6
Espagne	1er juillet 1886.	6.042	274.1	200.3
Portugal	" " "	2.821	89.3	39.3
Angleterre[1]	31 mars 1885.	17.829	737.5	740.2
Suisse	1er janvier 1886.	32	1.8	17.1
Serbie	13 juin 1886.	244	13.7	16.2
Roumanie	1er avril 1887.	729	59.2	28.5
Grèce	1er janvier 1886.	343	33	23
Turquie	1880–1881.	2.622	55.4	200
Bulgarie	1er janvier 1885.	....	2.1	
Finlande	31 déc. 1885.	65	5.9	6.1
Russie	" " "	18.028	1.038	982.1
France	31 déc. 1886.	31.000	1.336	859.5
Totaux		117.112	5.343.2	4.528.1

[1] D'après une note de l'honorable M. Hangcosck, de la Société de statistique de Londres, de fin mars 1884 à fin mars 1885, l'Angleterre paie comme intérêt 22.000.000 £ et 7.000.000 £ comme amortissement, soit au total 29.500.000 £.

Dans quelles proportions énormes les dettes publiques de toute l'Europe ne pourraient-elles pas être réduites si les dépenses de la guerre n'absorbaient pas tous les ans plus de 85 % de ces mêmes dettes? Toutes les puissances européennes ont des embarras financiers ; toutes ou presque toutes augmentent ou ont besoin d'augmenter leurs impôts. Toutes, sans exception, font des armements considérables. Cette situation présente les plus graves dangers et plus que jamais cependant, le maintien de la paix est nécessaire à l'Europe pour consolider son crédit, améliorer l'etat de ses finances, donner de l'essor et de la confiance au commerce et à l'industrie.

III. — LES CONVERSIONS DE RENTES À L'ÉTRANGER ET EN FRANCE.

Et cependant, malgré les charges de toute nature qui pèsent sur les États, les rentes de ces mêmes pays se sont négociées pendant l'année 1886 presque toutes aux plus hauts cours qu'elles aient cotés depuis 1870. Non seulement, grâce à l'abondance des capitaux et à l'abaissement du taux de l'intérêt, les fonds publics ont haussé, mais il a été réalisé, en matière de finances, des progrès considèrables.

Les États, non plus que les villes et les sociétés industrielles ou financières, n'hésitent pas à effectuer, sur une très large échelle, des opérations qu'on eût à peine osé concevoir il y a moins de trente ans.

Aujourd'hui des États, dont la puissance financière a toujours été relativement restreinte, peuvent contracter des emprunts qui dépassent de beaucoup ceux que naguère encore des nations riches n'eussent tentés qu'avec appréhension.

Toutes les combinaisons auxquelles peuvent prêter les finances d'État qui étaient si longtemps restées dans le domaine de la théorie, sont pleinement entrées dans la pratique et se réalisent couramment. Bien des préjugés économiques et financiers se sont dissipés ; bien des principes, encore contestés naguère, ont triomphé et se sont imposés.

Le crédit a acquis une force d'expansion inouïe ; les fonds publics, les valeurs mobilières se sont de plus en plus répandues, vulgarisées, démocratisées en quelque sorte. Leur grande facilité de circulation, leur mobilité, leur diffusion, leur accessibilité à toutes les fortunes, petites ou grandes, leur ont assuré une faveur, que l'on peut trouver excessive, mais qui est, à divers points de vue, très justifiée. Cet essor de la fortune mobilière a déterminé une véritable révolution dans les conditions financières de l'existence des peuples.

Emprunts, unifications de dettes, conversions, sont des opérations devenues familières même aux moindres États. Et, chose assez étrange, c'est la France qui, après avoir été, avec l'Angleterre, l'initiatrice des grandes réformes financières, a été depuis quelques années, parmi les nations, la plus timide à réaliser les combinaisons heureuses, légitimes, profitables, que la puissance et la solidité de son crédit lui rendent si faciles.

Rien, en effet, de plus curieux à observer, autour de nous, que les nombreuses opérations de conversion déjà accomplies avec succès ou en voie de préparation. Si on peut reprocher à certains États une propension trop grande à emprunter, il faut bien reconnaître qu'ils se préoccupent aussi, pour la plupart, de n'emprunter qu'au plus bas prix possible. Dès que leur crédit s'étend et s'améliore, ils s'efforcent de remplacer les anciennes dettes coûteuses, onéreuses, par des dettes plus légères, contractées à un taux moins élevé. Ce sont maintenant des puissances financières de second et de troisième ordre qui nos donnent l'exemple. Dans cet ordre d'idées et de faits, il n'est certainement pas inutile d'examiner comment se sont effectuées les conversions récentes et d'indiquer les divers procédés, jusqu'ici employés.

Depuis 1870, deux fonds d'États français ont été l'objet d'une conversion: l'emprunt Morgan et la rente 5%. On se rappelle comment elles s'effectuèrent: on offrit aux porteurs d'obligations Morgan 6%, le même revenu en rente 3%, moyennant une soulte de 124 fr. par obligation. Les porteurs de rentes 5% eurent à opter entre le remboursement à 100 fr. de leurs rentes et l'échange contre un nouveau titre de rente $4\frac{1}{2}$% non-convertible avant un délai de 10 ans qui expire en 1893.

La Belgique a opéré trois conversions: son $4\frac{1}{2}$ est devenu du 4%, puis du 3%. Pour la première opération, elle eut immédiatement recours à un syndicat de banquiers, qui se chargeait du placement de la rente nouvelle, tandis que l'État opérait le retrait de la rente convertie. Pour la seconde conversion, le gouvernement belge voulet opérer seul et émettre directement sa rente nouvelle; il n'obtint pas tout le succès désiré et dut, après des essais peu favorables, accepter le concours qui lui avait été donné précédemment.

Tout récemment, ainsi qu'on l'a vu dans le cours de cette étude, la Belgique a réalisé une trosième conversion en convertissant ses rentes 4% contre du 3½%. Cette opération, effectuée directement par le Trésor, obtint un plein succès.

La Suède a, elle aussi, transformé successivement son 4½ en 4 % et en 3½ % en recourant à l'intermédiaire des grandes maisons de banque. Celles-ci émettaient sur les marchés étrangers la nouvelle rente suédoise, tandis que l'État restait chargé du retrait des anciens titres.

On conçoit que l'intervention des syndicats et des groupes financiers soit, pour ainsi dire, l'unique moyen des petits États qui n'ont pas de marché national. Il est certain que la Roumanie, par exemple, n'a pu effectuer la conversion de sa dette 6 % que grâce au concours de puissantes maisons auxquelles elle s'est adressée. Ce sont ces dernières qui plaçaient la nouvelle rente tandis que l'État remboursait l'ancienne.

L'Espagne, lors de la récente conversion de ses emprunts de l'île de Cuba, s'est adressée à un groupe de banquiers : elle s'entendait avec eux pour le prix de la nouvelle rente à créer, et avec le produit du nouvel emprunt, remboursait des dettes anciennes contractées à plus gros intérêt.

Les grands États qui ont, presque tous, d'importants marchés financiers ne se croient cependant pas toujours assez sûrs de leurs propres forces pour dédaigner le concours des banques et des institutions de crédit. Sans ces hautes influences, aucune opération de crédit importante ne pourrait, sans doute, acquérir un caractère international et obtenir la participation des marchés extérieurs. Aussi toutes les conversions opérées dans de larges proportions ne l'ont-elles été qu'avec la participation des syndicats.

La Hongrie a effectué la conversion de sa rente 6 % en rente 4% en or et elle prépare, en ce moment même, une opération du même genre sur d'autres dettes. Ici, les banquiers, groupés en vue de cette transformation, se sont chargés à la fois et du placement de la rente nouvelle et du retrait de la rente ancienne. Le remboursement au pair n'est devenu obligatoire pour les porteurs de 6 % hongrois qu'à l'issue de l'opération qui s'est effectuée par fractions échelonnées. La loi, qui a fixé les conditions dans lesquelles cette conversion fût autorisée, était conçue presque dans les mêmes termes que le projet que nous formulions nous-même dès le mois d'août 1876[1] en vue de la conversion éventuelle du 5 % français.

---

[1] Voir notre étude : *La Conversion de la Rente 5%*. Paris, Dentu, édit., 1876.

En Allemagne, les conversions de fonds prussiens, bavarois et wurtembergeois se sont opérées par l'émission d'emprunts dont le produit a servi au remboursement des anciennes rentes.

A l'étranger, il nous reste à citer, au-dessus de tous, l'exemple des États-Unis qui ont accompli avec une habileté et un esprit de suite merveilleux des conversions successives dans les conditions les plus heureuses et les plus favorables, sans que les particuliers aient jamais eu à souffrir des conséquences de ces transformations répétées. Grâce à la prévoyance avec laquelle l'Amérique du Nord avait créé ses rentes par séries, des conversions partielles ont pu se succéder rapidement; et l'on a vu en peu d'années du 6 % se transformer en 5 %, puis en 4 %, puis en 3 %. Ces opérations nombreuses, les États-Unis les ont effectuées directement sur leurs propres marchés et à l'extérieur avec le concours de grandes maisons de banque.

Mais, en dehors des exemples que nous ont donnés les autres nations, nous pourrions rappeler ceux que, sous des formes diverses, nous ont offerts nos départements français et nos propres villes. Là, encore, nous trouvons des efforts très louables et des combinaisons très variées. Nous avons vu des villes recourir au remboursement au pair d'anciennes dettes et à des emprunts plus avantageux pour alléger leurs charges, les unes s'adressant au public, les autres s'assurant l'appui de syndicats, d'autres enfin traitant, sans autre intermédiaire, avec le Crédit Foncier de France qui leur garantissait à un taux maximum les capitaux dont elle avaient besoin pour rembourser la dette antérieure contractée à un taux plus élevé.

Nous avons vu enfin, plus près de nous encore, le Crédit Foncier de France profiter, pour son propre compte, et au grand profit de sa vaste clientèle d'emprunteurs, de l'abaissement du prix de l'argent, et convertir des obligations entraînant une annuité élevée par des titres n'exigeant qu'une annuité notablement inférieure. On sait avec quelle simplicité s'est effectuée cette opération : les porteurs des obligations à convertir avaient un droit de préférence dans la souscription des obligations nouvelles; ils restaient libres de n'en pas user, mais étaient dûment avertis du remboursement prochain et obligatoire des titres anciens.

Ainsi les nations qui nous entourent et, chez nous-mêmes, les provinces, les villes, les institutions de crédit, ont pratiqué avec empressement et avec succès, sous les formes les plus diverses, des conversions qui, toutes, ont été profitables. En ce moment même, de grandes opérations de ce genre sont à prévoir. Il n'est pas douteux, en effet, que l'Angleterre ne se prépare à une nouvelle conversion de ses Consolidés dont les cours sont au-dessus du pair ; dès que l'occasion sera propice, la transformation sera faite. En Italie, la conversion de la rente 5% est à l'ordre du jour, et il ne s'écoulera pas beaucoup de temps avant qu'elle ne soit réalisée. Déjà le gouvernement a préparé un projet pour convertir plusieurs dettes rachetables et offre du 4½ à la place du 5%.

Il est à remarquer que toutes ces conversions de rentes, qui ont diminué l'intérêt payé par les États à leurs prêteurs, n'ont nullement diminué les charges de ces divers pays. Pour être juste, équitable, toute conversion de rentes doit avoir pour conséquence une diminution d'impôts. Il n'en a rien été. Prenez tous les budgets des pays qui ont effectué des conversions ; comparez les chiffres des dépenses publiques et des impôts à ceux qui étaient inscrits avant et après les conversions, vous trouverez partout des augmentations de dépenses et d'impôts.

Il faut remarquer, d'autre part, que presque toutes ces conversions n'ont pu être réalisées avec succès qu'autant que la haute banque est intervenue et leur a donné son concours. Il convient enfin de dire que toutes ces opérations ont été facilitées par l'abondance toujours croissante des capitaux disponibles, et par la baisse du taux de l'intérêt, conséquence de cette abondance des capitaux.

IV.— *ABAISSEMENT DU TAUX DE L'INTÉRÊT DE L'ARGENT DEPUIS* 1870.

Depuis 1870, et surtout depuis le jour où, pour la première fois depuis la guerre, la rente 5% fut coté au pair, c'est-à-dire à 100, le 4 septembre 1874, des changements profonds se sont produits sur les marchés français et étrangers dans le taux de capitalisation. Successivement, d'année en année, lentement d'abord, puis par étapes vigoureusement franchies, les valeurs de premier ordre, de première sûreté, descendirent de 5% d'intérêt à 4½% ; les valeurs de second ordre, qui rapportaient 6½, 7 et 8%, descendirent à 5% et même au-dessous. A mesure que le capital de ces valeurs augmentait, leur revenu devenait naturellement moins élevé.

Au lendemain de la guerre, un capital de 100,000 placé en rentes 5% aurait produit 5.500 à 6.000 fr. de rentes. Le même capital, placé aujourd'hui en rentes françaises 3% produirait à peine 3.700 francs.

Depuis 1870, le 6% Américain a disparu ; converti d'abord en

5%, puis en 4%, le voilà maintenant en 3% en attendant une nouvelle conversion en 2½.

Le 4½ Belge, les fonds Allemands, tels que les 5% Badois, Bavarois, Wurtembergeois, etc., ont, sur la cote, cédé la place à des titres de moindre rapport, à des rentes de 3½ et de 3%, qui atteignent le pair.

Dans l'Europe entière, les rentes 4% qui ont été créées en remplacement de rentes 5% sont au pair et même au-dessus, ou ont été échangées contre du $\frac{3}{12}$ ou du 3%.

Des fonds étrangers, exotiques, comme l'on dit en Bourse, arrivent maintenant au taux moyen auquel se négociaient anciennement de bons crédits européens de second ordre. Les cotes anglaises nous donnent à cet égard, de curieux exemples.

Il y a dix ans seulement, voici, notamment, le 7% Japonais qui valait 100 fr. fin 1876 et qui maintenant vaut 113 ; à pareille date, le 6% Argentin 1868, coté aujourd'hui 101 à 102, valait 60 ; le 5% Brésilien valait fin 1876, 87 à 88 ; il est maintenant à 103, trois points au-dessus du pair.

Le 5% Italien qui ne donne net que 4,34, valait, fin 1876, 72 fr. : il était dans ces derniers temps à 102 fr. et même au-dessus, c'est-à-dire 20 fr. plus cher que le prix auquel nous émettions en 1871 notre rente française 5%.

Le 5% Roumain, qui valait 40 fr. fin 1876, et qui rapportait conséquemment 8%, se négocie au-dessus de 90. On évalue donc aujourd'hui le crédit de la Roumanie à un taux bien supérieur à celui auquel notre propre crédit était estimé en 1871 et 1872, puisque, dans ces deux années, la France émettait ses rentes 5% à 82,50 et 84 fr. 50.

La rente Autrichienne 4% or, cotée 89 à 90 fr. et qui, il y a peu de temps, s'est négociée même à 96 et 97 fr., est encore plus haut que nos rentes françaises en 1871. La rente Hongroise 4% or, a valu jusqu'à 88 dans ces derniers mois, alors que nous avons émis du 5% français 5 et 6 francs plus bas.

Voici, pour les principaux fonds d'États, la différence des cours cotés au 31 décembre 1869 et au 31 décembre 1886.

	31 déc. 1869	31 déc. 1886	
3% Français	70,05	82,20	
4,34 Italien	57,30	101,85	
6% Américain	84	134	(le 4%).
4½ Belge	102½	95,40	(le 3%).
5% Russe 1862	85	96	
3% Consolidés anglais	92⅝	101½	

V.—*MODES D'ÉMISSION ET TYPES DE RENTES EMPLOYÉS PAR LES GOUVERNEMENTS EMPRUNTEURS.*

Nous venons de montrer comment les conversions de rentes effectuées par les principaux États avaient été réalisées et comment la baisse du taux de l'intérêt et l'abondance des capitaux avaient facilité ces opérations. Il n'est pas sans utilité de faire remarquer aussi comment les divers pays effectuent leurs emprunts. On voit, d'après cette étude comparative des dettes européennes, combien est variée la diversité des types de rentes émises. L'Angleterre a du 3%, du 2½%, des anuites terminables ; l'Autriche, du 4,20% métallique, du 4% or, du 5% papier, du 5% argent, des lots à primes sans intérêts. La Belgique a eu du 4½, du 4%, du 3%. La Russie a émis des emprunts sous forme de rentes 6%, 5%, 4% ; la Hollande a des rentes 3½, 3%, 2½% ; l'Italie a du 5%, du 3% et vient de décréter du 4½% ; la Norwège a du 4½, du 4%, du 3½ ; le Portugal a du 5% et du 3% ; la Prusse a du 4% et du 3½%, la Roumanie a 7%, du 6%, du 5% ; la Saxe, du 3½ et du 3% ; la Suède, du 4½%, du 4%, du 3½% ; le Wurtemberg, du 4½, du 4%, du 3½%, etc. Parmi les fonds coloniaux, nous trouvons du 5% de la Nouvelle Zélande, du 5% Québec, du 6% Queensland, 4½, 4% et 3½% des Indes, du 4% du Canada, de la Jamaïque, de Tasmanie du 5%, 4½%, 4% Victoria. Quel enseignement tirer de ces faits ? C'est qu'on ne peut dire d'une façon absolue, c'est qu'il n'est pas scientifiquement ni pratiquement prouvé qu'il soit préférable pour un État de n'emprunter que sous un même type de rentes, et que la diversité de ces types de rentes peut nuire à leur plus-value. La vérité est qu'il en est des États comme des particuliers : le meilleur mode d'emprunt est celui qui coûte le moins cher et procure la plus grande somme des capitaux. Il peut être utile d'emprunter sous forme d'obligations ou sous forme de rentes ; en 4% ou en 3% ; en 5% ou en 4½%. C'est une question d'opportunité et d'appréciation. Tous les gouvernements ont choisi la forme d'emprunt la plus avantageuse aux intérêts de tous, sans s'astreindre à n'émettre qu'un type de rentes déterminé à l'avance.

Il en est de même pour le mode d'émission des emprunts. C'est la France qui, lors de la guerre de Crimée, généralisa le système des souscriptions publiques. Avant 1852, les emprunts d'Etat étaient soumissionnés par de grandes maisons de banque qui plaçaient ensuite les titres de rentes dans leur clientèle : plus tard, les gouvernements firent appel directement aux capitaux du public sans se servir de l'intermédiaire des banquiers. Cependant, des modifications sérieuses se sont produites dans le système des souscriptions. Nous voyons l'Angleterre pour ses emprunts coloniaux, pour ses emprunts de villes, effectuer des appels au crédit sous forme d'adjudication publique. Elle offre 4% d'intérêt, par exemple ; elle s'engage à servir d'abord les demandes de ceux qui se contentent d'un intérêt moindre. Ce système favorise les souscripteurs les moins exigeants, ne décourage pas le public par des mécomptes immérités à la répartition et permet à l'emprunteur d'obtenir les conditions les plus favorables ; ce genre de souscription rend les emprunts moins onéreux pour les emprunteurs. Les autres modes d'emprunts employés par les gouvernements sont des ventes fermes ou à option à des banquiers et à des établissements de crédit. Plusieurs États se sont bornés à charger des maisons de banque d'émettre les emprunts qu'ils désiraient effectuer, moyennant une commission. A l'exception de l'Angleterre et de la France, presque tous les gouvernements européens traitent encore avec des syndicats de banquiers pour leurs émissions.

VI. — DE LA RÉPARTITION DES FONDS PULICS ÉTRANGERS DANS LES PORTEFEUILLES FRANÇAIS.

Dans le cours de cette étude, nous avons essayé de connaître le montant approximatif des valeurs étrangères appartenant à nos nationaux. Les chiffres que que nous avons cités nous ont été donnés par les ministres des finances et les directeurs de statistique des gouvernements étrangers ; mais ils auraient besoin d'être complétés, et aucune autorité ne pourrait mieux que notre conseil supérieur de statistique obtenir et grouper des indications plus nombreuses sur ce sujet important.

A de rares exceptions près, et sauf des circonstances particulières telles que la hausse ou la baisse du prix du change sur des valeurs internationales, les capitalistes français qui possèdent des valeurs étrangères ne font pas recevoir le montant de leurs coupons d'intérêt à l'étranger : ils s'adressent à des banquiers et des établissements de crédit français, pour encaisser leurs coupons échus.

Nous sommes convaincus que MM. de Rothschild, la Banque de Paris, la Société Générale, le Comptoir d'Escompte, le Crédit

Lyonnais, le Crédit industriel et tous les banquiers — qui paient une patente spéciale comme effectuant des paiements de coupons étrangers, — répondraient sans difficultés à un questionnaire que le Conseil supérieur de statistique leur adresserait.

Ce n'est pas par simple curiosité que des documents semblables auraient besoin d'être mis au jour. Les questions financières et fiscales doivent, plus que jamais, prendre le pas sur les questions politiques. Or, ce que nos législateurs et la plupart de nos hommes politiques connaissent le moins, c'est l'exacte situation de la fortune publique de la France, le montant et la puissance de son épargne, la nature et le chiffre de ses placements soit sur des valeurs françaises, soit sur des valeurs étrangères. C'est à ce défaut de connaissances qu'il faut attribuer, pour beaucoup, les erreurs fiscales économiques et financières qui ont été commises dans l'etablissement, l'augmentation et la suppression de tel ou tel impôt de préférence à tel ou tel autre. A une époque où il est question d'impôt sur les rentes, d'impôt sur les valeurs étrangères appartenant à des Français, d'impôt sur le revenu, etc., ces renseignements sont indispensables si l'on veut éviter de dangereuses erreurs. Le Conseil supérieur ne doit pas hésiter, à notre avis, à faire la lumière sur ces questions spéciales: c'est du côté des statistiques financières, nous ne saurions trop insister sur ce point, que doivent proter les efforts et les travaux des hommes éminents qui font partie de la Commission.

VII.— DE LA COTE ET DE LA NÉGOCIATION DES RENTES FRANÇAISES AUX BOURSES ÉTRANGÈRES.

Nous devons aussi signaler une réforme que nous avons bien souvent réclamée et qui paraîtra sans doute utile à obtenir quand on se sera rendu compte de l'importance des emprunts étrangers contractés en France. A l'exception des fonds allemands, tous les fonds d'État étrangers, toutes les principales valeurs étrangères sont cotés à notre bourse; tous les gouvernements étrangers ont fait appel aux capitaux français. Or, aucune de nos rentes françaises n'est cotée ni à Vienne, ni à Saint-Pétersbourg, ni à Stockolm, ni à Christiania, ni à Rome, ni á Florence, ni à Madrid, ni à Lisbonne, ni à Athènes. Notre 3% est coté à Londres, Bruxelles et Amsterdam. Et c'est tout. Cette situation mérite qu'on y porte attention.

L'affluence des fonds d'État étrangers sua le marché français, la facilité avec laquelle ils s'y placent et s'y negocient, sont des faits financiers qui révèlent une tendance des capitaux contre laquelle il serait peut-être à las fois très difficile de tenter une réaction soudaine et violente.

Il est certainement regrettable que nos nationaux deviennent les créanciers d'États dont la solvabilité et le crédit sont douteux. Il est non moins fâcheux qu'aux capitaux lentement formés par les hommes d'épargne de notre pays se substituent des titres étrangers dépourvus de garantie sérieuse.

Mais, d'autre part, il ne saurait être mauvais et il est même nécessaire et utile, au point de vue financier et économique, que les nations honnêtes et notoirement solvables soient debitrices de la nôtre. Il ne saurait être mauvais qu'à un moment donne il y ait entre les mains des capitalistes français une certaine quantité de bon papier étranger, bien et dûment garanti, et facilement réalisable.

On conçoit cependant qu'il y a un certain équilibre financier international que ne saurait être rompu san inconvénient. On conçoit le peril qu'il y aurait pour la France à ne compter au dehors que des débiteurs et point de créanciers, à toujours absorber le papier et ne jamais en céder, à se saturer de valeurs étrangères tandis qu'elle ne placerait point dans les autres pays une quantité à peu près équivalente de valeurs françaises. On peut enfin mesurer le danger que notre pays pourrait courir le jour où les nations qui nous entourent gagneraient plus à notre ruine qu'à notre prospérité. Même au point de vu politique, ces considérations ne sont pas sans consistance.

Politiquement, aussi bien que financièrement, il est donc sage et désirable d'intéresser l'Europe à nos progrès, à notre dèveloppement national, à notre avenir économique.

Un des moyens les plus efficaces d'atteindre ce but est de placer parmi les capitalistes étrangers la plus grande quantité possible de rentes et de valeurs françaises.

Mais, dira-t-on, cette expansion des titres français s'opérera naturellement, grâce à la confiance si grande que le crédit de la France inspire aux autres peuples. Si bien qu'il n'y aurait qu'à laisser faire au temps, aux capitaux étrangers et à la sagesse des nations pour assurer un résultat si souhaitable pour notre avenir.

Ce raisonnement est d'une logique excellente et peut paraître très solidement fondé en theorie. Il est absolument vain, s'il n'est pas justifié par la pratique. Or, il ne l'est malheureusement pas.

Ce n'est pas tout de dire aux autres nations : " Moi, France, j'émets de la rente, offrant toutes garanties, pleine sécurité. Prenez-la ; il n'y a rien de meilleur. Vous connaissez ma richesse, ma puissance de production, mon amour du travail, ma probité reconnue. Vous savez que j'ai toujours payé et bien payé ; vous savez combien, même dans les circonstances les plus critiques, j'ai été ponctuelle à remplir mes engagements. Prenez de ma rente ! Quels meilleurs titres avez-vous chez vous ? Quels meilleurs placements ? Quel emploi plus productif et plus sûr."

Un tel discours n'aurait rien que de juste et d'exact. Tout le monde est pénétré de ces vérités et nous n'aurions à prêcher que des convertis.

Mais, pour que l'étranger prenne beaucoup de nos fonds d'État, encore faut-il qu'il sache où aller les prendre, où aller les acheter, et même où aller les vendre, le besoin échéant. Il faut les rendre accessibles à tous les capitalistes de l'Europe, et négociables facilement partout.

Or, c'est ce dont on ne nous paraît pas s'être suffisamment occupé.

Comme nous l'avons dit plus haut, nos rentes françaises ne sont pas cotées aux bourses étrangères. Dans ces dernières années, de grands emprunts ont été effectués chez nous notamment en rente 3% amortissable. On peut dire qu'à l'heure où nous sommes, cette rente est presque inconnue sur les grandes places financières de l'Europe. Il y a là une faute commise, une grave négligence qu'il faut se hâter de réparer. On doit faire pour nos rentes ce que les autres nations font pour leurs fonds d'État qu'elles prennent tant de soin de nous faire connaître et auxquels elles ouvrent accès sur tous les grands marchès européens.

VIII.— GUERRE, RUINE OU RÉVOLUTION INDUSTRIELLE ET ÉCO-
NOMIQUE.

Mais ce qui, à notre avis, ressort jusqu'à l'évidence du travail auquel nous nous sommes livrés, c'est que l'Europe entière, avec le poids de ses dépenses militaires, avec la surcharge des dettes publiques et d'impôts qui l'écrasent, marche, si elle persévère dans cette voie, à la guerre, à la ruine, à une véritable révolution industrielle et économique. Quel que soit le pessimisme d'une telle conclusion, nous ne pouvons taire nos impressions. La paix de l'Europe n'est, à vrai dire, qu'un état de guerre latent, et cette situation qui semble la condition ordinaire du vieux continent pèse de deux manières sur le monde civilisé : elle lui enlève, d'une part, une bonne partie des capitaux constitués par l'épargne annuelle, par le travail de tous, pour entretenir des soldats, acheter des fusils, des canons, des munitions, construire des forteresses, des navires ; d'autre part, elle l'empêche de se servir de ces capitaux énormes pour développer le commerce, l'industrie, le matériel de la production, diminuer les frais généraux de la nation. L'appréhension et les préparatifs de guerre deviennent aussi nuisibles et aussi coûteux que la guerre elle-même. Les finances de l'Europe sont tellement obérées qu'on peut craindre qu'elles ne conduisent fatalement les gouvernements à se demander si la guerre, avec ses éventualités terribles, ne doit pas être préférée au maintien d'une paix précaire et coûteuse. Si ce n'est point à la guerre que doivent aboutir les préparatifs militaires et les armements de l'Europe, ce pourrait bien être, ainsi que le disait, il y a vingt ans, lord Stanley, à " la banqueroute des États." Si ce n'est ni à la guerre ni à la ruine que doivent conduire de semblables folies, c'est assurément à une révolution induitrielle et économique.

La vieille Europe lutte contre la concurrence de pays jeunes, riches produisant à meilleur compte. Il est, au-delà de l'Océan, une République puissante, l'Amérique, qui a su éteindre une dette que les nécessités d'une grande cause lui avaient fait contracter ; elle offre au monde entier le spectacle d'une prospérité sans exemple. Tout récemment, le message du président Cleveland à l'ouverture du Congrès a traduit le sentiment d'un véritable embarras de richesses. En Asie, tous les peuples commencent à profiter des découvertes et des progrès que l'Europe a accomplis, et comme dans ces pays le prix de la main-d'œuvre et les charges publiques sont presque nuls, l'Europe entière éprouvera chaque année, de plus en plus, les affets de l'apparition sur la scène commerciale et industrielle, de tous ces peuples qui n'ont pas à payer, tous les ans, ni quatre milliards et demi pour les dépenses de la guerre, ni plus de cinq milliards pour les intérêts de leurs dettes publiques.

Le maréchal de Moltke disait récemment au Reichstag " qu'à la longue les peuples ne pourront plus supporter les charges militaires." Il aurait pu ajouter que le jour où les peuples se rendront compte de tout ce que leur coûte la guerre, même lorsqu'elle demeure à l'état de simple risque, lorsqu'ils considéreront la masse croissante d'intérêts que le progrès jette chaque jour du côté de la paix, les gouvernés sauront ce jour-là dicter leurs volontés à leurs gouvernants. Les 41 milliards d'augmentation des dettes publiques de l'Europe, depuis 1870, mis en regard des milliards de diminution de la dette de l'Amérique offrent un puissant enseignement. Non, les peuples ne pourront plus à la longue supporter de tels fardeaux ; non, ils ne pourront plus continuer à travailler, à peiner, à souffrir, à élever péniblement leurs familles pour que leurs biens, leurs ressources, leurs épargnes, les êtres qui leurs sont chers, soient sacrifiés et détruits par la guerre dans des luttes gigantesques. Ils veulent la paix, profiter des bienfaits qu'elle procure, échanger paisiblement leurs produits, commercer, travailler ; ils veulent tous une administration économe, des diminutions d'impôts.

A ces désirs, les gouvernements répondent en augmentant tous les ans les charges militaires, les préparatifs de guerre, les charges publiques.

Les peuples finiront par se lasser du maintien d'un tel état de choses qui nous ramène aux temps barbares : la civilisation qui a abattu les barrières entre les pays et les individus, rendu les communications plus rapides et plus faciles, établi des chemins de fer et des routes, creusé des canaux, percé des montagnes et des isthmes, imposera la paix aux sociétés modernes d'une façon aussi irrésistible que la guerre s'imposait aux sauvages et aux sociétés anciennes.— *Janvier*, 1887.

www.ingramcontent.com/pod-product-compliance
Lightning Source LLC
Chambersburg PA
CBHW020303240426
43673CB00039B/685